Practical Speech Fundamentals

Practical Speech

Fundamentals

EUGENE E. WHITE
The Pennsylvania State University

The Macmillan Company · New York

Ninth Printing, 1966

Library of Congress catalog card number: 60–5009

The Macmillan Company, New York
Collier-Macmillan Canada, Ltd., Toronto, Ontario

Printed in the United States of America

To Roberta and Genie

❦❦ *Preface*

This book is designed primarily for use in beginning under-graduate speech courses employing the fundamentals approach. It is divided into four major sections. Probably most teachers will wish to begin the semester's work with PART I AN OVERVIEW, the purpose of which is to help the student under-stand the nature and function of oral communication and acquire positive attitudes toward speaking. Thereafter, the pref-erence of the instructor will determine the sequence of chapter assignments. For instance, if he wishes to introduce at this time the fundamentals of personality, voice, physical delivery, pro-nunciation, or language, he may assign appropriate chapters in PART II THE SPEAKER. If he wishes to emphasize the audience-centered nature of speaking or the requisites for skilled listening-observing, he may assign the suitable chapter in PART III THE AUDIENCE. Or, if he wishes to take up one of the basic types of speaking—public speaking, oral reading, or group discussion—he may assign pertinent chapters in PART IV BASIC FORMS OF ORAL COMMUNICATION.

In the writing of this book I have attempted to motivate the student by focusing attention on the significance of each sub-ject as it is presented, and by offering concrete practical guidance in a simple and friendly fashion. While trying to keep the student's immediate needs and interests in mind, I have tried also to sensitize him to the requirements of effective speaking in the workaday world. In addition to stressing practical utility, I have tried to bring to the student's attention relevant philo-sophical implications, and have consistently emphasized the high ethical responsibilities which attend effective speaking. I have endeavored to couple full coverage with conciseness, solid theory with an informal style, individualized treatment of important concepts with the close integration of all materials, and the application of up-to-date experimental research with the time-honored principles of rhetorical practice.

During the several years spent in preparing this book I have enjoyed the generous assistance of several colleagues. I should emphasize my indebtedness to Dr. Clair R. Henderlider of Western Reserve University. A wise and gentle counselor, Professor Henderlider has given encouragement and guidance from the initial planning stage to the final polishing. I should also note my especial indebtedness to Dr. Orville Hitchcock of the State University of Iowa, who read the entire manuscript and offered numerous helpful suggestions. In addition, I should thank the following persons who criticized portions of the manuscript: Dr. Claude M. Wise of Louisiana State University; Dr. Earl W. Wells of Oregon State College; Dr. Johnnye Akin of Denver University; and Drs. C. Raymond Van Dusen and William L. Shea of the University of Miami. Despite this help, errors of fact or interpretation may still remain. For these I alone am responsible.

A final statement of appreciation: this book could not have been completed without the sympathetic understanding of my wife, Roberta Fluitt White.

Eugene E. White

Miami, Florida

❧❧ *Contents*

ix

x ❦❦ Contents

Group Discussion

I ❧❧ *An Overview*

1 ❦❦ *Oral Communication—*
Springboard to More Effective Living

By necessity and desire, man is a talkative creature! The amount of talking and listening done by the individual is astounding. Unless you are unusually unsocial or bookish, you probably utter more than 30,000 words a day. If you are a campus politician, a BMOC, a "hail-fellow," or a practice teacher, you may greatly exceed this total. When we consider that most of us listen more than we talk, the volume of communication that we receive and transmit is seen to be even more impressive. Are you skeptical that you talk so much? Think for a moment of a typical day in your life as a college student. Probably it goes something like this. Three or four hours are spent in the classroom listening to lectures, asking questions, and discussing ideas with instructors and classmates. Several hours are given to study, sometimes in the form of "boning-up" with several friends for a pending examination. Perhaps an hour or two in the afternoon or evening are devoted to glee club, band, debate, play rehearsal, fraternity business, intramurals, philosophy club, or some other extracurricular activity. Possibly considerable time is spent in "bull sessions" over coffee or coke with fellow students; if not, a part-time job may occupy these extra hours. Unless you eat too fast, two or three hours are reserved for meals, either with friends on the campus or at home with your family. A varying amount of time (usually not enough) remains for sleep. With the exception of sleeping and possibly studying, all of these activities, either by necessity or choice, involve talking, or listening, or both.

3

A little reflection should reveal that oral communication is indispensable in almost all other environments as well. Except for the recluse, talking and listening to others occupies much of the life of any person. As examples: a small boy begs his mother for a jar in which to keep a lizard recently captured under a bush in the garden; a surgeon, intent upon his task, snaps orders to his surgical nurse, "Suture"—"Rib shears"—"Rib spreaders" —"Lung retractors"—"Tourniquet"—"Suction"; a harassed business executive dictates letter after letter into a machine as the landscape streaks unnoticed past his Pullman window; a Great Books group tries to estimate the degree of Shakespeare's borrowing; a foreman passes among his men, giving instructions, asking questions, and boosting morale; a campaigning politician leans against a fence and praises the farmer for the sleek appearance of his sows.

In addition to conversational and discussional situations, much speaking is done under more formal speaker-audience relationships. You may be surprised to learn that in Cleveland, for example, at least sixty speeches are delivered at luncheon meetings in downtown hotels *each* day. Regular meetings, involving speeches, panel discussions, or parliamentary speaking, are scheduled by innumerable organizations, such as: Kiwanis, Rotary, Advertising Club, Institute of Electrical Engineers, American Welding Society, Academy of Medicine, and Council on World Affairs, as well as P.T.A. groups, hospital boards, women's clubs, and garden clubs.

With nearly every American family owning one or more radios and perhaps 85 per cent having television receivers, oral communication via the mass media has become a vital element in our mode of living. More than 100,000,000 persons may tune in an important speech by the President; many millions listen to favorite variety, dramatic, or give-away shows and to special events like the World Series and the Indianapolis Speedway race. As you well know, the members of the broadcast audience are endlessly bombarded by hucksters, comedians, masters of ceremonies, quiz masters, contestants, actors, lecturers, panelists, commentators, debaters, preachers, educators, politicians, and "interesting people chosen from the studio audience."

Obviously, we humans are not at a loss for words. What do we hope to accomplish with all this talk? While we may strongly suspect that some persons talk primarily to hear themselves or to keep others quiet, most of us speak when we have ideas we want others to hear. Our desire in speaking may be to impart information or to further understanding—as when we give directions to a tourist; our purpose may be to entertain or interest— as when we tell a joke to the office staff; or possibly our wish may be to influence belief or conduct—as when we urge an audience to contribute to the local cancer drive. Similar motives cause us to listen: to learn, to be amused, or to be counselled in solving problems and arriving at decisions. Therefore, *oral communication is prompted, for the most part, by the practical needs of individuals living together in a closely integrated society.*

The concept of a "closely integrated society" is basic to an understanding of the nature and function of communication and to a realization of the need for improving the efficiency of communication. Obviously our contemporary culture relies more upon communication than did the comparatively isolated and relatively self-sufficient, agrarian society of a century or so ago. The typical eighteenth century man dealt directly and often non-verbally with most of his problems of securing food, shelter, transportation, protection, clothing, etc. Over the generations since those times, the growing effectiveness of our systems of research, production, transportation, and distribution has developed an awesome industrial crucible that disgorges an increasing flood of gadgets, appliances, tools, machines, and weapons. This outpouring of material wealth has swept us to vastly higher economic standards and, at the same time, has radically altered both the mode and tempo of our existence. Electronics, mass production, and automation have forced us to substitute "interdependency" for "isolation" and "self-sufficiency." As you probably already appreciate, "interdependency" has increased both the volume and the importance of communication, oral and written. We now rely almost completely upon others to provide us with goods and services, and frequently we must make our selections on the basis of advertising. Although the future of our democratic government depends upon how intelligently we vote, we seldom are able to know the candidates firsthand. Furthermore, once in office the successful candidates must arrive at important decisions primarily by means of information gleaned from others. Thousands of pressure groups and special-interest combinations compete relentlessly for our support, our allegiance, our money, our time, and our energy. The scope of accumulated human knowledge and experience has expanded so greatly that an individual can hope to understand only the minutest fraction of it. And to secure most of what knowledge we have, we have had to rely upon communication.

To help us cope with our complex communication needs, science has produced many electronic marvels. Motion pictures record sound and image for mass consumption. The 100,000,000 telephones in the world bring Caracas, Bandung, Singapore, Montevideo, Cape Town, Ankara, and Oslo within reach of your voice. Some 6,000,000 miles of telegraph lines envelop the globe. The 200,000,000 telegrams sent annually in the United States do not include the traffic flowing over ticker systems, private leased wires, and press circuits. The world's 4,500 radio stations permit vocal communication to a possible audience of half a billion people. Television has stretched its coaxial cables to cover nations and eventually will link together all the world's people.

Despite remarkable advances in the means of communication, much avoidable misunderstanding and needless conflict still exist. Because of faulty *methods* of communication, interpersonal relations are strained, business encounters delays, campaigns fail, money is lost, time is wasted, and nations find it difficult to negotiate and as a consequence may resort to war.

The blame for failures in communication lies not in machines but in men, not in the means of communication but in its quality.

VALUES OF EFFECTIVE ORAL COMMUNICATION

As Ben Jonson pointed out, "Talking and eloquence are not the same: to speak, and to speak well, are two things." If the quality of oral communication matched its quantity, there would be no need for this and similar books. The ineffectiveness of the average speaker has led the *Cleveland News* columnist, Sidney Andorn, to complain that "if all our speakers-in-public were laid end to end, it would be a darn good thing for the public." Dwight P. Joyce, president of the Glidden Company, has declared that "more time is wasted in ineffective oral expression than in any other sphere of business activity." Everyone who is reasonably active in business, professional, or civic organizations has been subjected to much contentious wrangling, petty bickering, distortion of evidence, and other misuses of communication. Each day presents its large quota of immature speech habits: clouded thinking presented in ill-chosen words, stumbling inarticulateness, words blurted out without thinking, unpleasant voices, offensive speech personalities, speakers who soliloquize rather than communicate, and so on.

For those who are aware of these deficiencies but are unconcerned, we submit this statement by John Hoover, president of the B. F. Goodrich Chemical Company: "The ability to communicate effectively is essential to success in our workaday world, and, I might also say, to the success of a citizen in this country." As further support, here is the considered judgment of the President's Commission on Higher Education: "Without free, clear, and distinct communication a true meeting of minds does not occur, and understanding and cooperation are retarded if not prevented. . . . Few of the abilities men possess are of greater human significance than their power to order ideas clearly and to set these before their fellows by tongue or pen." [1]

If you are convinced that the ability to speak well and to listen efficiently does not "just happen" and if you are willing to work conscientiously to improve, both you and society will benefit. By developing your skill in oral communication you will achieve greater self realization, improve your social relationships, increase your professional and economic efficiency, and serve more effectively your community and nation.

A. Achieving Greater Self-Realization. At birth we possess various physical and mental potentialities. Within the limitations imposed by heredity, the extent to which we realize our potentialities is determined by our environment and our motivation. Although most persons are aware that concentrated effort is necessary to realize our fullest mental and physical capacities, many may take oral communication for granted. Childhood efforts to acquire speech have long faded from memory, and through the years we may have made no conscious effort to improve our oral skills. Unless someone has specifically directed our attention to this matter, we may have never realized that man is superior to other members of the animal kingdom primarily because he possesses a brain capable of rational and abstract thought and because he has developed a refined system of communication. Effective speech enables us to reveal our thoughts, our hopes, our knowledge to others. And the ability to listen effectively, not just hear, helps us to learn from the experience of others, to accumulate knowledge, to arrive at intelligent decisions, and to protect ourselves from trickery and high-pressure persuasion. Developing our ability to speak and to listen is essential to the realization of our greatest potential as mature individuals.

B. Improving Social Relationships. Almost everyone agrees that an individual's success and happiness depend primarily upon his ability to secure appropriate responses from others.

---

[1] Gail Kennedy, ed., "Higher Education for American Democracy," in *Education for Democracy* (Boston: D. C. Heath and Company, 1952), p. 27.

John D. Rockefeller valued this quality so highly that he once stated: "I will pay more for the ability to deal with people than for any other ability under the sun." Our social relationships depend largely upon the efficiency and appropriateness with which we communicate our wishes, attitudes, and sentiments and upon the accuracy with which we interpret the communications of others to us.

C. Increasing Professional and Economic Opportunities. Some persons erroneously believe that speech training is essential only in such professions as law, politics, the ministry, radio and television announcing, teaching, and the like. In almost every profession or vocation, however, effective communication is not just important—it is mandatory. In addressing a convention of educators, W. E. Bennett (Coordinator of Training, Cities Service Refining Company) described the importance of speech training to students in all fields:

I am told that in many cases the specialized students are required to take a semester of speech. . . . Those boys and girls are ambitious. They plan to become leaders, and they feel that the highroad to leadership lies in the technical courses, in the professions, in chemistry, physics, and engineering. Knowledge in these fields is undoubtedly the foundation upon which successful careers are erected, but coupled with that knowledge must be the ability to communicate—to share—that knowledge with other people, to make other people see through their eyes, to convince other people that their ideas and opinions are worth following. To get to the top they have to lead, but unless they are followed, they cannot lead. . . .

There is abundant evidence to prove conclusively that [skill in speaking] is essential to the college man's ultimate success. . . . One of the keys to our continued industrial progress is the development of more effective speech within our technological society.[2]

Executives generally agree that the most important single "success factor" is a superior ability to communicate with others. Writing in *Fortune,* Peter Drucker offers this advice to students:

What can you learn in college that will help you in being an employee? The schools teach . . . the one thing that is perhaps most valuable for the future employee to know. But very few bother to learn it.

[2] W. E. Bennett, "The Need for Effective Speech in a Technological Society," *The Southern Speech Journal,* September, 1951, pp. 28–29.

This one basic skill is the ability to organize and express ideas in writing and in speaking. . . . As soon as you move one step up from the bottom, your effectiveness depends on your ability to reach others through the spoken or written word. And the further away your job is from manual work, the larger the organization of which you are an employee, the more important it will be that you know how to convey your thoughts in writing or speaking. In the very large organizations, whether it is the government, the large business corporation, or the Army, this ability to express oneself is perhaps the most important of all the skills a man can possess.[3]

Whatever professional goal you have decided upon, be assured that your ability in speaking, or lack of it, will be a signal factor in determining how far and at what rate you will advance.

D. Serving More Effectively Your Community and Nation. Skill in oral communication is of tremendous consequence to democratic procedures. The capable, civic-minded citizen cannot escape the necessity for effective public utterance. A significant characteristic of us Americans is our gregariousness. We are a nation of joiners. Probably you now belong to several campus organizations. After graduation, you will undoubtedly join one or more professional, business, study, civic, or recreational groups. In time, you may acquire positions of responsibility and directorship in these organizations. Possibly you will assume leadership in some community efforts. As you become increasingly active your ability to communicate effectively will likewise become increasingly important to your community and nation.

Effective speech is a vital means of protecting our national freedoms. Perhaps our basic obligation as citizens in a democracy is to guard the principle of free speech. One of the best ways to preserve this inalienable right is to exercise it. Lincoln once said, "To sin by silence when they should speak makes cowards of men." Our democracy is predicated upon the belief that the individual citizen has the right and obligation to express himself upon matters of public concern. Should public communication become the sole prerogative of the "leaders," the spirit of democracy inevitably must wither. Furthermore, freedom of speech

[3] Peter Drucker, "How to Be an Employee," *Fortune,* May, 1952, pp. 126, 127, 168 ff.

is not true freedom for an individual if he lacks sufficient ability to express clearly his thinking and feelings. To achieve the fullest practical and idealistic concepts of democracy the individual citizen not only must be given the opportunity for public expression, he must also possess those skills necessary for effective public expression. Our freedom of speech is safe only as long as we use it actively, skillfully, and wisely. It is in grave danger if we neglect it through indifference, ineptitude, or cowardliness. If this basic freedom is lost, we shall swiftly lose our other precious rights, such as freedom to vote as we wish, freedom to worship according to our conscience, and freedom to work where we please and in a job of our choice.

THE CYCLE OF COMMUNICATION

What sequence of events occurs when one person speaks to another? What may cause the process of communication to break down? What role is played by—and what are the interrelationships among—the speaker, his message, his listeners, and the circumstances under which he speaks? Although you have talked with others since childhood, you probably have not had occasion to examine the basic nature of oral communication. Therefore, before beginning a program to improve your speech, you should study the following overview of the cycle of communication.

A. **The Sequence in the Cycle of Communication.** A spoken message cannot be delivered in the sense that a physical commodity is delivered. Depositing a quart of milk on a customer's front doorstep is infinitely easier than "depositing" one of your ideas in the mind of another person. Indeed, your thoughts and feelings cannot be directly transferred to your listener, because *nothing passes between you except waves of light and sound.* Because they carry symbolic values, these waves serve as stimuli which may stir up the desired meanings in the mind of your listener. However, even when he correctly interprets your words and actions, the act of communication is not yet complete. For the cycle to be consummated the listener must react in an observable manner, and, by some direct or indirect means, you must become aware of this response. Thus, the complete act of communication is not a one-way process, but an interacting pattern of stimulus and response. The speaker stimulates the listener to some noticeable response, which in turn influences the further behavior of the speaker. This circular response continues as long as communication occurs.

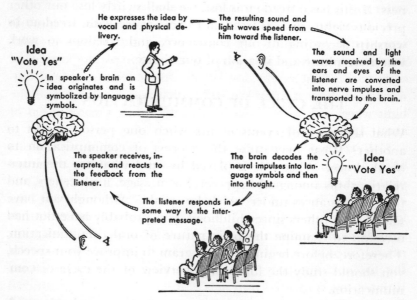

Fig. 1. The Cycle of Communication Is Not a One-Way Process, But an Interacting Pattern of Stimulus and Response.

To help clarify this concept, let us trace the stages in the complete cycle.

1. Thinking. Through some as yet unexplained neurological process, a thought originates in the mind of the speaker. As the initiator in the act of communication, he must have an idea which he wishes to convey to another person.

2. Symbolizing. The speaker must convert the idea into mental language symbols—words, phrases, and sentences.

3. *Expressing*. Having selected his words, the speaker must translate them into audible speech and appropriate physical action. To accomplish this, electric impulses, or directives, from the brain flash along nerve trunks to activate (a) the vocal mechanism, the muscles of which work in a complicated and spe-cialized fashion to produce sound waves; (b) the appropriate muscle groups which produce movements of the face and body (such as facial expression, gesture, and changes in posture) in order to supplement the sounds of language.

4. *Transmitting*. During this stage, the speaker's "idea" is represented by certain "disturbances" in the atmosphere sur-rounding him: the sound waves, which are invisible patterns of compression and rarefaction in the air molecules, spread out-ward from him at approximately 1,000 feet a second; and the light waves race away from him at the much greater speed of about 186,000 miles a second.

5. *Receiving*. When the sound waves impinge upon the ears of the listener, they set the ear drums into vibration. By means of the relaying action of the three small bones in the middle ear, the movements of the ear drums excite into "vibration" the fluids within the inner ear. In turn, the movement of the liquids stimulates the filaments of the auditory nerve. The resultant neural impulses speed along the nerve trunks to the brain of the listener. Similarly, the light waves strike the eyes of the listener, are converted into nerve impulses, and are conducted by the optic nerve to the brain.

6. *Decoding*. Conveyance of meaning from the speaker to the listener takes place only when the brain of the listener decodes the series of nerve impulses it receives via the auditory and optic nerves. This decoding process, which occurs at light-ning speed, must first translate the nerve impulses into mean-ingful language symbols and then into thought. If both the speaker and the listener share a relatively similar community of language experiences, the listener is able to attach to these sym-bols meanings which are roughly akin to those intended by the speaker.

7. *Reacting or "feeding back".* Once his brain has associated meanings with the incoming nerve impulses, the listener responds by further thought and/or by experiencing a feeling-tone or emotional state. His inner reactions may be accompanied by overt behavior, such as a smile, a perplexed frown, a blush, a yawn, a look of doubt, laughter, applause, restlessness, and so on. In discussion and conversation the response may also be vocal.

8. *Monitoring.* By watching the behavior of his listeners for clues as to how his message is being received, the speaker can make necessary adjustments in language, content, manner, mood, loudness, rate of speaking, voice tone, and so on. At the same time he is receiving the feedback of sound and/or light waves from the listener, the speaker's own neuromuscular system is providing him with a continuous stream of messages concerning his presentation, that is, the sound of his own voice and the kinesthetic feel of his physical activity feed back to him, greatly aiding him in monitoring his thought and delivery.

After reading the preceding discussion, perhaps you understand why famed scientist-philosopher Norbert Wiener characterized speech as "the greatest interest and most distinctive achievement of man." Instead of a simple one-way avenue, oral communication is a cycle involving eight almost unbelievably complicated stages. Now that you can appreciate better the intricate nature of the process of communication, let us quickly retrace the stages in the cycle in order to examine some of the more common causes for communicative breakdowns. (1) *Thinking.* Frequently the speaker's thinking is addled, fuzzy, or obtuse; he does not know precisely what he wants to communicate. (2) *Symbolizing.* As the President's Commission on Higher Education has asserted, "Experience indicates the close relationship that exists between thought and the symbols that express thought. Clear and precise thinking requires good language habits." If the speaker's thinking is confused, the language with which he clothes his thoughts will likewise be muddled.

Also, indifference, sluggishness, insensitivity, and/or a deficiency in language skills may cause him to select expressions which do not represent precisely what he wishes to say. (3) *Expressing*. In later chapters, we shall see that various inadequacies in the speaker's vocal and physical delivery may distort or destroy the meaning of his language. (4) *Transmitting*. The distance from the speaker-to-audience, intervening objects, and/or competing noises may block or interfere with the transmission of the sound and light waves. (5) *Receiving*. Faulty reception may be caused by failing eyesight or hearing loss. (6) *Decoding*. Sometimes the hearer is unable to interpret faithfully the language symbols he receives because of his inadequate vocabulary or insufficient mental associations. Furthermore, because a person interprets and evaluates language symbols in terms of his total experiences (motivations, attitudes, emotions, and interests), and because his experiences invariably are different from those of the speaker, his interpretations will involve overtones necessarily different from those of the speaker. Also, a prejudiced receiver may shut out part or all of what a speaker says, or may deliberately or subconsciously distort the meaning. (7) *Reacting* or "feeding back." In face-to-face speaking, the listener may fail to give adequate overt response or may respond in a manner which does not accurately represent his feelings. In telephoning, of course, the speaker does not receive visual clues from the listener. And in radio and television, the speaker has no immediate feedback from his hearers; in such cases the cycle of communication is not completed until letters, post cards, telephone calls, or ratings provide some understanding as to the reactions of the audience. (8) *Monitoring*. Because of insensitivity or self-preoccupation, the speaker may misinterpret or fail to observe the responses of his listeners. In addition, his attempts to monitor or adjust his presentation may be overdone, inadequate, or otherwise faulty.

B. The Constituents of the Cycle of Communication. Every act of speech possesses four dynamic, interrelated constituents: (1) a speaker delivers, (2) an idea or a series of ideas to, (3) a listener or group of listeners, (4) at a particular time and place.

These components are commonly referred to as the speaker, the message or speech, the audience, and the occasion. Because each speaking situation necessarily represents a unique combination of factors involving the four constituents, you must learn how to analyze yourself as the speaker, the message you wish to present, the audience which will receive your ideas, and the occasion which will exert a psychological effect upon both you and the hearers. Only in this way will you be able to make the most effective adaptation of yourself, your ideas, and your delivery to different communicative situations.

The following discussion will introduce you to each of the constituents of the cycle of communication. The remainder of this book will be devoted to analyzing these components in greater detail.

1. The audience.   Although the arrangement may possibly seem strange to you at first, let us begin with the audience. Since the function of an act of communication is to secure a desired response from the listeners, the effectiveness of the speaker is determined by his relative success in achieving that reaction. Therefore, *successful speaking is audience-centered.* All too frequently, the beginning speaker concentrates almost exclusively upon himself—his needs, his interests, his beliefs, his attitudes. This "I-centered" speaker fails to recognize that the purpose of his speaking is to influence others and that his own importance to the cycle of communication lies solely in his being the initiator of the process. If he is not preoccupied with self, the novice tends to focus primary attention upon his subject, ignoring the adaptation of his message to his hearers. This "subject-centered" speaker is more concerned with arguing a case or analyzing a principle than he is with reaching those who receive his message. Naturally, one should be concerned with his own interests, experiences, and convictions and should be anxious to present a worthwhile message. However, as long as it remains consistent with ethics, any spoken message should be developed and expressed in terms of the listeners' interests, needs, and capabilities.

In order to adjust your message and your presentation to the audience, you must first understand the basic principles of attention and motivation as they apply to the speaker-audience relationship. The effective speaker is a sensitive student of human nature. Secondly, you should develop skill in analyzing and evaluating those who will comprise your particular audience. Seek to acquire as accurate an insight as possible concerning the knowledge of the listeners about you and your subject and concerning their attitudes toward you and your subject. Usually you can secure significant clues by applying your knowledge of human behavior to these characteristics of your particular audience: the range of ages represented and the dominant age group; the ratio between men and women auditors; the number of persons in the audience; the educational and occupational backgrounds and the group affiliations of the listeners. (See Chapter 9.)

Of course, the audience has certain responsibilities to both the speaker and itself. Your speech course should help you to become a more efficient listener-observer. By applying the advice given in Chapter 8, you can improve your ability to understand, evaluate, and retain oral communication. In preview, the guides to effective listening-observing are: be co-operative and courteous; concentrate; be objective; be analytical and evaluative; and use the recommended techniques to promote retention.

2. The occasion. Under the general term "occasion" we can include all of the psychological and physical characteristics of the environment in which the communicative act takes place. To adjust successfully your speaking purpose, content, and delivery to the requirements of the occasion, you should analyze the basic nature of the meeting, the time and location, and the program. Ask yourself such questions as: Why is the meeting being held? What mood or atmosphere will probably pervade the gathering? When and where will the meeting occur? What are the physical characteristics of the room? How much time is available for my presentation? Am I the only speaker? If not, where do I fit into the program? Will activities other than speaking occur? How will all of these elements of the environment influence the receptivity and the expectations of my listeners? (See Chapter 9.)

3. *The message or speech.* The speaker's ideas as expressed in language, or "what he says," constitute his message. Any serious speech should fulfill these requirements: (a) It should be purposeful. (b) It should deal with significant, worthwhile ideas. (c) It should command attention and interest. (d) It should appeal to both logic and emotions. (e) It should be adapted to the total speaking situation.

a. An Effective Message Is Purposeful. It attempts to achieve a definite response from an audience. Instead of merely pointing at the general target of informing, entertaining, or persuading, the successful message aims at a specific, definite goal—the bull's-eye; it makes clear to the listeners precisely what the speaker wants them to know, enjoy, or believe. Without the focalizing influence of a main purpose, a message cannot possess unity, coherence, and emphasis, and usually is deficient in interest values.

b. An Effective Message Concerns Significant, Worthwhile Ideas. Inconsequential topics produce insipid speeches. Your message should "make a difference." It should present a challenge to you as the speaker and should concern some genuine want, interest, or desire of your listeners. Recognize that your speech class affords an unexcelled laboratory for intellectual growth. Probably no other undergraduate course places so high a premium on originality and maturity of thought. Many students complain that their university training has ignored current affairs; capitalize upon the opportunity offered by your speech course to broaden your understanding of, and acquire fresh insights into, the current political, social, religious, and economic problems. Many students complain that their academic work over-emphasizes rote memorization; accept this chance to think, philosophize, probe, sift, and apply the information you have gleaned from previous courses, from reading, and from life experiences. Your efforts will bring substantial rewards, both in the form of grades and in the more meaningful area of personal development.

c. An Effective Message Commands Attention and Interest. When an auditor ceases to give attention to your message, the cycle of communication is disrupted—just as inexorably and often just as completely as the lifting of a phonograph needle from a record interrupts the electronic circuit; although the disk may continue to spin, no sound is produced until the circuit is re-established by replacing the needle in its groove. In the case of oral communication, the distracted listener continues to receive your sound and light waves, but he no longer decodes them efficiently into thought. Your ideas cannot get through to his conscious awareness until his concentration returns and he begins again to decode the waves of sound and light which represent your message. Admittedly an audience may force itself to concentrate upon a dull speech because of respect for the speaker or for his position. Nevertheless, most of us can keep our audience listening only as long as our message maintains high attention and interest values.

d. An Effective Message Appeals to Both Logic and Emotions. Since nearly all of our beliefs and actions derive from a coalescence of reason and feeling, successful oral communication should be organized and developed in the most effective logical and psychological manner. Presently we shall take up the methodology involved in selecting, arranging, and supporting ideas. For the time being, however, the following telescoped treatment probably will suffice. To achieve your speaking purpose your message should carry the listeners smoothly, directly, and persuasively toward the desired reaction. All irrelevant, inconsequential, or ambiguous materials should be excluded. Unless the message is exceedingly brief it should be organized around a basic framework consisting of several major points, stages, contentions, or objections which directly support the specific speaking purpose. The amplifying materials which develop these major ideas provide the substance of the talk. All supporting elements should constitute a valid appeal to the reasoning and thinking of the listeners: they should clearly and logically reinforce the ideas they are designed to develop; they should be accurate and usually should be verifiable; any generalizations or implications which the speaker adds to the facts should be valid and should appear so to the listeners. Also, the supporting elements should capitalize upon the existing beliefs, wants, attitudes, and interests of the listeners; if possible, they should be so well adapted to the emotional predispositions of the auditors that the audience will *desire* to learn, believe, or do what the speaker wishes. Naturally, the message of the speaker must always remain consistent with sound moral principles and should appeal only to the higher motives of man's nature.

e. AN EFFECTIVE MESSAGE IS ADAPTED TO THE TOTAL SPEAK-ING SITUATION. In a sense, this principle embodies the previously listed requirements for an effective message. As we have already learned, oral communication should be audience-centered and should be adjusted to the physical and psychological characteristics of the occasion. In addition, your message should be suited to you as the speaker. Any speech is more effective if the listeners believe that the speaker has earned the right to talk on the subject. Of course, as a student you are not expected to be an authority on the major problems of society. Nevertheless, select for your speeches and discussions only those subjects on which you are already reasonably well informed. Also, if your message concerns a matter of vital meaning or interest to you, your presentation will be more dynamic and convincing. In developing your message, remember that, since you possess limited prestige and experience, you usually should rely more on documentary evidence and research than on personal opinions and experiences. This is especially true when addressing persons older than you.

4. The speaker. Perhaps the finest capsule definition of the ideal speaker was written some two thousand years ago by the Roman teacher Quintilian: "An orator is a good man skilled in speaking." In themselves, neither personal attributes nor speech techniques are sufficient to produce the consummate speaker.

Today, as probably never before, democratic society needs able persons who also are skilled in oral communication.

a. THE EFFECTIVE SPEAKER IS FIRST OF ALL A CAPABLE, MORALLY RESPONSIBLE PERSON. He possesses an honorable reputation, intelligence and broad knowledge, and desirable traits of character and personality such as sincerity, enthusiasm, confidence, modesty, and a sense of humor. In addition, he has appropriate attitudes toward himself, his message, and his audience.

What a man appears to be is sometimes the strongest factor in determining his degree of effectiveness as a speaker. If his motives seem to be questionable, if his reputation is unsavory, if he is disliked, or if his general competence is not established, a speaker may fail—even though he possesses many other abilities and attributes. Conversely, it is "easy to believe" the admired, trusted, well-liked person. The only abiding way to enjoy this persuasive advantage is to *be* a man of ability and character. Undoubtedly, some attributes can be feigned. While a good reputation is hard to fabricate, the charlatan may exude good will, appear to be competent, seem to have only the highest motives, and may be charming and likable as a person and a speaker. However, Lincoln and others have pointed out the folly of hoping to delude very many people for very long. As a speaker and a potential leader, start now to establish over the years a reputation for honesty, trustworthiness, and competency. The rewards are great and lasting, and extend beyond speaking success into all fields of human endeavor. (See Chapter 3.)

b. THE EFFECTIVE SPEAKER IS SKILLED IN APPLYING THE PRINCIPLES OF PREPARATION AND DELIVERY. Effective platform speaking looks effortlessly easy. Nevertheless, it is an extremely complex art involving numerous techniques of preparation and delivery. Perhaps a brief discussion of these skills will serve as an introduction to the remainder of the text and as a concise guide to the presentation of your initial class performances.

First, let us consider the general skills of delivery which are common to all forms of speaking: (1) Seek to understand more vividly and explicitly the nature of language and try to develop a mature and effective oral style. Effectual oral language is clear, direct, appropriate, graphic, and impressive. (See Chapter 4.) (2) Develop skill in the use of the audible code. The process of vocalizing the symbols of language is referred to as the audible code. It includes the audibility, pleasantness, fluency, and flexibility of the speaker's voice and the distinctness and correctness of his pronunciation. (See Chapters 6 and 7.) (3) Acquire polish in the use of the visible code. The visible code consists of the speaker's overt physical activity which reinforces his spoken message. Chapter 5 contains an analysis of the function and principles of effective bodily action as well as suggestions for improving posture, movement, gesture, eye contact, and facial expression.

Now let us turn to the basic elements of preparation and delivery as they relate specifically to public speaking, oral reading, and group discussion. Since these are the basic forms of speaking at public occasions, they are analyzed at length in Part IV. If you become proficient in their use, you will experience little difficulty in adapting your speech skills to associated activities such as radio and television speaking, interviewing, telephoning, parliamentary speaking, and conversation.

Public speaking. There are five steps in successful speech preparation: (1) Select a topic which is well suited to the audience, the occasion, and to yourself as the speaker. Determine whether you wish to inform, entertain, or persuade your listeners. Then, narrow this general purpose to a Specific Speech Purpose, that is, a definite, limited goal which you can reasonably hope to achieve with your audience. Probably the General Speech Purpose of your first talks will be to inform. Your Specific Speech Purpose might be to have your audience understand how tobacco is cured, how electronic "eyes" make rail travel safer, or how a case is handled by the United States Supreme Court. (See Chapter 10.) (2) Gather material by thinking over what you already know concerning the subject, by reading selectively, objectively, and analytically, by acquiring information from others, and, if possible, by using personal observation. (See Chapter 11.) (3) Organize the Body of the talk. Out of the materials you have accumulated, jot down in your mind or on paper the points you might want to present. From this Analysis List evolve two to five major divisions, topics, or arguments under which you can group supporting ideas. To keep your speech moving steadily toward its goal, the main headings of the Body should follow a logical progression or sequence of thought. (See Chapter 12.) (4) Develop the main headings of the Body. In themselves, the main divisions represent only a bare framework. Therefore, amplify them in terms of the logical demands of the subject and the psychological needs of the audience and occasion. To make the main points clear and persuasive, use examples, comparisons, statistics, testimony, explanations, reiteration, and visual aids. To promote audience attention, direct your materials toward the immediate needs and interests of the listeners, deal with matters that are significant, keep materials vividly concrete, avoid wearisome sameness in content or delivery, and employ appropriate humor. (See Chapter 13.) (5) Develop the Introduction and Conclusion. The Introduction stimulates favorable attention and orients the audience to the subject. The Conclusion summarizes the speech, promotes the proper mood, and, if necessary, attempts to impel the audience to act upon the speaker's recommendations. (See Chapter 14.)

Effective speech delivery depends upon adequate rehearsal. Unless you practice your speech at least four times, you may be unable to speak with maximum effectiveness. By rehearsing you can fix unforgettably in your mind the sequence of your ideas and can polish the vocal and physical aspects of delivery. (See Chapter 15.)

In presenting the speech, concentrate upon the process of conveying your ideas and feelings to your listeners. If you are deeply interested in your subject, are well prepared, and enthusiastically want to communicate, you probably will suffer little from negative feelings of inadequacy. (For methods of coping with speech fright see Chapter 2.) Keep your eyes on your listeners and speak directly to them in a sincere, modest, friendly, and lively manner. Feel free to gesticulate and to shift your position occasionally on the platform. Remember that the practice period, not the speaking platform, is the place to worry about specific techniques of delivery such as vocal inflections, gestures, pronunciation, and facial expression. When facing the audience, put everything from your consciousness except the process of communicating your message to your listeners. (See Chapter 15.)

Oral reading. In oral reading, one reads aloud either original material or that composed by another person. If you wish to prepare and read a speech from a verbatim copy, follow the five steps in speech preparation just discussed. Once the outline is completed, write an initial word-for-word draft of the entire speech; revise this and subsequent drafts until satisfied that you have phrased your ideas as accurately and as vividly as possible. Do not prepare an essay! During your writing, concentrate on composing a speech: keep sentences short and simple; employ contractions, personal pronouns, idiomatic expressions, and the other components of informal, direct oral communication. Type the final manuscript neatly; allow ample margins and two or three spaces between the lines; use only one side of the paper. In rehearsing, practice exclusively from the final script or duplicate; study the script carefully and read it through both silently and orally until intimately familiar with its sequence; then polish vocal and physical delivery. During the presentation, try to maintain a keen, direct sense of communication. Talk as conversationally as the size of the audience and the formality of the occasion permits. (See Chapters 16 and 17.)

If you wish to read aloud a speech, essay, or dramatic work prepared by someone else, follow these suggestions: (1) Choose a selection which is suitable to the audience, the occasion, and yourself as the reader. (2) Discover the author's intent. Particularly if the work possesses some depth, the process of determining the purpose of the writer may involve several steps: first, become adequately acquainted with the author, his motives, his reasons for writing the selection, and his attitudes as revealed in the composition; second, become sufficiently familiar with the historical context within which the plan of the work takes place; third, ascertain the intellectual and emotional meanings and the techniques of literary craftsmanship. (3) Develop appropriate attitudes toward the selection and the process of communicating it to the listeners. (4) Rehearse the selection until you feel that you can successfully project the emotions and thoughts of the author. (5) During the actual presentation, read to the audience in a natural, spontaneous manner; beware of artificiality and exhibitionism; and do not go to the extreme of acting. (See Chapters 16 and 17.)

Group discussion. As you will learn in Chapters 18 and 19, discussion is systematic, objective, and co-operative group deliberation for the purpose of investigating and solving problems. Because group discussion may take a variety of forms, the explanation here must be very general in character. Usually preparation for discussion involves these stages: (1) A chairman should be chosen by the participants, or by some other means. Ideally, the chairman should be well-informed on the topic for discussion; he should possess appropriate personality traits and should understand the techniques of leadership; also, he should be a skilled extempore speaker and an efficient listener. (2) A meaningful subject should be selected. It should be well suited to the occasion, the participants, and to the listeners, if any. (3) The subject should be phrased in such a way that it represents a specific, limited, and impartial question. (4) Relevant information should be acquired by each participant. (5) The discussion itself should proceed according to a logical progression of thought. Probably your initial discussions will attempt to evolve a policy or solution as an answer to some existing need. If so, your group will likely follow a sequence like this: first, attempt to clarify any potentially misleading or confusing terms in the question; second, analyze the alleged problem to determine its extent, severity, and causes; third, consider possible solutions to the problem, estimating the advantages and limitations of each;

fourth, decide which of the possible solutions is preferable; fifth, suggest means by which the program or solution can be put into effect.

Effective discussion emphasizes reflective thinking, valid reasoning, accurate information, and objectivity. Conversely, it minimizes emotionality, conflict, and competition. By means of cooperative talk, the discussants attempt to uncover the basic issues involved in a question and then to determine the most feasible answer(s). During the discussion, each person should maintain good manners, be a good listener, and attempt to present his ideas concisely, logically, and dispassionately.

SUMMARY

Most speaking is prompted by the practical needs of individuals living together in a closely integrated society. The volume and influence of oral communication make it an extremely important force in human relations. By developing your ability to speak effectively and to listen efficiently you can achieve greater self-realization, improve social relationships, increase professional and economic opportunities, and serve more effectually your community and nation.

The communicative process involves an interacting pattern of stimulus and response, commonly referred to as the cycle of communication. The complete cycle necessitates a sequence of eight stages: thinking, symbolizing, expressing, transmitting, receiving, decoding, reacting or "feeding back," and monitoring. Each cycle or act of communication possesses four dynamic, correlative components: the audience, the occasion, the message or speech, and the speaker.

EXERCISES AND ASSIGNMENTS

1. For an hour or two, record in a notebook the duration of each time you speak or listen. On the basis of this sample, estimate the number of words you utter and the amount of time you spend in oral communication during a day. Compare your results with those of your classmates. Indicate

in the notebook those acts of communication which were successful and those which were unsuccessful. In each case, try to determine the reasons for success or failure.

2. Prepare a detailed written report of the role of oral communication in your chosen vocation. If necessary, seek help from your speech instructor, major professor, academic advisor, and/or librarian. For instance, if you are considering a career in the foreign service, you will want to read articles such as Ben C. Limb's "Speech: The Life of a Diplomat," *The Quarterly Journal of Speech*, February, 1957, pp. 55–61. (You may be interested to know that Limb, who is Ambassador of the Republic of Korea to the United Nations, believes that "diplomacy is above all a profession of words—written and spoken—the diplomat is a man of words.") Present the highlights of your findings in a short speech to the class.

3. As you study the following seemingly unrelated quotations, try to link them to each other and, collectively, to one or more basic principles in this chapter. Then answer mentally the accompanying questions.

a. "A person possessing greater accuracy in social perceptions can act with more certainty and confidence in the consequences of his interpersonal behavior. He is in a position not only to achieve with more certainty the goals of others, but also the social goals that he has for himself." F. Loyal Greer, Eugene H. Galanter, and Peter G. Mordlie, "Interpersonal Knowledge and Individual and Group Effectiveness," *The Journal of Abnormal and Social Psychology*, July, 1954, pp. 411–414.

b. "Although the art of persuasion may play the dramatic role in making a sale, the primary and really important thing for a salesman to do is on a more mundane, common-sense level. That job is to learn the prospect's viewpoint and adapt to it. In the words of L. Morton Morley, Vice President in Charge of Sales . . . Minneapolis-Honeywell Regulator Company: 'I believe that all the other qualities of a true salesman are of lesser importance. He can have enthusiasm, stamina, intelligence, personality, sincerity, and all the other attributes of a salesman, and still be a failure if he does not have the knack of finding the *points of common interest.*' And the important points, Mr. Morley adds, are those which are of chief interest to the prospect—not to the salesman." J. M. Hickerson (President, J. M. Hickerson, Inc., advertising agency), "Successful Sales Techniques," *Harvard Business Review*, September-October, 1952, pp. 33–46.

c. "Television audience-participation programs are systems of social interaction involving both audiences and performers . . . both audience and performers exert control over one another's responses. . . .

The social-psychological processes involved in an audience's subjective participation in the television program are not radically different from those occurring in everyday social activity. . . ." Donald Horton and Anselm Strauss, "Interaction in Audience-Participation Shows," *The American Journal of Sociology*, May, 1957, pp. 579–587.

Thought questions: Why is it necessary for the leader to understand the relevant wants, needs, attitudes, and interests of those whom he would lead? In what sense is the speaker a leader? Do you agree with Greer, Galanter, and Mordlie that leaders are more accurate in judging the needs of their followers than is the average person? Give reasons for your answer. How does the audience help to control the presentation of the speaker? Is this shaping influence comparable to that exerted on the public expressions of a political or civic leader by his followers? Explain. In what ways is the salesman's customer-centered "sales pitch" similar to the audience-centered nature of the public speaker's act of communication? In what ways different? What are some of the similarities and differences between the face-to-face audiences of public speaking, group discussion, or oral reading and the studio audiences of television audience-participation programs?

4. Prepare a short talk (or prepare to engage in class discussion) on the ethics of effective speaking. Perhaps this quotation of I Corinthians xiii:1 may serve suitably as your "text": "Though I speak with the tongues of men and of angels, and have not charity, I am become *as* sounding brass, or a tinkling cymbal."

2 ❦❦ A Positive Approach to Speaking

The value that you derive from your speech course, or from any learning situation, depends upon your native ability, previous experiences, and your desire to profit from the training. Although you have no control over the background of experience which you bring to the class or over your capacity for development, you can do much to condition your receptivity. To acquire maximum benefits from your speech training, adopt and maintain positive attitudes toward yourself as a speaker, toward the course, and toward your classmates and instructor.

APPROPRIATE ATTITUDES TOWARD YOURSELF AS A SPEAKER

A. Gaining Confidence.   Charles Dickens once complained: "Oh the nerves, the nerves, the mysteries of this machine called man! Oh the little that unhinges it: poor creatures that we are!" Few crises so utterly "unhinge" our body machinery as does the fear of speaking in public. Few fears are so unfounded as speech fright, yet are so prevalent and so tenacious.

When examined within the framework of cause and effect, speech fright ceases to be a mysterious, uncontrollable malady. First, let us examine the effects. Every experienced speech teacher has listened sympathetically as novices describe their struggles with tension. Sometimes the symptoms take extreme form, such as: "My feet weighed fifty pounds each and I could hardly move them"; "I ached all over"; "My head seemed about to burst"; "I couldn't eat for two days before my speech." Sometimes, anxiety reveals itself in less obvious ways. One nervous person may talk too much in discussion, another may bubble and simper in conversation, and others may be belligerent, flippant, excessively humble, too anxious to please, cool and disdainful, hypercritical, dictatorial, or unwilling to listen to others. Although it may sometimes serve to cloak the speaker's insecurity from his listeners, such compensatory behavior is a negative adjustment and nearly always reduces one's potential effectiveness.

What provokes the emotional disturbance affecting nearly all of us to some extent when we speak in public? (1) *Social fear.* The basic cause from which all others stem is social fear. We do not experience tension when conversing with associates or with members of our family. We may feel only mild apprehension, if any, when talking to a client about a purchase, to a professor about a report, or to an employer concerning a change in work routine. However, when the number of persons listening to us increases into a group, when the speaking situation becomes more formal, and when the cycle of communication assumes a speaker—silent-audience relationship, we are more inclined to suffer strong social fears. Instead of thinking of the audience as being composed of various individuals, the beginning speaker tends to consider the audience as an aggregate body sitting in judgment. The size of the audience, the unfamiliarity of the experience, the importance of "doing well," and the unpredictability of the listeners' response combine to stimulate fear reactions in the speaker. (2) *Limited experience.* Weren't you nervous at your first prom? On the initial appearance at your first job? Of course. Poise and assurance are acquired by continued and successful exposure to a situation. As the sense of strangeness wears off and as the individual recognizes that he is coping satisfactorily with the challenge, he naturally develops self-confidence. (3) *Unpleasant previous experiences.* You may have been negatively conditioned by one or more unsuccessful or embarrassing experiences, such as forgetting your lines in a high school play, "drawing a blank" when reporting to your Sunday school class, being laughed at when making a serious point at a club meeting, or receiving severe criticism from a teacher, parent, or friend. Thereafter, speaking at any public occasion might serve to elicit a fear response. (4) *Feelings of social inadequacy.* Many individuals suffer from a general sense of social insecurity. Often such attitudes impair assurance when facing an audience. As you probably know, inferiority feelings frequently arise from an underestimation of one's true worth. For example, young people are inclined to be unduly sensitive about their "undesirable" personal characteristics, such as: obesity, thinness, shape or length of the nose, prominence of the Adam's apple, bad complexion, dialect, guilt feelings, absence of sex appeal, lack of "hail-fellow" gregariousness, and so on. (5) *Factors in the particular speaking situation.* Speech fear may be engendered by inadequate preparation, the importance of the meeting, the prestige of the listeners, unfamiliarity with the location, or by the speaker's belief that the audience holds him in low esteem or is hostile to him personally or to his ideas.

We have inspected the symptoms of speech fright and have diagnosed some of the causative factors. To explain how to relieve apprehension is the next step. Unfortunately, there is no magic prescription which will immunize you against the fear virus. However, the following psychological advice may help you to reduce the virulence of your emotional disturbance.

1. Face up to speech fright. Recognize that you may experience some nervous strain preceding and during your first platform performances, and resolve that no matter how severe your emotional disturbance may become you will accept each opportunity to speak. Resist any temptation to escape tension by dropping the course, skipping the class when scheduled to talk, feigning illness, or pretending to be unprepared. (Now and then a student who is adequately prepared may avoid speaking by claiming he is not ready.) Occasionally a student becomes so apprehensive over speaking that he develops a genuine, if psychosomatic, illness such as a sore throat or an upset stomach. If this happens to you, do not let such an indisposition keep you from speaking. Any direct or subconscious avoidance of speaking will condition you negatively; it will serve to increase your tension when confronted with a speaking situation which you cannot avoid. The only way to master speech fright is to face up to it.

2. *Apply these psychological antidotes to counteract speech fright.* The following suggestions should help you to function efficiently, even though you are nervous.

a. OTHERS SHARE YOUR FEELINGS OF TENSION. For several years the author has asked the members of his beginning classes the question: "What do you consider to be your most important single speech need?" A large majority have responded in effect: "To gain poise and assurance when facing an audience." In a survey of students enrolled in communication skills classes at the University of Iowa, Floyd I. Greenleaf found that between 84 and 89 per cent experienced mild to severe stage fright when speaking in public. Milton Dickens and William Parker found that the strain of addressing an audience "measurably affected" the pulse and blood pressure rates of over 90 per cent of the student speakers tested at Redlands University.[1]

Naturally emotional misgivings are not restricted to students; they are shared by most public performers. After more than sixty years of entertaining distinguished audiences, the world's greatest cellist Pablo Casals confessed that he still suffered from "the jitters" prior to a concert. The beloved singer Madam Schumann-Heink once sighed, "I grow so nervous before a performance, I become sick, almost. I want to go home." Following many years of combating nervous tension, the famed actress Cornelia Otis Skinner asked her father, "How long does one have to be in the theatre before one loses stage fright?" His reply was, "I have been in the theatre for fifty years and have never failed to have some stage fright." Nearly every veteran public

---

[1] Milton Dickens and William R. Parker, "An Experimental Study of Certain Physiological, Introspective and Rating-Scale Techniques for the Measurement

speaker, who has expressed himself on the matter, has admitted to being keyed up before important addresses. The roll of distinguished, successful speakers who experience such heightened tension includes: Harry S. Truman, Adlai E. Stevenson, Ralph J. Bunche, Billy Graham, and Dwight D. Eisenhower.

The knowledge that your anxieties are by no means unique should help you to avoid exaggerating the seriousness of your plight.

b. You Appear More Assured Than You Are.   Tension is easier to bear if you realize that the symptoms of speech fright are usually well concealed. Even speech instructors often believe that a speaker is more confident than he feels. Although you may be painfully conscious of the "butterflies" in your stomach and the pounding in your chest, such symptoms may be unnoticeable to others. Unless you give some overt clues, no one will know that your heart is racing or that your head aches; unless you are demonstrating some visual aid that requires precise handling, no one will observe slight tremors of your fingers; if your voice is somewhat tense, many persons will not notice it. Some experienced speakers admit that they remain nervous during an entire presentation; but, because they have learned to perform effectively despite tension, only the performers themselves are conscious of their inner excitement.

c. Tension Is a Potential Friend.   When Edmund Burke wrote "No passion so effectively robs the mind of all its powers of acting and reasoning as fear," he was referring to paralyzing panic, terror. Naturally if you so dread the act of speaking that you work yourself into a state of profound agitation, such extreme stress will restrict your effectiveness. However, by applying the psychological antidotes given in these pages, you should be able to substitute the asset "heightened tension" for the liability speech fright. Nature's method of preparing us for an emergency is to generate nervous energy—power—by stimulating the flow of various endocrine secretions, stepping up the heart rate, and increasing physical tonus. Be thankful that the anticipation of speaking activates your neuromuscular system to become more alert and more responsive. Put your nervous energy to work for you, instead of letting it react against you, by channeling it into positive outlets such as vigorous, enthusiastic vocal and physical delivery. If you do, your presentation will be more dynamic, your flow of language will be smoother, your personality will project itself to the listeners more effectively, and your mental reactions will be faster, clearer, and more accurate.

d. AUDIENCES ARE FRIENDLY.   Since speech fright is basically caused by the dread of unfavorable audience reactions, you should feel encouraged to know that audiences, particularly your classroom group, want the speaker to succeed. Beginners are sometimes poor interpreters of the feedback they receive from their listeners. Because they fear negative responses, they are inclined to be overly suspicious. Frequently they distort an innocuous facial expression or shift in posture into an evidence of hostility or boredom. After his first speech, one student said, "They seemed to be just sitting there waiting for me to make some mistake so they could laugh or sneer at me." Do not be guilty of such a misjudgment of the feedback. Unless actively hostile to you or your ideas, an audience will not desire your failure as a speaker. Only the ill-bred auditor indicates obvious disapproval of a speaker who is doing his best. Usually listeners are friendly and want you to do well. In fact, they tend to be embarrassed and to suffer in empathy when a speaker seems upset. The average auditor will be pulling for you if for no other reason than that he feels better psychologically when you do creditably. Your classmates will be especially sympathetic and encouraging. After all, most of them are waging their own individual struggles against tension.

e. SYSTEMATIC PROCEDURES WILL MINIMIZE TENSION.   If you apply the suggestions concerning the various forms of speaking (as briefly sketched in Chapter 1 and fully treated in Part IV), you will reduce the likelihood of an onset of excessive tension. (1) Select only those subjects on which you are already well informed and which are interesting and meaningful both to you and to the listeners. If you have had long experience with a subject, you probably have developed mature attitudes toward it and a storehouse of knowledge about it. This thorough background provides a strong psychological comfort. During your talk you will be much less likely to forget; and, if you should be unable to recall a particular point, a substitute idea will probably flash to your consciousness. When excited about a subject, you are less inclined to be self-conscious. Your eagerness to speak tends to crowd out the negative reaction of fear. If your listeners are interested, they automatically will respond more favorably to your message. Their positive reactions will prove highly encouraging to you. Because you recognize that your presentation is getting across, you will enjoy better poise. (2) Prepare conscientiously. Aside from the rewards to the audience, careful preparation will strengthen your confidence in your ability to cope with the speaking situation. Gather more material than you can use; then select that which will be most interesting and meaningful to the listeners. Arrange your ideas in a logical manner so that you and the listeners can easily remember the development of thought. Try to complete your gathering and organizing of materials sufficiently in advance of speaking so that the ideas and the sequence can "set" or mature in your thinking. Warning: You are inviting speech fright if you pick a subject at random, prepare superficially by reading an article or two in *Coronet* or *Reader's Digest,* or complete your preparation just before speaking. (3) Rehearse your presentation so that you know perfectly the idea sequence of your speech. As you go over the material orally and silently several times, the neural patterns in the brain become firmer and are less likely to be disrupted by emotional tension. (4) On the day of your presentation, follow these guides to prevent the building up of pre-speech tension. Arrive at class a little early and engage in casual conversation with several of your acquaintances. Your platform presentation will be merely an expanded form of such social conversation. Most authorities suggest that after the meeting gets underway you should concentrate upon the proceedings. If you give close attention to the announcements and the other events on the program, your attention will be distracted from yourself and you may pick up some relevant observations which may serve as an interesting springboard into your presentation. Some speakers, however, use the pre-speech period to condition themselves to speak, much as a boxer uses the pre-bout period to prepare himself to fight. Jack Dempsey used to warm up for his fights by shadow boxing in his dressing room while he snarled, "I can lick that so and so." You might use your warm-up period to give yourself a pep talk. You might tell yourself: "I have something to say that has genuine meaning for my listeners, and I want to share my ideas with them. Because of long-term interest and intensive preparation, I know more about the subject than my hearers. I am in a position to be of real service to them." As you await your turn to speak, breathe deeply, slowly, and regularly. Try to relax the muscles of your jaws, neck, and shoulders. If you can do so unobtrusively, stretch and yawn several times. (5) When your turn comes to speak, walk briskly to the platform. Take a comfortable stance near the front of the stage and midway between the two sides. As you pause for a moment, look directly at several friends in the audience; if you feel like smiling, do so; if not, at least try to seem friendly and animated. As you launch into your speech be dynamic and enthusiastic. Your listeners will appreciate your sincere eagerness to reach them and will respond accordingly. Look at and talk to each individual in the small classroom audience. If you feel tense, change position on the platform, try some gestures, use greater volume, or increase the animation of your voice. Attempt to forget about yourself as you concentrate upon the process of conveying your message to the audience. Do not worry about negative considerations such as: "How do I look? Will I forget? Does my voice quaver?" A strong fear reaction cannot set in as long as your mind is occupied with the positive thoughts involved in reaching your listeners.

3. Maintain faith in your eventual triumph over speech fright. Surviving your first speaking experiences should bolster your confidence and reduce your apprehension. Even if you do not speak as effectively as you wish, consider your efforts to be valuable learning experiences and expect to do better as the term progresses. Under the skilled handling of an experienced instructor, students rarely fail in early speeches. However, if you believe that you have discredited yourself, take comfort in the optimistic prediction of producer Stanley Kramer, who has seen many victims of camera fright catapult to stardom: "Failure gives you a feeling of solidity. When you climb back on your feet, you have a confidence that comes from surviving failure. It's a confidence you can't get in any other way." After you discover that you can perform adequately though tense, your fear of nervous stress will recede, and you will gradually learn to control it instead of letting it control you. In a study of beginning speech students at the University of Minnesota, Stanley Paulson found that both men and women showed "significant increases in confidence" during their training and that the acquired poise was retained even when they spoke to audiences composed of strangers.[2] Accept the inspirational value of this assurance from The Second Epistle of Paul to Timothy: "For God hath not given us the spirit of fear; but of power, and of love, and of a sound mind."

B. Being Modest. In comparison to the host of those who lack sufficient confidence, only a rare few are arrogant, supercilious, condescending, or disdainfully aloof. Successful speaking experiences will, of course, develop self-confidence. However, your self-appraisal should be tempered by a recognition of your limitations and by a genuine respect for the intrinsic worth of others. As a rule, successful, psychologically secure persons experience little need for a defensive facade of superiority, and typically they possess at least a touch of humility. A realistic person can hardly fail to be modest. On the one hand, he realizes the vastness of accumulated knowledge, the complexity of modern problems, and the relatively large supply of keen, well-

[2] Stanley Paulson, "Changes in Confidence During a Period of Speech Training," *Speech Monographs,* November, 1951, pp. 260–265.

educated, highly skilled persons; on the other hand, he has rationally evaluated his own capacities, accomplishments, and limitations. Except for most unusual cases, the university student is relatively untried and untested; he has yet to make a significant impression upon his times. For him to indulge in over-confidence is to limit his personal growth. If you are inclined to view your speaking with self-satisfied complacency, you might be interested in learning that, following each of his speeches, Adlai Stevenson evaluates critically his content and delivery. How does he feel after such an analysis? "I am always depressed," he says. "I shouldn't say that I am never satisfied, but I am always wishing I had done better. I think a speaker really makes four speeches: the speech he thinks about ahead of time; the speech he writes; the speech he gives; and the speech he gives on the way home." [3]

APPROPRIATE ATTITUDES TOWARD THE COURSE

Occasionally, beginning students harbor misconceptions about the nature of a course in speech. Perhaps an analysis of some of these misconceptions will help you to derive the maximum benefits from your study.

A. "Are Speakers Born, Not Made?" At the outset, you may be struck by the disparity in the speech skills of your classmates. In your other courses, like history or philosophy, striking differences in the initial ability of the students may not be so obvious. However, in courses involving basic skills, such as applied art, applied music, physical education, acting, and speech, individual variations in ability are easily noticeable. Some speech students reveal pleasant voices, clear pronunciation, facility in language, and well-adjusted personalities; others display less skill; and a few may exhibit irritating vocal quality, slovenly pronunciation, barbarous language, and/or unattractive speech person-

[3] Russel Windes, Jr., and James A. Robinson, "Public Address in the Career of Adlai E. Stevenson," *The Quarterly Journal of Speech*, October, 1956, p. 230.

ılities. Do these variations indicate that speakers are born, not made? No, they demonstrate merely that individuals inherit dissimilar capabilities and that some develop their potentialities more rapidly than others.

If all performers were born and not made Norman Vincent Peale would not have become one of the most successful speakers of our times and Humphrey Bogart would never have won an Oscar. Several years ago in an interview at the Marble Collegiate Church, Dr. Peale was asked: "Were you born with a natural facility for self-expression or have you been forced to cultivate it?" His reply was, "I doubt that anyone was ever less likely to become an effective speaker than I. I definitely was not endowed with superior linguistic skill. In fact, as a boy in Ohio, I was exceedingly shy and inarticulate. One of my most important early battles was to acquire adequate poise in ordinary social situations." [4] Humphrey Bogart displayed so little talent as a young actor that to the experienced eye of Alexander Woollcott one of Bogart's performances "could be mercifully described as inadequate." Undoubtedly many adequate speakers and some exceptional ones have acquired their talent without conscious effort. Conversely, some persons even after extensive study and experience remain ineffectual, bumbling performers. Nevertheless, most persons need directed training under competent guidance. With training, experience, and the desire to improve, the average student can become a good speaker and the individual who is richly endowed with natural talent can become an outstanding speaker. Of course, few students can become Daniel Websters, Winston Churchills, or Franklin Roosevelts. For that matter, few golfers can become Ben Hogans or Sam Sneads. However, individuals of average ability become effective speakers with greater frequency than duffers become par-breaking golfers. Furthermore, even the Roosevelts and the Churchills improve with training, practice, and study.

[4] Eugene E. White and Clair R. Henderlider, "What Norman Vincent Peale Told Us About His Speaking," *The Quarterly Journal of Speech*, December, 1954, p. 408.

B. "Is a Silver Tongue More (Less) Important than Significant Ideas?" The conflict over which is more important, subject matter or presentation, is probably as old as speechmaking. When Demosthenes was asked to name the chief requisite in eloquence, he assigned first place to action, or delivery. Cicero was more explicit when he wrote, "Delivery, I say, has the sole and supreme power in oratory; without it, a speaker of the highest mental capacity can be held in no esteem; while one of moderate abilities, with this qualification, may surpass even those of the highest talent." Although he recognized that delivery "contributes much to the right impression of a speech," Aristotle believed that the worth of a message should be judged by its logical contents. If space and your patience permitted, we could trace this argument over the centuries. Indeed, it still continues. Now and then a student claims, "If you have something worthwhile to say, the manner in which you say it is unimportant. Lots of empty-headed fools are fascinating speakers. The world needs more people with significant messages and fewer mediocrities who can charm audiences with nonsense." As might be expected, this point of view is usually advanced by a studious, thoughtful pupil—one who is more interested in ideas than in salesmanship, who is introverted rather than garrulous, shy rather than aggressive. A more common point of view is expressed by the student who says, "If you ask me, the important thing in speech is good delivery. A man with a good voice, a likable personality, and a gift of gab can just about write his own ticket." This attitude is common among confident, gregarious students who enjoy talking and mixing with people. Usually such a student is primarily interested in action rather than ideas, and he rarely has designs on a Phi Beta Kappa key. Both of these viewpoints contain elements of truth. If the speaker's ideas are vitally important or compellingly interesting, listeners may tolerate incredibly bad delivery; conversely listeners may occasionally be so mesmerized by the polished manner of the speaker that they tend to be uncritical of his content.

Controversy over the relative merits of content and delivery is as meaningless as debate over which is most important in base-ball—pitching, hitting, or fielding—or which parent is more important to a successful home. We do not attempt to resolve the issue here. We merely suggest that you should be vitally concerned with both what you say and how effectively you say it. Skillful delivery should not be wasted on inconsequential ideas, and significant material should not suffer from inadequate presentation.

C. "Is Speech a Snap Course?" Professor Claude E. Kantner has pointed out that the educated man is not "a stuffed sausage who has been through a four-year grind and comes out filled from end to end with knowledge, neatly packaged and ready for the waiting job market." Learning is an active, not a passive process. The benefits you receive from your speech training, or from any learning experience, are directly proportional to the intensity of your efforts. If you slide through the course and yet receive a passing grade, either you are unusually talented or the standards used by your instructor or your institution are too low. Your speech course deserves your best efforts. If you are indifferent to improving your speech, you have underestimated the significance of oral communication to your future and to society. Make the most of this opportunity to develop your oral skills.

D. "Will the Course Make Me an Orator?" Some students expect a one-semester course in speech to accomplish miracles. As examples, a student believed that the course would enable her to develop an "entirely new personality"; another hoped to acquire a voice "exactly like that of Edward R. Murrow"; a third expected to be "able to handle the King's English the way Adlai Stevenson does"; a fourth thought that he would "never again be at a loss for words"; and a fifth believed that the course would convert him into a professional lecturer. At the opposite extreme, some students begin a speech course resigned to defeat. As one such student said, "I'll try my best, but I don't really expect to improve much, if at all." What is a reasonable prognosis for your development of speech skills? Experience with thousands of students indicates that any person who exerts a conscientious effort will improve but that a pupil should not expect a miraculous transformation. A single semester of history will not produce a historian, nor will a semester of speech transform even a talented student into an orator. Highly competent speaking requires a maturation of thought, a richness of philosophy, a depth and breadth of knowledge, and a superb skill in the application of a host of rhetorical abilities—all of which must be acquired by extensive experience over a considerable period of time. The degree of improvement you will achieve depends directly upon the intensity of your desires and the amount of time that you are willing to devote to study, preparation, and practice.

APPROPRIATE ATTITUDES TOWARD YOUR CLASSMATES AND YOUR INSTRUCTOR

After the first meeting or two of your speech class you will know your class members' names and something about their backgrounds, hobbies, and aspirations. In his various speaking assignments, each student will reveal facets of his character and personality. He will share with you many of his beliefs, attitudes, biases, and interests. As you get to know your colleagues better, your relationships probably will develop into a positive *esprit de corps*. Close friendships often develop and occasionally even romance blossoms.

The closeness of the relationship and the informality of the atmosphere require that you exercise tact and maintain politeness. Recognize that you will have an important part in the growth of each individual as a speaker and as a person. By being attentive, objective, and analytical listeners, you and the other students will serve as a testing laboratory for each speaker's ideas and manner of presentation. Moreover, you will be training yourself in a skill essential to effective living—that of understanding and interpreting communications directed at you.

Along with listening and observing, you may have another obligation to your classmates—to help in the evaluation of their abilities as speakers. You may be asked to assess aloud or in written reports the strengths and weaknesses of other speakers' performances. If you are invited to augment your instructor's critiques, frame your comments discreetly and make them constructive. Stifle any inclination to deliver a cutting or belittling remark which may reduce the speaker's confidence and security. Many centuries ago, Aristotle pointed out that such caustic criticism is basically an unwholesome attempt to expand one's own ego. Moreover, it may backfire: your resentful victims may begin to take nasty digs at you. With the enthusiastic cooperation of each member, a speech class can be a rewarding experience in democratic living.

Your instructor's function entails more than acquainting you with subject matter; he must guide your personal development of a complex skill. Naturally, this necessitates that he offer constructive suggestions. Welcome the recommendations of your instructor. He will be diplomatic and considerate of your feelings. His only motive is to help you become a better speaker. To close your mind to advice places an artificial limitation upon your chances to improve. Receive any suggestions graciously; analyze them objectively; then, if you feel so inclined, accept them and try to profit accordingly.

SUMMARY

To secure the maximum benefits from your speech course, adopt and maintain appropriate attitudes toward yourself as a speaker, toward your speech course, and toward your classmates and instructor. More specifically, face your speech training with confidence and modesty; also, recognize that effective speech is not a gift but an acquirable skill, that you should be concerned with both what you say and how you say it, that by expending maximum effort you will derive commensurate returns, and that you can realize the greatest values from the

course only by achieving a healthy and cooperative relationship with your classmates and instructor.

EXERCISES AND ASSIGNMENTS

1. When the English journalist William T. Stead, who had never spoken
to large audiences, was called upon to address a series of public gatherings,
he asked his friend Cardinal Manning for advice. The Cardinal's suggestion
was: "Be full of your subject and forget yourself." Thought questions: What
do you consider to be the merits and limitations of this advice? How helpful
do you believe it would be to the typical beginning speaker? If you were
offering suggestions to a person subject to speech fright, what additional
guides, if any, would you give? (You might enjoy reading Joseph O. Baylen
and Patrick G. Hogan's article, "W. T. Stead on the Art of Public Speaking," *The Quarterly Journal of Speech,* April, 1957, pp. 128–136.)

2. In the course of your reading, attempt to discover instances of speakers
who experience speech fright. Bring at least one such example to class. As
samples: In an article concerning Billy Graham's television sermons, *Time*
quoted the evangelist as admitting, "Although I have a deep inner peace,
I have an exterior fear before every program and get perspiration on my
palms." The columnist Mary Margaret McBride wrote this human interest
story concerning one of her speech experiences:

> It sounds rather pretentious, I'm afraid, but I'm going to say it anyway:
> the most stimulating dinner partner I ever had was an ex-President of
> the United States.
> This came about when I went to Kansas City to make a speech before
> Theta Sigma Phi honorary journalistic organization. . . .
> That evening at dinner, I found myself actually seated next to Harry
> S. Truman.
> The one time I diet is when I have to speak in public. That's because
> I'm too scared to swallow.
> And on such occasions I literally never hear what anybody says to me
> in the way of admonition, comfort, or persiflage. But somehow this was
> different, for Mr. Truman understood.
> "Eat a little," he urged. "It'll do you good," and added comfortingly,
> 'Everybody feels like that."
> "Not you?" I asked in astonishment. "Even messages to Congress?"
> The former President nodded and suddenly I felt so much better that
> I choked down a little chicken.

3. Some speech experts believe that attitudes are more important than
aptitudes. Make a detailed list of the various attitudes that you believe the

successful speaker should possess. As you read the list to the class, defend each of your items and explain how each might be developed by the beginning speaker. Before executing this exercise, you might wish to read Chapter 3. Also, you might enjoy reading this article prepared by two businessmen, Donald E. Baier and Robert D. Dugan, "Factors in Sales Success," *Journal of Applied Psychology*, No. 1, 1957, pp. 37–40. (Baier and Dugan say that "A salesman's belief in his product and his motivation are more important than technical knowledge in determining how well he does his job. Length of service is unrelated to job success.")

4. In a three-minute speech to the class, describe frankly your symptoms of anxiety both before and during your class presentations. Talking candidly about your fears should have a wholesome cathartic effect. However, if you hesitate to express yourself in this way before an audience, do not feel compelled to do so.

5. Attend a social function and observe carefully the behavior of those present. Did some persons reveal symptoms of social fear? What kinds of defensive or compensatory behavior did you notice? Report your observations to the class. Be careful, of course, to protect the identities of the persons involved.

6. Prepare a short essay explaining your reasons for taking a course in speech. If required to take the class, explain why you favor or oppose this requirement. Such an analysis should aid you in clarifying your own motivations and may help your instructor to meet more effectively your personal needs.

II ❦❦ *The Speaker*

3 ❧❧ *Personal Attributes*

The preceding section introduced the study of oral communication. We are now ready to consider the personal characteristics and the basic delivery skills necessary for effective speaking. Here is a preview of what lies ahead in Part II: This chapter explains the desirable personal attributes of the speaker, which include broad knowledge, appropriate traits of personality and character, and suitable appearance and conduct. Chapter 4 suggests ways in which you can improve your understanding and use of language. Chapter 5 offers guides to the effective use of bodily action. Chapter 6 explains how to cultivate the audibility, pleasantness, fluency, and flexibility of your voice. Chapter 7 presents a program for improving the clarity and appropriateness of pronunciation.

THE EFFECTIVE SPEAKER IS
INTELLECTUALLY PREPARED

A. The Importance of Broad Knowledge to the Speaker. The intellectual nudist is rarely an effective speaker. The successful speaker has something worth saying. Usually he is a mature person who possesses wide knowledge and human understanding. A facetious student once explained, "A good speech is something like hash—it's accumulated over a period of time." Although somewhat strained, this analogy illustrates the point that successful speaking is usually the product of an accumulated storehouse of information. By personal experience or persevering study, the persuasive speaker has earned the right to talk on his subject. Of course, the young college student does not need to

49

abstain from speaking in public until his conjectures ripen into mature judgments. However, as we have suggested before, for his speeches, discussions, and oral readings he should select topics within his range of personal or acquired experience. Furthermore, he should seek constantly to increase his background of knowledge. In Part IV of this text, we shall discuss the preparation needed for specific acts of communication. Now, however, let us consider briefly the lifelong problem of acquiring and preserving a broad, rich reservoir of information.

B. The Establishing of a Program of Self-Improvement. Evidence indicates that the most successful speakers have never ceased in their acquisition of a liberal education. Your present academic program should make a significant contribution to your general knowledge. However, you may find it desirable to supplement course work with an independent improvement program, especially if you are specializing in a technical field like electrical engineering or physics. Following graduation, you should expand your project for general self-betterment. The acquiring of interests in and knowledge of a wide variety of subjects will increase your areas of intellectual sensitivities, will make you a more mature and better balanced individual, and will provide a fund of background information which will serve you well in the future when preparing for specific speaking assignments.

In addition to improving your general store of knowledge, concentrate on becoming an authority in the area of your future vocation. When you leave school, most of your speaking in public will be directly related to your type of employment, that is, usually an editorial writer will be invited to speak on current events, an investment broker on economics, and an AFL-CIO official on labor-management relations.

How do you conduct such a program of self-betterment?

1. Become an insatiable, selective reader. As Francis Bacon said, "Reading maketh a full man." Reading opens limitless, magnificently rewarding vistas. (a) Plan to investigate at least a few of those ideas which have shaped civilization. The greatest thoughts of the most profound philosophers are available to you in such works as John Locke's *On Civil Government,* John Stuart Mill's *On Liberty,* Saint Thomas Aquinas' *Treatise on Divine Government,* Francis Bacon's *Novum Organum,* Plato's *The Republic,* and Auguste Comte's *The Positive Philosophy.* (b) Enjoy the romance and adventure available in the great masterpieces of world literature. Perhaps an earlier exposure to literature in high school proved unpleasant? Now, you are several years older and should be better equipped to understand and to enjoy the best writings of our rich literary heritage. As an experiment, read several outstanding plays, novels, tales, and epic poems. If you have difficulty deciding where to start, try both ends of the alphabet with *Andersonville* by MacKinlay Kantor and *The Yearling* by Marjorie Kinnan Rawlings. (c) Read historical works. When well-written, history is vivid, compelling, and dramatic. By means of the printed page you can experience vicariously the great events of recorded times. You can struggle over the passes of the Alps behind Hannibal's elephants; you can witness the climax of the first politico-constitutional conflict in English history when the English barons forced King John at Runnymede to accept the Magna Charta; you can stand in Fraunces' Tavern, New York, as General George Washington took final leave of his officers; you can join General Wingate's raiders as they push through the stifling Burmese jungles, climb jagged ranges, and slip through the elephant grass in the valleys. Perhaps you might like to start your reading in history with one of these books: Catherine Drinker Bowen's *The Lion and the Throne,* Ray West, Jr.'s *Kingdom of the Saints,* Bruce Catton's *A Stillness at Appomattox,* David Lavender's *Bent's Fort,* Arthur M. Schlesinger, Jr.'s *The Crisis of the Old Order,* Earl S. Mier's *The American Story,* or *The American Heritage Book of the Revolution.* (d) Explore the fascinating worlds of science, sociology, psychology, political science, and economics. Learn about the nature of matter, the structure of the earth, the origin of life, and the requisites for interplanetary travel. Read about man's greatest scientific inventions and medical discoveries; about painters, sculptors, and musicians; about cybernetics; about rational and sub-rational behavior; about America's granaries, stock markets, and steel mills; and about the world's governments, peoples, and religions. As a beginning, try one or more of these books: C. W. Ceram's *Gods, Graves and Scholars,* Thor Heyerdahl's *Aku-Aku,* Vance Packard's *The Hidden Persuaders,* E. H. Gombrich's *The Story of Art,* Edward Steichen's *The Family of Man,* John K. Galbraith's *The Affluent Society,* or Willy Ley's *Rockets, Missiles & Space Travel.* (e) By means of newspapers and magazines keep up with current events. Read at least one of these magazines each week: *Time, Newsweek, U.S. News and World Report, Life, Look,* or *The Reporter.* Also become familiar with *Fortune, The Atlantic,* and *Harper's Magazine.* (f) Read intensively in the literature of your field. Almost every area of specialization has its professional and semi-professional journals, special bulletins, monographs, and bibliographic aids.

2. *Supplement the printed page by becoming a skilled and constant observer.*   Acquire knowledge of life and humanity by becoming highly tuned to your environment. William Blake has pointed out that "The fool sees not the same tree that a wise man sees." Many persons are automatons, going about their routine daily activities with only a sluggish awareness of what is happening about them. Others, who possess a searching, probing intellect, are sensitively alert to their surroundings. Observe the different types of people you encounter, notice how they behave under different circumstances, and listen to what they have to say and how they express themselves. Take advantage of the opportunities in your area to observe at close range man's problems of traffic congestion, slums, race relations, legislation, and the dispensation of justice. Visit the outstanding scenic attractions in your region. Become acquainted with the business, industrial, scientific, and cultural activities of your community. Avoid the intellectual vacuity displayed by the student from New York City who had never visited the United Nations Headquarters, the student from Detroit who had never toured an industrial plant, or the student from Washington, D. C., who had never visited the Library of Congress or the Smithsonian Institution. One important type of observing can be accomplished in your own home by the selection of rewarding programs on radio and television.

3. Occasionally set aside brief periods for reflective thinking. According to the publisher John S. Knight, "What we really need is a reform movement to give serious reading and sober reflection a touch of respectability—and for the ladies—a fashionable facade. The word THINK would then become something more than a motto on the desk." Admittedly both America's standard of living and world leadership depend to a considerable extent upon the bustling energy of its people. Nevertheless, one is inclined to agree with the satirist who wrote that "These days there are too many persons in too many cars in too much of a hurry going in too many directions to nowhere for nothing." For the sake of intellectual growth and emotional stability, pause occasionally to reflect upon what you have learned, what you are doing, and what the future holds for you. Such periods of quiet meditation will enable you to know yourself and others better, to make mental associations, and to acquire new values and concepts.

4. Preserve significant materials. A few individuals seem to be gifted with photographic memories enabling them to retain vast amounts of specific data. For most of us, however, knowledge is transitory. The illustrations, quotations, statistics, jokes, and other material, which at one time may seem compellingly vivid gradually fade into indistinctness and finally into oblivion. The only practical method of preserving materials for ready reference is to follow the practice of many writers, journalists, and speakers: record the information in a permanent file. As examples: David Lloyd George "carried a small book in which he noted any thought or phrase which might fit into a speech." [1] For many years, Franklin D. Roosevelt maintained an extensive

[1] Thomas Jones, *Lloyd George* (Cambridge: Harvard University Press, 1951), p. 266.

"Speech Material File," organized according to subject matter.[2] When a "happy phrase" occurs to Prime Minister Harold Macmillan, "he jots it down for use later—a process he calls 'hatching eggs'—and deposits it in what he calls 'the egg box.' " When composing a speech, he often "fishes out" an appropriate reference or quotation.[3] Dorothea Michaelson, staff lecturer for the National Gallery of Art, told a University of Miami speech student: "If I hear or observe something that might be useful to my speaking, I make a mental note of it. As soon as circumstances permit, I record the observation on a 3″ by 5″ card. If, after a period of time, it still seems valuable, it becomes a part of my files. Otherwise, I discard it. I would stress the importance of keeping reference material to anyone who wants to become an effective speaker." For the person who speaks frequently, a constantly expanding file provides an invaluable, immediately accessible reservoir of previously assimilated material. (The process of note-recording will be discussed in Chapter 15.)

THE EFFECTIVE SPEAKER POSSESSES DESIRABLE TRAITS OF PERSONALITY AND CHARACTER

Successful oral communication requires more than knowledge and skill in speaking. The speaker should possess desirable attributes of personality and character. Although exceptions immediately come to mind, we may suggest that, as a general rule, an individual is no better speaker than he is a person. The intrinsic worth of an individual tends to be mirrored in his oral utterance. This principle has long been recognized by rhetoricians. Aristotle argued that a speaker's reputation is one of the most potent of all the means of persuasion. Cicero added, "It contributes much to success in speaking that the morals, principles, conduct, and lives of those who plead causes . . . should

[2] For a detailed explanation of the nature, purpose, and acquisition of this material, see the study by Earnest Bradenburg and Waldo W. Braden, "Franklin Delano Roosevelt" in *A History and Criticism of American Public Address* (New York: Longmans, Green & Co., Inc., 1955) , Vol. III, Marie K. Hochmuth, ed.

[3] *Time,* January 21, 1957, p. 21.

be such as to merit esteem." Although sometimes a speaker may successfully camouflage his true nature, considerable truth exists in Ralph Waldo Emerson's dictum, "What you are . . . thunders so that I cannot hear what you say." [4]

Among the attributes of personality and character which a speaker should possess are sincerity and honesty, animation and enthusiasm, assurance, modesty, objectivity, and a sense of humor.

A. Sincerity and Honesty. In school, business, industry, government, and in the family, interpersonal relations depend upon the honesty and reliability of the individual. Without faith in one another, society as we know it could not endure. On the public platform, as elsewhere, there is no substitute for integrity. As Harry S. Truman has said, "mere talent without intellectual honesty . . . is not enough to make a successful speaker. . . . Sincerity, honesty, and a straightforward manner are more important than special talent or polish." [5]

The sincere and honest speaker believes what he says. Unlike the Grecian sophists, skilled in making the worse appear the better cause, the ethical speaker advances only those causes in which he believes. Earnest conviction generates a personal power which reveals itself in numerous ways in the speaker's delivery.

---

[4] Recent experimental studies reinforce the traditional importance of desirable traits of personality and character in the speaker. A study by Berlo and Gulley demonstrates that "the favorableness with which" a speaker "is viewed is of prime importance in securing acceptance of a substantive point of view." David K. Berlo and Halbert E. Gulley, "Some Determinants of the Effect of Oral Communication in Producing Attitude Change and Learning," *Speech Monographs,* March, 1957, pp. 10–20. A study by Osgood and Tannenbaum concludes that: "The more favorable the attitude toward a source, the greater the effect of a positive assertion on raising attitude toward the concept and the greater the effect of a negative assertion upon lowering attitude toward the concept. Strongly unfavorable sources have just the opposite effects." Charles E. Osgood and Percy H. Tannenbaum, "The Principle of Congruity in the Prediction of Attitude Change," *Psychological Review,* January, 1955, pp. 42–55. Also, see Harold B. Gerard, "The Anchorage of Opinions in Face-to-Face Groups," *Human Relations,* August, 1954, pp. 313–325 and Carl I. Hovland, Irving L. Janis, and Harold H. Kelly, *Communication and Persuasion* (New Haven: Yale University Press, 1953), Chapter 2, "Credibility of the Communicator," pp. 19–55.

[5] Eugene E. White and Clair R. Henderlider, "What Harry S. Truman Told Us About His Speaking," *The Quarterly Journal of Speech,* February, 1954, pp. 37–42.

Honesty thus provides its own reward, because as the Trinity College professor John Lawson pointed out in the eighteenth century: "You cannot be much affected by what [a speaker] says, if you do not look upon him as a man of probity, who is earnest, and doth himself believe what he endeavoreth to make out as credible to you."

The sincere and honest speaker rejects the philosophy that the end justifies the means. He recognizes the many-sided nature of all serious problems; he respects the laws of adequate evidence and logical reasoning; he attempts to appeal to the higher motives in human nature rather than to the lower ones; and he presents accurate facts free from deliberate distortion. He rejects as dishonest the techniques of the demagogue and the unethical advocate.

The sincere and honest speaker talks in a simple, direct manner, without artifice or sham. His purpose in speaking is to convey his ideas and feelings to others. Therefore, he speaks from the mind and heart, avoiding the indirectness of elocutionary delivery and the artificiality of feigned emotions and attitudes.

B. Animation and Enthusiasm. Charles S. Woolworth, the five-and-ten-cent-store tycoon, once said, "A man can't succeed at anything unless he has enthusiasm for it." Certainly in no area of our activities are animation and enthusiasm of greater importance than in oral communication. Enthusiasm is catching; usually a speaker's eagerness to communicate is reflected to some degree in his listeners. Conversely, spiritless speaking usually produces listener apathy and inattention.

The animated, enthusiastic speaker is a vital, alert person. Such an individual not only is a refreshing personality, he may also be a magnetic speaker. On the other hand, the negative, wet-blanket type of personality repels rather than attracts, thus making more difficult the process of communication.

The animated, enthusiastic speaker has a compelling interest in his subject. Since the successful simulation of interest is difficult and hypocritical, a speaker should select only subjects in which he has an absorbing and continuing interest. A subject which is dull to the speaker almost inevitably results in a flat, insipid presentation.

The animated, enthusiastic speaker possesses a keen desire to communicate his message. Not only must he have something to say, he must also eagerly want to say it to his particular audience. A speaker may have a deep, even dedicated, interest in his subject, but, because he lacks a strong desire to reach his listeners, may still have a vapid, uninspiring delivery.

C. Assurance. In order to guide listeners into new areas of understanding, intellectual agreement, or emotional feeling, the speaker must demonstrate a high level of leadership. One cannot be a forceful leader of others until one can lead oneself. In addition to possessing skill in delivery and a knowledge of what he wishes to accomplish, the speaker must also have faith in himself. Although everyone experiences periods of trepidation and uncertainty, when one faces an audience the time for positive action has come. The effective speaker is a positive thinker. He expects to do well. He believes that what he says has genuine meaning for his listeners. Because he has prepared as carefully as possible for the public performance, he feels that he has earned the right to talk. He has confidence in the reliability of his evidence and the validity of his reasoning. He has respect for himself as a person and believes that he is entitled to a courteous hearing by others. He appreciates the intrinsic worth of his listeners and expects them to respond favorably to him. The beginning speaker might find comfort in this story about General Stonewall Jackson. Jackson was explaining to his staff the plans for an attack against the Union forces in the Shenandoah Valley. One of his staff members was so fearful of failure that the General called him aside. Placing his hand on the other man's shoulder, Jackson said, "Never take counsel of your fears. Always counsel with faith." In speaking, as in military science, to anticipate failure is to encourage defeat.

D. Modesty. As defined by *Webster's,* modesty "denotes an absence of all undue confidence in oneself or one's powers."

Modesty is the counterpart of assurance. The well-integrated, mature personality evidences an appropriate balance between confidence and humility. Self-assurance should be tempered by a respect for others and by a recognition of one's own limitations. Self-preoccupation interferes with a speaker's concentration on the process of communication and, if obvious, will alienate his listeners. By his manner, the arrogant speaker indicates that he is more concerned with himself than with his auditors and thereby violates what William James called "the deepest principle of human nature"—the desire of everyone (including members of audiences) to feel respected and appreciated.

E. Objectivity. Complete and perpetual objectivity is neither possible nor desirable. Such a state of mind would tend to produce a condition of permanent indecision. We inevitably develop positive or negative attitudes toward everything possessing significant meaning in our lives. Such emotional and intellectual pre-conditioning gives direction to our lives and furnishes the foundations for our moral and ethical codes. Is it possible to be completely objective about cruelty, evil, home, honor, country, or God? Once he has arrived at a conviction a person cannot possess complete objectivity; he has found the "truth"; he is no longer a "seeker" but is a "believer." In persuasive speaking, the speaker has taken a position of advocacy or opposition and attempts to convert others. A pleader cannot have the objectivity of the detached neutralist. Nevertheless, he can be fair. He can refuse to use questionable evidence, to distort supporting materials, to substitute rationalization for logic, or otherwise to circumvent intellectual honesty. The speaker can be sufficiently objective about himself to analyze calmly his assets, limitations, motivations, and convictions. In this way he can direct his efforts toward improving himself as a person and as a speaker. He can be sufficiently objective about his listeners to respect their sincere opinions and attitudes. Objectivity helps to produce the intellectual honesty and human understanding necessary for effective speaking.

F. Sense of Humor. A sense of humor is a valuable asset for the speaker. It provides the resilience to bounce back from the disappointments which unavoidably attend the process of learning to talk in public. It enables one to view his speaking endeavors in better perspective, to accept failures more philosophically, and to resolve to do better next time. Also a sense of humor makes one a more interesting speaker. Few listeners can dislike or remain indifferent to the speaker who stimulates them to laughter. Of course, some speaking situations are so extremely serious that a suggestion of levity would be inappropriate. However, a touch of humor frequently serves to lighten tension for both speaker and audience, to renew interest, and to identify the speaker as being a person of good will.

THE EFFECTIVE SPEAKER DRESSES AND CONDUCTS HIMSELF APPROPRIATELY

One of the primary methods by which listeners estimate a speaker's personal qualities is by observing his appearance and behavior.

A. Dress and Grooming. To many students the following guides for suitable dress and grooming may seem like a belaboring of the obvious. However, years of experience in observing public speakers indicate that a significant number of persons need this advice.

1. Dress should be suitable to the occasion. Students sometimes ask if they should "dress-up" for classroom speaking. The answer depends partly upon campus custom. At some colleges men traditionally wear jackets and ties to class, and women wear dresses or suits. At other institutions the men wear jeans, corduroys, or moleskins and "T" shirts; the women, skirts, sweaters, and low-heel shoes. Probably your appearance should not drastically violate the expectations of your classmates. Obviously, do not wear jeans and sweat shirt if customary campus attire is jacket, dress shirt, and tie. Probably a safe rule for classroom speeches is to dress somewhat more formally than usual, but not conspicuously so. For most off-campus speaking situations, a man should wear a suit and necktie, and a woman should dress according to customary social dictates. Regardless of the nature of the occasion, your apparel must be neat, clean, and in good repair. Clothes should be well-pressed, properly buttoned, and free from dandruff or food stains. Shoes should be polished and in good condition. Do not handicap your effectiveness with careless or unsightly dress, such as a frayed or soiled collar, crooked tie, twisted hose seam, or bulging pockets.

2. *Dress should be appropriate to the speaker.* Audiences do not expect a young man to dress as conservatively as the middle-aged, distinguished speaker, nor do they expect the matron to dress in the casual, informal air appropriate for a teen-age university freshman. In addition to dressing appropriately for your age, choose those styles, cuts, and colors which are best for your height, weight, and coloring.

3. *Dress should not call undue attention to itself.* If your clothing is obviously very expensive, striking, slovenly, or overly elaborate, it may distract attention from your message. As you know, in the majority of circumstances you will be correct to wear a business suit or dress of relatively conservative form and color. Since current styles stress informality, casualness, and brighter colors, do not feel compelled to wear dark, somber clothes; on the other hand, avoid ostentatious or eccentric dress. Ultra-modern or unusual styles and loud or clashing color combinations attract unnecessary attention. Women should avoid huge sweep-brimmed hats, veils, cumbersome purses, and the vulgar display of jewelry.

4. *Grooming should be above reproach.* Perhaps no single feature more quickly alienates the typical audience than does poor grooming on the part of the speaker. If he has proper respect for the audience and the speaking occasion, the speaker will be solicitous about the minute details of his personal appearance. Hair should be combed and trimmed; hands and finger nails should be clean. Men should be clean-shaven.

B. Platform Etiquette and Conduct. This topic will be discussed in Part IV under the basic forms of speaking. Here we simply note the importance of poised, courteous behavior. Be a considerate, co-operative listener while waiting for your turn to speak and after your presentation. As you are speaking, try to avoid distracting mannerisms; harness your nervous energy by concentrating enthusiastically on the process of conveying your message to the listeners; be respectful of your listeners' opinions and prejudgments, even though such views may clash sharply with your own. Remember that a speaker cannot compel his auditors to believe or accept, he can merely lead; and he can lead only when others are willing to follow.

SUMMARY

The desirable personal qualities of the speaker include broad knowledge, appropriate traits of personality and character, and suitable appearance and conduct. To develop a rich storehouse of knowledge, become an insatiable, selective reader and a skilled and constant observer; set aside brief periods for reflective thinking; and preserve significant materials. The attributes of personality and character which you should possess include sincerity and honesty, animation and enthusiasm, assurance, modesty, objectivity, and a sense of humor. In addition to being suitable to the occasion and to your age and physical characteristics, your dress should not call undue attention to itself; of course, your grooming should be above reproach.

EXERCISES AND ASSIGNMENTS

1. Compile a list of twenty books you plan to read in the coming year or two for the purpose of broadening your knowledge in a variety of fields. List both fiction and non-fiction and include selections from at least four or five basic areas of knowledge. Read the list to the class and be prepared to defend your selections.

2. Prepare a detailed analysis of your own speaking attributes. Your instructor will be glad to arrange a personal conference to help you plan a program of self improvement.

3. Interview a prominent local person who is considered to be an effective speaker. Discover how he "earned the right to speak." What are his views on the importance of broad knowledge and human understanding for the speaker? Prepare a written or oral report, depending upon the preference of your instructor.

4. In your reading of newspapers, news magazines, and historical works, be alert for references to the long-range educational training of prominent speakers. Bring at least one relevant quotation to class. Here is a sample item which appeared in *Time's* feature story on Prime Minister Harold Macmillan, one of England's most effective orators: "He reads prodigiously, found time last summer between official papers to read all of George Eliot, Lucretius (in Latin), several Trollope novels, and Stendhal's *Le Rouge et Le Noir* in French. (In Flanders, wounded and pinned down in a shell hole, he had whiled away the time by reading a volume of Aeschylus in the original Greek.)"

5. Study a prominent speaker to determine his long-term program for intellectual self-betterment. (Consult your instructor or librarian.) Attempt to discover the nature of his academic and informal training, the sources of his basic premises, and the extent and limitations of his intellectual powers. Assess his personality, character traits, and speaking skills. Estimate the influence which his personal attributes have exerted upon his development into an outstanding speaker.

6. Listen to a radio or television speech, or attend a public speaking occasion. In preparing a written report, which evaluates the speaker's personal attributes, utilize both your previous knowledge concerning the speaker and your impressions concerning his appearance, delivery, and subject matter.

7. Possible topics for speeches, panels, or informal class discussions: (1) What distinguishes ethical from unethical persuasion? (2) Under what conditions are appeals to the emotions ethical? Unethical? (3) How can a student achieve the maximum long-range benefits from his college experiences? (4) Which one of the various character and personality traits is the most important to effective speaking? Why? (5) Can the persuader ever be completely intellectually honest? How far can a speaker slant evidence in his favor before he becomes mendacious? How can an audience detect intellectual dishonesty in the speaker? (6) How liberal is the current stereotype concerning suitable dress and appearance of the public speaker? How closely should the speaker's dress and appearance approximate this stereotype? If he violates the stereotype, what may be the result? Do you consider this stereotype an abridgment of your personal freedoms?

4 ❧❧ *Language*

Many beginning students subscribe to rather limited concepts of the place of language in speech. *Mr. Curt and Quick* has as his motto: "Say it briefly and get it over with." Influenced by our efficient but hurried society, he has neither the time nor the interest to develop a broader concept of language. *Mr. Glib and Smooth* is primarily concerned with developing fluency. If he can produce words which flow freely and smoothly, he is satisfied. The possibility that such words may be ill chosen is to him of minor concern. *Mr. Word Worshipper* is basically interested in words for their own sake rather than as vehicles of thought. He likes to use "purple" passages and verbal niceties. What language *is* has become more important to him than what language *does*. Valuing words more highly than the thoughts they symbolize, he would rather hear the comment, "You can certainly handle the King's English," than the response, "I think you had some good ideas in that speech." The foregoing concepts of language are limited, but not entirely erroneous. We know that economy in style is desirable; few will deny the importance of fluency; and an abiding interest in words and style should lead to skill in oral language. But the speaker's insight must be deeper and his understanding greater if he is to comprehend fully the nature and functions of language in communication.

Without language you probably could not think, for thinking is done by talking silently to yourself. The communication of your thinking to a listener demands the selection of words which possess the maximum of clarity, appropriateness, and vividness, *not only to you, but to your listener*. When asked to define effective language style, Dean Swift replied that it is simply "proper words in proper places." What is "proper" (effective) in a given situation is always determined by the listener. How to use words with maximum listener-effectiveness is, then, the subject of this chapter. To develop an effective oral style, however, one must begin with an awareness of certain basic concepts.

THE NATURE OF LANGUAGE

A. Words Are Only Symbols.   Although the symbolic nature of language is relatively easy to comprehend, many persons do not react to words as symbols; instead, they conceive of words as *being* the objects, ideas, or facts which the words represent or "stand for." Examples: the woman who thought pigs were well named because "that is exactly what they are"; the man who asked how astronomers discovered the name of a newly observed galaxy; the student who wondered how Dr. Alexander Fleming was sure the drug he discovered was penicillin and not some other drug. (This student undoubtedly would be shocked to learn that at least one pharmaceutical company rents the services of an "electronic brain" to expedite the creation of thousands of new words needed for naming products.) Such is the thinking of those who confuse the world of words with the world of things.

Sometimes labels are regarded as more important than the realities they represent (or misrepresent). A man who is called a "failure" may as a result believe that he is one, not realizing that to be *labeled* a "failure" does not necessarily mean *being* one. Similarly, the normally hesitant, non-fluent child who is *called* a "stutterer" may become so emotionally disturbed in attempting to achieve adult levels of fluency that he actually *becomes* a stutterer. The power of words is apparent in the damaging potential possessed by labels such as "traitor," "coward," "egghead," "atheist," and the like.

Words are not always used to vilify or destroy; frequently they are used to dignify. In lieu of a raise in pay, many a stenographer has been satisfied by a change in title to, let us say, "executive secretary," and a garbage collector may be given a decided raise in morale by changing the name of his occupation to "sanitation engineer." The woman who rebels at being called a "housewife" accepts the label "homemaker." For similar reasons the "rat killer" becomes a "rodent exterminator"; the "press agent," a "public relations counselor"; the "repairman," a "maintenance expert"; the "criminal child," a "juvenile delinquent"; the "service station," a "lubritorium." The "poor" become the "underprivileged"; the "bar" or "saloon" becomes a "cocktail lounge"; the "toilet," a "washroom" or "rest room" or "powder room"; and the "second hand" item, a "reconditioned" product. Executives are rarely "fired"; instead they "resign" or take an "extended leave"; nations are not "conquered"; they are "liberated," and a "disorganized retreat" is called an "orderly, strategic withdrawal," or vice versa. In each of the above instances of word-juggling, observe that only words, not realities, have been changed. But such is the power of words that by changing them one may *seem* to have altered reality.

To understand language reject the identity of label and reality. A clear differentiation between the world of words and the world of things is mandatory.

B. Words Cannot Transmit (or Transfer) Meaning; They Can Only Stir Up Meanings. In Chapter 1, we noted that nothing passes between a speaker and a listener but sound and light waves. Unlike a bag of groceries, meaning cannot be delivered. If it could, a large majority of the common language problems would not exist, and the communication of precise meanings would be a simple matter—you could be sure, for example, that when you say "the American way of life" your listener would know exactly what you mean. Unfortunately, words can only stir up meanings in the minds of your listeners. Such meanings may not be identical with yours.

Because every person has had different experiences in connection with a given word, as many meanings may be attached to the expression as there are persons who know it. Communication of precise meaning is possible only when words stir up closely similar meanings in the minds of both speaker and listener. It is small wonder that misunderstanding occurs so frequently.

C. Words Do Not Tell the Whole Story. One word may tell us more than another, but any term says very little about the idea or thing to which it refers. Suppose we choose a simple, common word such as "pen." When a speaker uses this word, the context of his remarks will probably reveal which of the common basic meanings was intended, that is, a writing instrument which uses ink, an enclosure, or the slang abbreviation for "penitentiary." If "writing instrument" was intended as the meaning, the word "pen" does not reveal whether the speaker refers to a fountain pen, a "post-office scratcher," a ball point, or a quill. Furthermore, it fails to reveal the size, shape, weight, color, design, manufacturer, cost, durability, writeability, and a vast number of further details or characteristics. Instead of "pen," suppose the speaker had said "a black ball-point ladies' pen, manufactured by Scriptex, Series 48E." In that case, the listener would know considerably more about the pen the speaker had in mind (although many more words necessarily were used). But even in an era of precision mass production, not all Scriptex ladies' black ball-point pens, Series 48E, are precisely alike. Each pen is slightly different in age, performance, durability, and in a number of other characteristics. It is not always necessary, of course, to distinguish "pen$_1$" from "pen$_2$." If one says, "The boss grabbed a pen and hurriedly signed the letters," additional knowledge of the pen is not needed. Of signal importance, however, is the speaker's awareness that words always give an incomplete picture of reality.

Be particularly prudent in using all-purpose words such as "honor," "beauty," "democratic," "liberal," and "progressive." Abstract words tend to emphasize similarities and minimize differences, even when differences are great. Such words may not possess sufficient specific meaning for one to predict how a listener may interpret them. If you are careful to reconcile abstractions with concrete facts, your communication has a better chance to be meaningful.

D. Words Are Static; Meanings Are Dynamic. When a speaker uses the word, "Republicanism," what does he mean? A speaker who condemns "Republicanism" may have McKinley in mind, but some listeners may be thinking of Eisenhower. Is Texas (1939) the same as Texas (now)? Obviously not. Unless he differentiates, however, the speaker with Texas (1939) in mind may mislead or antagonize a listener who thinks he means Texas (now). When you talk of the "home town" you haven't visited in ten years, does your listener hear, "It's a wonderful place to live," or "It *was* a wonderful place to live"? What distance is covered in "an overnight trip"? How fast is "fast"? What do the majority of people consider to be "morally right"? The answers depend partly upon when the words are spoken.

Remember that while words remain the same the objects and ideas to which they refer are undergoing constant change. As Franklin P. Adams has said, "Words mean one thing on Monday and another on Tuesday." The danger lies in reacting to words as though the things they represent are changeless.

E. Words Have Both Denotative and Connotative Meanings. Suppose we take the word "war." A dictionary might define it as "a state of conflict between nations or states." But to many persons "war" has additional vivid meanings based upon memory and experience. To Ken, a forty-year-old veteran of the Korean War, "war" recalls an officer's commission, pleasant work, good food, some leisure time, new experiences, excitement, freedom from former civilian responsibilities—in short, "never having had it so good." To Fred, another veteran, "war" recalls foxholes, combat fatigue, a nightmare of anxiety and deprivation, and a Purple Heart. To Mary, in her late teens during the Korean engagement, "war" recalls little more than memories of not enough fellows around to date.

Words have two kinds of meaning, and therefore affect us in two ways. Literal, dictionary meanings, which are relatively dispassionate and objective, are called *denotative* meanings. Personalized, emotional meanings growing out of experiences and memories are called *connotative* meanings.

With the exception of words such as *the, a,* and *but,* all language possesses varying degrees of connotative meaning, the amount and strength of which depend upon the individual. Terms which possess unusually rich emotional coloration are called *loaded words.* Words like *mother, father, sweetheart, traitor, coward, racketeer,* and *bureaucrat* usually secure an emotional response from the majority of listeners. Some persons tend to react more strongly than others to connotative meanings. Moreover, a given individual may tend to emotionalize concepts in certain areas of thought to a greater extent than those in other areas. For example, a scientist whose attitude toward his work is rational and dispassionate may be essentially emotional in his reaction to his hobby, his friends, his favorite football team, and his children.

THE ATTRIBUTES OF EFFECTIVE ORAL LANGUAGE

A mature and effective oral style possesses these four characteristics: (1) clarity, (2) directness, (3) appropriateness, and (4) vividness and impressiveness.

A. Effective Oral Language Is Clear. Meaning may be obscured by the use of poor grammar and syntax, words with multiple meanings, abstract terms possessing obscure referents, and words bearing little or no meaning to the listener. If language is to be clear, it should have the following attributes.

1. Correctness. This attribute of clarity primarily concerns grammar and syntax. The rules for correct usage may be found in any of the English handbooks or grammars. Even though such principles sometimes lag behind accepted usage, they lend a needed stability to our language.

Although breaking the rules of grammar does not always impair clarity, it may cause you to lose status among literate listeners. Each of the following sentences and phrases illustrates one or more commonly heard but incorrect usages. Can you identify the error in each case? Are you able to correct it?

We did it ourself.	Where were you at?
Stop it already.	The data is revealing.
There's likely to be two men coming.	I was absent due to illness.
Each of them took their time.	I got it second handed.
He don't care.	He was considerable disturbed.
He has the capacity to do the job.	He ran like he had never run before.
She aggravates me.	Two friends and myself were there.
I feel badly.	He's nowhere near good enough.
Set down and relax.	You hadn't ought to do that.
He looks different than he used to.	It's real exciting.
That's all the faster I can write.	The reason is because he's lazy.
Who amongst us is innocent?	Everybody has their license.
Irregardless of the fact.	She's not too good of a singer.
We had planned on coming.	Those kind of people cause trouble.

The use of mangled syntax may make language incomprehensible. A student speaker compared the accuracy of two types of gauges for measuring rainfall in this way:

The government gauge which is used which is a glass tube the same as the gauges put out by the seed companies look the same, but the edge of the tube where the water drops and is measured has an edge as sharp as a razor blade which splits the raindrops, but the seed companies' rain gauges are flat on edge and when a drop hits the edge it may have the tendency to splatter, thus not catching the full drop but only a part of it.

How many times did you have to read the passage above before you were sure of its precise meaning? The speaker's audience had only one chance. Another student was shocked when a recording of his speech revealed this tortuous construction: "He wrote an exam that was twice my length that I took in half the time that he took for it." Even the speaker was not sure what he had meant. Another said, "Playing a trumpet is a difficult instrument." Misplacing a modifier may change radically the meaning of an idea. For example, seven different meanings can be conveyed by successively inserting the word *only* before each of the seven words in this sentence: *She told me that she loved me.*

2. *Accuracy*. The second attribute of clarity, accuracy, results from precise word choice. Imprecision may result from the use of all-purpose words such as: "document," "area," "definitive," "formalize," "implement," "projection," "directive," and "finalize." Such words carry little precise meaning. Imprecision may result from the use of abstract words. In a revealing "Profile" of the Ford Foundation, *The New Yorker* lifts from one of the Foundation's annual reports two sentences which illustrate how abstract language conveys little or no precise meaning: (1) "The Trustees of the Ford Foundation believe that a healthy economy is essential if American democracy is to function effectively," and (2) "The Ford Foundation believes that the advancement of human welfare depends on the partnership in progress of all free men." *The New Yorker* further notes that the ambiguity is so great that the gist of each sentence is not materially changed by reversing it in this manner: (1) "Democracy is essential if a healthy economy is to function effectively," and (2) "The partnership in progress of all free men depends on the advancement of human welfare." [1] In order for the sentences above to communicate precise meaning, almost every word would require lengthy explication. Compare them with this typical example of the concrete, specific language employed by *Time:*

In a New Orleans hotel suite sat an unkempt man, his flesh folding in rolls above his belt. He sipped contentedly from a jar of pure honey, bestirring himself now and then to waddle across the room, or to scratch himself, or to snap his suspenders, while the returns from the Democratic primary election for governor dinned into his ears: "Long 112,261 . . . Morrison 87,128 . . . Preaus 25,948 . . . Grevemberg 16,863 . . . McLemore 18,227." "Looks good," he croaked. "It's in the bag."

As the evening wore on, it grew clear to all that the unkempt man, Earl Kemp Long, had been elected for four years as governor of the great state of Louisiana.[2]

Imprecision may result from the indiscriminate use of exaggeration. Often we are tempted to use carelessly the superlatives

[1] *The New Yorker*, December 10, 1955, p. 62.
[2] *Time*, January 30, 1956, pp. 16–17.

popularized by Hollywood and advertising agencies, such as "colossal," "stupendous," "the best," "terrific," and the like. Or we may fall into the language habits of some clubwomen, whose social conversation would be crippled without the constant and indiscriminate use of words such as "lovely," "charming," "wonderful," "adore," and "exquisite." Imprecision may also result from the use of generalizations when accuracy demands specificity. Don't say "everybody thinks he's wonderful," when you mean "several of my friends have commented to me about how courteous they think he is"; if twenty-three states have ratified an amendment, be careful not to say "most of the states"; in reporting the financial condition of a company use specific data rather than the ambiguous statements: "It is doing well," or "Business has been good."

To achieve clarity in language, have a clear concept in your own mind of the idea you wish to symbolize. Then choose the word or words you believe will be most likely to stir up a closely similar meaning in the minds of your listeners.

3. Simplicity. To achieve the third requisite for clarity in the use of language, simplicity of style, observe the following suggestions:

a. Use No More Words Than Are Necessary to Express Adequately a Given Idea. In discussion and conversation, as well as in public speaking, the tendency toward verbosity is widespread. Wordiness not only wastes time but often impairs intelligibility, destroys emphasis, and reduces punch. In a guest appearance on "Meet the Press," Senator Frank Lausche of Ohio was asked if he voted for Senator Taft in his race against Joe Ferguson in Ohio's 1950 senatorial election. Lausche replied, "If I would say that I did not vote for Bob Taft I would not be telling the truth." A simple answer to the question would have been "yes." Bennett Cerf reports the following admonition by a jurist

Beware of platitudinous ponderosity. Let your communication possess coalescent consistency and concatenated cogency. Eschew all flatulent garrulity and asinine affectations. Use intelligibility and veracious vivacity without rodomontade or thrasonical bombasity. Sedulously avoid all prolixity and psittaceous vacuity.[3]

Translated into simple language this advice means, "Be clear, think for yourself, and be brief." While admittedly an extreme example of both wordiness and the use of uncommon words, the passage illustrates how verbosity can cloud meaning.

Beware of tautology or redundancy. The following illustrates this language defect:

Meet Tautological Tessie. She's planning to *redo her house over.* A man she trusted turned out to be a *dishonest crook.* She likes to know the *true facts,* and doesn't care to drive at a *fast speed.* At parties she serves *sherry wine.* She was once courted by a *rich millionaire* and she thinks *young teenagers* are cute. It is her conviction that when studying a new subject you should learn the *basic rudiments.* She always sends flowers to *sick invalids,* and if there's anything she hates it's a *gloomy pessimist. Fragrant perfumes* attract her. A neighbor of hers was held up and robbed by a *crazy psychopath.* You'll never catch her going to see *sad tragedies,* as she much prefers *funny comedies.* At a sideshow once she saw a *tall giant.*[4]

In addition to avoiding redundancy, eschew the phrase or sentence which "says the obvious." One of the best known obvious remarks is Calvin Coolidge's declaration that when a great many people are out of work the result is unemployment. In similar vein is the television commercial which declares that "Pleasure helps your disposition," the Children's Bureau pamphlet which advises that "The time to replace shoes is when the child has outgrown them," and the Department of Agriculture report which predicts that "The year will bring considerably better conditions for farmers in areas that were seriously affected by drouth last year—if precipitation increases in those areas."

b. Do Not Use a Fifty-Dollar Word When an Inexpensive One Will Do. Provided it accurately symbolizes your meaning, a short, simple, common word is nearly always more effective than a long, unfamiliar word. If you are more interested

---

[3] *This Week.*
[4] Eleanor Clarage, "Main Street Meditations," *Cleveland Plain Dealer*, January, 25, 1956.

in impressing listeners with your large vocabulary than in "getting through" to them, this is difficult advice to follow. Some of our greatest literature, however, is expressed in short, simple words. The Twenty-Third Psalm contains 118 words, of which 92 are one syllable, 21 are two syllables and 5 are three syllables. Of the first 118 words in Hamlet's "To be or not to be" soliloquy, 99 are one syllable, 13 are two, 4 are three, and 2 are four syllables. Your chances for achieving clarity will be greater if you choose the most commonly used terms which will adequately represent your thinking. Why say "I visualized an apparition," when "I saw a ghost" will do? Isn't "wait" more likely to be clear to more people than "hold in abeyance"?

c. Use Short and Simply Constructed Sentences. Speakers often become lost in a labyrinth of extended complex, compound, or complex-compound sentences. The chances of clarity are greatly enhanced if the majority of sentences average no more than ten or twelve words and contain a minimum number of subordinate clauses. The sentence, "Reduction in taxes, financially feasible only because of lowered governmental expenditures, will go into effect, it is planned, this month," is a bit complex for the hearer. Rearranging the thought into two sentences eases the task of understanding: "Taxes are to be lowered beginning this month. This reduction was made feasible only by reducing the cost of government."

4. Understandability. Up to this point we have seen how meanings may be clouded by inaccurate, incorrect, complex, and ambiguous language. In addition, language sometimes carries either the wrong meaning or no meaning at all to the listener. Such is the case when the definition of a term or process is needed and not supplied, and when technical jargon, specialized slang, or uncommon foreign words are indiscriminately employed.

Some geography textbooks devote an entire chapter to "topsoil" without once explaining what it is, and refer to the climate of the United States as "temperate" without elaborating on the term. Youthful readers in the Midwest, who may experience

extremes of 110° and —20° in a typical year may find the term
"temperate" (which probably means to them "moderate") a
bit confusing.

Every area of knowledge has its own glossary of terms which
have precise meanings to those trained in the field but which
may be gibberish to the uninitiated. For instance, in explaining
the optical qualities of his new Rolleiflex camera a student used
the terms "parallax compensation," "halation," "diopter,"
"solarization," and "focal plane shutter." A check at the conclusion of the speech revealed that only one listener knew the
meanings of all those terms.

Use sparingly the specialized slang of your profession, class,
culture pattern, or age group. The Commerce Clearing House
reports the following examples of slang in use among members
of labor organizations: "pie card," "therblig," "galloping rate,"
"bob-tailing," "stick-and-carrot technique," "PM," "scabwag,"
and "honeymoon contract." At this writing, urban teen-age
slang, an extremely fluid and transitory code, includes in its
glossary: "kicky," "oogley," "scooches," "slodges," "flutter bum,"
"lurp," "chrome dome," and "crusted."

Some foreign words, such as *fiance,* are widely used and understood in the United States. Other foreign expressions are employed primarily by literate persons. Unless your listeners are
unusually well educated, you should beware of uncommon foreign terms such as: *fin de siècle, avant garde, vis-à-vis, cap-à-pie,
de rigueur, Wanderjahr, sine qua non,* and *de gustibus non est
disputandum.* In any event, use such foreign words sparingly,
or your listeners may feel you are "showing off."

B. Effective Oral Language Is Direct and Conversational.
To some persons a speech is an essay or theme wired for sound.
Indeed, some students do not even attempt to disguise the fact
that they are presenting almost word-for-word a theme written
for English 101. A student speaker made one concession to the
oral situation by changing the word "reader" to "audience" in
the sentence, "It is essential that the reader be informed of the
reasons for the inadequacies suffered by many in attempting to

read quickly their evening newspaper." Such a construction, however, ignored the presence of flesh-and-blood listeners. Awareness of the listener could have been achieved by changing the language to "You should know why it may take too long for you to finish reading your evening paper." Another student speaker used the transition "as was noted above," instead of "as I mentioned earlier." Again, this was language meant for a reader, not a listener.

Language for speech should be chosen for its oral qualities. Make liberal use of personal pronouns. Speak of "our problem," "your schools," "my point." Say "we can improve," "you can help," "I believe." For interest and emphasis, employ the direct and the rhetorical question. The direct question is answered by the speaker, for example "Do you know how much money is wasted each year by the city government?" The rhetorical question is answered silently by the listener, for example "Would you be interested in a plan which can save you $1,000 each year?" Oral language ordinarily makes much greater use of contractions than does written language. Say "don't" rather than "do not," "wouldn't," rather than "would not," "can't" rather than "cannot."

To increase the likelihood of instant comprehension, keep your oral language conversational and idiomatic. The language of discussion and most platform speaking should sound as much like conversation as is consistent with the formality and impressiveness of the occasion and with the size of the audience.

C. Effective Oral Language Is Appropriate. Since the speaker's focal point is his listeners, he must choose language to meet their needs and expectations. Many factors determine the language patterns a listener prefers—among them his age, education, breeding, occupation, and sex. Also, the nature of the speaking occasion often influences a listener's concept of appropriateness. A member of a crowd at a pep rally is conditioned to expect language which is greatly different from that which he hears during a devotional service at church or during a lecture at the university. A listener also expects language to be appropriate to the speaker. Probably you expect a different oral style from each of these persons: a foreman at a local furniture factory, a college professor, your mother, a steady date, your sister, your roommate. Finally, language must be appropriate to the purpose of the speaker. Accuracy and objectivity in word choice are of paramount importance when the speaker's purpose is to inform or to examine rationally a problem. However, the persuader may employ sweeping generalities, loaded terms, familiar slogans, and powerful assertions to arouse the emotions of his listeners and incite them to desired action. In each of the following pairs of phrases the first would be more appropriate to the informative speaker and the second to the persuader who is addressing a receptive audience: (1) compulsory health insurance—socialized medicine; (2) persons earning less than $2,000 per year—the exploited, downtrodden poor; (3) the rulers of Russia—the Godless, power-mad racketeers in the Kremlin; (4) Florida—the Sunshine State; (5) Cleveland, Ohio—the best location in the nation.

D. Effective Oral Language Is Vivid and Impressive. To hold attention, maintain interest, and achieve a lasting impression, language must be vivid and impressive. Such attributes may be realized by employing concreteness, figurative words, originality, and variety.

1. Concreteness. Although many kinds of symbols evoke imagery, we are concerned here with only the use of language symbols. Vividness is almost inseparable from concreteness, because imagery is specific, not general. Abstraction has no form or substance. Therefore, since we think in images, we have difficulty in conceiving "beauty," "sin," etc., but can picture specific incidents or examples. The wise speaker will attempt to make abstractions vivid by the use of concrete and descriptive terms which relate directly to the listeners' experience, and which arouse sense imagery.

The appeal to types of imagery may correspond to the various physical senses. Vividly descriptive words may enable the listener to experience vicarious reactions which are similar to those which he would experience in the presence of actual sensory stimulation such as the following: (1) *Visual:* a mountain meadow, a reproduction of the Sistine Madonna, the smile of a boyhood pal, the colorful action at a circus. (2) *Auditory:* the cacophony of a busy intersection, the roaring flow of a mountain stream, the striking of a grandfather clock, an aria from an opera, the voice of a friend. (3) *Gustatory:* the taste of cold pop on a July afternoon, of mince pie, of lemon juice, of smoked oysters, of fried chicken. (4) *Olfactory:* the pungency of cleaning fluid or gasoline, the musty air in an unused room, and the fragrance of Chanel No. 5, of a pile of freshly cut lumber, or of brewing coffee. (5) *Tactual:* the soft give of a thick carpet, the roughness of sandpaper, the sharp edge of a carving knife, the smoothness of a highly polished table top, the sponginess of a foam rubber pillow. (6) *Kinaesthetic:* the feeling of movement in shooting a basket, kicking a football, swinging a bat, striking a punching bag, dancing a mambo, vaulting a fence, bowing a violin.

2. Figurative words.   Give vividness to language by employing figurative expressions. Among the many figures, *simile* and *metaphor* are perhaps the most common and most useful to the speaker. They are alike in that each compares objects or concepts essentially unlike; they differ in that a simile *states* a likeness between two objects or ideas, while a metaphor directly identifies the two on the basis of a common likeness. "Highways are like arteries" is a simile; "highways are arteries" is a metaphor. In either case, of course, the figure "arteries" is so well known and widely used that much of the vividness is lost. In contrast, the following figures are sufficiently striking to arrest attention and impress most listeners.

Similes

1. Robert Frost described the writing of free verse as "like playing tennis with the net down."

2. Arguing that it is fallacious to assume that a given TV viewing hour is a favorite simply because more people look at television at that time,

Robert Lewine, program director of ABC-TV, said, "Putting your best shows on at 8 o'clock and then saying the public likes that hour is like corraling sheep into a pen and saying they like to stick together. Actually you drove them together."

3. Regarding the convolutions involved in dancing the mambo, Arthur Murray had this comment: "It's like doing the backstroke without water."

Metaphor

1. The world is too big an egg for the American eagle to hatch.

—Samuel B. Pettengill

2. Shakespeare was an intellectual ocean whose waves touched every shore of thought.

—Robert G. Ingersoll

3. A word is not a crystal, transparent and unchanged; it is the skin of living thought and may vary greatly in color and content according to the circumstances and the time in which it is used.

—Oliver Wendell Holmes

3. Originality. Certain words and phrases once striking and original have become hackneyed and trite from excessive use. Unfortunately, such words often are the first to come to mind when the speaker or discussant expresses himself. Avoid using the following phrases and ones similar to them:

hit the nail on the head	busy as a bee
view with alarm	too numerous to mention
fit as a fiddle	conspicuous by his absence
mountain out of a molehill	only too glad
black as pitch	bated breath
in a nutshell	slow as molasses in January
proudly presents	last but not least

Originality in language does not necessitate using new or unusual terms. Sometimes a striking rearrangement of words produces a sharp and lasting effect. Consider the following examples:

1. We have built machines which act like men and have become men that act like machines. . . . The danger of the future is that men may become robots.

—Erich Fromm

2. Don't smoke in bed! The ashes falling on the floor may be your own.

—Svenska Dagbladet

3. Democracy in American higher education can lead to the nurture of mediocrity or of ability. It will lead to mediocrity if we admit to our colleges great numbers of students who lack intellectual ability and interest, and then water down the curriculum so that they may splash through the courses without drowning.

—C. H. Cramer

Another way to achieve originality is to coin new words out of old ones. Adlai Stevenson once attacked the foreign policy of Secretary of State John Foster Dulles with these words: "We hear the Secretary of State boasting of his brinkmanship—the art of bringing us to the edge of the nuclear abyss." Among the experienced practitioners of word creating is Walter Winchell. An individual seeking a Reno divorce is, in his terms, "Renovating." A construction company used the same device when it called its imaginative engineering "imagineering." The famous answer given by Senator Penrose to the two philandering senators who protested against serving with the Mormon member, Senator Smoot, derives its originality from shortening two nouns into unusual verbs: "Personally, I'd rather deal with a polygamist who doesn't polyg than with a monogamist who doesn't monog."

Admittedly, figurative and picturesque language is not readily at the tip of the average speaker's tongue. We advise you to store in your mind striking maxims, comparisons, and figures for ready use when the occasion is appropriate.

4. Variety. Because it lacks vivid impressiveness and variety, monotony in choice of words kills attention values. Using a relatively small group of adjectives, verbs, and nouns again and again is a common failing of most persons. A limited speaking vocabulary and the force of habit are largely responsible. In noting the victory of an athletic team, most speakers would use one of the following verbs: *win, defeat, beat.* A look at the sports pages of a metropolitan daily, however, would reveal many other words to express *victory: upset, trim, sweep, notch, romp, nip, jolt, trip, edge, halt, sink, capture, clip, triumph, slaughter.* In the sparkling style of *Time* magazine an individual rarely just *says* something; he *snaps, chortles, chuckles, cracks, intones, drawls, grumbles, blurts, drones,* or *purrs.* Moreover, in *Time* a person seldom gets into a car and just *drives;* he either *snakes, streaks off, swerves along, speeds away, flashes by, hurries dustily on,* or *coasts.*

Speakers seem to be especially unimaginative in the words they choose to link together major points. Even though ideas may be well prepared, the speaker frequently fails to plan how to couple one to another. The result is overdependence upon connectives such as *and, also, another thing, another point, for example,* and *in other words.* For the sake of variety, add to your speaking vocabulary these and other connectives: *moreover, furthermore, nevertheless, nonetheless, in consequence, inasmuch as, on the contrary, thereupon, meanwhile, however, on the other hand, whereas, in addition to.*

In addition to a weary sameness in the choice of words, many speakers employ an inflexibility of sentence structure which robs communication of attention values and reduces the impressive quality of language. Suggestions: (1) Vary the length of sentences. A series of long sentences should be interspersed with occasional short, crisp ones—some perhaps no longer than two or three words. (2) Do not neglect the periodic construction. Interest and suspense might be added to the loose arrangement, "You will increase your chances of enjoying lasting health if you watch your diet, get adequate rest and exercise, and cultivate a serene mental outlook," by reversing the order so that the meaning of the main clause is not completed until the end of the sentence: "If you watch your diet, get adequate rest and exercise, and cultivate a serene mental outlook, you will increase your chances of enjoying lasting health." (3) Instead of relying almost entirely on the declarative form, make occasional use of interrogatory, exclamatory, and imperative sentences. (Direct and rhetorical questions were discussed earlier in the chapter.) An exclamatory sentence such as "It couldn't possibly be true!"

or "Drunken drivers should be jailed!" is welcome as a change of pace and as an attention getter, but must not be overused. Listeners often respond strongly to the command of an imperative sentence, particularly when action is demanded by the speaker. Example: "Stop frowning and start smiling! Turn toward the person sitting next to you and smile. Now! Broaden your smile! Don't you feel your tensions easing? When you leave this room, keep smiling! Open your heart to others and embrace them with a radiant smile! If you do, I promise you a tranquil mind, a good digestion, and a widening circle of friends."

SPECIFIC GUIDES FOR IMPROVING ORAL STYLE

A careful reading of the previous portions of this chapter should have given you a more sensitive awareness of the symbolic nature of language and a better understanding of the attributes of effective oral style. However, facility in the use of language cannot be developed by the mere reading of this chapter; you must initiate a long-term personal program. Perhaps the following suggestions will prove helpful to you in conducting such a project.

A. Developing a Continuing, Analytical Interest in Language. To improve language skills, you must become a student of words and their usage.

1. Become word conscious. Develop an active curiosity concerning words—their meanings, etymology, synonyms, and antonyms. Perhaps "the dictionary habit" affords the best means of acquiring an interest in, and an understanding of, words. If you do not own a recent edition of a good dictionary, buy one and keep it handy at your desk. Heed the words of John Ruskin, "get into the habit of looking intensely at words, and assuring yourself of their meaning, syllable by syllable—nay, letter by letter. . . . Whenever you are in doubt about a word, hunt it down patiently. . . . Never let a word escape you that looks suspicious." In addition to the dictionary, consult guides such as Roget's *Thesaurus of English Words and Phrases,* Fowler's *Dictionary of Modern English Usage,* Crabbe's *English Synonyms, Antonyms, and Prepositions,* Kin's *A Dictionary of American Maxims,* and Reifer's *A Dictionary of New Words.* If time permits, study the development of language from primitive man to the present, the grammatical structure of language, and the relationship of English to other languages—ancient and modern. These references may provide an interesting start: Mario Pei, *The Story of Language;* R. M. Estrich and H. Sperber, *Three Keys to Language;* Irving J. Lee, *The Language of Wisdom and Folly;* George O. Crume, *English Grammar;* Herbert Read, *English Prose Style;* James L. Jackson, "Air Force Language in the Making," *The Quarterly Journal of Speech,* February, 1956.

2. Study the language style of skilled writers and speakers. As you were advised in Chapter 3, read widely, selectively, and critically in fiction as well as non-fiction. Study the style in quality periodicals such as *The New Yorker, The Saturday Review, Time, Harper's Magazine, The Atlantic,* and others. Examine carefully the model speeches in *Vital Speeches* magazine and in collections like A. Craig Baird's *Representative American Speeches* and *American Public Addresses: 1740–1952,* Harold F. Harding's *The Age of Danger,* and Wayland M. Parrish and Marie Hochmuth's *American Speeches.* Read regularly a good newspaper to observe the sprightly, economical style of the seasoned reporters, columnists, and editorial writers. Listen analytically to the language style employed by successful lecturers, preachers, political figures, and radio-television performers. Seek the company of mature conversationalists among your classmates, teachers, church and club members, and dormitory or fraternity mates—and learn from their example.

B. Increase Your Vocabulary. Occasionally a student expresses doubt that a large vocabulary is important to the speaker. He may point to his ten-year-old sister who finds her limited vocabulary no barrier to loquacity; or he may cite an accomplished "off-the-cuff" speaker noted for his fluency despite a limited vocabulary. The effective speaker, however, is concerned with more than the flow of language; he is aware of the need for using in a given situation the particular words which express his ideas most precisely and most vividly. Although many believe that a given concept may be symbolized equally well by any one of possibly a dozen words, usually one of these words represents the concept most clearly and vividly to a specific audience on a particular occasion. Thus it is important to the speaker to have at his instant command the best possible word among a group of synonyms. The effective speaker, therefore, seeks to increase his stock of readily available words for extempore communication. How does one go about building a vocabulary? (1) As already indicated, *become word conscious.* (2) *Jot down new words.* When reading or listening, if you encounter a new word or one whose meaning is unclear to you, record it on a small pocket pad. (3) *Learn the meanings of these new words.* At the first opportunity, after entering a new word in your notebook, look up its meaning and pronunciation in a dictionary; copy them on the pad. Also, if the definition includes a sample sentence using the word, record this sentence. (4) *Incorporate these new words into your writing and speaking.* Deliberately insert a suitable new word or two in each speech you make. After using a new word a few times, it should become an active, useful part of your speaking vocabulary. By adding only four or five new words a week, you will be surprised and gratified at the enrichment of your vocabulary in only a few months.

C. Practice Writing and Speaking. Make a determined and systematic attempt to improve the clarity, directness, appropriateness, vividness, and impressiveness with which you employ language. Consider each act of written or oral communication an opportunity to develop your language skills.

Although important differences exist between written and oral style, the essential elements are similar. Conscientious practice in writing will produce an increased language facility which has carry-over value to speaking. Refuse to dash off a report, theme, or term paper with only scant attention to the requisites of effective style. Rework each composition until it represents your thinking precisely and attractively. Join the reportorial staff of your college newspaper; you will find the experience stimulating and rewarding. Also, practice writing speeches in manuscript form. Either deliver the speeches in class or give the copies to the instructor for suggestions on style.

Although during a specific act of oral communication you should not be unduly conscious of your use of words, you can utilize every speech, discussion, or conversation as a means of improving your oral style. How? Immediately after each speaking experience, ask yourself questions such as: How efficient was my use of language? In what ways could I have improved grammar? Syntax? Simplicity? Accuracy? Understandability? Vividness? Conversational quality? Suitability to the listener, to the occasion, and to myself as the speaker? Also, you should arrange to record some of your speech presentations during rehearsals and in class. With the assistance of a competent critic, listen analytically to the playbacks.

SUMMARY

Development of a mature oral style must be based upon an understanding of certain basic concepts about language: (1) words are only symbols; (2) words do not transmit meaning—they can only stir up meanings; (3) words cannot represent completely the things they symbolize; (4) words are static, while meanings are dynamic; (5) words have both denotative and connotative meanings.

The attributes of effective oral language are clarity, directness and conversational quality, appropriateness, and vividness and impressiveness. For language to be clear, it must be correct, accurate, simple, and understandable. For language to be direct and conversational, it must be informal, idiomatic, and instantly intelligible. For language to be appropriate, it must be well suited to the audience, the occasion, the speaker, and the speaker's purpose. For language to be vivid and impressive, it must be rich in sense imagery and figurative expressions, varied in word choice and sentence structure, and, when possible, original in word usage.

To improve your oral style, initiate this self-help program: (1) Develop a continuing, analytical interest in language by becoming word conscious and by studying the language style of skilled writers and speakers. (2) Increase your vocabulary. (3) Practice writing and speaking.

EXERCISES AND ASSIGNMENTS

1. Prepare a written report on semantics and its application to the beginning student of speech. Or, substitute for a written report either an oral presentation or a group study project culminating in an informal panel discussion presented to the class.

2. (a) List ten or twenty words whose meanings have changed in the last century. (b) List as many words as you can which were in standard use some years ago which are now archaic or obsolete. (c) List ten or fifteen words or phrases which were once original but are now commonplace.

3. During one round of speeches, jot down the hackneyed words and phrases used by your classmates. Opposite each enter a more vivid usage which conveys the same idea.

4. Evaluate the language in a speech printed in Baird's annual compilation of *Representative American Speeches,* Baird's *American Public Addresses: 1940–1952,* Harding's *Age of Danger,* Parrish and Hochmuth's *American Speeches,* or *Vital Speeches.* Use as your criteria: (1) clarity, (2) appropriateness, (3) directness and conversational quality, and (4) vividness and impressiveness. Support your judgments with examples from the speech. Your evaluation may be presented in either a written or an oral report.

5. Make a list of the loaded words in a political speech, in a series of newspaper advertisements, or in a series of radio or TV commercials. Do these words mask faulty reasoning? In each case, substitute a more objective word or phrase. Does this weaken the overall persuasive power of the speech or advertisement? Report your findings for class discussion.

6. Accumulate a list of unusual figurative words, phrases, and maxims. Attempt to use one or more of them in each of your remaining class speeches or discussions.

7. Record a short extemporaneous speech or a ten-minute segment of one of your group discussions. Listen to the playback for (1) awkward syntax, (2) ambiguous terms, (3) involved sentence structure, (4) redundancies and needless repetition. Take notes instead of relying on memory, and listen to the playback several times, if necessary. Use your findings as a basis for improving your extemporaneous style.

8. List at least fifty words which are not now a part of your speaking vocabulary but whose meanings you know. Attempt to use at least three of them in your next speech or group discussion in class. Incorporate others into future performances.

5 ❧❧ *Bodily Action*

At a crowded luncheon table in the school cafeteria we crane our necks to look at a person talking to us from the far end of the table; in group discussions we make careful seating arrangements so that each person may see every other person without effort; when attending a speechmaking event we look for the best seats and avoid those affording a poor view of the speaker; when a prominent speaker uses the mass media most of us prefer to tune in the speech on television rather than on radio. When we listen to someone we like to see him; and when we talk we like to see our listeners.

In Chapter 1 we noted that communication occurs as the result of the transmission of sound and light waves between speaker and listener. The sound waves transmit the audible code (what the listener *hears*), and the light waves transmit the visible code (what the listener *sees*). In this chapter we shall discuss the visible code—the use of posture, movement, gesture, eye contact, and facial expression to communicate meaning.

THE FUNCTIONS OF BODILY ACTION IN COMMUNICATION

The physical act of speaking is the product of muscular activity. However, bodily action beyond the minimum required to produce vocal sounds is considered by some theorists an exhibitionistic frill. If such were the case there would be no point in devoting a chapter to physical delivery. Here are some important reasons for developing effective bodily action in speech.

87

A. Bodily Action Helps You to Adjust to the Speaking Situation. Excessive nervous tension, as we have noted earlier, is one of the problems confronting many beginning speakers. We all know that to exercise a taut muscle usually relaxes it. Tension in the neck muscles may be relieved by moving the head around repeatedly in a circular motion; and muscle cramps can be worked out with exercise. Unfortunately, when speaking to an audience, you have little chance for exercise unless you are, let us say, demonstrating calisthenics. However, by using appropriate gestures of the head, trunk, and arm, and by moving occasionally on the platform, you may achieve a degree of muscular relaxation which will relieve the trembling of rigid muscles and help to put you at ease. Of course, in group discussion you will not have much opportunity to move about. However, you may gesticulate. Fortunately, most people are more relaxed in group speaking than in platform speaking.

Being "keyed up" sometimes may immobilize the beginning speaker into a rocklike rigidity or may drive him to seek release in distracting activities such as wiggling, stroking his hair, rubbing his nose or chin, jingling his coins or keys, tossing a piece of chalk, drumming on the lectern, buttoning or unbuttoning his coat, and so forth. Recognize that nervous energy cannot be completely suppressed or destroyed, but must find expression in some form. Cultivating the use of vigorous, purposeful bodily action will provide a useful outlet for excessive energy and will serve to minimize random muscular activity.

B. Bodily Action Helps to Reveal to the Listener Your Personality, Emotional State, and Intent. Inevitably, your listeners draw inferences from your physical presence, or "the way you look." Your posture, movement, gestures (or lack of them), eye directness, and facial expression—all offer a myriad of overt and covert clues to the nature of your personality and character. Consciously or unconsciously, the viewers interpret these clues, thereby formulating judgments concerning your likability, sincerity, enthusiasm, poise, modesty, and objectivity. Also, your use of the visible elements of delivery tells much about your attitudes toward the audience, the occasion, the subject, and toward yourself.

Your physical behavior should conform to the positive stereotypes held by the audience and should avoid negative ones. Narrowed eyes darting furtively in many directions mean to many listeners that the speaker has something to hide and may not be trustworthy; excessive random action and aimless movement may be associated with a lack of certainty or conviction; a hang-dog look, a listless walk, and a vapid mien may indicate lack of interest; a glowering, fierce expression coupled with a menacing body-set may frighten fellow committee members into silence; an airy, lighthearted manner on a solemn, dignified occasion may be interpreted as inappropriate; likewise a ponderous, heavy-handed approach on a joyous occasion will not be well received.

Bodily action does not always mirror the inner feelings of the speaker. Faulty habits, ignorance, or fear may cause a speaker's physical delivery to misrepresent his purposes and attitudes. For instance, the speaker with a serious purpose may employ a manner which invokes a humorous response. Conversely, one who hopes to entertain may inadvertently defeat his intention by using physical behavior which does not fit his listeners' conception of the entertaining speaker.

C. Bodily Action Helps You to Get and Hold Attention. Sometimes the attention of a listener may be secured and held solely by means of the intrinsic meaning of the words being uttered. Usually, however, language is not sufficiently compelling to maintain consistent attention unless it is accompanied by effective vocal and physical delivery. Everyone has heard significant ideas presented so ineffectually that listening was a distinct effort.

Physical delivery helps to secure and maintain attention in two important ways—by offering visual symbols in motion rather than at rest, and by facilitating empathic release in the listener.

We all pay attention to movement. If other interest factors are equal, the moving object nearly always will command greater attention than the stationary one. We usually are attracted more strongly by an animated TV commercial than by a slide, by a speedboat churning through the water than by one moored to the dock, or by an animated Christmas display than by one which doesn't "do anything." Also, we are more easily held by a physically active speaker than by one who is almost motionless.

Empathic response is the tendency to enter into the feeling or spirit of the objects of our attention. When watching a boxing match on TV we are likely to follow with our bodies the action in the ring, wincing when blows are landing, jerking perceptibly to propel other blows to their mark. In watching a play we tend to identify ourself with the actors to the extent that we mimic their facial expressions and feel the same emotions they portray. In watching a speaker who is alert, energetic, active, and dynamic we tend to feel the same way. By using bodily action appropriate to the response sought, the effective speaker makes his listeners active participants in communication.

D. Bodily Action Helps You to Secure Desired Listener Response. Effective physical behavior aids the speaker in clarifying meaning, attaining emphasis, and arousing emotions.

1. Clarifying meaning. Sometimes words are inadequate to communicate full, complete meanings. Therefore, when feasible speakers should make use of pictures, diagrams, charts, maps, working models, and other visual aids. In addition, they should employ expressive bodily action to clarify meaning, particularly when using narration, exposition, and description. Concepts such as distance, size, shape, direction, and speed become more vivid and meaningful, as do certain manual techniques and processes. Here are some examples of concepts which may be clarified by bodily action: the *distance* between two passing cars, or how far from the eyes a newspaper must be held to be read by a farsighted person; the *size* of a steak, a speckled trout, a cakepan, a book; the *shape* of a house, a swimming pool, a tree, an ashtray; the *direction* of a jet fighter's climb, a spiral staircase, a hairpin turn, the trajectory of a bullet, the whirling, dipping funnel of a tornado; the *speed* of a flying insect, a hopping frog, a turning spit, a passing car. Consider also the importance of expressive action in explaining such techniques as mounting a horse, conducting an orchestra, serving a tennis ball, catching a football, using an electric shaver, or cleaning a fish.

Listeners have largely sterotyped the meanings conveyed by certain specific movements, such as the shrugged shoulder, the curled lip, the clenched fist, the raised eyebrow, and the nod. Thus, such actions are useful to the speaker in conveying specific meanings.

2. *Attaining emphasis.* The physical behavior of the speaker helps to emphasize ideas in a variety of ways. In platform speaking, movement toward the audience may serve notice that an important point, perhaps the climax, is approaching. A step or two to either side may help to indicate a transition from one major topic to another. A series of important words may be accentuated by a decisive head movement accompanying the delivery of each word. A succession of points may be enumerated on the fingers, and a clenched fist may strike the table to drive a point home. Leaning forward from the waist is often a cue that an important idea is forthcoming. Also, appropriate facial expression aids the speaker in emphasizing his feelings and the character of the point he is making.

3. *Arousing emotion.* We have noted the importance of empathy in maintaining attention. Empathic response from the listener indicates that he is emotionally involved. When the speaker exhibits the visible characteristics of the emotional state he wishes to rouse, his listeners tend to reflect his feelings. Thus, if the speaker experiences a genuine sense of horror and excitement as he describes a tragic fire in a convalescent home, his feelings should be manifested naturally and unaffectedly in his own physical behavior; the listeners observing his manner will subconsciously tend to share his sentiments. In addition to arousing emotions, the physical behavior of the speaker may also be helpful in keeping emotions in check. In situations demanding a rational, objective approach, a relaxed, dispassionate demeanor on the part of the speaker tends to beget a similar mood in his listeners.

THE PRINCIPLES OF EFFECTIVE BODILY ACTION IN COMMUNICATION

A. Bodily Action Is an Inherent Part of the Act of Communication. Students sometimes ask, "When should one use bodily action?" or "Did I use bodily action in that speech?" Such questions reveal a misunderstanding of the concept. Although a speaker may choose either to employ or to avoid hand or arm gestures, he cannot choose to use or not to use physical delivery. Complete immobility or flaccidity is impossible in speaking. Even the comparatively inactive person uses discernible movements of the mouth and jaws to form words, moves his eyes and head occasionally, and shifts his weight from time to time. Furthermore, one cannot speak to a visible audience without communicating visible meaning. By virtue of his lack of physical animation, the sluggish or inhibited speaker inevitably reveals something of his personality and his attitudes toward his audience and his speaking. Physical delivery is an inherent part of the communicative process.

B. Effective Bodily Action Is Closely Integrated with the Entire Act of Communication. For physical delivery to be effective it must be smoothly integrated into the total process of speaking. The effective speaker responds to the intellectual and emotional meaning of his message and to the other elements of the speaking situation with appropriate posture, movement, facial expression, and gesture. He does not insert gestures for their own sake. To do so is exhibitionism, and calls attention to delivery at the expense of ideas. Planned gestures often are poorly timed and appear artificial.

C. Effective Bodily Action Results from Carefully Developed Habit Patterns. Usually, effective action doesn't just happen. Nor will speaking experience guarantee it. Repeated experience often means only the repeating of bad habits and the consequent strengthening of their hold. When you observe a speaker with

effective action, notice his gestures, his manner of movement, his posture, and his expressive face. Then observe your
appearance in a mirror. Try smiling, frowning, knitting the
brows, looking surprised, and a number of other facial expressions. Does your face express your feelings? Execute a number
of the common hand and arm gestures. If watching your reflection does not prove psychologically discomforting, practice
before the mirror until you develop muscular patterns of appropriate physical delivery. Co-ordination, timing, integration,
and the other characteristics of effective action do not often
occur automatically; they are physical skills which have to be
developed.

**D. Effective Bodily Action Is Not Mechanical; It Is Spon-
taneous and Appears Effortless.**   Several generations ago speech
students were taught to use their bodies according to a set of
rules. Movement on the platform was carefully prescribed.
Gestures were to be made according to exact rules providing for
every muscle movement and were to be executed at precise
points in the speech. While sometimes highly polished, the resulting delivery often seemed mechanical, stilted, and artificial.
Since then, speech educators have abandoned the belief that
there is a single correct way to execute bodily action. Today's
teacher stresses spontaneity and naturalness. The student is
usually told to gesture only when he feels like doing so and to
execute gestures and movement in a way which seems natural
for him. Unfortunately, a gesture that seems natural to the
speaker often is ineffectual.

Although you should reject the rigid prescriptiveness of elo-
cution, do not carry too far the "whatever is natural is good"
theory. *Develop through practice those habit patterns which
produce effective use of bodily action. Then depend primarily
upon the desire and impulse of the moment to produce the kind
and amount of bodily action suited to the audience, the speech,
the speaker, and the occasion.*

E. Effective Bodily Action Is Appropriate.   (1) *To the audience.* In communicating with a child, abundant descriptive

literal gestures and vigorous facial expressions aid in getting ideas across. The adult, however, finds such action unnecessary and perhaps annoying; he prefers more subtle bodily activity. The teen-ager falls somewhere between the extremes. Because he leads a vigorous life, he will consider positive, dynamic action appropriate; however, he will not appreciate the more obvious literal expressiveness expected by the child. Also, the well-educated, sophisticated audience seems to prefer a more subtle, controlled type of action than would appeal to an unselected group. Remember: the most effective action is that which produces an empathic response in the listener—that which the listener might use to express the same idea. Therefore, adapt action to your listeners' pattern of expectation. (2) *To the occasion*. We have come to regard certain characteristics of physical delivery as being appropriate to a certain type of occasion. Thus, an audience at a pep rally expects energetic action from a speaker. The members of a learned society anticipate that a report on scientific research will be delivered with dignified restraint. The discussants in an informal business conference would consider strenuous physical action unnecessary and inappropriate. A lethargic, well-fed after-dinner audience may drift into a condition of semi-consciousness unless the speaker employs considerable physical action. On the other hand, an expectant group of students awaiting the announcement of awards or the outcome of a contest or election will listen intently to the speaker regardless of his manner of physical expression. (3) *To the speaker*. We expect women to be somewhat less vigorous than men. Also, we consider abundant and forceful action normal for youthful speakers; restraint and subtlety seem more in keeping with mature adulthood.

TYPES OF BODILY ACTION IN COMMUNICATION

From the functions and basic principles of bodily action we turn now to a more specific treatment of the various types of physical behavior in speech. Although these types of action tend to overlap and are closely integrated in the act of speaking, for purposes of discussion they can be classified roughly into five categories: (1) posture, (2) movement, (3) gesture, (4) eye contact, and (5) facial expression. The relationship of each to the process of communication will be analyzed and suggestions will be offered to improve your use of each.

A. Posture. Most public platform speaking is done while standing, while group speaking ordinarily takes place in the sitting position.

1. The characteristics of good posture. To some extent, your stance and carriage will depend upon the formality and physical characteristics attending the occasion, the size and composition of the audience, the nature of your message, and your age, physical make-up, and personal prestige. In general, however, your posture will be acceptable when you are erect, yet appear relaxed.

When standing, you should directly face the audience; the feet should be slightly apart (perhaps six to twelve inches), with the weight fairly evenly distributed on each foot; and the trunk should be carried comfortably erect. Another acceptable stance is to place one foot slightly back of the other and rest most of the weight on the rear foot; in using this stance be careful to avoid letting the body twist awkwardly out of line. Unless using the arms for gesticulation, you may let them hang naturally at your sides. Other acceptable hand positions are: (1) either hand in a pocket; (2) both hands in jacket pockets; (3) hands clasped behind you; (4) either or both hands grasping the rear corners or side edges of the lectern. For visual variety, change your hand positions occasionally.

When sitting, keep the spine reasonably erect without seeming to be unnaturally stiff. You can remain somewhat relaxed when erect by resting your shoulders and trunk against the back of the chair. If seated at a table, you may rest your arms on the table and, if you wish, clasp your hands. In very informal group discussions you may even occasionally rest your cheek in the palm of your hand; however, if such posture is accompanied by a blank look and infrequent participation, fellow discussants may conclude that you are bored and indifferent.

2. What to avoid. (1) *Slouching.* Whether standing or sitting, the speaker who slouches may give the impression that he is tired, lazy, indifferent, or disrespectful. As a rule, none of these is the cause. Habit usually is responsible for slouching. (2) *Leaning.* Many speakers grasp for any available object which will support most of their weight. They have become so habituated to leaning on tables, lecterns, backs of chairs, and the like, that they are ill at ease on an empty platform. Of course, in informal situations effectiveness may not be reduced by occasionally leaning on the lectern or against a table. In extremely casual circumstances, some successful public speakers may sit momentarily, or possibly for extended periods, upon a table. Instead of decreasing effectiveness, such informality conceivably might promote closer rapport with the listeners. Nevertheless, we strongly urge that, at least while learning to speak, you maintain good posture. (3) *Excessive stiffness and erectness.* The military bearing, whether seated or standing, seems pompous and often ludicrous to the listener. Furthermore, to maintain this position is excessively taxing for the speaker. (4) *The lowered head.* Keep your chin off your neck. Unless you do, eye contact will be difficult. In any case this position leads the listener to believe that you are timid, insecure, or unfriendly.

3. How to acquire good posture. Posture is largely a matter of habit. If your posture is bad while communicating, probably it is generally unsatisfactory. Check yourself in a full-length mirror. If you are slouching, straighten up and try to "stand tall." Note whether your weight is distributed evenly on both feet to prevent throwing your body out of line. When you see that you have achieved a pleasing bearing, try to get the kinesthetic "feel" of that position, so that you can achieve it without checking in a mirror. Then attempt to maintain the position at all times except during periods of complete relaxation. Good speaking posture is not easily attained unless proper bearing has become habitual.

B. Movement. We are concerned at this point with gross bodily movements, such as moving about or walking to and from the platform. Movement which is more limited in scope is usually called gesture, and will be discussed in the next section. Although these two forms of activity have been separated for purposes of convenience, a sharp line of distinction cannot be drawn between movement and gesture. Obviously, movement is primarily the concern of the platform speaker rather than the group discussion speaker, who, as you know, is usually seated. Even the discussion participant, however, may occasionally move to a blackboard or chart, or for some other reason change his position in the room.

1. The characteristics of effective movement. Changing positions on the platform should be done smoothly and naturally. A medium walking rate is preferred, although rate of speed may be changed to meet the particular requirements of the ideas spoken.

Students frequently ask how often they should move. The amount of movement which is appropriate depends upon the totality of the particular speaking situation, that is, your age, sex, and physical vigor, the character of your message, the size and mood of the audience, the impressiveness of the occasion, the presence or absence of a microphone, and so forth. As a general rule, do not feel compelled to stand in exactly the same spot for an entire speech, especially if the talk lasts more than five minutes. Move as frequently as you wish, *provided* your shifts do not interfere with communication.

Where should one move? Again, variable circumstances prevent a categorical answer. If using a lectern, try an occasional move from behind to either side. Upon reaching the side, you may temporarily rest a hand upon the lectern, if you wish. You may proceed even farther and stand in front of the lectern, if space permits. However, do not move more than a step or so to the rear of the lectern. In some cases more than two steps to the rear will block your face from the vision of some auditors in the front rows. When moving to the right, shift the weight to the left foot and step out first with the right one; in this way you avoid the awkward crossing of the left leg in front of the right. When moving to the left, take the first step with the left foot. If you move to a blackboard or chart, stand to one side facing the audience and point with the hand nearer the visual material. Use a pointer if one is available. Do not block the visual material with your body.

The novice sometimes forgets that speeches neither begin with the first word spoken nor conclude with the last; they start as soon as the speaker is introduced and continue until he has returned to his seat. Effective movement to and from the platform is important, because first and last impressions occur at these times. When introduced, proceed briskly to the lectern or the center of the platform. Do not hurry anxiously nor saunter lazily. Avoid both the cocky swagger and the timid, hesitant step. Pause for a moment before beginning to speak. At the end pause momentarily and return to your seat.

2. *What to avoid.* (1) *Immobility.* Particularly if you speak for more than ten minutes, beware of remaining rooted to one spot the entire time. (2) *Too much movement.* Pacing back and forth can be as boring as absence of movement, and considerably more distracting. (3) *Swaying.* A widespread habit among speakers is that of rhythmically moving the body from side to side or backward and forward. The first pattern occurs when the weight is repeatedly shifted from foot to foot, and the second when the weight is shifted from the balls of the feet to the heels and return. Swaying is sometimes so distracting that listeners focus upon it rather than upon the speaker's words. (4) *Jerky and mechanical movement.* Some speakers move more like wind-up toys or puppets than like human beings. Nervous tension is frequently the cause. (5) *Slow and shuffling movement.* Lackadaisical shufflers should cultivate light and spirited movements to help keep audience interest.

3. How to develop effective movement. If your instructor
has suggested the need for improvement, you might check your
movement in a full-length mirror. Also, in an unoccupied classroom, practice walking from a seat to the lectern and return;
practice moving from behind the lectern to the sides and front,
and return; remove the lectern and practice shifts on the empty
platform. Move to the blackboard and point out various aspects
of a real or fictitious visual aid while speaking to the imaginary
audience. Develop habits of movement which can be executed
naturally and effortlessly when speaking.

C. Gesture. A gesture is a purposive movement of the
fingers, hands, arms, head, shoulders, or trunk which serves to
convey meaning and secure emphasis. A *descriptive* gesture, as
stated earlier, helps to clarify concepts such as speed, distance,
direction, size, and shape. A *suggestive* gesture, such as a shrug of
a shoulder or a toss of the head, carries implied meaning. An
emphatic gesture strengthens the impact of an idea. Some
common gestures of emphasis: (1) The clenched fist may be extended, shaken several times, or used to "pound" the table or
lectern. In "striking" the table, stroke vigorously but weaken
the force of the blow just before contact to avoid distracting
noise. (2) The open palm pushed away from the body may serve
to signify disapproval or rejection. (3) The vertical palm may
be moved from one side to another in order to emphasize limitations or the division of ideas or evidence into different categories. (4) The turned-up palm may be extended as a mild reinforcement of a point or as an appeal for support. (5) The pointed
finger may reinforce a verbal accusation or a warning. In using
this gesture, point slightly above the heads of the listeners
rather than directly at someone.

1. The characteristics of effective gestures. (1) *Complete-
ness.* Most effective hand and arm gestures involve three stages:
the *preparation,* the *stroke,* and the *return.* The preparation is
that movement which brings the arm or hand to the point
where the stroke is begun. The stroke, usually the most vigorous
and rapid part of the entire gesture, carries most of the meaning,

particularly in gestures of emphasis. The stroke and its preparation may be repeated several times before the gesture is completed. The return consists of bringing the arm back to the original position. In some gestures the preparation is omitted, or may be considered a part of the stroke. For example, the shrugged shoulder is executed by lifting the shoulders (stroke) and returning them to the position of rest (return); extending both arms outward with palms up (symbolizing indifference, ignorance, or indecision) also involves only the stroke and the return. (2) *Definiteness.* The stroke should be strong, smooth, and unmistakable; this does not imply that all gestures should be made swiftly; many require slow and deliberate execution. All, however, should be decisive—not weak or vague. (3) *Timing.* Occasionally a speaker may gesticulate during a vocal pause. The purpose of such a gesture is to prepare the listener for the words to come or to give added meaning to words just spoken. As examples, the speaker might stab an index finger at his listeners just before saying "Try it sometime!" Or he might shake his head immediately after asking "Is there any other solution?" In all other situations, the stroke of the gesture should be timed to occur simultaneously with the word or phrase to be reinforced. Lagging behind or "jumping the gun" usually destroys the effectiveness of a gesture and may cause the speaker to appear ludicrous. (4) *Proper placement.* Although this suggestion should be interpreted with considerable flexibility, most hand and arm gestures probably should be executed in front of the body—rather than far out to the sides—and in the zone between the waist and shoulders. (5) *Variety.* The novice frequently relies upon one or two gestures which he invariably executes with the same hand. In contrast, the skilled speaker achieves much greater physical expressiveness by using a variety of gestures and by employing both hands, singly as well as simultaneously.

   2. What to avoid. (1) *Random action.* We have noted that because of excessive nervous energy, many beginning speakers tend to engage in various types of meaningless muscular activity.

To help rid his delivery of distracting random gestures the speaker should work conscientiously to develop habits of effective gesticulation. (2) *Inhibition.* Occasionally students attempt to repress any natural inclination to gesture because they consider that "talking with one's hands" is not polite or that gesticulation is "arty" and "dramatic." Such attitudes indicate a misconception of the place of gestures in speaking. Visible language is a basic part of the communicative process. (3) *Perpetual motion.* Some persons gesticulate from the beginning of the speech until the end. Ceaseless action is distracting and, sometimes, irritating. Furthermore, the monotonous overuse of gestures reduces their effectiveness in clarifying and emphasizing meaning. Gestures should be used discriminatingly as a means of punctuating ideas, not as an omnipresent accompaniment to words. (4) *Mechanical artificiality.* Admittedly, some experienced speakers plan specific gestures for execution at particular places in their addresses. However, if the beginner adopts this procedure, his actions will nearly always appear mechanical and artificial. Gesticulation should occur on impulse—its impetus should arise unpremeditatedly from the desire of the speaker to communicate clearly and forcefully his ideas and feelings. Unless a gesture is a spontaneous expression of the speaker's thoughts and emotions, the rest of his body may not be closely integrated with the muscular pattern of the gesture. Thus, a raised fist might seem to indicate that the speaker is angry but, if it is accompanied by a slumped, placid body-set, the listeners will recognize that he is not genuinely concerned.

3. *How to acquire effective use of gesture.* Practice executing various gestures until the movements come easily and naturally. When rehearsing a speech, gesticulate freely whenever you have the slightest urge to do so. When delivering a speech, concentrate on your ideas and your listeners and let gestures come, if they do, spontaneously. Try to incorporate into your platform speaking the same readiness to gesture that is characteristic of your speaking in animated conversation.

D. Eye Contact.   One of the most important ways by which a speaker establishes contact with a listener is by looking at him. Each member of an audience likes to believe that the speaker is talking directly to him, at least some of the time. If a speaker look excessively at his notes, the floor, the ceiling, or out the window, his listeners are likely to lose interest in him and his message. After all, such a speaker appears to have little interest in communicating with his listeners.

1. The characteristics of good eye contact.   How much of the time should you look at your listeners? As a general rule, keep your eyes on your listeners except for necessary reference to your notes, manuscript, or visual aids. Of course, under somewhat unusual circumtances, a speaker might deliberately break eye contact. For instance, in an attempt to arouse a desired emotional response or to create a mood, he might peer into the distance briefly or look at the floor in dejected fashion.

To whom should you address your gaze? For small audiences, like your speech class, look directly at each person several times during even a short speech of four or five minutes. To achieve genuine rapport with these listeners, look into their eyes. Persons within ten or twenty feet of you can easily detect whether you are looking at them or "through" them. For audiences of hundreds or thousands, you cannot look at each person, even in a relatively extended speech. In such cases, divide the room into a number of sections and address your remarks to those in one section and then to those in another, and so on. In each section focus upon a few individuals successively; when you return your gaze to a section, focus upon a different series of individuals. Probably you should concentrate most of your attention on those seated in the central portion of the audience, but do not ignore those on the periphery. Also, if certain individuals in your audience seem uninterested, you might direct especial attention to them; perhaps if they sense that you are indeed genuinely concerned with reaching them, they will respond more favorably.

How long should you focus your gaze upon one individual? As usual, avoid extremes. Do not permit your eyes to flit from one person to another so rapidly that you give the impression of not really looking at anyone; on the other hand, do not look at an individual for so long that he begins to feel uncomfortable. As a general practice, maintain eye contact with a listener for at least a second; within a few seconds move on to another person.

2. *What to avoid.* Because of timidity and fear, a few beginning speakers refuse to look at the audience. A larger number direct only unfocused glances at their hearers and see nothing but a blur of shapes. Such students occasionally adopt as psychological crutches the practice of looking at the foreheads or just above the heads of the listeners instead of into their eyes. These and similar devices are essentially negative. Presumably, you have something important to tell the listeners. If you are well prepared, sincere, and reasonably enthusiastic, you will want to look at them while you talk.

3. *How to acquire good eye contact.* If you have inadequate eye contact when speaking to an audience, ask yourself if you also tend to avert your eyes when engaging in conversation. If so, deliberately force yourself to look directly into the eyes of each person with whom you converse. When rehearsing speeches, direct a steady gaze at the empty chairs in the room, or upon various other objects within your vision; be sure that you actually focus upon each. When delivering classroom speeches, begin by singling out a friend to whom you will speak for a few seconds; shift your eyes to another person; and keep repeating the process until the speech is over. With practice, the average person can develop good habits of eye contact.

E. Facial Expression. As you know, the face is capable of unusually expressive action which aids greatly in clarifying meaning, revealing attitudes and personality, and in achieving emphasis. Facial expression is not the same as eye contact; one can possess excellent eye contact and yet be facially inexpressive.

1. *The characteristics of good facial expression.* As for all other elements of physical delivery, facial expression should appropriately reflect the intellectual and emotional meanings of the accompanying words and should appear natural and genuine, rather than contrived.

2. What to avoid. (1) *Insufficient expression.* In the ordinary communicative situations of daily living, most persons are facially expressive. However, in platform speaking nervous strain may inhibit the flexibility of normal facial action. Instead of reflecting appropriately the intellectual and emotional meaning of his language, the inanimate face of the self-conscious speaker directs attention to his problems of personal adjustment. (2) *Exaggerated facial expression.* Because of an overly demonstrative nature or because of poor communicative attitudes, a few speakers tend to exaggerate facial expressions. Such grimaces distract attention from what the speaker is saying. (3) *Random facial expression.* Speakers who fail to channel excessive nervous energy into productive outlets may occasionally indulge in random activity of the facial muscles. Naturally such contortions usually impair the speaker's effectiveness.

3. How to develop appropriate facial expressiveness. (1) Attempt to free yourself from inhibitions to the extent that natural facial expressions may manifest themselves. (2) In practice sessions, attempt to express with your face various common emotions and meanings; perhaps ask your parents or close friends whether your facial expressions reinforce the meanings and moods intended. (3) Do not plan and rehearse specific facial expressions for use in a given speech. Depend upon the speaking situation and the meanings of your message to elicit your natural expressiveness.

SUMMARY

Visible action helps the speaker to (1) adjust to the speaking situation, (2) reveal his personality and emotional state, (3) attain and hold audience interest, and (4) secure audience response by clarifying meaning, emphasizing ideas, and arousing emotions. Physical action is an inherent part of the process of oral communication. When effective, it possesses these characteristics: (1) it is closely integrated in the entire act of communication; (2) it is spontaneous and appears effortless rather than mechanical, although it may be acquired by carefully developed habit patterns; (3) it is appropriate to the audience, the ocasion, the speaker, and his purpose. The types of bodily action include (1) posture, (2) movement, (3) gesture, (4) eye contact, and (5) facial expression.

EXERCISES AND ASSIGNMENTS

Practicing Bodily Action

1. Rehearse several times and deliver in class a "how to do it" or "process" talk. For suggested topics, see page 262.

2. Deliver a short class speech demonstrating effective and ineffective posture, movement, eye contact, facial expression, or gesture.

3. Prepare a pantomime (communication by action alone) for class presentation. Suggestions: (1) teach an imaginary person to play tennis, dance the rumba, use judo holds, operate an elevator, use a microscope; (2) demonstrate how to eat spaghetti, trim a hedge, wash a dog, change a tire, cut an obstreperous boy's hair; (3) impersonate a nervous speaker, a baseball coach, a cheerleader, a flamboyant lawyer, a public official, a well-known campus personality.

4. With two or three classmates, select or write a short playlet for a group pantomime. Stories of adventure, mystery, or melodrama frequently afford the opportunity for considerable physical action. Assign a single part to each performer and rehearse the pantomime once or twice before presenting it to the class. Following the presentation, determine whether the class was able to follow the plot.

Evaluating Bodily Action

5. Your instructor may arrange to take motion pictures of each member of the class both at the beginning and at the end of the term. If your school does not own a camera and projector, they may be available for rent at the local library. Also, students occasionally own such equipment. If money for film is not available from the university, the members of the class may be willing to contribute the necessary funds.

(1) Film about thirty seconds of each person's speaking.
(2) To minimize self-consciousness, the camera operator should not make obvious to the speaker the precise moments during which the camera is activated.

(3) When showing the pictures, stop the projector after each speaker for comments and evaluations by the instructor and the class.

(4) This film should be shown again at the end of the term for the purpose of comparing it with the pictures taken at that time.

6. In a written or oral report to the class, evaluate the physical delivery of a speaker whom you have recently observed at a public meeting off-campus or have seen on television. Explain specifically how his use of facial expression, eye contact, posture, movement, gesture, and body tonus contributed to or detracted from his effectiveness.

7. Spend an hour or two watching the bodily action of television performers. When the sound is turned off, can you identify the emotions which the performers are evidencing? Periodically turn on the sound to determine how closely you have been able to follow the speakers' thoughts. Several times when the sound is turned on close your eyes and listen to the oral presentation; then open your eyes and watch the picture in addition to hearing the sound. Do you believe that the combination of sight and sound significantly improves the clarity and vividness of the speakers' communication? Report your findings to the class in a brief oral report.

6 ❦❦ *Voice*

Among the various personal characteristics which influence our judgments of others the voice seems to be one of the most important. Think for a moment about your friends and associates. Don't most of those who are popular and successful possess better than average voices? Conversely, don't you hear a disproportionately large number of unpleasant, weak, or monotonous voices among those persons who seem checkmated by fate or who experience difficulty in maintaining effective interpersonal relations? Remember the impressions you formed of your fellow students during the first meeting of your speech class? As the period began you looked around the room to size up your classmates. Soon you knew them better—each introduced himself to the class. Dick, the first speaker, walked with brisk assurance to the front of the room. Muscular, square-jawed, almost handsome, he turned to face his audience and began to speak. But after a few words, your attention shifted to his thin, tense, high-pitched voice. Such an inappropriate voice seemed almost a negation of his many positive attributes. Barbara spoke next. An unusually attractive girl might be expected to have a correspondingly pleasing voice. Again disillusionment! Barbara's voice was harsh, strained, and almost masculine; she talked too loudly and much too rapidly. As other pupils introduced themselves, you heard relatively few clear, expressive, pleasant voices—voices which were easy to listen to, which encouraged you to like the speaker, and which gave to language a warm, living quality. As your turn approached, you wondered how you would sound to others. Your voice was so much a part of you that in the past you had been scarcely aware of it. But you were now convinced that your classmates would be as sensitive to your voice as you had been to theirs. You realized that your evaluation of each individual as a speaker and as a person had been strongly conditioned by hearing his voice. By the end of the period you were perhaps convinced that an effective voice is singularly important to successful oral communication.

AN INTRODUCTION TO VOICE TRAINING

Probably during the first class meeting your instructor asked you to read Chapter 1, "Oral Communication—Springboard to More Effective Living." In Chapter 1, you learned that the vocal mechanism produces the sound waves which carry audible symbols (words) to the ears of the listeners, that the effective voice gives to language shades of meanings and emotional overtones by varying pitch, force, quality or tone, and rate of utterance, and that the voice provides clues concerning the speaker's state of health and his attitudes toward himself and his audience.

A. Become Acquainted with the Elements Which Help to Determine the Nature of Your Voice. Up to this point, no attempt has been made to answer the question frequently asked by students of speech: "Why does my voice sound as it does?" Here are several of the determining factors.

1. The physical structure of the organs used for speech. At your next class or during a walk across the campus, observe in the people about you the diversified sizes and shapes of the various mouths, jaws, teeth, and "Adam's apples." Corresponding variations exist among the internal structures such as the tongue, hard and soft palates, and larynx. Such structural dissimilarities help to account for differences in pitch level and vocal quality among the voices; to some extent they also limit the changes in vocal production which can be effected by training. Thus, a man cannot become a bass if, because of his small larynx, he is a "natural" tenor. But he can improve the flexibility and richness of his voice within its natural pitch range.

2. *Your past and present environment.* As a small child you unconsciously echoed the vocal qualities, inflections, stresses, and rates used by your parents and older siblings. Later on, you were influenced, consciously or unconsciously, by your playmates, classmates, teachers, and other close associates. Perhaps you deliberately imitated the vocal style of an admired friend, a counselor, a movie star, or a TV personality. The locality in which you were reared also exerted considerable influence upon your vocal habits. Experts can determine from your voice and pronunciation the area in which you spent your formative years, and often can identify your cultural and national background.

3. *Your basic personal adjustment.* Various deep-seated personality manifestations may reveal themselves in the voice. If you experience chronic tension resulting from emotional disturbances (such as hostility, timidity, defensiveness, submissiveness, or anxiety), or, conversely, if your neuromuscular system maintains an appropriate body tonus resulting from positive emotional adjustments (such as contentment, optimism, and friendliness), you may expect that such emotional states will be reflected to some extent in the tone, pitch, and force of the voice and in the rate of your utterance.

4. *Your reactions to the particular act of communication.* Your attitudes toward the act of communication directly affect the degree of your muscular tension. And since speech is produced by muscular activity, changes in body tonus may influence the voice. Examples: The nervous speaker may have difficulty in achieving the controlled breathing necessary for firm vocal tones; also the involuntary muscles of his speech mechanism may become so tense that his voice assumes a harsh or thin quality and his pitch rises unnaturally high. The bored, indifferent speaker talks with a dull, lifeless, monotonous voice. The angry speaker may be so disturbed that the musculature of his throat and pharynx mirrors his emotional stress, producing a raspy, strident voice. The confident, enthusiastic speaker reveals his positive orientation by maintaining his customary control over voice quality and flexibility. In any communicative situation, you must meet three requirements if you wish to speak with an animated, pleasant, expressive voice: you should possess suitable habitual vocal characteristics; you should channel nervous energy into productive outlets; and you should have appropriate attitudes toward yourself, your listeners, and your message.

B. Apply the Following Systematic and Positive Approach to Achieve Maximum Benefits from Your Study of the Voice.

1. Learn what sound is and how it is produced. Often a student is unconvinced of the need for understanding the basic principles of sound or the process by which the vocal mechanism functions. He suspects that many well-known speakers and actors with excellent voices know little or nothing about acoustics or the "hows" and "whys" of vocal production. Such is undoubtedly the case. However, understanding the structure and operation of the vocal mechanism will facilitate the detection of improper vocal habits, help you to determine the causes of various defects and shortcomings, and permit you to make fullest use of both the criticisms given by your instructor and the various exercises he may assign. An intelligent approach to voice training necessitates an elementary knowledge of sound, the anatomy and physiology of the speech organs, and the processes which produce speech—respiration, phonation, resonation, and pronunciation.

2. Know the attributes of the effective voice. Most persons can readily judge which voices they like and which they do not like. But often they are unable to explain the reasons for their judgments. In order to improve your voice, you must know what constitutes a desirable voice. The attributes may then serve as goals. The effective speaking voice is audible, pleasant, fluent, and flexible. Presently these attributes will be discussed in detail and procedures will be recommended to help you achieve each.

3. Make an objective, accurate evaluation of your voice. This is more difficult than you may think. In the first place, you may never have consciously listened to your voice. Secondly, like most persons, you may tend to hear what you want to hear and may be resentful of criticism. With the aid of recordings of your voice, cultivate the ability to analyze objectively and accurately your own voice. Condition yourself to profit from your instructor's evaluations. With proper attitudes and with the help of your instructor you should be able to determine the specific vocal improvement needed.

4. Initiate a program of planned and directed practice. Do not expect to achieve significant vocal improvement simply by delivering an occasional speech, participating in a series of group discussions, or by engaging in the customary amount of daily talk. Successful voice training involves systematic, concentrated effort perhaps over a protracted period. Study carefully the remainder of this chapter, particularly as it relates to your own vocal needs. Then, with your instructor, map out a program which concentrates on only one problem at a time, requires daily drill, and provides for frequent checks on your progress. You say you haven't the time? Much of the practice can be accomplished in the time you now idle away or while you are engaged in automatic activities such as showering, dressing, driving a car, and other daily tasks.

UNDERSTANDING THE BASIC PRINCIPLES OF SOUND

Before taking up the structure and effective operation of the vocal mechanism, we should become acquainted with certain elementary principles of sound. All sounds—*whether the shrill whistle of a donkey engine, the slap of uneasy waters lapping at piling, the plop of a newspaper landing on the doorstep, the unintelligible announcements blaring over a railroad depot public address system, or the rich bass notes of Tennessee Ernie singing an "old time" hymn*—are produced in essentially the same manner and have certain common perceptual properties.

A. Requisites for Sound Production. The creation of any sound involves a source of energy which acts upon an object setting it into vibration. These vibrations result in sound waves.

In order to have carrying power those sounds which are weak at their source require reinforcement by electonics or by some type of resonance.

1. *The source of energy* which activates an object into vibra tion may be a blow (clapping hands, clanging bell, or an ax blade biting into a log), a pluck or scrape (the stringed instruments or sand paper being applied to a surface), an explosion (nuclear weapons, rocket or automobile engines, or firearms), the force of rushing air (referee's whistle, the reed in wind instruments, the human voice), and so on.

2. *The vibrating body, or sound source,* may be anything capable of oscillation, such as reeds, pipes, strings, plates, or columns of air. The vocal folds in the larynx (voice box) are the vibrators for the human voice.

3. The forward and backward motions of the sound source produce in the surrounding air particles invisible physical vibrations which are called *sound waves.*[1] The forward motion of the sound source pushes the immediate air particles outward, causing them to become packed more closely together. The displacement of these molecules brings them into collision with adjacent molecules which, in turn, hit other molecules. This process continues until the energy contained in the original wave is dissipated. The elastic nature of air causes the compressed molecules to bounce rapidly back past their original position and then to rebound forward and backward in decreasing oscillations. Thus, alternating patterns of condensation (greater density or compression of air particles) and rarefaction (lesser density or a thinning out of air particles) swiftly spread out in all directions from the sound source. These waves of pressure continue to travel until the energy which was imparted to the initial wave by the sound source has been dissipated. Your especial attention is directed to two considerations: (1) The air

---

[1] For practical reasons we shall assume that the transmitting medium is air. However, sound waves also travel through other gases, solids, and liquids. As was stated in Chapter 1, sounds travel through the atmosphere at about 1,100 feet per second. They travel through solids and liquids at greater speed and are carried over wires at the speed of light, about 186,000 miles per second.

particles disturbed at the sound source do not speed directly through the air to convey the sound. Only the disturbance, or the wave, travels. After activating adjacent air particles, thereby pushing the wave along, the molecules return quickly from their period of compression to their center of equilibrium. (2) The sound wave represents longitudinal not transverse movements; that is, the vibrations of the air particles are back and forth excursions along a course stretching directly from the sound source. Roe M. Heffner explains that the nature of the longitudinal wave may be compared to "the propagation of the bump from a switching engine down a long line of freight cars, none of which moves appreciably from its original position. Still more convincing as a demonstration of the propagation of energy is the return of this bump from the free end of the train to the engine when the train remains standing still." [2]

4. Reinforcement of the sound waves, *resonation,* may be accomplished by means of sound boards (as the sounding board in the piano) or by passageways or cavities (as the tubular structure of wind instruments, the hollow structure of most stringed instruments, and the throat, mouth, and nasal cavities in the human voice).

B. Perceptual Properties of Sounds. All sounds possess four interrelated properties: frequency, amplitude, wave composition, and duration. These characteristics are interpreted by our neuromuscular systems as *pitch, force, quality,* and *time.*

1. Pitch. The rapidity with which a sound source vibrates determines the rate or frequency with which it produces sound waves. For our purposes, we can consider that the greater the number of vibrations in a given unit of time, the higher the pitch; conversely, the fewer the number of vibrations, the lower the pitch. (We should also recognize, however, that pitch is partially dependent upon the intensity and overtone composition of the sound.) For example, the ear identifies a sound vibrating at a frequency of 256 cycles per second (c.p.s.) as

[2] Roe M. Heffner, *General Phonetics* (Madison: University of Wisconsin Press, 1949), p. 42.

middle C, one at 384 c.p.s. as G, and one at 512 c.p.s. at C above middle C. A given number of vibrations per second will be heard as the same pitch whether played on the violin, sung by the human voice, or blown on a toy trumpet. Most of us probably cannot hear sounds below 16 c.p.s. or above 18,000 c.p.s., and our sensitivity to high frequency sounds (those over 2,400 c.p.s.) tends to decline with age.

2. Force. Although the force (intensity or loudness) of a sound is partly dependent upon its frequency and overtone structure, force is primarily determined by the amount of energy exerted on the vibrator. The greater the energy exerted, the greater tends to be the amplitude of movement of the vibrator. The greater the displacement of the vibrator, the greater the amplitude of the sound waves produced. As mentioned earlier, the ear interprets amplitude as force. Try this experiment: pluck a guitar string, first gently then forcibly; note the wider visible vibration and the louder sound after the forceful pluck.

3. Quality. Quality is that characteristic which enables us to distinguish between two sound sources producing the same note with the same degree of force and the same duration of time. Although partly dependent upon frequency and intensity, the quality of a sound is determined basically by the composition of its wave. Have you ever wondered why all tuning forks of the same pitch produce identical sounds? Their complete lack of distinctive quality results from their construction: each prong of the fork can move forward and backward only as a complete unit, thus producing simple waves or pure tones. Nearly all sound sources, however, vibrate both in "complete units" and in sections or segments, thus creating complex waves. In such cases, the *fundamental* or "complete unit" vibrations dominate the sound and basically determine the pitch; the segmental vibrations produce higher frequencies, *overtones,* which give the sound its timbre or quality. For example, a violin string vibrates as a whole (producing the fundamental) and also in segments (producing the overtones). The overtones are not heard as separate pitches. They blend with the fundamental to create the quality of the violin tone. Thus one may distinguish a violin from a viola, even though both play the same note on the musical scale with the same degree of loudness. We shall soon see that in comparison to most musical instruments the greater complexity of the vocal mechanism permits a much larger variation in the possible combinations and relative intensities of the overtones. Therefore, although two violins of comparable construction may produce tones of almost identical quality, probably no two human voices are exactly alike. For this reason you easily recognize familiar voices on the telephone, even though that instrument does not reproduce sounds with high fidelity. Possibly you have also experienced hearing voices in the distance and readily identifying them, despite not being able to understand what was being said. (Of course, other factors such as intonation, pitch, and pronunciation are also involved in such identification of voices.) The overtones which determine the quality of the voice are weak and would be lost without reinforcement. As will be discussed presently, resonance provides the amplification necessary to give each voice its unique timbre.

4. Time. Each sound must have a beginning and an end; the intervening period during which sound waves are uninterruptedly produced is known as the duration of the sound.

We have now identified the perceptual properties common to all sounds: pitch, force, quality, and time. Any program of voice training must of necessity attempt to improve the usage of one or more of these acoustic characteristics. To facilitate such vocal alterations, you should learn how the voice is produced.

LEARNING HOW THE VOICE IS PRODUCED

As you know, the production of speech requires the interdependent operation of four processes: *respiration, phonation, resonation,* and *pronunciation.* You may not have considered, however, that the mechanisms responsible for these processes were designed primarily for vegetative duties directly concerned with the sustaining of life—not for the production of speech. The basic function of the lips, teeth, tongue, larynx, diaphragm, lungs, and the other organs of speech are biological and include aerating the blood, chewing, swallowing, gagging, coughing, sucking, and aiding in the function of elimination and heavy lifting. To speak at the same time one is performing any of these functions (with the exception of aerating the blood by breathing) is either difficult or impossible. The fact that speech is an *overlaid* or "secondary" function helps to explain some of the difficulties a speaker may experience in developing an effective vocal delivery.

A. Respiration. We have noted that sound waves occur only when the application of energy forces an object into vibration. The source of energy for the voice is the stream of air exhaled from the lungs.

1. The structure of the breathing mechanism. The thoracic framework is formed principally by the spinal column, the sternum or breastbone, and twelve pairs of ribs. In the rear, the ribs are attached to the vertebral column. In the front, the upper six pairs are joined to the sternum; the next four pairs are coupled directly to each other and indirectly to the sternum by connecting lengths of flexible cartilage; the bottom two pairs are free from anterior attachments and are called floating ribs. The rib cage is not a rigid structure. Its lower portions, especially, are capable of limited upward and outward movement. Of the organs within the thoracic cage we are most concerned with the lungs and trachea. The lungs are mistakenly believed by some to "suck in" and "push out" the air in the breathing process. However, the lungs have no muscle tissue and, therefore, play no active part in respiration; they serve only as passive reservoirs for the air which is inhaled and exhaled. Breathing is accomplished by the action of various muscles which change the size and shape of the thorax. To identify and discuss each muscle would complicate unnecessarily our study. Perhaps it is sufficient to say that breathing involves the action of various thoracic muscles, the diaphragm (a large double-dome-shaped sheath of muscular and fibrous tissue which forms the floor of the thorax and separates it from the abdomen), and the abdominal muscles.

2. *The functioning of the breathing mechanism.* We turn now to a comparison of respiration for life with that for speech.

a. BREATHING FOR LIFE. The process of *inspiration* (inhalation) is accomplished by enlarging the size of the thoracic cavity, thus reducing the air pressure within. To equalize the pressure, air rushes in through the nose and/or mouth, down the pharynx (throat), through the trachea (wind pipe), and into the lungs. Enlargement of the thorax may be brought about by three kinds of related action. (1) The diaphragm, the most powerful and important muscle of inspiration, contracts to become somewhat flattened and to force its rear portions downward and forward. This action causes the diaphragm to push down on the abdominal organs, thereby lengthening the chest cavity. (2) Various thoracic muscles contract to lift the ribs and sternum, enlarging the lateral dimensions of the chest cavity. (3) In an undesirable method of breathing, the neck and clavicle (collar bone) muscles pull the rib cage upward, increasing the vertical dimensions of the chest cavity.

The process of *expiration* (exhalation) is accomplished by relaxing the muscles which were used for inspiration. The diaphragm relaxes and, under pressure from the partially compressed abdominal organs, returns quickly to its original position. When the muscles which have enlarged the rib cage relax, the weight of the cage causes it to descend. Thus, breathing to sustain life is basically a matter of alternately enlarging and decreasing the size of the air cavity. When your body is at rest, a complete respiratory cycle occurs smoothly and regularly every 3.5 to 4 seconds, or approximately fifteen to eighteen times per minute. Inspiration and expiration require nearly equal periods of time.

b. BREATHING FOR SPEECH. Breathing for speech differs in several ways from breathing for life. (1) Since voice is produced during exhalation, this process becomes active. To produce an out-going column of air strong enough and steady enough to serve as the vocal motor, two related and concurrent processes are required. First, the diaphragm and the thoracic muscles of inhalation relax, thus permitting the progressive reduction in the size of the chest cavity. Secondly, the abdominal muscles and certain thoracic muscles contract. Their combined action pulls the rib cage downward and exerts pressure upon the viscera, which are pushed upward against the diaphragm. As you can readily see, a precise balance must be achieved between the pressure exerted by the contracting abdominal muscles and the gradual relaxation of the thoracic muscles and the diaphragm. (2) In contrast to the equal duration of the inspiration—expiration periods in vegetative breathing, speech requires a more rapid period of inhalation and usually a longer period of exhalation. In speaking, the ratio time between inspiration and expiration varies from one-to-one to perhaps thirty-to-one, depending upon the nature of the thought being expressed. (3) The rhythmical nature of normal vegetative breathing is disrupted in speaking. During speech, the length of the respiratory cycle varies greatly, depending upon the mood of the speaker and the nature of his message. Snidecor found that although the average duration of the respiratory cycle for oral reading was 4.2 seconds and for extempore speaking was 4 seconds, the length of individual cycles varied between 1.25 seconds and 9.95 seconds.[3] (4) Breathing for speech requires a slightly deeper inhalation than does normal vegetative breathing. However, as we shall soon see, the control of exhalation and the other elements of voice production are far more important to the speaker than deep inhalation.

Before turning to the application of breathing to good voice production, we should explore the question, "Is there a best way to breathe for speech?" Conclusive evidence cannot be cited to prove the superiority of any one method of breathing. *The*

---

[3] John C. Snidecor, "Temporal Aspects of Breathing," *Speech Monographs*, November, 1955, pp. 284–289.

important considerations are that you inhale sufficient air, that you exert a strong degree of control over the speed and the steadiness with which it is used during vocalization, and that you prevent excessive nervous tension. The one type of breathing which you should avoid is the clavicular. In this method, considerable expansion occurs in the upper chest. Such breathing is so shallow that the speaker's breath supply is inadequate either to produce sounds of adequate strength or to maintain a smooth easy flow of speech. The "clavicular breather" often has to pause awkwardly in mid-phrase to catch his breath. Furthermore, because clavicular breathing stimulates excessive tension in the neck and throat, the voice may seem strained and flat.

3. The importance of controlled breathing in good voice production. In addition to serving as the motor which sets the vocal folds into vibration, controlled breathing enables you to achieve better voice usage: (1) *By helping to regulate force.* Changes in vocal force help the speaker to convey special intellectual and emotional meanings and to prevent monotony in vocal utterance. An increase in force results primarily from a corresponding increase in the amplitude of the sound wave, which in turn is occasioned by the wider vibration of the vocal folds. To accomplish the latter, one must strengthen the pressure of the column of air pushing against the folds. A decrease in force results basically from an equivalent weakening of the out-going breath stream. (2) *By helping to achieve firmness of tone.* You are familiar with the tremulous voice of fear. Any other strong emotion which causes an increased physical tonus may disturb the balance between the progressive relaxation of the muscles of inspiration and the gradually applied pressure of the muscles of exhalation. A vocal tone can be no steadier than the flow of air producing the tone. If the breath stream is unsteady, a resultant quaver will be heard in pitch and loudness. (3) *By helping to control timing and rate.* Both shallow and overly deep breathing tend to impair effective rate and timing. If you take into your lungs an insufficient amount of air, you may be forced to stop for breath in the middle of the phrase. On the other hand, if you breathe in excessive amounts of air, the oversupply may cause you to lengthen the stream of words uttered in one breath and perhaps to increase your rate inappropriately. Platform speaking probably requires somewhat deeper inhalations than does vegetative breathing. However, even when speaking vigorously you do not use more than one-fifth of your total lung capacity in a single respiratory cycle.

Exercises to improve control over the muscles of breathing appear on pages 131–132.

B. Phonation. The production of voiced sounds is called phonation. We have noted earlier that such sounds are created when the exhaled air stirs the vocal folds into vibration.

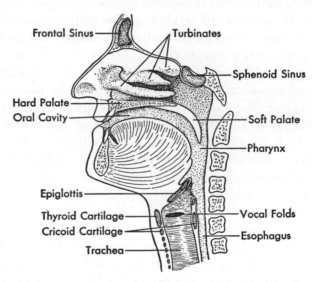

Fig. 2. Mid-Line Section of Head and Throat Showing Nasal, Oral, Pharyngeal, and Laryngeal Cavities.

1. The structure and functioning of the phonatory mechanism. The vocal folds are located in the *larynx*, a cartilaginous air pipe connecting the trachea with the pharynx (throat). Although the larynx is composed of nine cartilages, we need be concerned with only three. The *thyroid* cartilage consists of two

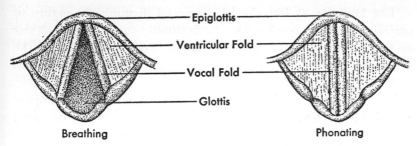

Breathing   Phonating

Fig. 3. Position of the Vocal Folds During Breathing and Phonating.

relatively large plates which are fused in the front and spread toward the back like butterfly wings. Also known as the "Adam's apple," this structure may easily be felt with the fingers. It protrudes noticeably in most males. Beneath the thyroid and articulated with it by muscles and connective tissue is the *cricoid*

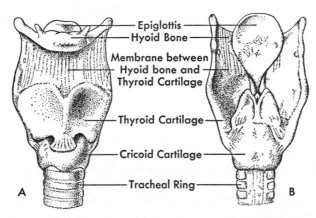

Fig. 4. The Larynx and Trachea. *From Jon Eisenson, Basic Speech (New York: Copyright by The Macmillan Company, 1950). Used by special permission of The Macmillan Company.*

cartilage. Unlike the thyroid which is open in the rear, the cricoid forms a complete ring, wider in the back than in the front. Placed atop this widened posterior portion of the cricoid are the paired *arytenoids,* small, triangular-shaped cartilages which serve as the rear attachments for the vocal folds.

The larynx may be raised or lowered through the action of certain *extrinsic* muscles. One such muscle connects the larynx to the hyoid bone (a horseshoe-shaped bone at the base of the tongue) and during swallowing pulls the larynx upward and slightly forward so that it presses against the back of the tongue; this raising action of the larynx also exerts a pull upon the opening of the esophagus enlarging it so that it receives more easily

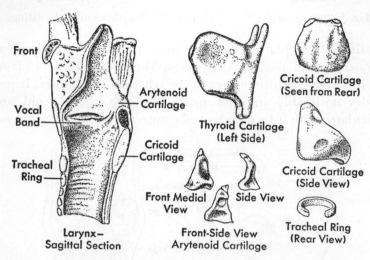

Fig. 5. The Cartilages of the Larynx. *From Jon Eisenson,* Basic Speech *(New York: Copyright by The Macmillan Company, 1950). Used by special permission of The Macmillan Company.*

the food and drink that pours over the top of the protected larynx. A second important extrinsic muscle connects the larynx to the sternum; its contraction pulls the larynx downward. We shall see presently that the action of these muscles may influence the quality and pitch of the voice.

Alternation in the position and tension of the vocal folds is provided by the action of certain *intrinsic* muscles. The most important of the intrinsic muscles are the vocal folds themselves, which are called the thyro-arytenoid muscles. The folds are attached at the front and sides to the inside walls of the thyroid and at the rear to the vocal processes of the arytenoids. As seen from above, the folds appears to be two flat ledges of muscles with inner rims overlaid with white connective tissue. As seen from below, the folds appear to be rounded bulges or swellings protruding from the laryngeal walls. During vegetative breathing the folds are relaxed, leaving a triangular opening (glottis) with the vertex in front. During certain other biological activities, as well as during phonation, the glottis must be closed to permit the building up of air pressure in the trachea. The closing of the folds is accomplished by the integrated action of various intrinsic muscles which cause the arytenoid cartilages to slide together and to pivot inwardly on their ball and socket-like attachments. These movements bring the folds together so that their edges touch, effecting a closed valve. To open the glottis, other muscles pull the arytenoid cartilages apart and rotate them outwardly.

This valve action of the vocal folds protects you by guarding the entrance to the trachea and aids in the performance of various biological functions. As an example, when a foreign body enters the air passage immediately above the larynx, the glottis closes, thereby impounding the air coming up from the lungs; the abdominal muscles contract to increase the air pressure beneath the folds; the folds abruptly separate and the air escapes upward in an explosive cough, expelling the foreign matter. As another example, the automatic closure of the folds with the attendant increase in infra-glottal pressure produces a firm chest foundation for your arms when you are engaged in brief, vigorous muscular action, such as lifting a heavy weight.

The valve operation required to produce voiced sounds is considerably more complicated than that required for simple biological functions. In phonation, the edges of the folds are brought lightly together so that they touch throughout their complete length. This closure must be sufficiently tight to prevent the escape of any air except that representing genuine thoracic pressure. It should not be so tight, however, that it precludes the free excursions of the folds when set into motion by the breath. When the force of the air stream becomes strong enough to overcome both the resistance of the folds and the air pressure above them, the folds are forced apart and a puff of air escapes between them, setting their inner edges into vibration. The puff of air, converted into a wave of condensation and rarefaction by the movement of the folds, continues up the throat and out the mouth and/or nose. Immediately after the puff of air has passed between the folds the pressure below the glottis drops and the glottis is quickly closed. After the pressure has been re-established, it again forces apart the folds and another wave is produced. If this alternate opening and closing of the glottis occurs more rapidly than about fifty times a second, a vocal tone is produced. When phonation is concluded, intrinsic muscles return the arytenoids to their original station, thus separating the folds. (As you will see in Chapter 7, the process of phonation applies only to voiced sounds; voiceless sounds, like *p, t, k,* and *s,* are produced by driving the breath stream under pressure through narrowed oral passageways.)

2. *The importance of the phonatory mechanism in good voice production.*

a. THE PHONATORY MECHANISM HELPS TO DETERMINE THE PITCH OF THE VOICE. As stated previously, pitch depends primarily upon the relative rapidity of the fundamental vibrations by which the sound is produced; the greater the number of cycles per unit of time the higher will be the pitch, while the fewer the vibrations the lower the pitch. In the human voice, the interrelated action of various muscles determines pitch changes by altering the length of the folds and the thickness and tension of the inner edges of the folds. (1) When the folds are *shortened* or *lengthened,* the pitch tends to be raised or lowered accordingly. In like manner, the violinist alters pitch by pressing a finger upon the string to shorten or lengthen the vibrating segment, and the harpist plucks strings of different lengths to produce different notes. (2) An increased *thickness* of the folds tends to produce a lowered pitch and a decreased thickness a raised pitch. Perhaps you have noticed that the lower notes on the piano, harp, or guitar are produced by strings possessing greater girth. (3) Because changes in length and thickness tend to neutralize each other, changes in the *tension* of the folds are possibly the most important single agent in altering pitch. As tension is increased the pitch tends to be raised, and as it is decreased the pitch lowered. Similarly, stringed instruments are tuned by increasing or decreasing the tension of the individual strings.

Although you have only limited control over the individual muscles which determine the length, thickness, and tension of the folds, you can improve your utilization of pitch by applying the suggestions given later in this chapter and in Chapter 16. Basically such a program involves freeing the throat and neck muscles from excessive tension, training the ear to listen critically to your own voice and to the good voices around you, developing a kinesthetic feeling for the various kinds and degrees of muscle tension needed to produce different pitches, determining whether you are using the general pitch level most suitable for your vocal mechanism, and drilling on exercises to widen your usable pitch range and to improve the flexibility of your use of pitch.

b. The Phonatory Mechanism Helps to Determine Voice Quality.   You know that the distinctive quality of every voice is determined by the composition of the sound wave—the number, frequencies, and relative intensities of the overtones—and by the resonation which the sound receives. Pleasant quality can be produced only by elastic, healthy vocal folds possessing sufficient tension to effect close approximation, but free from excessive tension. Flabby, inelastic folds allow too much air to escape between them during phonation, causing a husky, breathy tone. Excessive tension in either the intrinsic or extrinsic muscles or in the larynx produces harshness or hoarseness.

C. Resonation.   As you know, without some means of amplification the sound produced by the vibration of the vocal folds would be weak and colorless. To demonstrate the need for reinforcement of a tone, strike a tuning fork and place the end upon the top of a table; note the difference in the strength of the sound when contact is made. Or remove the mouthpiece from a saxophone or clarinet and blow into it; you will hear a weak, reedy tone contrasting sharply with the characteristic sound of the instrument. The process by which sounds are amplified and enriched is called resonation.

1. The nature of the resonating process. Resonance is produced in three ways: by reflected vibrations, by sympathetic vibrations, and forced vibrations.

a. REFLECTED VIBRATION. When a sound wave strikes a surface it is reflected. If the surface is hard and smooth, as exemplified by the tubing and flared opening of the saxophone, the reflection is more efficient. We shall soon see that in the production of the human voice the sound waves are reflected by the inner surfaces of the throat, mouth, and nasal cavities and that the surface texture of the cavity walls helps determine the amount of reflection and the type of frequencies to be reinforced.

b. SYMPATHETIC VIBRATION. Perhaps you have been annoyed by a metallic humming which occurs periodically in your radio or television set during a musical program. If you listen carefully, you may discover that the humming is caused by a loose wire or a piece of metal inside the receiver which vibrates only when a particular note is played or sung. This phenomenon is called sympathetic vibration. An object begins to vibrate if a nearby vibrating source is "tuned to the same frequency." Of signal importance to voice production is the principle that the column of air in a cavity may be stirred into sympathetic vibration. The frequency to which a given body of air will respond sympathetically is decided by the size and nature of the cavity and by the size and shape of its opening(s). For instance, the longer and the larger the cavity—the lower are the frequencies to which it will respond; conversely, the larger the opening—the higher is the pitch level to which the cavity is best adapted. In human beings, the throat and mouth are capable of assuming many shapes and sizes, thus making possible the resonating of a large variety of pitches and the production of wide variations in vocal quality.

c. FORCED VIBRATION. This type of amplification occurs when a vibrating sound source comes into actual contact with another object, forcing it into oscillation. In the violin and cello, the bridge conveys the vibrations of the strings to the body of the instrument. In the human voice, the role of forced vibration has not been clearly established. Although forced vibrations occur in the rib cage, skull, and thyroid cartilage during speech, such vibrations probably cannot penetrate through flesh, skin, and clothing to affect materially the loudness or quality of the sounds.

2. The structure and function of the resonating mechanism. Before the sound waves produced by the vibrating folds can find egress through the mouth and/or nose, they must pass through two or three resonating cavities: the *pharyngeal cavity* (throat), the *oral cavity* (mouth), and the *nasal cavity* (nose). Let us examine the nature of each cavity and explain how each helps to determine the strength and quality of the voice.

a. THE PHARYNGEAL CAVITY. The pharynx is a pipe about five inches long, extending from the top of the larynx upward to the nasal cavity. It is commonly divided into three parts. The lower extremity (*laryngopharynx*), which connects with the larynx and esophagus, stretches from the top of the larynx upward to the base of the tongue. The middle section (*oropharynx*), which opens into the oral cavity, is the only part of the pharynx which is visible when you look into a mirror and say *AH*. It extends upward from the laryngopharynx to about the soft palate. The upper extremity (*nasopharynx*) reaches from the top of the oropharynx to connect with the nasal cavity.

The pharynx is an extremely versatile resonator. On high-pitched tones the lifting of the larynx shortens the length of the column of air in the pharynx so that it may reinforce sympathetically the higher frequencies. On low-pitched tones the larynx is pulled downward, lengthening the pharyngeal air column so that it may resonate the lower frequencies. The length of the pharynx may also be decreased by raising the soft palate against the rear wall of the throat, thereby sealing off the upper section— the nasopharynx. In addition to influencing the length of the air column, the action of the soft palate helps to control the openings of the pharynx: the contracted velum blocks the entrance to the nasal cavity and causes the air to be emitted through the mouth. The relaxed velum permits the nose to serve as an outlet while the mouth functions as a resonating cavity. Furthermore, even the diameter of the pharynx and the texture of its walls may affect the quality of the tone produced. If the muscles lining the walls of the pharynx (called *constrictors*) contract vigorously, the passageway is narrowed and the tension of the surface is increased. The harder surface and the smaller diameter of the constricted pharynx resonate efficiently the higher frequencies, producing a hard, tense voice quality. On the other hand, a rich, mellow quality may be produced if the constrictor muscles are relatively relaxed; the resultant wider passageway and walls of softer texture damp some of the higher overtones and give greater prominence to the lower ones.

b. The Oral Cavity. The oral cavity is visually the most familiar of the resonators. Its parts, readily seen in a mirror when the mouth is opened wide, include: (1) the *hard palate* which forms the bony roof over the front part of the mouth; (2) the *velum* which is the fleshy ceiling over the rear half of the mouth and which, because it possesses muscle fibers, can be lifted upwards and backwards against the pharyngeal wall, closing the passage into the nasal cavity; (3) the *pillars of fauces* which are paired muscular arches coming down on each side from the velum and which can be contracted to help reduce the size of the opening into the pharynx; and (4) the tongue which, as you know, is a large, muscular structure capable of phenomenally rapid, diverse, and precise action.

Like the pharynx, the mouth is a versatile resonator permitting numerous adjustments in its size, shape, and openings. Such variations are important in resonating the voice and, as we shall see in Chapter 7, in modifying the breath stream so as to produce the vowels and most of the consonants.

c. THE NASAL CAVITY. The nasal cavity connects with the nasopharynx in the rear and terminates frontally at the nostrils. Actually a pair of cavities, the nasal area is partitioned by a thin wall of bone and cartilage called the *septum*. Protruding from the cheek wall of each cavity are bony convolutions known as *turbinates*. A glance at diagram 2, page 120, will indicate that, although the overall size of the nasal structure is comparatively large, the inner passage is relatively small, because of the obstruction of the septum and the turbinates. Unlike the pharynx and the mouth, the nasal cavity is severely limited in the alterations which can be made in its size, shape, and openings. Although the size of the rear opening may be altered by movements of the velum and that of the front by constriction of the nostrils, the nasal cavity itself cannot undergo changes in shape.

The nasal cavity serves as the primary resonator for only three sounds—*m, n,* and *ng*. When these sounds are produced, air is prevented from escaping through the mouth (by either lip or tongue action as explained in Chapter 7); the velum is relaxed leaving the nasopharyngeal port open, thus allowing the air to be emitted through the nose. During the production of sounds other than *m, n,* and *ng*, the velum is raised so that it touches, or nearly touches, the rear wall of the pharynx—directing the air chiefly into the oral cavity. When the nasopharyngeal port is left slightly open, the nasal cavity supplements the resonation of high frequency overtones in the non-nasal sounds.

3. The proper use of the resonating mechanism. The major impediment to effective amplification and enrichment of voice is inappropriate muscle tension. All muscles of the throat should be relaxed except those properly engaged in the production and resonation of the sound. Inappropriate muscular contractions may impair resonance in three ways: (1) By obstructing the passageway through which the sound must travel to the outside atmosphere. Proper resonance requires that the air pipes be kept well open. A muffling and damping of the voice occurs when the tongue is unnecessarily humped backward into the throat, when and faucial pillars are contracted to reduce the opening from the pharynx into the mouth, when the constrictor muscles are excessively activated, consequently pinching the pharynx, and so on. (2) By causing the texture of the pharyngeal walls to become extremely firm and, thereby, producing a strident quality. (3) By hindering the flexibility of movement of the pharyngeal and oral cavities. To make the most of "tuned" resonance, these cavities must be capable of wide variations in size and shape. However, if the throat musculature is excessively tight, such delicate and rapid adjustments may be difficult or impossible.

Later in the chapter we shall find methods of improving several common defects in vocal quality caused by improper resonation. Also, since the speaker should employ the general pitch level which is most effectively resonated by his particular mechanism, we shall learn how to determine one's optimum pitch.

D. Pronunciation. After the sound waves have been produced at the larynx and resonated in the throat, mouth, and perhaps the nose, they must be modified by the articulators to become the various vowels and consonants of speech. When combined in proper sequence and given suitable stress, these sounds become the auditory symbols of our spoken language. Chapter 7 explains in detail how the various articulators, such as the lips, teeth, tongue, and palate, alter the breath stream so that speech sounds are produced. That chapter also contains suggestions which will help you to improve the clarity and appropriateness of your utterance.

ACQUIRING THE ATTRIBUTES OF THE EFFECTIVE VOICE

You have learned how the vocal mechanism produces the four characteristics of sound: pitch, force, time, and quality. Now let us apply this knowledge to a discussion of the attributes of the effective voice: *audibility, pleasantness, fluency,* and *flexibility.* The remainder of this chapter is given to explanations of these attributes, advice on acquiring them, and exercises to develop them.

A. The Effective Voice Is Audible. Many persons do not use sufficient projection to insure that every word will be heard without strain under the various circumstances in which they speak. To maintain easy audibility, the speaker must adjust his volume to the size of his audience, the acoustical properties of the room in which he is speaking, and to competing noises.

Students sometimes believe that the carrying power of the voice depends exclusively upon the force with which the air from the lungs strikes the vocal folds. However, projection is also dependent upon the efficiency with which the laryngeal sound is resonated and the clarity with which the articulators modify the sounds into language symbols. Follow some or all of these suggestions when you wish to improve projection: increase volume; try to speak with an "open" throat (see page 135); hold your head erect and speak directly to your listeners; reduce your general rate if it is excessively fast; shorten your thought phrases (see page 141 and Chapter 16); articulate with greater preciseness.

To improve audibility, practice on the following exercises.

To Improve Breath Control

1. Place your hands on your sides below the ribs and above the pelvis; extend your thumbs backward and fingers forward on the abdomen. As you execute a series of quick inhalations, note the feel of the frontal and lateral expansion. Keeping your hands in position, pant sharply several times. Do a series of quick coughs. Substitute numbers for the pants or coughs and count from one to four; project each number vigorously as though you were a platoon leader counting cadence.

2. Breathe deeply and utter the vowel *A* as you exhale. Hold it as long as you can maintain a steady, clear tone. Repeat, using other vowels: *AH, E, I, OO,* and *AW.* Now, see how long you can produce a smooth, steady hissing sound—*s-s-s.*

3. Inhale deeply and count as far as you can on one exhalation. The

tone should be firm even though supported by minimal air pressure. Do not waste air by permitting the voice to assume a breathy quality or by letting air escape between numbers. If you are practicing with someone, count in unison with him to see who can count farther.

4. Inhale while mentally counting to ten and exhale on the count of one. Repeat, inhaling to the mental count of nine and exhaling to the count of two. Continue this procedure, each time subtracting a number from the inhalation and adding one to the exhalation, until inhalation is done to the count of one and exhalation to the count of ten.

To Improve Projection

1. Inhale deeply and produce a sustained *AH*. Begin the sound softly. Then, slowly and steadily increase the volume until the sound is very loud. Maintain the same pitch throughout and increase the volume by steadily strengthening the muscular contractions of the abdominal muscles. Work to keep an open and relaxed throat and try not to waste air. Practice variations of this exercise: (1) Use other vowel sounds. (2) Begin softly; for a few seconds, steadily increase the volume; then gradually decrease the sound to its original intensity. (3) Begin loudly; diminish volume gradually; then build up to the original loudness.

2. Utter a simple statement, such as "Please stop what you are doing," four times—each on a different breath. The first time, say it as though you were talking confidentially to a person three or four feet away; the second time, as though you were conversing with an informal group of twenty people around a large table; the third time, as though you were speaking to an audience of fifty people scattered within a periphery of twenty or thirty feet; the fourth time, as though you were addressing an audience of several hundred people in a large auditorium. Try to keep the same pitch in each case and to maintain a relaxed throat. Take a slightly deeper breath for each successive statement and contract more vigorously your abdominal muscles.

3. Select several ten-minute excerpts from speeches, essays, or dramatic works and, over a period of weeks, practice delivering them in an auditorium, large barn, or some secluded place out-of-doors. Imagine that you are speaking to an audience of three or four hundred persons. Station a friend at some distance and ask him to raise a hand whenever your presentation becomes inaudible. As you strive for good projection, also endeavor to maintain a keen sense of communication. Be as direct and conversational as possible.

B. The Effective Voice Is Pleasant. Pleasantness is essentially a matter of personal taste. In general, we tend to prefer those vocal qualities, rates of speed, types of pronunciation, and patterns of inflection to which we have been accustomed. Thus, the nasal twang of some New Englanders may be unnoticed by many others in that region but may irritate a Southerner. Furthermore, to some extent pleasantness of voice is associated with the speaker's personality, appearance, likability, motives, and ideas. If we rate the speaker high on these counts, we may be somewhat less inclined to be critical of his vocal characteristics. Nevertheless, when asked what qualities of voice they prefer, persons typically respond with such expressions as "resonant," "well-modulated," "smooth," and "mellow." Also, most persons agree that voices like the following are unpleasant: "whiny," "nasal" "raspy," "shrill," "husky," "breathy," "tense," and "weak."

To produce pleasing vocal quality, the speech mechanism must be sufficiently relaxed. Since speech is the product of muscular activity, it consequently requires some muscle tension. However, you should strive for *selective* relaxation and tension—only those muscles needed for appropriate vocal production should be actuated. The muscular energy and coordination necessary to become a successful major league batter is considerable; yet great hitters like Ted Williams appear to be unusually relaxed and "loose." Effective speakers, singers, and actors have achieved the same delicate balance between relaxation and tension.

If an analysis of your voice quality indicates the need for improvement, consult your instructor in planning a program of regular practice. The following exercises may serve as the core of such a program. If possible, make periodic recordings of your voice to provide a check on your progress. Also, endeavor to train your ears so that you readily recognize the acoustic difference between good vocal timbre and your present quality.

To Achieve Optimum Pitch

Because of the physical structure of his larynx and resonating cavities, each speaker has one or possibly two pitch levels at which his voice sounds most pleasant and functions most effectively. A voice which uses a general pitch level either significantly above or below its optimum pitch usually sounds strained, lacks adequate flexibility of pitch, and is inadequately resonated. As a rule, abnormally high-pitched voices are the result of habit or muscular tension. Somtimes, because he admires deep voices or hopes to improve timbre, a speaker will force his voice downward to an ab-normally low pitch. Other causes for unnaturally low-pitched voices include lethargy, lassitude, and habit. The following exercises are designed to help you discover your habitual and optimum pitch and, if meaningful differ-ences exist between the two, to make the optimum pitch your customary level.

1. The term *"habitual pitch"* does not mean unchanging pitch but refers to the note you use most often in your speaking. It is the pitch at which you are most apt to start or conclude a phonation. To discover your habitual pitch read a page from this book in a natural, informal manner. Listen for the pitch level used most frequently—the one at which the largest number of inflections begin and end. When you believe that you have dis-covered it, sustain the note while attempting to locate it on the piano key-board. Record the pitch. Repeat this experiment daily for several days, noticing the piano note each time. If the note varies, an average of the pitch levels should give an approximation of your habitual pitch. Your instructor will help you if necessary.

2. You may use one or both of these methods to determine your *optimum* or *natural* pitch. (a) Sing a tone in your middle range. Find this note on the piano. Accompanied by the piano, sing *AH* down the scale as far as you can go without forcing your voice or losing clarity of tone. Now, go steadily up the scale until you reach the highest note you can produce without excessive strain. Your optimum pitch is located about one-third, or pos-sibly one-fourth, of the way up your total range, starting from your lowest pitch. By simple arithmetic locate on the piano the note which is one-third of the distance up your complete range. At this pitch sing a prolonged *AH* sound and then utter in a monopitch a simple sentence, such as "This is my right pitch." Try the vowel and the sentence one note higher—two notes higher—one note below the original—two notes below. The level at which your voice has greatest clarity and fullness of tone and at which the vowel mechanism seems most comfortable is your optimum pitch. (b) Follow the same procedure as in the first method, except that you simply count up four keys on the piano from your lowest pitch. Your optimum pitch may possibly be this note, or one note higher, or one note lower.

Probably you will wish to consult your instructor in executing this exer-cise and in making the final judgment.

3. Compare your habitual pitch level with your optimum level. If they are different, seek to adjust the habitual level to correspond with the optimum pitch. As you sound the optimum pitch key on the piano. prolong

successively the vowels *AH, E, I, OO,* and *AW*. Strike the note again and utter a simple sentence on the pitch. Repeat a number of times. Then, first striking the note, begin a sentence on the optimum pitch and continue—not with a monopitch—but with normal inflections. Repeat many times, striking the proper pitch on the piano at the beginning. To avoid monotony, you may vary the sentences. Eventually you will not need to use the piano—you will have memorized the pitch. Continue this exercise until you have incorporated the desired pitch into your speaking as your habitual level.

To Promote Effective Resonance

Open Throat Resonance:

1. Relax the tongue blade, letting it lie on the floor of the mouth with the tip behind the lower front teeth (the position for the *AH*). Relax the jaw muscles; lower the jaw; and inhale slowly and gently as if beginning to yawn. Especially if the inhaled air is cooler than the body temperature, you should be distinctly aware of the inward rush of air into the throat. Try to "memorize" the feel of the rising action of the velum and the growing opening at the rear of the mouth. Do you see this motion take place as you do this exercise before a mirror? If so, you are experiencing the open throat essential for effective reflection and sympathetic amplification of the voice. Repeat the gentle yawnlike inhalations until you are keenly sensitive to the kinesthetic sensations of the open throat.

2. After a gentle yawnlike inhalation, vocalize the vowel *AH* on the exhaled breath. Try to produce a richly resonated tone. Follow the same procedure with other vowels: *E, I, OO, AW,* and *A*.

3. On the exhalation, following a yawnlike inhalation, combine a consonant (*b, v, t, h, w,* or *z*) with a vowel (*AH, E, I, A, OO,* or *AW*) in a manner something like this: *bAH, hE, Av, tI,* or *wOO*. Try to aim the sound at the upper front gum. As you will recall from the previous discussion, one cannot place a sound anywhere except in the larynx where it is produced. However, if you think of yourself as focusing the sounds in the front part of the mouth rather than in the rear portion, you probably will utilize a more open throat, thereby improving the clarity and brilliance of the tone.

4. Select a simple prose passage. Before reading each sentence, draw in the breath by means of the gentle yawnlike inhalation. Try to direct the tones against the upper front gum and seek to avoid any tightening of the throat musculature.

Nasal Resonance:

As you know, the nasal cavity is a bony structure and, hence, cannot be altered in size or shape. However, its restricted passageway can easily become partially or completely blocked by accumulated secretions or by inflamed mucuous membranes. To provide for suitable nasal resonance, maintain the structure in as healthy a condition as possible. See exercises on pages 138–139 for correcting nasality and denasality. Also read the discussion in Chapter 7 concerning the nasal sounds and practice on the accompanying word lists.

To Correct Common Faults in Vocal Quality

As indicated previously, a person's voice is a barometer of his emotional maturity and stability. More than a simple matter of muscular contractions, your voice is a reflection of your basic emotional adjustments and your reactions toward the speaking situation. If unhealthy mental attitudes cause unsatisfactory vocal quality, emotional reorientation should precede voice training. However, if you have no physical or emotional impediments, the following guides should help you to overcome any of the common defects in vocal quality.

Correcting Breathiness:

A study by Charles F. Diehl and Eugene T. McDonald suggests that the breathy voice interferes more seriously with a speaker's ability to communicate information than does the harsh or hoarse voice. Breathiness is a defect in phonation caused by improper glottal closure. As you already know, for air pressure to build up beneath the folds prior to phonation, the folds must be closely approximated. When initiating a phonation, even a very slight delay in closing the glottis will permit the escape of unvocalized air, producing a breathy effect. Furthermore, the tonus of the folds must be sufficient to permit a genuine trachial pressure to develop before blowing the folds apart. Otherwise full vibrations cannot be attained. In the breathy voice the tone is fuzzy and somewhat like a half-whisper. Also, the speaker with breathy quality usually has difficulty projecting his voice any distance. Although irregularities on the edges of the vocal folds may cause breathiness, the most common cause is the inefficient use of the larynx.

1. Review the previous exercises for controlled breathing, projection, phonation, and resonation.

2. Cough sharply several times. Get the kinesthetic sensation of the closed glottis prior to the cough.

3. Begin a prolonged *AH* as a whisper and then gradually add vocal fold vibrations until the sound is completely free from breathiness. Repeat several times using the various vowels.

4. In the following word pairs, the *h* sounds in the first half of each column are correctly made without vocalization. Be careful, however, not to let their aspiration carry over into the production of the vowels. Before

initiating the words in the second-half of each column, bring the folds together as though you were going to cough.

hand—and	hark—ark	hill—ill	heave—Eve
hale—ale	her—err	his—is	hate—ate
harm—arm	hat—at	has—as	ham—am

Correcting Harshness:

A distressingly large number of persons limit their personal effectiveness by speaking in irritatingly strident tones. Although occasionally the result of pathologies, the harsh voice is usually caused by excessive tension throughout the vocal mechanism. The folds may be brought together so tightly and maintained under such pressure that they cannot vibrate freely—thereby impairing phonation. Excessive muscular contractions may pinch the throat and increase the firmness of the pharyngeal walls, thereby reducing the ability of the pharynx to resonate the lower overtones and accentuating the higher ones. Sometimes laryngeal tensions may become so great that friction noises are produced in the tube above the folds. Often the extrinsic muscles are hyperactivated so that the larynx is held either in an abnormally high position, producing a shrill, cutting quality, or in an unnaturally low position, producing a hard, grating quality.

1. Very frequently harshness results from a general state of hypertension which, in turn, arises from basic and continuing emotional conditions such as aggressiveness, frustration, or lack of human warmth. In such cases, the speaker should take a personality inventory and attempt to resolve his emotional conflicts.

2. Refer to the exercises previously prescribed for *relaxation, controlled breathing,* and the *open throat.* They may help to relax the musculature and alleviate harshness.

3. By consulting with your instructor and by using a mirror, attempt to determine whether your larynx is pulled unnecessarily high or low in the throat. If such proves to be the case, experiment with different pitches and vocal qualities that cause the larynx to rise and lower and attempt to memorize the feel of the larynx at the different levels. By continued practice you can learn to tell by muscle "feel" when your larynx is riding too high or too low in the throat.

4. Relax the tongue on the floor of the mouth; lower the jaw and open the mouth as though you were going to yawn; and gently inhale and exhale several times. Once you believe that the musculature is relatively relaxed, begin to read orally any simple material, prolonging the vowels and attempting to maintain an open throat. During the reading if you experience an onset of throat tension, return to the gentle inhalations and exhalations just described. When the tightness subsides, resume your reading.

Correcting Hoarseness or Huskiness:

Some evidence exists that listeners are more apt to label the hoarse voice as undesirable than they are the harsh, nasal, or breathy voice. A husky voice sounds like a harsh voice with a breathy component added to the tone. Because hoarseness is often related to infections or inflammations of the vocal folds, a physician should be consulted before voice training is attempted. When organic causation can be dismissed, hoarseness is probably caused by excessive tension, habitual pitch cast at an abnormally low key, or by emotional problems such as shyness or inferiority feelings. Practice on the exercise for *relaxation, controlled breathing, optimum pitch, open throat, breathiness,* and *harshness.*

Correcting Throatiness:

In throatiness the sounds seem to be "placed" too far back in the mouth, and the tone is muffled or swallowed and often guttural. The immediate cause of throatiness is a constriction of the resonating passage, usually taking the form of a pinching of the lower pharynx or the protruding of the rear part of the tongue into the throat. Such a stenosis may result from excessive tension, habit, imitation, a deliberate depression of the larynx to deepen the voice, or negative psychological attitudes. To help correct throatiness, review the exercises for *relaxation, optimum pitch, open throat,* and *harshness.*

Correcting Nasality:

Nasality is characterized by a stuffy, "through the nose" voice quality and is the result of cul-de-sac resonance. (A cul-de-sac resonator is one with a single opening or with an entrance larger than its exit.) As you know, for all sounds except *m, n,* and *ng,* the entrance into the oral cavity should be closed or very nearly closed. If its entrance is smaller than its exit at the nostrils, the nasal cavity will serve as an appropriate supplementary resonator of the "non-nasal" sounds. However if the velum relaxes to the extent that the passage through the nasopharyngeal port is larger than the exit through the nose, the nasal area serves as a cul-de-sac resonator and the voice becomes excessively nasal. Frequently, inadequate velar contractions are accompanied by one or more of the following: a humping of the dorsum of the tongue so that it restricts the size of the opening between the throat and the mouth; insufficient oral activity; and inadequate mouth opening. Occasionally nasality may be present even when a tight velopharyngeal closure is effected. In such cases excessive muscular tension has probably caused one or more abnormal cul-de-sac pockets to form—perhaps between the base of the tongue and the epiglottis, between the cheeks and the gum ridges, or elsewhere in the mouth or throat.

1. To alleviate the excessive muscular tensions of the tongue, faucial pillars, and throat which often attend nasality, practice on the exercises for *relaxation, controlled breathing,* and the *open throat.*

2. Using a mirror, inspect the normal relaxed position of the velum. Now yawn and note the resulting action of the velum as it moves upward and backward to block off the nasal cavity. Yawn repeatedly until you have memorized the feel of the rising velum.

3. While continuing to observe the interior of your mouth in the mirror, utter a prolonged *AH.* Your velum should rise as you begin phonation and remain elevated until you stop. Now deliberately relax the velum while saying *AH.* Do you hear the resulting nasalization? Repeat raising and lowering the velum while sustaining *AH* until you can produce at will either a pure or a nasalized *AH.*

4. As you sustain an *AH,* use your fingers to compress and release your nostrils. If your velum is raised, pinching the nares should cause no appreciable difference in quality. Practice producing the different vowels at various pitches until the pinch test indicates that nasality has disappeared.

5. Prepare for oral drill a list of paired words in which one word contains a nasal sound and its mate does not. Examples: bean—beet; fame—fate; ping—pit.

6. Prepare a series of sentences containing no nasal sounds. As you read them aloud, occasionally apply the pinch test to check the presence of nasality.

Correcting Denasality:

Denasality refers to that "all stopped up" quality caused by the inadequate nasal resonance of the *m, n,* and *ng* sounds. It occurs when the nasal passages are obstructed or closed by enlarged adenoids or a deviated septum. It may also result from a head cold or some allergic condition which causes the membranous lining of the nose to swell and become inflamed. In many cases, alleviation of denasality depends upon medical or surgical correction. Following the elimination of organic causes, however, the speaker may continue to produce denasal tones through habit or, if his velum has been accustomed to inactivity, may begin to speak with extreme nasality. In either case, the speaker should refer to the exercises given earlier for establishing good nasal resonance and for eliminating nasality.

C. The Effective Voice Is Fluent. Stemming from the Latin *fluere,* meaning "to flow," fluency refers to the smooth, easy, and ready flow of language. Unfortunately, some beginning speakers confuse fluency with glibness or volubility. Glibness connotes excessive fluency devoid of sincerity or careful thought; it frequently arises from the devious desire of the speaker to over-whelm his listeners with a constant stream of words in order to conceal, divert, or deceive. Volubility implies a great torrent of speech, often insincere and usually shallow and verbose. Of course, you remember from your reading of the first three chapters that glibness, or any other type of subterfuge, lacks the integrity of thought and purpose necessary for long-term effectiveness and that conciseness is a requisite for vivid, direct utterance.

1. To be fluent, employ a suitable general rate. All of us have experienced listening to speakers who use distracting extremes in tempo—those who race headlong through words in an incomprehensible, irritating manner, and those who dawdle so much that listening becomes tiresome and irksome. A "smooth, easy, and ready flow of language" can be produced only if you use a general rate somewhere in the wide middle ground between these undesirable extremes. As we shall see presently, the appropriateness of your speed of utterance is conditioned by factors other than fluency: your general tempo should be correlated with all the elements involved in the cycle of communication—the audience, the occasion, the message, and yourself as the speaker. In terms of the requisites for speaking gracefully and seemingly effortlessly, your overall pace might be somewhere between 100 and 185 words a minute. Because of individual differences of age, temperament, physical condition, etc., a specific rate cannot be arbitrarily prescribed as best for fluency. We expect a teen-ager to speak faster than a septuagenarian, a vibrant, physically vigorous person faster than a deliberate, slow moving one, and so on. For most public speakers, however, the rate that will enable them to speak extemporaneously most easily and most effectively is probably between 120 and 150 words a minute. In the oral reading of simple prose, the rate may be somewhat faster. Caution: during your early class performances you may be inclined to speak more rapidly than you are able to clothe your ideas with appropriate language.

2. To be fluent, make appropriate use of pauses. Fluency does not require an uninterrupted stream of words. "Conveyor belt" vocal delivery, particularly when it moves rapidly, is monotonous to the listeners and wearing upon both them and the speaker. Furthermore, delivery without pauses fails to extract maximum intellectual and emotional meaning from language and usually impairs fluency.

a. Pauses Are the Punctuation Guides to Speech. The effective speaker recognizes that words must be arranged into thought units. Since vocal phrasing is discussed in detail in Chapter 16, perhaps it is sufficient to introduce the concept here. The essential point is that by grouping together those words containing a common core of meaning and by separating that group from others, the speaker facilitates audience understanding and retention. The basic method of setting one thought phrase apart from another is by a brief period of silence, or pause. Over three-fourths of the silence occurring in speaking takes place between phrases and sentences. To discover how silence serves as the punctuation of oral speech, read the following sentence orally, pausing briefly at each slanted line: "He rose from his chair,/ put on his coat,/ turned off the TV,/ opened the front door,/ and departed." Effective vocal phrasing requires both a discriminating sense of timing and an exact knowledge of the meaning of the point being expressed and its relationship to preceding and subsequent ideas. When reading materials orally, you will discover that grammatical punctuation is a helpful, although not an infallible, guide to phrasing.

b. Pauses Aid in Attaining Emphasis. Pauses for emphasis which occur within phrases usually either precede or follow the word to be emphasized. For example, "All we have to fear is/ fear itself" uses a pause to *precede* the word to be emphasized; conversely, this sentence utilizes the pause *following* an important word to focalize maximum attention on the word and heighten its dramatic effect: "This will end in suicide/ unless we act now!"

c. Pauses Provide an Unobtrusive Means for the Speaker to Inhale. If the speaker stops for breath in the middle of a phrase, the rhythm of speech is disrupted and meaning may be obscured. However, by drawing breath during the pauses for emphasis or oral punctuation, he can replenish his air supply without disturbing the flow of language.

3. To be fluent, reduce hesitations. Unlike the pause which is deliberate and purposeful, hesitations usually occur when the speaker cannot think of the proper word or when he loses his train of thought. A pause does not disrupt fluency; a hesitation, being a mental derailment, momentarily interrupts communication.

Eliminating or reducing hesitations is largely a matter of improving symbolic formulation—in other words, cultivating the ability to think of the right word at the moment it is needed. This ability can be developed by practicing extemporaneous speaking, discussion, and conversation. Fluency does not require an enormous vocabulary, as is sometimes believed, but rather a ready supply of words which come easily to the tongue.

As previously suggested, adjustments in rate can also be helpful in reducing hesitation. An extremely fast tempo tends to magnify the duration of any interruptions which occur. Furthermore, in extempore speaking and discussion the greater the speed the more stringent the need for a rapid choice of words. The compulsion to select words in rapid sequence increases the probability of awkward breaks and helps to account for the tendency of many rapid speakers to talk in a jerky, stop-and-go manner. A moderate pace not only allows greater time for symbolic formulation, but also helps to reduce the obviousness of a hesitation.

Finally, do not put such a high premium on fluency that, instead of searching momentarily for an appropriate word, you resort to meaningless fill-ins (such as "I mean" and "and-uh"), to hackneyed, vague, or favorite words which come quickly to mind, or to redundant and ambiguous expressions. An occasional hesitation is far less undesirable than preserving fluency at any cost!

D. The Effective Voice Is Flexible. Few deficiencies are as detrimental to effective communication as vocal inflexibility. Unfortunately, this shortcoming is exceedingly common. All too prevalent are speakers who (1) rarely vary their pitch more than a tone or two upward or downward, or (2) maintain a fixed speed from the beginning of an oral message to the end, or (3) use almost the same degree of force regardless of what is being said, or (4) employ a single voice quality to express all moods, emotions, and meanings. Without variability in pitch, time, force, and quality, even a clearly produced and richly resonated voice will be monotonously dull. Flexibility helps to hold attention, clarify meaning, and to secure desired response. The use of the variable factors of voice should be governed by the meaning and mood to be conveyed. The radio or television reporter who relays each news event—whether trivial or momentous—in the same staccato, rapid-fire delivery, and the oleaginous announcer who delivers all commercials—whether for life insurance or mattresses—in the same throaty, orotund manner, may be just as guilty of inflexibility as the speaker who uses monopitch.

In the following section we shall learn how one can achieve appropriate variation in the use of *pitch, time, force,* and *quality.* Although these variables operate in conjunction with each other to produce the flexible voice, each may be studied and practiced separately.

1. Flexibility of pitch. As you know, pitch is the location of the voice on the musical scale. The process of raising or lowering the voice on this scale constitutes pitch variability. The inflexible voice tends to restrict this upward and downward movement to the extent that monopitch may be closely approached. In a study of 226 speakers, George M. Glasgow found that monopitch significantly restricts one's oral effectiveness. As he reported: "The experiment reveals that level monopitch decreases audiences' comprehension of spoken language by approximately 10 per cent in comparison with their comprehension of the same and similar materials when spoken with good intonation." [4]

The flexible voice employs an adequate range of pitch. Sometimes the beginning speaker mistakenly assumes that he is compelled by the nature of his speech mechanism to talk in a near monopitch. Of course, one's upper and lower extremities of pitch are limited by the size of his vocal folds, the structure of his larynx, and the size of his resonators. Nevertheless, a narrow range of only a few tones is basically a functional, not an anatomical, problem. With training and practice you should develop a usable reach of at least an octave. And if you become highly skilled in speaking or acting, your range may exceed two octaves.

These guides will explain how to determine your existing pitch range and, if necessary, how to expand it:

By executing the exercises on pages 133–135 "To Achieve Optimum Pitch," you will be able to determine the extent of your present range as well as your habitual and optimum pitch levels. If your habitual level is significantly below the optimum level, changes in pitch are necessarily restricted chiefly to movements above your customary level; your habitual pitch is already nearly as deep as your mechanism will permit. The reverse is true if your habitual pitch is well above your optimum level: changes will tend to be confined to notes below your unnaturally high habitual pitch.

Over a period of time repeat the following exercise frequently. As you sound a sustained *AH,* move up the scale from your lowest comfortable note to your highest. Inhale and move gradually down the scale. As you practice this drill, attempt to stretch your range both upward and downward. Substitute for *AH* other vowels, numbers, or words. Begin and end on different notes of the scale. Vary the speed at which you move up and down the scale. Do not feel compelled to inhale after every scale run.

Choose a selection which contains *strong, vigorous, out-going* emotions and which concerns some topic of considerable interest to you. Read several lines adhering rigidly to a monopitch. Read the next few lines, limiting pitch changes to three or four notes. In reading the remainder of the selection, try to let yourself go. Attempt to enter into the emotional feelings and work for the widest possible range of pitch.

[4] George M. Glasgow, "A Semantic Index of Vocal Pitch," *Speech Monographs,* March, 1952, pp. 64–68.

In animated oral communication pitch is almost always moving upward or downward. Such changes express both intellectual and emotional meanings and, even in platform speaking, should be much like the pitch variations of animated conversation. Be careful in your speaking to avoid objectionable patterns such as the "sing-song" melody, in which upward and downward movements in pitch are alternated. Also avoid indiscriminately using upward inflections to end sentences (often causing declarative sentences to sound like questions); beginning nearly every sentence with a sharply rising inflection and closing with a slowly falling glide; employing the ministerial chant, which may sound as much like song melody as speech melody and tends to interfere with the communication of meaning.

Variations in pitch occur by means of *inflections* and *steps*. The *inflection* is a gradual, continuous slide either upward or downward during a syllable or a series of syllables, or is a combination of upward and downward slides within a syllable. The step is an abrupt change in pitch occurring between phonations, that is, between syllables, words, phrases, and sentences. Both the inflection and the step are useful tools to indicate shifts in feeling or thought and to aid in achieving emphasis. *For exercises and further advice on developing flexibility of pitch, see pages 383–387.*

2. Flexibility of time or rate. Effective speech is characterized by variety in rate. (1) Regulate your speed of utterance to fit the speaking situation. As examples: If participating in a small, informal discussion group, you should employ a faster tempo than in making an announcement before an audience of several thousand persons. If exhorting the sales staff of the school literary magazine in a small conference room, you should use a more rapid rate than in delivering a Fourth of July oration in a ball park.[5] (2) Also, make appropriate adjustments in tempo to promote interest values and clarify meaning. If a specific

[5] In studying 184 male speakers, Black found that their rate was automatically and significantly affected by the size of the room. John W. Black, "The Effect of Room Characteristics upon Vocal Intensity and Rate," *The Journal of the Acoustical Society of America,* March, 1950, pp. 174–176.

section of a speech or reading is complex, if the ideas grow solemn in mood, or if certain material needs special emphasis, reduce your rate. Conversely, if ideas are light or exciting, if the material is easy to understand, or if you wish to hurry through subordinate ideas, increase the pace.

Flexibility in the use of rate depends upon your utilization of the two variable elements of time: pauses and duration of sound.

a. VARIATION IN PAUSES.   Your speaking rate depends partly upon the number and duration of pauses. When a decrease in tempo seems appropriate, you may increase the length and, in many cases, the number of pauses. Thus, if you were addressing a large formal audience, the problem of projection and the sobriety of the occasion would suggest a stretching of your pauses and a reduction in the length of your thought phrases, increasing the number of pauses. When a general increase in rate is desired, the duration of the pauses may be reduced and sometimes the length of the thought units may be increased, reducing the number of pauses. As a workable rule of thumb, the longer the duration of a pause the greater becomes its effectiveness in focalizing attention and promoting understanding. (However, do not prolong an interval of silence to the point of diminished or negative returns.) Therefore, the length of a pause should bear a direct relationship to the complexity, significance, solemnity, and length of the thought being expressed.

b. VARIATION IN DURATION OF SOUNDS.   The second means of altering rate is to vary the amount of time consumed in producing the individual sounds. When you speak rapidly you tend to shorten most of your sounds, and when you decrease the tempo, to prolong them The sounds permitting the least amount of variability in their production are the plosives, such as *p, t, b, d, g,* and *k*. Other consonants such as the continuants *r, m, n, l,* and the sibilants *z, s,* and *sh* can be lengthened or shortened at will. The most important instruments of duration or quantity of sound, however, are the vowels. Alterations in their length provide the quantitative differences essential to controlling general rate, promoting emphasis, and conveying special intellectual and emotional meanings. For instance, you should deliver more slowly the words of a phrase containing a crucial argument or presenting an involved concept, and may hurry over the words of a subordinate amplifying phrase. In the following three-phrase sentence, the middle unit should be subordinated by a decreased duration of sounds: "The wise driver,/ as you all know,/ is always careful."

See pages 387–393 for further discussion of flexibility of time and for illustrative drills.

3. Flexibility of force. Although the voice should always be clearly audible, variations in the degree of loudness and intensity should occur. Constant use of any level of force—soft, medium, or strong—tends to bore listeners. Moreover, mono-force does not indicate thought relationships nor reflect changes in the mood of the subject matter or of the speaker. An increase in loudness and intensity usually indicates that the words so stressed have greater ideational significance or intensified emotional values. You should also be aware that a lowered level of loudness, while intensity is maintained or increased, may bring about a similar effect.[6] This device, known by actors as "underplaying," may be used effectively by the skilled speaker in sharpening attention or in driving a point home. For example, "You wouldn't dare!" delivered in an intense manner with subdued volume may carry greater meaning than if delivered in a loud voice.

In working for greater flexibility of loudness and intensity, you should understand and try to make appropriate application of the three basic types of vocal force: the *explosive,* the *effusive,* and the *expulsive.* Before the three forms are discussed, it should be made clear that they do not constitute rigid categories. Instead, the *explosive* and the *effusive* represent opposing extremes, and the *expulsive* represents the more frequently em-

[6] This intensity-loudness dicotomy is serviceable, though technically inexact. As used here, intensity depends more upon wave composition and loudness more upon wave amplitude.

ployed mean. (1) *Explosive* force, as the name implies, refers to a powerful general level of intensity and usually of loudness, and to the employment of abrupt, sometimes violent, explosions of intensity and loudness. Explosive force is appropriate when the speaker feels violent emotions concerning his message, or when he senses the need to awaken or startle a lethargic audience. It is inappropriate for the majority of dignified and polite occasions, and always should be used sparingly and judiciously. Careless or excessive use of explosive force reduces its potency and may irritate the listeners. (2) *Effusive* force is smooth, regular, and sustained. It may be either powerful or soft as the situation requires, but rarely changes abruptly either from loud to quiet or from quiet to loud. Instead, alterations in force are made gradually. Effusive force expresses calmness, serenity, assuredness, and repressed emotions such as sadness, depression, and gloom. It is used appropriately in the oral interpretation of certain types of prose and poetry and in public speaking to express certain emotions and moods. (3) Unlike effusive force, *expulsive* force is characterized by numerous changes in the degree of intensity and loudness; unlike explosive force, *expulsive* force is characterized by relatively moderate rather than extreme, staccato-like explosions of intensity and loudness. *Expulsive* force is used in lively conversation and is appropriate for the majority of public speaking and group discussion situations. Because we are so accustomed to hearing expulsive force, we may be unaware of the almost constant changes in the degree of force which characterize it.

For further analysis of flexibility in the use of force and for exercises, see pages 393–396.

4. Flexibility of quality.   Should pleasant quality ever be altered? Although richness of timbre is one of the vocal attributes, the shifts in the speaker's moods should be reflected by appropriate changes in vocal quality. Examples: in using dialogue, your timbre should change somewhat to indicate the different characters; in delivering light, humorous passages, your vocal quality should be correspondingly bright and "sunny"; in castigating an opponent or an institution, your tone should take on a cutting edge; in evoking divine guidance, your timbre should reflect the solemnity and sacredness of the supplication. Such modifications are not artificial, but will occur naturally and unpremeditatedly—if you possess a flexible voice and are emotionally identified with the language you are expressing. As you know, changes in quality are produced by interrelated adjustments of your speech mechanism, such as alterations in breathing, changes in the tension of the vocal folds, and modification in the size, shape, and surface tension of the resonators. The best way to increase flexibility of quality is to experiment while speaking and reading aloud. Try to create those qualities of voice which point up the meanings and emotions you wish to communicate. *Also, read the further discussion on pages 396–399 concerning flexibility of quality and practice on the accompanying exercises.*

SUMMARY

The voice is one of your most important attributes. Its nature is determined by the physical structure of the organs used for speech, your present and past environment, your basic personal adjustment, and your emotional reactions to the specific act of communication. To achieve maximum benefits from your voice training, you should learn what sound is and how it is produced by the voice; understand the attributes of the effective voice; make an objective and accurate analysis of your voice; and initiate a program of planned and directed practice.

All sounds are produced in essentially the same manner: a source of energy causes some object to vibrate, producing sound waves. Often such sounds are reinforced by some type of resonance. Also, all sounds have certain perceptual properties, namely pitch, time, force, and quality.

Speech is an overlaid function which is produced by four closely related processes: respiration, phonation, resonation, and pronunciation. When these activities operate appropriately, the resulting voice is audible, pleasant, fluent, and flexible. The voice is audible when it is easily heard; it is pleasant when the tone is agreeable to the listeners; it is fluent when it flows smoothly, easily, and readily; and it is flexible when it possesses suitable variations in pitch, time, force, and quality.

7 ❦❦ *Pronunciation*

Distinct and appropriate pronunciation is an essential character-istic of the cultured and educated person. In addition, it is extremely important to the smooth functioning of our highly integrated society. If a spoken message is slurred or mumbled, or if it is characterized by incorrect pronunciation, the cycle of communication may be disrupted; misinterpretations and costly mistakes may result.

LEARNING HOW THE SOUNDS OF SPEECH ARE MADE

As was stated in Chapters 1 and 6, the production of an audible, pleasant, expressive voice is achieved by three basic processes. (1) Respiration: the motive power for speech is provided by the expiration of air from the lungs. (2) Phonation: the air passes upward from the trachea through the larynx setting the vocal folds into vibration. (3) Resonation: the resonating cavities (the pharynx, mouth, and nose) serve to improve selectively the quality and strength of the tone as the vibrating air continues upward and is emitted through the mouth or nose. To achieve speech, a fourth process is required: pronunciation, or the moulding and shaping of sounds of language, as distinguished from random sounds. Pronunciation is concerned with both *intelligibility* and *acceptability*. Sounds must be formed clearly and distinctly; and they must be given values, sequences, and stresses which listeners will accept as meeting conventional standards of correctness.

A helpful step in improving pronunciation is to learn how

speech sounds are made. This necessitates an introduction to the organs of pronunciation and to the International Phonetic Alphabet (IPA).

A. Inspecting the Organs of Pronunciation. To produce language sounds, the speech mechanism modifies the breath stream after it leaves the trachea and before it passes out the mouth opening or the nose. Some sounds are given the feature of voicing, accompanied by modification through the alteration of the size and shape of the resonating cavities; some sounds, both voiced and voiceless, require an interruption or constriction of the breath. The most important organs involved in the manipulation of the breath stream are the lips, teeth, alveolar ridge,[1] hard palate, soft palate (velum), tongue, lower jaw, vocal folds, and the resonating cavities of the throat, mouth, and nose. (See figures on pages 120 and 121.)

In helping to form sounds, the *lips* may be rounded, protruded, stretched, tensed, relaxed, brought together, or separated. Also, the lower lip may be raised against the upper teeth. The *lips, teeth, alveolar ridge, hard palate, soft palate,* and *tongue* may function as valves (such valvular action involves the use of two or more organs in combination, as: both lips, lower lip and upper teeth, tip of tongue and alveolar ridge, blade of tongue and hard palate, and rear of tongue and soft palate) to stop, restrict, or divert the breath stream. Unlike the *hard palate,* which is a bony structure covered by mucous membrane, the *soft palate* is composed of muscular tissue and has a capacity for limited movement. For all sounds except the three nasal consonants [m], [n], and [ng], the soft palate should be pulled upward and backward, blocking off the nasal cavity; the breath should be forced out the mouth with little or none of it escaping through the nose. For the nasal sounds, the breath should be permitted to pass through the nasal cavities and out at the nose.

The *tongue* is the most important single organ of pronuncia-

---

[1] For our purposes, the alveolar ridge may be considered that part of the gum ridge which is just above and behind the upper front teeth.

tion. Muscular contractions enable the tongue to alter the longitude and latitude of the passageway through the mouth cavity. The *lower jaw* may be raised or lowered, thus aiding the tongue to assume its various positions and helping the lips to form the variety of mouth openings.

In producing the vowels, diphthongs, and the voiced consonants, the *vocal folds* are set in vibration by the breath stream. For the nine voiceless consonants,[2] the folds do not vibrate, and the resultant sound is composed exclusively of the noise of friction. In order to understand phonation better, try two experiments. First, place the fingers lightly on the Adam's apple. Pronounce the voiceless (s) and then the voiced (z), being careful to pronounce the sounds and not the letter names. Your fingers should feel vibrations during the production of (z). The difference between the (s) and the (z) should be even more striking in the second experiment. Stop up your ears and make the (s) and then the (z) sound. If the difference is not obvious, you are probably making the letter names instead of the sounds.

B. Understanding the International Phonetic Alphabet. As you have known since childhood, our alphabet comprises twenty-six spelling symbols. Possibly you do not know, however, that instead of twenty-six sounds, Americans use approximately forty-four. To represent these forty-four sounds we employ about two hundred and fifty common spellings. One spelling letter may represent as many as eight different sounds; conversely, one sound may be spelled in perhaps fifteen different ways. As an example of the phonetic unreliability of our spelling, the vowel sound in "he" is represented by the following letters: *eat, me, key, creek, field, police, either, people, quay, Caesar,* and *amoeba.* The spelling symbol "e" is pronounced differently, or not at all, in these words: be, pretty, end, bear (as pronounced by nearly all Southerners and some Easterners), sergeant, Georgia, rheumatism, were, river, sew, they, height, move, garden, bones, and drowned. Consider the wide variance

[2] Consult the chart on page 161 and the description of the individual sounds as presented later in this chapter.

between pronunciation and spelling in words like *knight* and *colonel*. Perhaps the most widely quoted example of the spelling absurdities of English is George Bernard Shaw's spelling of "fish": G-H-O-T-I. Pronounce the "GH" as in "enough," the "O" as in "women," the "TI" as in "nation," and you have F-I-S-H.

Because conventional spellings do not closely represent speech sounds, some system of phonetic aids is necessary for the student who wishes to improve his pronunciation. The most accurate and least confusing system is the International Phonetic Alphabet which is based upon the principle of one symbol per sound and one sound per symbol.[3] Improvement in pronunciation is possible only after an individual develops the ability to hear and to analyze his own deficiencies. In these endeavors, a knowledge of the IPA is extremely helpful.

C. **Making the Vowels.** A vowel is a voiced speech sound which is nearly free from audible friction noises. In producing a vowel, the velum blocks off the nasal passages and the breath stream passes out of the mouth, encountering relatively little obstruction. Variations in the position of the tongue constitute the most important factor in the production of the different vowels. Figures 6 and 7 indicate the approximate position of the highest part of the tongue in the formation of the various vowels: in the *front vowels* the highest point of the tongue arch is in the front of the mouth; in *central vowels* the arch is in the center of the mouth; in *back vowels* the tongue is elevated in the rear of the mouth.

1. Front vowels. In going down the list of front vowels from the highest (i) to the lowest (a), the high point of the tongue arch moves progressively downward and backward away from the alveolar ridge. This movement is accompanied by a

---

[3] More accurately, the IPA provides, in rough approximation, for one symbol per *phoneme*. A given sound, such as (g), is produced somewhat differently by each individual speaker. And in one's own speech the acoustic nature of a sound is influenced to some extent by the production of adjacent sounds. However, as long as the variations are relatively slight, the listener identifies them as belonging to the appropriate phonemes. See Claude M. Wise, *Applied Phonetics* (Englewood Cliffs, N. J.: Prentice-Hall, Inc., 1957) pp. 74–78.

progressive enlargement of the mouth opening and a lowering of the jaw. For each front vowel, the tongue tip remains behind the lower front teeth.

The vowel (i) [key word—"b*e*"] is produced with the high point of the tongue arched toward the alveolar ridge. The sides

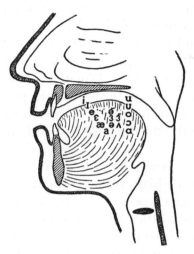

Fig. 6. Representative Tongue Positions for Vowels of American Speech. This placement of the vowels is intended to be indicative, not prescriptive. Authorities differ on the proper characteristics of the vowel diagram. Also, individuals vary considerably in tongue placement for the several vowels. Figures 6, 7, and 8 utilize the standard vowel trapezium suggested by Daniel Jones. See his *Pronunciation of English* (London: Cambridge University, 1950), 3rd edition, pp. 18–21. Also, see Gordon E. Peterson, "The Phonetic Value of Vowels," *Language*, No. 4, 1951, pp. 541–553; Martin Joos, "Acoustic Phonetics," Language Monograph No. 23, *Supplement to Language*, April-June, 1948, pp. 49–59.

of the tongue lie against the inner surfaces of the upper teeth. The mouth opening is unrounded. The lips and tongue are tense.

In forming the vowel (ɪ) [key word—"b*i*t"], the forward arch of the tongue is slightly lower and farther back in the mouth than for (i), resulting in a vertically larger passage for the breath stream. The jaw descends slightly; the mouth opening is a little larger and somewhat less slit-like; the lips and tongue are more relaxed. In comparison with (i), the (ɪ) is usually a shorter sound.

For the vowel (e) [key word—"ch*a*otic"], the tongue arch is still high in the front of the mouth but is slightly lower than for (ɪ). The entire tongue remains somewhat retracted, with its sides resting against the inner surface of the upper teeth. The mouth opening is unrounded and perhaps a little larger than for (ɪ); the lips and tongue are somewhat more tense; and there is a lowering in the elevation of the jaw. The pure (e) is used only in unstressed syllables. When it occurs in syllables of primary or secondary stress, the (e) loses its pure vowel form and develops a glide from (e) to (ɪ). Although the latter sound is touched very lightly, the discernible diphthong (eɪ) results. (See page 159.)

To produce the vowel (ɛ) [key word—"l*e*t"], the tongue is humped in a middle-high, front position, forming a horizontal and vertical passageway somewhat larger than for (e). Also, the mouth opening is a little larger and less narrow. The sides of the tongue maintain contact with the upper molars. The lips and tongue are less tense than for (e).

In making the vowel (æ) [key word—"*a*t"], the highest point of the tongue is in a low-front position. The tongue blade lies low in the mouth and has no contact with the upper teeth. The vertical and horizontal passageway for the breath stream is greater than for the middle and high front vowels. The tongue is relaxed and the lips only slightly tense. The mouth is well open, but the lips are unrounded. The elevation of the jaw is considerably lower than for (ɛ).

Most Americans use the vowel (a) only in combination with (ɪ) to form the diphthong (aɪ). (See pages 159–160.) However, some persons in eastern New England and in eastern Virginia substitute (a) for (æ) in words like "dance," "ask," and "path," and (a) for (ɑ) in such words as "Harvard," "bar," and "father." The (a) is made with the tongue low in the mouth and very slightly arched between the middle and the tip. The passage for the breath stream is much greater both vertically and horizontally than for the mid-front and high-front vowels. Also, the mouth is opened wider. The lips and tongue are relaxed, and the lips are not rounded.

2. *Central vowels.* For the five central vowels, the arch of the tongue is in the central part of the mouth cavity. The mouth opening is relatively small. The lips are unrounded.

In forming the vowel (ʌ) [key word—"t*on*"], the tongue position is probably lower than for any other central vowel; its greatest elevation is slightly back of the center. The lips and tongue are fairly relaxed. Although it is a short sound, the (ʌ) *never appears in unstressed or unaccented syllables.*

The vowel (ə) [key word—"*a*bove"] serves as an unaccented substitute for almost all of the other vowels. *It appears only in unstressed or unaccented positions.* To produce the (ə), the tongue is more relaxed than for (ʌ), with the arch slightly higher and a little farther forward. The duration of sound is noticeably shorter.

Except for some New Yorkers and New Englanders and most Southerners,[4] Americans use the (ɚ) [key word—"fath*er*"] to represent the pronunciation of *unstressed* syllables ending in "r." In forming the (ɚ), two different positions may be utilized: the tongue blade may be arched in the central part of the mouth; or, the tongue tip may be elevated and curled slightly backward (retroflected) toward the roof of the mouth. The lips and tongue are relatively relaxed.

When the spelling combinations "er," "ear," "ir," "or," "our," "ur," and "yr" occur in stressed syllables, most Americans use the vowel (ɝ) [key word—"b*ir*d"]. However, many New Englanders and Southerners, and some persons living in New York City use the vowel (ɜ). Although the (ɝ) is a stronger and much longer sound than the (ɚ), it is produced in much the same manner: the tongue blade may be arched in the central part of the mouth, or the tongue tip may be elevated and turned slightly backward toward the center of the hard palate. In making the (ɜ), the lips are unrounded, or partially rounded, and may be

---

[4] Such speakers would use (ə) instead of the (ɚ).

somewhat more tense than for the (ɝ). A retroflection of the tongue tip toward the palate is not used; instead, the tip lies behind the lower front teeth and the blade is elevated in the central part of the mouth cavity.

3. Back vowels. In going down the list of the five back vowels from (u) to (ɑ), the high point of the tongue arch moves progressively downward toward the floor of the mouth, the mouth opening becomes larger and less rounded, and the jaw is gradually lowered. For each back vowel, the tongue tip remains in a low position behind the lower front teeth.

The vowel (u) [key word—"b*oo*m"] is produced with the back of the tongue humped in a high position, nearly in contact with the velum. The mouth opening is smaller than for any other back vowel. The lips are rounded and protruded. The lips and tongue are tense. The vertical passage for the breath stream is narrow, but the horizontal passage is wide.

In forming the vowel (ʊ) [key word—"b*oo*k"], the tongue is elevated somewhat less high in the back of the mouth than for (u), thereby forming a greater vertical passageway. Likewise, the mouth is opened a little wider, the lips are somewhat less rounded, and the lips and tongue are more relaxed.

To make the vowel (o) [key word—"*o*bey"], the tongue is arched a little lower in the rear of the mouth than for (ʊ), and the mouth opening is probably a little larger. The lips are rounded and the lips and tongue are tense. Like the front vowel (e), the (o) is used only in unstressed syllables. When the (o) occurs in syllables of primary or secondary stress, it develops a glide form. After the (o) is produced, the tongue glides upward to the position for (ʊ), and the diphthong (oʊ) results. (See page 160.)

In making the vowel (ɔ) [key word—"*o*r"], the tongue is low and is arched slightly in the back of the mouth. The lips are less rounded than for (o). The mouth is well open, and the lips and tongue are relatively tense.

For the vowel (ɑ) [key word—"c*a*lm"], the lowest of the back vowels, the tongue lies on the floor of the mouth with a slight

elevation in the mid-back portion. Horizontally the oral passageway is wide, and vertically it is greater than for any other
back vowel. Lips and tongue are relaxed. Although the mouth
is well open, the lips are not rounded.

D. Making the Diphthongs. The term "diphthong" refers
to the continuous sound which is produced by a rapid blending
of two vowel sounds within the same syllable. In comparison
with the second vowel, the first vowel of a diphthong invariably
is longer in duration and more strongly stressed. Also, the

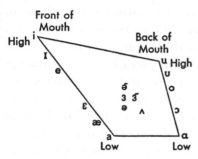

Fig. 7. Vowel Diagram.

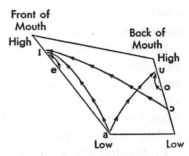

Fig. 8. Diphthong Diagram. This
chart illustrates the shift in the
position of the tongue arch in
making the standard diphthongs:
(eɪ), (oʊ), (aɪ), and (ɔɪ).

mouth opening is larger and the position of the tongue lower
for the first vowel. In addition to the diphthongs (eɪ) and (oʊ),
which we introduced earlier in connection with their pure vowel
forms (e) and (o), American English includes these standard
diphthongs: (aɪ) as in "p*ie*," (aʊ) as in "*ou*ch," and (ɔɪ) as in
"b*oy*."

To make the initial vowel of the diphthong (eɪ), the tongue
is arched relatively high in the front of the mouth. Then, without any interruption in phonation, the arch moves slightly upward and forward, producing the (ɪ).

To form the diphthong (aɪ), the tongue initially lies low
in the mouth with a slight arch near the front, thereby pro-

ducing the (a). The tongue arch then shifts rapidly upward until it assumes a high-front position for the (ɪ). An acceptable and very common practice is to substitute the low back vowel (ɑ) for the (a), thus producing the similar-sounding diphthong (ɑɪ).

The diphthong (aʊ) starts with the uttering of the vowel (a). The tongue arch then glides smoothly and rapidly to its position high in the back of the mouth for (ʊ). So many persons pronounce the first element of the diphthong as (ɑ) that it must be considered an acceptable variant.

To pronounce the diphthong (oʊ), the tongue is humped relatively high in the rear of the mouth, forming the (o); then, the tongue arch moves slightly upward into position for the (ʊ).

In making the first vowel of the diphthong (ɔɪ), the blade of the tongue lies nearly flat with a slight elevation in the rear of the mouth; the lips and tongue are tense; and the lips are somewhat rounded. After the (ɔ) is uttered, the tongue arch slides rapidly to its high front position for the (ɪ); the lips become slit-like; and the lips and tongue lose much of their tension.

E. Making the Consonants. As we learned earlier, in the uttering of a vowel sound the vocalized breath stream encounters slight obstruction as it passes through the oral cavity and out the mouth; the resultant sound is sonorous and relatively free from friction noises. In contrast, to produce most of the consonants the breath stream is hindered, diverted, or interrupted; sonority varies from the unphonated, hissing noise for (s) or (f) to the rich, vowel-like quality for the nasals and the (l).[5]

1. Plosive consonants. "Stop-compression-plosive" is a more comprehensive term than "plosive." To produce a plosive, the

---

[5] The differentiation between vowels and consonants on the basis of sonority provides a simple, serviceable formula. However, because some consonants possess as much (or even greater) sonority as some vowels, this distinction is not completely accurate. The careful student may appreciate the following definitions, which, although complicated, offer an accurate method of separating vowels and consonants. A vowel or diphthong is a sound capable of being the nucleus of a syllable, cf., "let," "lode." [When (r, l, m, n, ŋ) become nuclei of syllables, they take the forms (ɝ, ɚ, m̩, n̩, ŋ̍), and in these forms are vowels, cf., "murder (mɝdɚ), "stop 'em" (stɑp m̩), "button" (bʌtn̩), "thinkin' of it" (θɪŋkṇ ɑv ət).] A consonant is a sound capable only of accompanying the nucleus of a syllable. See Wise, *op. cit.*, pp. 73–74.

CHART OF CONSONANT SOUNDS

	BILABIAL		LABIO-DENTAL		DENTAL AND POST DENTAL		VELAR		GLOTTAL
	Voiceless	*Voiced*	*Voiceless*	*Voiced*	*Voiceless*	*Voiced*	*Voiceless*	*Voiced*	
Plosives	p	b			t	d	k	g	
Nasals		m				n		ŋ	
Fricatives			f	v	s ʃ θ	z ʒ ð			h
Affricates					tʃ	dʒ			
Glides	ʍ	w				rᵃ j			
Lateral						l			

ᵃ Other classifications which have been used for (r) include retroflected continuant, rolled consonant, semivowel, fricative, and non-fricative.

breath stream is completely stopped by closing off the naso-pharynx with the velum and by blocking egress through the mouth; air pressure is built up; suddenly the breath is released, the compressed air escaping through the mouth opening (some speakers permit part of the air to pass through the nose). When such a consonant occurs before a pause in connected discourse, the explosive phase may be modified or even omitted.

For the voiceless (p) [key word—"*p*at"] and its voiced counter-part (b) [key word—"*b*at"], the lips are closed lightly but firmly. The breath stream is forced up from the lungs into the mouth, increasing the pressure. Abruptly the lips are parted, and a small amount of air is exploded in a puff. Typically the (p) has more plosive force than the (b).

In making the voiceless (t) [key word—"*t*op"] and its voiced analogue (d) [key word—"*d*og"], the escape of the breath is pre-vented by placing the tip of the tongue against the alveolar ridge and the edges of the tongue against the inner surfaces of the upper teeth. When the tongue tip is depressed, a puff of air escapes through the mouth opening.

For the voiceless (k) [key word—"*c*ap"] and its voiced counter-part (g) [key word—"*g*ate"], the contact of the back of the tongue against the velum provides the necessary articulatory dam. The tongue tip lies behind the lower front teeth. When the rear of tongue is suddenly lowered, the impounded breath is exploded.

2. Nasal consonants. The identifying characteristic of the three nasal sounds (m) [key word—"*m*op"], (n) [key word—"*n*ot"], and (ŋ) [key word—"ba*n*k"] is the expulsion of the vocal-ized breath stream through the nose instead of through the mouth. As we found earlier, for all the sounds of English except the nasal consonants the velum is raised, thereby preventing the breath stream from entering the nasopharynx.

The (m) is produced by closing the lips and permitting the vocalized breath to pass up from the throat and out the nose. The tongue, which plays no part in the formation of this sound, may lie relaxed on the floor of the mouth. Or, if the (m) is immediately followed by a vowel, the tongue may assume the position for that vowel.

In making the (n), the position of the tongue is identical with that for (d); that is, the tongue tip is placed against the alveolar ridge and the edges of the tongue maintain contact with the inner edges of the upper teeth. The vocalized breath stream is resonated as it passes by the restricted oral cavity and then is emitted through the nasal passages. Usually the lips are separated.

As in the production of the plosive (g), to form the (ŋ) the back of the tongue is elevated against the soft palate, completely blocking the breath stream. However, for the (ŋ) the velum is in a lowered position; the vocalized breath stream is emitted smoothly through the nasal passages, instead of being abruptly released through the mouth as for the (g). Typically the tongue tip lies on the floor of the mouth behind the lower front teeth. The teeth rows are usually somewhat separated, as are the lips.

3. Fricative consonants. The nine fricatives are produced by forcing the air in a continuous stream through a restricted passageway. The resultant noise of friction gives this group of consonants its name.

To form the voicless (f) [key word—"*f*at"] and its voiced mate (v) [key word—"*v*ain"], the lower lip is placed lightly against the upper front teeth, and the breath stream is forced through the extremely restricted opening between the upper teeth and the lower lip.

For the voiceless (s) [key word—"*s*eat"] and its voiced counterpart (z) [key word—"*z*ero"], the upper and lower front teeth are brought almost into contact, making a very narrow opening. The edges of the tongue are pressed against the upper side teeth and gum ridge; the blade of the tongue is grooved down the mid line; the lowered tongue tip may be pointed toward either the upper or lower front teeth, or it may be placed against the insides of the lower front teeth. The breath stream is forced through the restricted oral passageway between the rows of teeth. Both of these sounds are very frequently misarticulated by both children and adults.

In making the voiceless (θ) [key word—"*th*ink"] and its voiced correlative (ð) [key word—"*th*em"], the sides of the tongue are pressed against the upper molars, and the tongue tip rests lightly against the lower edges of the upper front teeth. The breath stream is forced through the narrow space between the tongue tip and the edges of the upper teeth. The lips are parted and unrounded.

For the voiceless (ʃ) [key word—"*sh*oe"] and its voiced counterpart (ʒ) [key word—"lei*s*ure"], the sides of the tongue are pressed against the inner surfaces of the upper teeth. The body of the tongue is flattened and is raised toward the hard palate and the alveolar ridge. Although the position for the tongue tip is variable, usually it is lower than for the (s) and (z) and forms a wider groove. The lips are slightly rounded and somewhat protruded. The breath is forced through the oral passageway and out the mouth.

In producing the (h) [key word—"*h*ot"], the only glottal sound in the English language, the vocal folds are brought almost together, and the breath stream is forced between the folds producing a light but audible noise of friction. The folds, however, do not vibrate, but remain motionless as the air passes between them.

4. Affricates. An affricate is a consonant combination composed of a plosive followed immediately by a fricative. The articulatory mechanism combines the movements for the plosive and the fricative so rapidly that the two sounds are heard as a single unit. The voiceless (tʃ) [key word—"*ch*air"] and its voiced counterpart (dʒ) [key word—"*j*ump"] are the most common affricates in English. The (tʃ) is made by taking the position for (t), building up pressure, and then exploding the air through the opening characteristic of (ʃ). The (dʒ) is produced in similar fashion, with the articulators initially forming the dam for the (d) and the following explosion assuming the characteristics of (ʒ). The (tʃ) and the (dʒ) may be regarded as single phonemes.

5. *Glide consonants.* As we found earlier, the lips and tongue remain in a relatively fixed position for the uttering of fricatives; for plosives and affricates, the mechanism moves with a sudden "jerk" during the emission of the sounds. In contrast, the four glides are produced by a smooth but marked and rapid movement of the articulators during the production of the sound.

To make the (r) [key word—"*r*ed"], the sides of the tongue are in contact with the inner surfaces of the upper teeth. The tongue tip may be pointed toward the palate, or the middle of the tongue may be raised toward the roof of the mouth. The vocalized breath stream is forced through the small aperture between the tongue and the palate. The mouth opening is narrow, and the lips are slightly protruded. During the production of the sound the tongue gradually moves into position for the following vowel.

In making the (j) [key word—"*y*es"], the tongue is placed in a position similar to that for the vowel (i). The tongue then glides into place for the following vowel. Frequently the consonant (j) appears in combination with the vowel (u). Examples: "*b*eauty," "*E*urope," "*f*ew," "*v*iew," "*u*se," "*y*ule," "*y*ew," "*y*outh."

To form the voiceless (ʍ) [key word—"*wh*en"] and its voiced correlative (w) [key word—"*w*in"], the back of the tongue is raised toward the soft palate, similar to the position for (u). The lips are well-rounded, forming a small mouth opening. From this initial position, as the breath stream continues to be forced over the tongue and through the mouth, the tongue and lips glide into position for the following vowel.

6. *Lateral consonant.* The only lateral sound in English is the (l) [key word—"*l*ate"]. In making the two variations of this consonant, the tip of the tongue is pressed lightly against the alveolar ridge; the vocalized breath stream passes laterally over both sides of the tongue and out the mouth. In Southern and Eastern speech, when the (l) occurs before a front vowel, the tongue *blade* assumes the position for the vowel (i) and a "clear"

(l) results. When the (l) occurs in the General American dialect area, and with the exception of its position before a front vowel, when it occurs in Eastern and Southern, the back of the tongue usually is humped toward the soft palate as for the vowel (u) or (o) and a "dark" (l) is produced.

IMPROVING THE CLARITY OR DISTINCTNESS OF PRONUNICIATION

Intelligibility of utterance depends upon the distinct production of the individual speech sounds. Many words depend upon a single sound for identification. If that sound is improperly produced, is muffled, or is slurred, comprehension will be delayed and misunderstanding may result.

In beginning a program for improving the clarity of pronunciation, the first step is to determine whether you typically misform, omit, or substitute particular sounds. Read aloud to your instructor the following test passage, which contains all of the vowels and consonants, and many of the consonantal combinations.

You have asked about my three boys. They work afternoons in an oil station. Each knows the modern language well; but each often displays cloaked resentment against studying an ancient language. Like most people, each brother prefers that which is familiar and dislikes that which is strange and unusual. Yet, when we reflect philosophically, they typically have a pronounced feeling of respect for those neglected items of their education. They know that in later life nearly everyone has wished he had taken such courses. Sometimes one of my sons asks me for books of Shakespeare's tragedies. He, himself, thinks much pleasure can be gained by reading and has often urged others to read more. For a long time, another boy has been a great admirer of the Black Mountains region and has read widely on that subject. Each winter vacation, except once or twice when circumstances prevented, he has visited the mountains. He speaks of his long walks over the icy ground beside swiftly flowing mountain streams and slowly moving valley brooks. Our third son wants to be a physician like his old father. All are grand chaps who always answer life's demands with zestful spirits.

If the reading of the test passage reveals minor faults of

formation or substitution which are due to bad habits,[6] the following suggestions may serve as helpful general guides to correction: (1) By reading the test passage to your instructor, determine all sounds causing you difficulty. (2) Learn to recognize the difference between the defective sound and the correct one. Ear training is extremely important: unless you can hear the difference between the correct and the incorrect versions, you cannot remedy the difficulty. Inability to discern differences may indicate a hearing loss. If you or your instructor suspect such a loss, arrange immediately with an otologist or with the university's speech and hearing clinic for an audiometric test. (3) Learn how to make the sound correctly in isolation. Drill until you are able to produce the sound easily, without flaw. (4) Develop the ability to incorporate the sound into simple one- and two-syllable words. (5) The final, and perhaps most difficult, step is to integrate the sound into your normal flow of language. Continued practice will build appropriate new habits.

Although most students probably do not have specific "defects" of articulation, almost everyone needs to improve the general distinctness of pronunciation. Carelessness, "tongue laziness," and excessive speed are the most common obstacles to clarity. In mumbled or muffled speech, the individual sounds are "cloudy"; utterance seems "mushy" and "hidden in the throat." In slurred speech, the sounds are telescoped so that some are indistinctly formed and others are omitted. Almost inevitably, impaired comprehension results from slurring such as "djaseeagameasite?" for "Did you see the game last night?" To produce sounds distinctly, the organs of articulation must move accurately, swiftly, and with precision.

To improve the general distinctness of pronunciation, follow these guides: (1) If possible, make periodic recordings and check your progress with your instructor. (2) If your general rate is excessively rapid, make a conscious and persistent attempt to

---

[6] Serious speech problems such as dysphasia, cleft-palate speech, or the inability to form certain sounds, are beyond the scope of this text; they require remedial training under the direction of a speech therapist.

slow down. Occasionally ask friends if your conversational speaking rate is sufficiently moderate for clear pronunciation. Each evening read orally for several minutes; read both very slowly and at a moderate rate, endeavoring to enunciate all words distinctly. (3) If you have fallen into habits of careless articulation, convince yourself that such speech is a serious social, psychological, and economic handicap. Then attempt to sensitize yourself to the differences between crisp, distinct pronunciation and slovenly, blurred pronunciation. Energize yourself so that you will attempt at all times to speak clearly. Read aloud daily. Sometimes, for drill purposes, exaggerate the enunciation of individual sounds. Of course, be certain that this exaggeration does not carry over into normal speaking situations. Also, practice on word lists containing difficult sound combinations. (4) If you are handicapped by sluggish articulators, attempt to activate the entire speech mechanism. To improve control over the lips, tongue, lower jaw, and velum, drill repeatedly on exercises such as the following.

EXERCISES TO IMPROVE MUSCULAR CONTROL OF THE ORGANS OF ARTICULATION

1. Protrude the lips and round them tightly. Pull the lips back and to the side until they are stretched thin and tight. Repeat several times slowly, then increase speed until the movements are rapid.

2. Stretch upward the right side of the upper lip; return the lip to its normal position. Do the same for the left side of the upper lip. Stretch downward the right side of the lower lip; relax the lip. Do the same for the left side of the lower lip. Repeat, varying the speed and the order of movements.

3. Extend the tongue and slide the tip around the outside of the mouth, making the complete circle. Repeat a number of times, varying the speed and the direction of the rotation, that is, clockwise, counterclockwise, etc.

4. Push the tongue strongly against the alveolar ridge. Then curl the tip backward and press it strongly against the palate. Relax and repeat several times.

5. Move the lower jaw in a clockwise circular movement. After several circuits, rotate the jaw in the opposite direction.

6. Yawn repeatedly; whistle; blow up balloons; blow vigorously out the

mouth. All such activities require that the velum be pulled back against the pharyngeal wall.

DIFFICULT SOUND COMBINATIONS

If your reading of the test passage on page 166 indicates that you have difficulty in articulating any of the consonant clusters, drill on appropriate word lists which you can easily find in standard references such as Johnnye Akin, *And So We Speak: Voice and Articulation;* Jon Eisenson, *The Improvement of Voice and Diction;* Charles K. Thomas, *Handbook of Speech Improvement.* Nearly everyone can improve the clarity with which he articulates difficult combinations like the (d) of (nd) and (ld); the (t) of (ft), (st), and (pt); the whole clusters (sk), (sks), (skt) [from "sked"], (sp), (sps), (spt) [from "sped"], and (sts). Practice on these sample words:

la*nd,* sa*nd,* behi*nd,* ba*nd,* maintai*ned,* dema*nd,* arou*nd,* u*nd*er, ope*ned,* buil*d,* tol*d,* fiel*d,* worl*d,* hudd*led,* mai*led,* sca*ld,* ti*lled,* a*ft*er, si*ft,* the*ft,* gi*ft,* fi*ft*een, li*ft,* lau*ghed,* la*st, st*age, again*st,* mi*st*ake, pa*ssed,* toa*st,* we*pt,* sle*pt,* ste*pped,* o*pt*ical, cre*pt,* ski*pped* gul*ped,* ba*sk*et, a*sk,* *sc*amper, *sc*ore, ma*sk,* ri*sks,* fla*sks,* de*sks,* ta*sks,* tu*sks,* a*sked,* ba*sked,* hu*sked,* ri*sked,* *sp*eech, wi*sp,* cri*sp,* de*sp*air, ho*sp*ital, *sp*ell, ga*sps,* cla*sps,* ra*sps,* gra*sps,* li*sped,* wi*sped,* ga*sped,* mi*sts,* po*sts,* ne*sts,* conte*sts,* gue*sts.*

TONGUE TWISTERS

In your first rendition of the accompanying exercises read slowly and articulate each sound distinctly. In successive readings, attempt to maintain clarity while you steadily increase the speed of utterance. Practice until you can read each exercise with rapidity and with preciseness of pronunciation. Invent additional tongue twisters.

1. A three-toed tree-toad loved a two-toed she-toad. Unfortunately the two-toed she-toad did not love the three-toed tree-toad. The three-toed tree-toad tried three times to win the love of the two-toed she-toad, but the two-toed she-toad told the three-toed tree-toad that she loved only a fat, fickle frog.

2. Six, slim, silver, slinking coyotes slyly slipped through the side fence. The surprised and sleepy farmer seized his gun and shot sixteen shells in senseless frenzy. One sick coyote sank in the slimy marsh, but the others escaped.

3. Riding to his wedding over the wet roads, Fred raced rapidly in his little red Willis. A white rat ran right under the Willis. The already wilted Fred winced, but soon realized that the white rat had really run between the wide rear wheels.

4. Amidst the mists and fiercest frosts
   With barest wrists and stoutest boasts
   He thrusts his fists against the posts
   And still insists he sees the ghosts.

We should not leave this section on improving the clarity of pronunciation without offering an important caution. In attempting to improve distinctness, avoid becoming overprecise, ostentatious, or artificial. Overprecise speech may be as detrimental to communicative effectiveness as indistinctness; overprecision calls attention to itself at the expense of the ideas being expressed. If unduly conscious of the clarity of utterance, a speaker tends to make excessive use of the articulators, to stress normally unstressed vowels, articles, and prepositions, and to use abnormal patterns of accentuation and loudness. In uttering the sentence, "They have taken the picture to the sofa" the artificial speaker might say: ðeɪ hæv teɪkɛn ði pɪktʃuɝ tju ði soʊfɑ. In contrast, the standard informal pronunciation would be: ðeɪv teɪkən ðə pɪktʃɝ tə ðə soʊfə. Remember: when talking to others concentrate on the process of communicating ideas and feelings. The habits of precise pronunciation, developed during practice periods, will automatically function for you as you engage in oral communication.

IMPROVING THE CORRECTNESS OR APPROPRIATENESS OF PRONUNCIATION

A. Background Explanations. Now that we have studied how the sounds may be clearly and distinctly produced, let us turn to the correctness or appropriateness with which the individual sounds are combined to form the words of connected discourse. As stated earlier, in oral communication sounds must be given values, sequences, and stresses which will be accepted as meeting conventional standards of correctness.

1. What is correct pronunciation? Of necessity, "correct pronunciation" is an elastic term which does not lend itself easily to accurate, clear definition. Perhaps the most precise explanation possible is to say that a pronunciation is correct if it is used by large numbers of educated, cultured persons.

2. Who determines the standards of acceptability in pronunciation? The authority for appropriate standards of pronunciation resides in the people who use the language. In its preface, *Webster's New World Dictionary of the American Language* [7] states: "With pronunciation, as with all other aspects of lexicography, it cannot be repeated too often that dictionaries are not the lawmakers—they are merely the law-recorders. A pronunciation is not 'correct,' or standard, because it is given in a dictionary; rather, it should be found in a dictionary because good usage has already made it standard." *The American College Dictionary* [8] makes the same point in more picturesque language:

> This dictionary records the usage of the speakers and writers of our language; no dictionary . . . can prescribe as to usage; it can only inform on the basis of the facts of usage. A good dictionary is a guide to usage much as a good map tells you the nature of the terrain over which you may want to travel. It is not the function of the dictionary-maker to tell you how to speak, any more than it is the function of the mapmaker to move rivers or rearrange mountains or fill in lakes.

If a majority of cultivated persons pronounce a word in a particular manner, that pronunciation must be accepted as "correct." Obvious hazards exist in determining standards of acceptability: any judgment of what constitutes a "cultivated"

---

[7] Published by The World Publishing Company of Cleveland; copyright, 1956.
[8] Published by Harper & Brothers of New York; copyright, 1953.

person is necessarily subjective; any estimation of the number of persons using a particular pronunciation is uncertain. Dictionary makers are aware of such difficulties and exert strenuous efforts to make their editions as reliable as possible. The publisher of any standard dictionary maintains a staff of language scholars who gather and file millions of references concerning word usage and pronunciation, send out hundreds of questionnaires to persons recognized as good speakers, and study the pronunciations of numerous speakers on radio and television. Unfortunately, the most definitive system of lexicography cannot insure complete accuracy. Furthermore, because of the fluxional nature of pronunciation and the extended time period necessary to compile a dictionary, by the date of publication a dictionary edition is already somewhat behind current pronunciation practices. Despite these, and other limitations which will be discussed later, the standard dictionaries do a magnificent job of determining and recording the predominant pronunciations used by careful speakers.

3. Is there a single standard of American pronunciation? Perhaps even the most rustic individual is aware of regional differences in speech. In John Steinbeck's *The Grapes of Wrath*, this dialogue takes place between an Oklahoman and a Kansan:

"I knowed you wasn't Oklahomy folks. You talk queer kinda—that ain't no blame, you understan'."

"Ever'body says words different," said Ivey. "Arkansas folks says 'em different, and Oklahomy folks says 'em different. And we seen a lady from Massachusetts, an' she said 'em differentest of all. Couldn't hardly make out what she was sayin'." [9]

Instead of a single national pattern, the United States may be divided into three standard regional variations or dialects. As a serviceable formula, we can consider that the Eastern dialect is used primarily in New York City, and in New England east of the Connecticut River and the summits of the Green Mountains,

---

[9] John Steinbeck, *The Grapes of Wrath* (New York: The Viking Press, 1939), p. 184.

that the Southern dialect is spoken in the states which formed the Confederacy, and that the General American dialect prevails in the remainder of the United States.[10]

Each of the three regional patterns has its unique beauty. Students should not consider one dialect superior to another, but should attempt to follow the best pronunciation usages of their region.

4. What are the basic regional variations? Less difference exists among the *standard* dialects than is generally supposed. Much of the dialectal speech head on radio, on television, and in the movies is extreme regionalism and would be considered substandard by the careful speakers within the geographic area represented. For example, the pronounced diphthongization, the exaggerated intonation pattern, and the thick, cotton-in-the-mouth drawl are less characteristic of the educated Southerner's speech than many Northerners believe.

---

[10] Careful students may appreciate having the boundaries of the various areas drawn more precisely. In his *A Word Geography of the Eastern United States* (Ann Arbor: University of Michigan Press, 1949), Hans Kurath suggests that, instead of being confined to New York City and the eastern portion of New England, the Eastern (or, as he calls it, "The North") speech area includes all of New England and New York, the northeastern half of New Jersey, the northern third of Pennsylvania, and at least the northeastern corner of Ohio. According to Kurath, the line separating the Southern speech area from the remainder of the United States begins on the Delaware coast about the latitude of Dover; it follows a northwestwardly curving course to the north of Baltimore, and then bends southwestward, crossing the Potomac below Harper's Ferry; it continues southwestward along the Blue Ridge until it reaches the latitude of Lynchburg, Va., where it veers first to the southeast and then to the southwest passing between Charlotte, N. C., and Columbia, S. C. Here, for want of adequate data, Kurath's line ends. In several letters to the author and in his *Applied Phonetics*, Claude M. Wise has projected the line "speculatively on the basis of non-statistical data." Wise considers that the line curves around the base of the Appalachians in northern Georgia and northeastern Alabama and then swings north, separating the hill from the cotton country, until it reaches the Ohio River in the vicinity of Louisville and Cincinnati; it then turns down the Ohio to the Mississippi, cuts across the southeast corner of Missouri, runs south across Arkansas separating the eastern cotton country from the western hill country, continues southward into Louisiana and then swings northwestward around the Louisiana hill country, crosses the Louisiana-Texas line near Shreveport, and then bends southward to the Gulf. That portion of the United States which is not included in the Eastern or Southern areas may be considered General American. It should be emphasized that, although we have been using the word "line," regional borders are actually strips of land which vary in width from a few miles to perhaps more than two hundred.

Space does not permit a detailed description of the regional differences. However, the following analysis presents some of the more obvious variations in the standard speech of the three major dialects.

a. Perhaps the most obvious difference among the dialects is that the General American speaker nearly always pronounces the "r" when it appears in the spelling of a word. On the other hand, speakers using the Eastern and Southern dialects pronounce the "r" only under certain circumstances, that is, when the "r" is in a linking position.[11] Furthermore, Southerners and Easterners use the vowel (ɜ) where the General Americans use (ɝ) in words like "b*i*rd," and the vowel (ə) where the General Americans use (ɚ) in words like "hung*er*."

b. In a group of about 150 "broad a" words, persons from the General American and Southern regions use the vowel (æ); those living in the Eastern dialect area use (æ), (a), or (ɑ). In most "broad a" words, the letter "a" immediately precedes either: one of these voiceless fricatives (f), (s), or (θ); or a nasal sound which is followed by a voiceless fricative or a plosive. Examples: "*a*fter," "cl*a*ss," "gr*a*ph," and "*a*nswer."

c. In words like "absurd" and "greasy," Southerners and perhaps Easterners are somewhat more likely to use a (z) than are General Americans.

d. Eastern and Southern speakers tend to use (ju) instead of (u), when the spellings "u," "eu," and "ew" appear immediately after (t), (d), or (n). Examples: "*tu*be" (tjub), "*dew*" (dju), "*neu*tral" (njutrəl). In each of these words, most General American speakers use (u).

e. In Eastern speech, a low-back vowel (ɒ) is sometimes used where General American speakers use (ɑ), or perhaps (ɔ) or (ʌ), in such words as "h*o*t," "n*o*t," "g*o*t," "c*o*mmon," "wh*a*t," "w*a*s," "h*o*bby," "r*o*tten," "c*o*ffee," and "d*o*ctor." The sound (ɒ) is made with the tongue slightly higher in the rear of the mouth

---

[11] In standard Eastern and Southern speech, the "r" is pronounced when it is *immediately* followed by a vowel. The vowel may occur in the same word or may be the initial sound in another word which is spoken without an intervening pause.

than for (ɑ), but somewhat lower than for (ɔ); the tongue is a little more tense than for the (ɑ) but less so than for the (ɔ).

f. When the letter "a" appears before a final "r" or before an "r" which is followed by a consonant, some Eastern speakers use the vowel (a) instead of (ɑ). Examples "*far*" (fa:),[12] "*hard*" (ha:d), "*carb*on" (ka:bən), and "*art*" (a:t).

g. In the spellings "or" and "arr" plus vowel in certain poly-syllables like "*forest*," "*torrid*," "*forehead*," and "*warranty*," the Eastern and Southern speakers prefer to use (ɑ) for the first vowel: (fɑrɪst, tɑrɪd, fɑrɪd, wɑrəntɪ). Other Americans probably use the (ɔ) as: (fɔrəst, tɔrəd, fɔrəd, wɔrəntɪ).

h. In words like "Mary," "scary," "marrow," and "character," most General American speakers probably use the vowel (ɛ). Examples: (mɛrɪ, skɛrɪ, mɛro, kɛrɪktɚ). A majority of Easterners use (æ), and Southerners use (æ), (eɪ), or (ɛ).

5. *What is the difference between formal and colloquial pronunciation?* Formal pronunciation is that usage which is suitable for unusually dignified situations, such as the reading of a judicial decision in a courtroom, a funeral sermon, and a speech to a large audience. Colloquial pronunciation represents that usage which is appropriate for conversation and most public speaking occasions. In recent years, public speakers have moved steadily away from the formal or literary style and toward the informal or colloquial. A colloquial pronunciation is considered standard if it is accepted by the careful speakers of the region; it is incorrect if rejected by the cultured speakers. Standard colloquial speech should be used in all except the limited num-ber of situations demanding a dignified, relatively slow utter-ance.

In differentiation from the colloquial, formal pronunciation has these characteristics: its general rate of utterance is somewhat slower; consonants are typically articulated with greater distinct-ness; most vowels tend to be given greater length. For formal speech, the sentence "Your boys have to go" would be pro-

---

[12] The symbol (:) indicates that the (a) sound is held slightly longer than usual in order to compensate for the dropping of the (r).

nounced: (jʊr bɔɪz hæv tu gou). In most communicative situations such pronunciations would seem stilted and unnatural. Therefore, standard colloquial usage would be: (jɚ bɔɪz hæv tə gou). Under formal conditions, the sentence "I could have done it and I know it" would be pronounced: (aɪ kʊd hæv dʌn it ænd aɪ nou it). In contrast, the normal, standard colloquial expression would be: (aɪ kʊd əv dʌn ət n̩d aɪ nou ət).[13]

6. What guides or cautions should be observed in using the pronunciation guides of a dictionary? (1) The function of a dictionary is to record as faithfully as possible those pronunciations prevailing among educated, cultured persons. The dictionary attempts to report accurate, factual information; it does not deliberately seek to dictate or create arbitrary standards. (2) When several pronunciations are widely used for a word, dictionaries place first the preferred form, that is, the one occurring most frequently. However, do not pay slavish respect to the order of listing because all forms which are offered are in general cultivated use, and often two or more of the variations may be heard with approximately equal frequency. When offered a choice, select the pronunciation you hear most often in the speech of the educated persons around you. (3) Since dictionaries inevitably are somewhat behind current practices, avoid being hypercritical about the usage of forms not mentioned in your dictionary. Perhaps a forthcoming edition will list the seemingly aberrant form, or possibly a dictionary published by a different company will include it as an acceptable variant. (4) In recording pronunciations, most dictionaries make little or no recognition of regional differences. Recognize, therefore, that a particular word, bearing a given set of diacritical marks, might be pronounced differently by persons living in other dialect areas. (5) Be certain that you understand the diacritical or phonetic symbols and that you pronounce correctly the key words. A mispronunciation of the key word will result in a mispronunciation of the word you are checking. (6) Dictionaries

---

[13] The appearance of the (ˌ) under a consonant as in (n̩) indicates that the consonant represents a syllable.

tend to reflect a more formal speech than standard conversational usage. In part, this practice arises from the lexicographer's perplexing problem of representing in *isolation* the pronunciation of words which typically occur only in the flow of connected discourse. As you have learned, the context in which a word appears may alter the stress pattern of the vowels and the articulation of the consonants. In many cases, the dictionary maker leaves to the reader the task of converting the formal pronunciation into the colloquial.

B. A Program of Self-Improvement in the Correctness or Appropriateness of Pronunciation. Initiate and maintain a program to improve the acceptability of your pronunciation. Listen carefully to the speech of others on the campus, at work, and on radio and television. Carry with you a pocket-size notebook and enter any words which you believe may have been mispronounced. Also, in the course of your reading, record each word the pronunciation of which you are uncertain. Every evening check in a standard dictionary the list of words you have accumulated during the day. Do more than merely "look up" the words: transcribe each one in phonetic or diacritic symbols; pronounce each aloud several times; compose a sentence containing the word and say it aloud several times. Periodically review your lists.

With the aid of voice recordings, analyze your own speech to discover pronunciation errors. Pronunciation faults may be conveniently classified as omissions, additions, inversions, substitutions, and misplaced stress. The errors most frequently committed are those of sound substitutions and misplaced stresses. As part of your speech inventory, read carefully the following discussion, pronouncing each word in the various drill lists and completing the suggested exercises.[14]

1. Avoid omitting necessary sounds. Be vigilant to include in your pronunciations all those sounds considered necessary by

---

[14] In the following word lists, unless the error being discussed relates particularly to the Eastern and/or the Southern dialects, the phonetic transcriptions will utilize the General American pronunciations.

conventional usage. Study the following examples of omission errors. If you tend to commit any of these mistakes, drill on the suggested words and prepare an extensive list of words for further drill.

a. SOUND OMISSIONS OCCUR MOST FREQUENTLY IN WORD END-INGS. Do you make any of these errors?

The omission of the sounds (t) and (d) in words like slep*t*, shap*ed*, lapp*ed*, slack*ed*, lurk*ed*, fel*t*, mel*t*, bol*t*, dar*t*, smar*t*, las*t*, pas*t*, cross*ed*, fish*ed*, lash*ed*, jabb*ed*, logg*ed*, hugg*ed*, sco*ld*, foil*ed*, slav*ed*.

The omission of one or more sounds in combinations such as (sks), (skt), (sps), (sts), (kts), (kst), (nst), and (ndz). Practice on the following words: a*sks*, ma*sks*, ta*sks*, hu*sks*; a*sked*, ma*sked*, ta*sked*, ba*sked*; gra*sps*, cla*sps*, ha*sps*, ra*sps*; mi*sts*, wai*sts*, boa*sts*, po*sts*; a*cts*, detra*cts*, affe*cts*, reje*cts*; ne*xt*, he*xed*, ta*xed*, fle*xed*; lan*ced*, dan*ced*, pran*ced*, again*st*; lan*ds*, pretend*s*, mound*s*, len*ds*.

In the Southern dialect, the omission of (ə) from (oə), of (ɪ) from (aɪ), and of the linking (r): f*our* (foə) not (fo), d*oor* (doə) not (do), sn*ore* (snoə) not (sno), bef*ore* (bɪfoə) not (bɪfo), sc*ore* (skoə) not (sko); I (aɪ) not (a), h*igh* (haɪ) not (ha), fr*y* (fraɪ) not (fra), sk*y* (shaɪ) not (ska); f*ar* *in* (far ɪn) not (fa ɪn), h*er* *a*pple (hɜr æpḷ) not (hɜ æpḷ), c*ar* *a*t (kar æt) not (ka æt), d*oor* *o*pen (dour oupən) not (dou oupən).

b. NECESSARY SOUNDS ARE OFTEN OMITTED IN THE INTERIOR OF WORDS.

Persons in all three dialects may omit one or more medial sounds in such words as: Mississippi, somewhere, veteran, gentleman, diamond, government, February, matriculate, medieval, grocery, recognize, Philippine, prominence, regiment, everywhere, particular, frequently, arctic, library, isn't, primitive, pronunciation, memorial, declaration, association, everybody, company, interested, didn't.

Persons in the various dialect areas sometimes omit the sound (l) when it appears in a medial position: Wi*ll*iam (wɪljəm) not (wɪjəm), ye*l*p (jɛlp) not (jɛp), gu*l*f (gʌlf) not (gʌf), a*l*ways (ɔlweɪz) not (ɔweɪz), he*l*p (hɛlp) not (hɛp). Sometimes Southerners omit the linking (r) when it appears in the middle of a word: ve*r*y (vɛrɪ) not (vɛɪ), be*r*ry (berɪ) not (beɪ), ma*r*riage (mærɪdʒ) not (mæɪdʒ), dai*r*y (derɪ) not (deɪ).

Some Southerners may erroneously omit the (ə) from (oə), the (ɪ) from (aɪ), and the (ɪ) from (ɔɪ), when they appear in a medial position: f*ourteen* (foɔtin) not (fotin), doorman (doɔmən) not (domən), morning (moɔnɪŋ) not (monɪŋ); height (haɪt) not (hat), right(raɪt) not (rat), light (laɪt) not (lat), defiant (dɪfaɪənt) not (dɪfaɔnt); coil (kɔɪl) not (kɔl), boil (bɔɪl) not (bɔl), spoil (spɔɪl) not (spɔl).

c. THE OMISSION OF NECESSARY SOUNDS OCCURS MUCH LESS FREQUENTLY IN THE INITIAL POSITION THAN IN THE MEDIAL OR FINAL. However, sounds, such as (ə), (h), (ɛ), and (ɪk), occasionally are omitted from the beginnings of words:

across (əkrɔs) not (krɔs), among (əmʌŋ) not (mʌŋ), about (əbaʊt) not (baʊt); heat (hit) not (it), happen (hæpən) not (æpən), hay (heɪ) not (eɪ), hand (hænd) not (ænd); escapade (ɛskəpeɪd) not (skəpeɪd), expiration (ɛkspəreɪ-ʃən) not (spəreɪʃən), explanation (ɛkspləneɪʃən) not (spləneɪʃən); extinct (ɪkstɪŋkt) not (stɪŋkt), extension (ɪkstɛnʃən) not (stɛnʃən), expressman (ɪkspresmən) not (spresmən).

2. Avoid adding unnecessary sounds. This error is the exact opposite of the one just discussed. Read orally the following lists to determine whether your speech includes unnecessary vowels and consonants.

a. THE ADDITION OF UNNECESSARY VOWELS.

Some persons in the three dialect regions erroneously add the (ə) vowel in words like these: athlete (æθlit) not (æθəlit), umbrella (ʌmbrelə) not (ʌmbərelə), chimney (tʃɪmnɪ) not (tʃɪmənɪ), cathedral (kəθidrəl) not (kəθidərəl), elm (ɛlm) not (ɛləm).

In the South and in eastern urban centers, the vowel (ɪ) is sometimes intruded before the vowel (u) and is sometimes added after the vowel (ɜ): tool (tul) not (tɪul), to (tu) not (tɪu), fool (ful) not (fɪul), school (skul) not (skɪul); bird (bɜd) not (bɜɪd), curb (kɜb) not (kɜɪb), disturb (dɪstɜb) not (dɪstɜɪb), worth (wɜθ) not (wɜɪθ), heard (hɜd) not (hɜɪd).

Some Southerners tend to add either the vowel (ɪ) or (ə) after the vowel (æ), and the vowel (o) after the vowel (ɔ): past (pæst) not (pæɪst), lamp (læmp) not (læəmp), camp (kæmp) not (kæɪmp) pants (pænts) not (pæɪnts); walk (wɔk) not (wɔok), talk (tɔk) not (tɔok), cough (kɔf) not (kɔof), ought (ɔt) not (ɔot).

b. THE ADDITION OF UNNECESSARY CONSONANTS.

The error of adding unnecessary (t) and (d) sounds is widespread. It occurs in such words as: across (əkrɔs) not (əkrɔst), wish (wɪʃ) not (wɪʃt), twice (twaɪs) not (twaɪst); drowned (draʊnd) not (draʊndəd), gown (gaʊn) not (gaʊnd), attacked (ətækt) not (ətæktəd).

The addition of the intrusive (r) occurs in all dialect areas, possibly appearing least frequently in General American speech. As the terminology indicates, an intrusive (r) is one which "intrudes," that is, one that is not spelled but is pronounced. Examples: Chicago (ʃɪkago) not (ʃɪkargo), ought (ɔt) not (ɔrt), China (tʃaɪnə) not (tʃaɪnɚ), idea (aɪdɪə) not (aɪdɪɚ), wash (waʃ) not (warʃ).

Sometimes in Southern speech the consonant (j) is inappropriately inserted. Sample words: hat (hæt) not (hæjət), gas (gæs) not (gæjəs), column (kaləm) not (kaljəm), class (klæs) not (klæjəs).

The addition of (g) or (k) after (ŋ) is an error which is heard with greatest frequency in urban centers. Examples: long (lɔŋ) not (lɔŋg), running (rʌnɪŋ) not (rʌnɪŋg), blinking (blɪŋkɪŋ) not (blɪŋkɪŋk), darling (darlɪŋ) not (darlɪŋk), singer (sɪŋɚ) not (sɪŋgɚ).

c. MISCELLANEOUS ERRORS OF ADDITION. The following list contains a number of common mistakes. If you find that you ordinarily mispronounce any of the examples, bring to class a list of similar words.

almond (amənd) not (almənd), psalm (sam) not (salm), calm (kam) not (kalm), it (ɪt) not (hɪt), statistics (stətɪstɪks) not (stəstɪstɪks), Worcester (wʊstɚ) not (wɜtʃestɚ), Westminster (westmɪnstɚ) not (westmɪnɪstɚ), family (fæmlɪ) not (fæmblɪ), height (haɪt) not (haɪtθ), beneficial (bənəfɪʃəl) not (bənəfɪʃɪəl), overalls (ovɚɔlz) not (ovɚhɔlz), grievous (grivəs) not (grivɪəs).

3. *Avoid inverting the proper position of sounds.* Although this error probably does not occur as frequently as other pronunciation faults, it is sufficiently common to warrant careful attention. The following list contains words often subject to inversion. Pronounce each word clearly and distinctly. For several days listen critically to the conversations about you and bring to class those inversions you hear.

perspiration (pɚspəreɪʃən) not (prespəreɪʃən), prescriptive (prɪskrɪptɪv) not (pɚskrɪptɪv), hydrant (haɪdrənt) not (haɪdɚnt), pretend (prɪtend) not (pɚtend), prevent (prɪvent) not (pɚvent), modernize (madɚnaɪz) not (madrənaɪz), patronize (peɪtrənaɪz) not (peɪtɚnaɪz), pattern (pætɚn) not (pætrən), pretty (prɪtɪ) not (pɜtɪ), ask (æsk) not (æks), officer (ɔfəsɚ) not (ɔsəfɚ), secretary (sɛkrətɛrɪ) not (sɛkɚtɛrɪ), introduce (ɪntrədus) not (ɪntɚdus), integral (ɪntəgrəl) not (ɪntrəgəl).

4. *Avoid erroneously substituting one sound for another.* Sound substitutions are very common in American speech. Also, they represent a type of pronunciation which is often difficult to correct. As a part of your self-improvement program, examine the accompanying lists to determine whether you commit any of the substitution faults mentioned. If you detect errors, collect and transcribe in phonetics or diacritics a large number of words which contain the sound in question. With the aid of voice recordings, drill on the word lists. Make a determined effort to incorporate the correct pronunciation into your habitual speech practices; to determine your success in this attempt, check periodically with your instructor.

The following discussion includes some of the more common forms of vowel, diphthong, and consonant substitutions. A review of the section "Learning How the Sounds of Speech Are Made" will make the ensuing passages more meaningful.

a. Vowel Substitutions.

(ɛ) for (ɪ):
Sometimes speakers, especially those living along the border between the Southern and General American speech areas, replace the vowel (ɪ) with the vowel (ɛ) in words such as: sl*i*m, beg*i*n, br*i*nk, h*i*m, s*i*nce, th*i*nk, m*i*nk, p*i*nk, s*i*mmer, *E*ngland, s*i*n, J*i*m, h*i*nder, th*i*n, h*i*nge.

(ɪ) for (ɛ):
The substitution of (ɪ) for (ɛ) probably occurs most frequently in the South. These words should be pronounced with (ɛ): t*e*n, s*e*nd, p*e*ncil, l*e*nd, fr*ie*nd, p*e*nny, *e*nd, r*e*member, f*e*nce, d*e*nt, B*e*n, w*e*nt, c*e*nter, D*e*cember, surr*e*nder, m*e*ntion, *a*ny, m*a*ny, t*e*n, g*ue*ss, p*e*nalty, sl*e*nder.

(eɪ) for (ɛ):
Although occurring in all three dialects, the replacement of (ɛ) by (eɪ) perhaps happens most often in the South. Words for drill: b*e*d, s*ai*d, N*e*d, d*ea*d, n*e*phew, f*e*d, l*e*dge, l*e*d, b*e*t, h*ea*d, *e*gg, m*ea*sure, n*e*gative, g*e*t, b*e*ck, d*e*ck, wr*e*ck, p*e*ck, M*e*xico, tr*e*k.

(æ̃) for (æ):
The substitution of a nasalized (æ̃) for the low front vowel (æ) is a common occurrence in all three dialects. Instead of making the (æ) with the tongue

low in the mouth, some persons arch the tongue toward the palate. When this happens, the velum may tend to drop, permitting a portion of the breath stream to pass through the nose. In the following sample words, be sure you do not use disagreeable nasality: hand, stand, family, lamp, man, gap, rant, stamp, can, tank, spank, damp, sample, bank, plan, bat, hat, platter, fat, ramp, scamp, sat, tap.

Miscellaneous substitutions for (æ):
As is illustrated in this list, a variety of vowels is sometimes substituted for (æ): rather (ræðɚ) not (rʌðɚ), bad (bæd) not (bɛd), stamp (stæmp) not (stɔmp), can (kæn) not (kɪn), can't (kænt) not (keɪnt), guarantee (gærənti) not (gɑrənti).

(æ) for (a):
We found on page 156 that the vowel (a) is widely used by cultivated speakers in the East. Sometimes, however, Easterners raise the tongue arch too high in the mouth, producing an (æ) instead of (a). The use of (æ) in the following words would constitute an error: part, carpet, guardian, Harvard, tarpaulin, smart, art, barter, cart, start, carpenter.

(ɚ) for (o) and (ə):
Speakers using the General American dialect sometimes substitute (ɚ) for (o) or (ə) in word endings. Sample words: window, jello, potato, swallow, tobacco, bellow, fallow, hula dancer, pillow, fellow.

(ou) for (ɔ):
For a limited number of words, some Southerners tend to replace (ɔ) with (ou). Some of these words are: on, gone, want, upon, donkey.

(ɔ) for (ɑ):
In the Southern dialect area, in that portion of the General American region which borders on the Southern, and in the East the vowel (ɑ) is sometimes replaced by (ɔ). Avoid using (ɔ) in words like these: hard, farm, carpenter, alarm, dart, far, start, car.

(ɪ) for (ə):
As we found earlier, the unstressing of vowels in unaccented syllables is a standard, common occurrence in English. Occasionally, however, such unstressing leads to the incorrect substitution of (ɪ) for (ə). The endings of the ollowing words should be pronounced with (ə): soda, Georgia, Florida, Alaska, opera, Alma, vanilla, America, hyena, extra.

.) for (ju), (jʊ), or (jə):
Faulty unstressing causes some persons to use (ə) in such words as: debutant, herculean, indissoluble, municipal, museum, reputable, salutary, contribute, disputation, interlocutor.

b. Diphthong Substitutions.

(a) and (ɑ) for (aɪ):
In the South and in the border country, separating the General American and Southern dialect areas, the vowel (a) or (ɑ) is sometimes substituted for the diphthong (aɪ). Sample words subject to this error: *I*, *my*, *fly*, *cry*, *tie*, *hire*, *tire*, *mired*, *liar*, *ironed*, *Irene*, *fire*, *Irish*, *Hiram*, *retire*.

(ɔɪ) for (aɪ):
Inhabitants of rural New England sometimes substitute (ɔɪ) for (aɪ) in such words as: *wife*, *skies*, *strife*, *nice*, *kite*, *lice*.

(ε) for (eɪ):
In Southern speech the vowel (ε) is sometimes substituted for (eɪ) in words like: *take*, *naked*, *bake*, *rake*, *grade*, *made*, *layed*, *lake*, *brake*, *stayed*, *shake*, *strayed*, *fake*, *forsake*, *break*, *flake*.

(aɪ), (oə), (ɔɪ) and (ɝ) for (ɔɪ):
Sometimes in rustic speech the diphthong (ɔɪ) is incorrectly replaced by (aɪ) or (oə). In urban speech, some persons substitute (ɔɪ) or (ɝ) for (ɔɪ). Use (ɔɪ) in words like: *oysters*, *joint*, *deploy*, *boil*, *doily*, *oil*, *choice*, *poison*, *destroy*, *appoint*, *Troy*, *rejoice*, *noise*, *spoiled*, *voice*, *toy*, *annoy*, *poise*, *boiler*, *boys*.

c. Consonant Substitutions.

(d) for (t):
Use (t) and not (d) in such words as: *little*, *protestant*, *betting*, *matter*, *mantel*, *certain*, *water*, *butter*, *botany*, *better*, *kitty*, *cattle*, *veteran*, *battle*, *lighter*, *letter*, *beautiful*, *antelope*, *aesthetics*, *potato*, *partner*.

(n) for (ŋ):
Perhaps the most common substitution error is that of (n) for (ŋ) in verb forms ending with "ing." Students should recognize that this represents a case of sound substitution and not one of omission: no (g) sound is heard in the "ing" endings, and therefore could not be omitted. Frequently the vowel substitution of (ə) or (i) for (ɪ) accompanies the substitution of (n) for (ŋ): an example, "doing" (duɪŋ) may become (duən) in careless speech or (duin) in the speech of some persons trying to say (ɪŋ). Drill words: *running*, *singing*, *saying*, *praying*, *dancing*, *speaking*, *drinking*, *sighing*, *flying*, *jumping*, *batting*, *sleeping*.

(t) for (θ):
The replacement of (θ) by (t) is somtimes heard in Southern and in urban speech. Use (θ) in these words: *Beth*, *death*, *youth*, *bath*, *both*, *math*, *think*, *thimble*, *through*, *thick*, *tooth*, *thin*, *thirty*, *birth*, *thing*, *three*.

(d) for (ð):
Like the immediately preceding error, the substitution of (d) for (ð) is a characteristic of sub-standard Southern and urban speech. Drill words: *the*, *mo*ther, *bro*ther, *fa*ther, *the*m, *tho*se, *the*se, *thi*s, *tha*t, *wi*th.

(tʃ) for (dʒ):
The substitution of the unvoiced (tʃ) for its voiced counterpart (dʒ) is a common error of foreign accent. These words should be pronounced with (dʒ): colle*ge*, bul*ge*, dama*ge*, coura*ge*, stora*ge*, ca*ged*, pa*ged*, enga*ged*, wa*ged*, ima*ge*, smu*dge*, *j*eer, *j*eweler, enra*ged*, *j*ump, he*dge*, ple*dge*, langua*ge*.

(s) for (z):
The replacement of the voiced (z) by its voiceless analogue (s) occurs especially frequently in word endings. Use (z) in such words as: doe*s*, dai*s*y, surpri*s*e, mu*s*eum, surmi*s*e, despi*s*e, sud*s*, ball*s*, run*s*, lo*s*e.

(z) for (s):
Although many cultured speakers use (z) for (s) in words like "absurd" and "greasy," (z) is considered undesirable in such words as: ba*s*eball, pri*c*e, preciou*s*, de*s*cribe, fa*c*e up, le*ss*, Mi*ss*, mi*s*appropriation.

(s) for (ʃ):
This error occasionally occurs when the letters "sh" are immediately followed by an "r." Sample words: *shr*ew, *shr*iek, *shr*ill, *shr*imp, *shr*ine, *shr*ink, *shr*ivel, *shr*oud, *shr*ub, *shr*ug, *Shr*eveport.

(w) for (ʍ):
This substitution probably does not occur frequently in the Southern or General American regions. In the East, however, it is so widely used that authorities generally consider it standard. Unless an Easterner, you should use (ʍ) when the letters "wh" appear in an initial position.[15] Sample words: *wh*en, *wh*ether, *wh*at, *wh*ere, *wh*ence, *wh*imper, *wh*ich, *wh*y, *wh*ip, *wh*ine, *wh*ippet, *wh*im, *wh*iff, *wh*ale, *wh*ack, *wh*eel, *wh*istle.

5. *Avoid misplacing stress.* To rid your speech of all errors of misplaced stress may require conscientious effort over a period of time. However, a good beginning for such a program can be secured by reading aloud the following lists and by devising similar ones. (The following word lists utilize the General American pronunciations as recorded in John S. Kenyon and Thomas A. Knott, *A Pronouncing Dictionary of American English. Note:* Kenyon and Knott transcribe the (eɪ) and (oʊ) as pure vowels (e) and (o) rather than as diphthongs.)

[15] With the exception of words like: *wh*o, *wh*om, *wh*ole, *wh*oop, *wh*olly, *wh*olesale.

WORDS OF TWO SYLLABLES

ACCENT ON FIRST SYLLABLE: [16]

bestial (bɛstʃəl)
blackguard ('blægə̆d)
bodice ('bɑdɪs)
brigand ('brɪgənd)

damask ('dæməsk)
despot ('dɛspət)
dulcet ('dʌlsɪt)
hostile ('hɑstļ)

piquant ('pikənt)
pristine ('prɪstin)
respite ('rɛspɪt)
ribald ('rɪbļd)

ACCENT ON SECOND SYLLABLE:

abyss (ə'bɪs)
assent (ə'sɛnt)
cabal (kə'bæl)
Detroit (dɪ'trɔɪt)

devise (dɪ'vaɪz)
digress (də'grɛs)
direct (də'rɛkt)
discuss (dɪ'skʌs)

escape (ə'skep)
estate (ə'stet)
estrange (ə'strendʒ)
event (ɪ'vɛnt)

WORDS OF THREE SYLLABLES

ACCENT ON FIRST SYLLABLE:

atrophy ('ætrəfɪ)
cerebral ('sɛrəbrəl)
credulous ('krɛdʒələs)
deprecate ('dɛprə,ket)

diffidence ('dɪfədəns)
dolorous ('dɑlərəs)
efferent ('ɛfərənt)
epaulet ('ɛpə,lɛt)

impious ('ɪmpɪəs)
impotent ('ɪmpətənt)
labyrinth ('læbə,rɪnθ)
myriad ('mɪrɪəd)

ACCENT ON SECOND SYLLABLE:

caloric (kə'lɔrɪk)
clandestine (klæn'dɛstɪn)
equator (ɪ'kwetə̆)
inclement (ɪn'klɛmənt)

Italian (ɪ'tæljən)
medallion (mə'dæljən)
phlegmatic (flɛg'mætɪk)
secretive (sɪ'kritɪv)

sonorous (sə'norəs)
systemic (sɪs'tɛmɪk)
tangential (tæn'dʒɛnʃəl)
united (ju'naɪtɪd)

ACCENT ON THIRD SYLLABLE:

apropos (,æprə'po)
assignee (əsaɪ'ni)
attaché (,ætə'ʃe)
debonair (,dɛbə'nɛr)

diagnose (,daɪəg'nos)
dispossess (,dɪspə'zɛs)
guarantee (,gærən'ti)
legionnaire (,lidʒən'ɛr)

masquerade (,mæskə'red)
palisade (,pælə'sed)
repartee (,rɛpə̆'ti)
statuesque (stætʃu'ɛsk)

WORDS OF FOUR SYLLABLES

ACCENT ON FIRST SYLLABLE:

amicable
('æmɪkəbļ)
comparable
('kɑmpərəbļ)
dirigible ('dɪrədʒəbļ)
exigency ('ɛksədʒənsɪ)

formidable
('fɔrmɪdəbļ)
lamentable ('læməntəbļ)
malefactor
('mælə,fæktə̆)
malleable ('mælɪəbļ)

millinery ('mɪlənɛrɪ)
predatory ('prɛdə,torɪ)
solecism ('sɑlə,sɪzəm)
systematize
('sɪstəmə,taɪz)

[16] In using phonetics, primary accent is indicated by (') and secondary stress by (,), each of these symbols being placed *before* the syllable to which it refers.

ACCENT ON SECOND SYLLABLE:

autocracy (ɔ'takrəsɪ)	diminutive (də'mɪnjətɪv)	euphonious (ju'fonɪəs)
bureaucracy	emolument	fatuity (fə'tjuətɪ)
(bju'rakrəsɪ)	(ɪ'maljəmənt)	hyperbole (haɪ'pɚbəlɪ)
circuitous (sɚ'kjuɪtəs)	encomium (en'komɪəm)	impiety (ɪm'paɪətɪ)
corporeal (kɔr'porɪəl)	epitome (ɪ'pɪtəmɪ)	

ACCENT ON THIRD SYLLABLE:

catastrophic	esoteric (ˌɛsə'terɪk)	syncopation
(ˌkætə'strafɪk)	machination	(ˌsɪŋkə'peʃən)
deprecation	(ˌmækə'neʃən)	therapeutic
(ˌdeprə'keʃən)	panegyric (ˌpænə'dʒɪrɪk)	(ˌθerə'pjutɪk)
detestation (ˌditɛs'teʃən)	soporific (sopə'rɪfɪk)	transmutation
diabetes (ˌdaɪə'bitɪs)	supplication	(ˌtrænsmju'teʃən)
	(ˌsʌplɪ'keʃən)	

SUMMARY

Distinct and appropriate pronunciation is essential to effective oral communication. The sounds of language must be formed clearly and must be given those values, sequences, and stresses which meet conventional standards of correctness. A self-improvement program in pronunciation involves three steps. (1) Learn how the speech sounds are made: a working knowledge of the speech mechanism and the International Phonetic Alphabet is a prerequisite to the study of the standard methods of producing the vowels, diphthongs, and consonants. (2) Drill to improve the clarity with which the sounds are uttered: this phase of your program should include exercises to improve muscular control of the organs of articulation and word exercises containing difficult sound combinations. (3) Analyze your speech to eliminate inappropriate pronunciation characteristics: first, recognize what constitutes suitable standards of pronunciation for your region of the United States; then, study your speaking habits to discover and to eradicate any errors of omission, addition, inversion, substitution, and misplaced accents.

III ❧ *The Audience*

8 ❧❧ *Listening and Observing*

Recently a national press service carried this story. At the cash register of a Long Beach, California, supermarket a neatly dressed stranger engaged the manager in conversation. As he chatted, the stranger casually wrote a check for $100. Mindful that for months the police had pleaded for help in curtailing the passing of bad checks, the merchant requested identification. Smiling affably, the customer offered an impressive-looking document with the heading "Long Beach Police Department." Later, when the manager attempted to cash the check, it bounced. Upon complaining to the police, he learned that the "impressive-looking document" was an ex-convict registration. In addition to causing him embarrassment, failure to listen and to observe effectively cost this merchant time and money.

As you read in the first chapter, communication is not a simple one-way process in which a speaker "gives" ideas to passive listeners. Communication is a *cycle* involving highly complex functionings on the part of both the speaker and the receiver. In such a cycle, the listener-observer is as important as the speaker. What is the nature of the role played by the listener-observer? How does listening differ from hearing? How does observing differ from seeing? How important to the individual is the ability to listen-observe effectively? How can habits of listening-observing be improved? The following discussion contains answers to these questions.

The differences between "listening" and "hearing" are patent. For our purposes, a person "hears" if he is conscious of having received the sound waves produced by the speaker. A person "listens" if, in addition to being aware of such stimuli, he attaches appropriate meanings to them. "Hearing" is a passive process, "listening" an active one. Likewise, "observing" means more than merely "seeing": in "observing," one interprets and evaluates the visible symbols emanating from the speaker, that is, his posture, gestures, and facial expressions, his use of visual aids, etc. Since speakers utilize both the visible and audible codes, the receiver of an act of communication must be a skilled listener and a discerning observer.

A conscientious application of the guides discussed in this chapter can help you to develop your ability to understand, retain, and evaluate oral communication. Increased skill in acquiring and retaining information will improve your grades, your chances for job success, your capacity for friendship, and your general efficiency. Increased skill in critical evaluation will help you to protect yourself from trickery, sham, and high-pressure persuasion and will help you to remain calm in times of hysteria.

Only systematic, persistent effort can produce the mental discipline necessary for effective listening-observing. Utilize your speech class as an excellent listening-observing laboratory. During the semester, in addition to your own opportunities to speak, you will hear many performances by other students. The time spent as an auditor can be largely wasted. However, by concentrating closely you can help provide a stimulating speaker-audience relationship, receive considerable worth-while information, and can improve your own speaking and listening-observing techniques. For every classroom performance, ask yourself such questions as these: What response is the speaker attempting to achieve? Does his talk move logically and psychologically toward the accomplishment of that goal? Does he have distracting mannerisms? Is his choice of language clear, direct, appropriate, and vivid? Are his attitudes well-adjusted toward himself, his material, and his audience? In what ways could his vocal delivery be improved? Remember that the analysis of a poor performance may be as rewarding as the analysis of a good one. By participating actively as a listener-observer you can help make each class period a stimulating learning experience.

Apply the guides for effective listening-observing in your other classes, at your job, at club meetings, in social conversations, and while listening to radio and television. Embark on a long-range program for self-improvement. The rewards are well worth the expenditure of time and energy.

BEING CO-OPERATIVE AND COURTEOUS

To receive the greatest possible benefits from a speaking situation, one should be cooperative and courteous.

A. Consider Yourself an Important Participant in the Cycle of Communication. Speaking is purposive. The speaker wishes to effect some change in the auditor: to inform, entertain, or persuade him. The speaker is important because he is the source of visible and audible stimuli; the listener-observer is equally important because he receives, interprets, and evaluates the stimuli supplied by the speaker. Both the speaker and the listener-observer share the responsibility for effective oral communication. As Oliver Wendell Holmes wrote in *The Poet at the Breakfast Table,* "It is the province of knowledge to speak and it is the privilege of wisdom to listen."

B. Determine to Profit from the Discussion. Avoid judging in advance that the subject is dull and uninteresting. If the topic for a panel, lecture, oral reading, or debate appears dull or sterile, adopt a practical attitude. Resolve to secure something of value from the presentation. Instead of throwing up mental road blocks, ask yourself: Could this subject have potential cultural value for me? Could it have some application to my present or future occupation? Could it add to my knowledge of current affairs or help me in my academic training? Could it make me a better person?

C. Indicate by Your Attitude that You are Interested. The listener-observer constantly communicates with the speaker by such means as smiles, applause, laughter, and shifts of position.

By being a sympathetic, co-operative listener-observer, you stimulate the speaker to do his best. Realizing that his efforts are being appreciated and that his hearers are co-operating to make the speaking situation as successful as possible, the speaker becomes more relaxed, more confident, and more stimulating. Should he attempt a touch of humor, encourage him with a smile, or perhaps a chuckle. If he scores a particularly impressive point, nod your head in agreement, or, if it seems appropriate, applaud. Sit in a fairly erect but comfortable position. Keep your eyes focused on the speaker. Remember that listening-observing is an active process; use the energy necessary for efficient receiving.

D. Avoid Obvious Demonstrations of Disapproval. A speaker is no better than his audience permits him to be. In social conversations, interviews, and in telephone speaking, negative attitudes on the part of one person can make successful communication impossible. In public performances the indifference or hostility of a significant portion of an audience may affect adversely both the thought processes and the delivery of the speaker. Obvious demonstrations of disapproval are insulting to the other members of the audience as well as to the speaker. By making the communicator's task more difficult, the negative auditors reduce the profit others may receive. Evident indifference on the part of a few makes concentration more difficult for others, even if they wish to pay attention. If the speaker is doing his best, he is entitled to a courteous reception. Avoid such manifestations of disapproval as yawning, stretching, frowning, smirking, drumming fingers on a chair, shuffling feet, unnecessary coughing, reading from a magazine or newspaper, frequent shifts of posture, derisive laughter, talking or whispering, and staring vacantly out the window. Of course, only the boor resorts to boos and catcalls.

E. Except Under Unusual Circumstances, Do Not Fake Attention. Several students were bragging about their ability to camouflage inattention. One claimed that he could go to sleep while keeping his eyes focused on the lecturer. Another stated that she deliberately sat behind a large football player. Periodically she would move her head to one side and smile animatedly at the professor as though fascinated by the lecture. Then she would gradually draw back to her shelter behind her bulky classmate where she could daydream undetected. A third said that she spent class time writing letters, instead of taking notes. Were the professors fooled? Possibly, but probably not. In the classroom and elsewhere, the successful faking of attention is exceedingly difficult. Since listening-observing is an active process the body responds appropriately by providing an increased flow of adrenalin, a higher muscle tonus, a somewhat faster heart beat, and so forth. Likewise, the passivity of inattention may be reflected in the glazed stare, vacant facial set, limp body, and so on. When taken in the aggregate, the covert signals emanating from the auditor usually report the degree to which he is attending.

F. Make Allowances for Deficiencies in the Speaker's Delivery and Appearance. Many persons permit a personal distaste for a speaker's manner of presentation or his physical appearance to interfere with effective listening-observing. Although such limitations and deficiencies on the part of the speaker may render listening-observing more difficult, they do not necessarily affect the logical worth of what is said. If each of us would make an objective evaluation of our own appearance and speech skills, we would probably be more sympathetic toward others.

Unfortunately, some persons unfairly contrast the amateur, inexperienced speaker with the professional performer on radio or television. In comparison to a network announcer, many of our most brilliant and most important citizens appear deficient in oral communication. Furthermore, few men speakers possess the youthful handsomeness of an Eddie Fisher, and few women have the sophisticated charm of a Betty Furness or a Laraine Day. Such shortcomings, if they may be so catalogued, do not impair the wisdom or the importance of the spoken message.

Avoid permitting dialects, grammatical errors, or inefficient use of language to condition you emotionally against a speaker or his message. Also, resist being negatively influenced by such physical factors as the width of the nose, the shape or size of the ears, facial blemishes, scars, height, or girth. Except for his weight, a person can do relatively little to alter physical characteristics. It is illogical and unfair to discriminate against a person for peculiarities beyond his control. Naturally, if a speaker dresses inappropriately or is not well groomed, one might question his discernment in other regards. Nevertheless, one should give him an objective hearing.

FOSTERING CONCENTRATION

A. Remember That Listening-Observing Is an Active Process. As the rather tired proverb puts it, "Nothing worth having comes without effort." Except in instances when the duration of the communication is short, the speaker unusually skillful, or the subject especially interesting, effective listening-observing is hard work. The processes of analysis, evaluation, and synthesis require mental effort of a high order. While no completely painless methods exist, the following suggestions may facilitate concentration.

B. If Possible, Read, Talk, and Think About the Topic Beforehand. Precondition yourself to listen-observe by acquiring general information about the subject. In addition, seek relationships between the topic and your primary fields of interest, academic specialties, general background of knowledge, cultural needs, and so forth. If you possess some information about the subject and see significant relationships to your interests, you will experience less difficulty in concentration.

C. Select a Suitable Seat for Listening and Observing. In social conversation, choose a comfortable seat where you can see and hear the other speaker(s) easily; avoid sitting in a draft or in a light glare. In radio and television listening, sit at the proper distance from the set for good viewing and/or listening; adjust all necessary dials and the lighting of the room beforehand; seek to prevent or reduce interfering noises. At public performances, arrive sufficiently early to select your seat; in general, sit in the central part of the auditorium, toward the front; try to avoid sitting behind posts, in acoustically dead spots, in light glare, or close to the entrance doors.

D. Minimize Distractions. When possible, reduce or eliminate distractions; when this is impossible, attempt to ignore them and work harder to grasp what is being said.

E. Recognize That, Like Reading, Listening-Observing Has Various Purposes or Objectives Which Require Different Degrees of Concentration. Each of the three general purposes of communication, to entertain, to inform, and to persuade, requires a somewhat different type of listening-observing.

1. Listening-observing for entertainment. Ordinarily our basic purpose is enjoyment when we engage in conversation and when we listen to humorous after-dinner speeches, variety shows on radio and television, popular movies, plays, and soap operas. This type of listening-observing usually requires little if any forced concentration. We attend because it is a pleasure to do so.

2. Listening-observing for information. Usually this is the type of listening-observing done during classroom lectures, newscasts, conferences, reports at board meetings, the reading of the minutes, and so on. Understanding and retention are the primary goals of informative speaking.

3. Listening-observing to form judgments. When speaking on controversial subjects, the advocate attempts to convince his audience, deepen existing beliefs and feelings, or impel action. Persuasive speaking presents the greatest challenge to the listener-observer. Most of us react emotionally rather than intellectually to discussions of controversial issues. To form rational judgments, the effective listener-observer should attempt to be objective, analytical, and evaluative.

The remainder of this chapter will concern the two more difficult purposes of listening-observing: to acquire information and to form judgments.

F. Keep Mentally Alert. According to some experimenters, the mind of the listener-observer works about four times as rapidly as the average person talks. Utilize this ratio to promote a better understanding and a more accurate evaluation of what the speaker is proposing. (1) *Correlate the speaker's ideas with your own thinking and experiences.* For instance, if the speaker discusses crowd psychology, supplement and compare what he says with your own recollections of crowd behavior at football games, at bus stops during rush hours, and so on. Reflect whether the speaker's evidence corresponds with what you have heard or read. Formulate questions or comments to offer during the forum period. (2) A correlative of the first point is to *analyze and evaluate the speaker's evidence and reasoning* (see pages 200–205). (3) *Attempt to chart the course of the speech* (see page 208). (4) *Make mental summaries or take notes* (see page 209).

BEING OBJECTIVE

A. Attempt to Be Objective Toward the Speaker. (1) As previously suggested, *be charitable toward the speaker's appearance or deficiencies of delivery.* (2) *Although you should consider who the speaker is and what interest groups he may represent, give him a fair hearing.* You would be unwise to accept the position of Aristotle that an audience should give no thought to the previous character or reputation of a speaker. Nevertheless, you should not permit favorable, or hostile, prejudgments about a speaker to prevent a careful analysis of what he says.

B. Attempt to Be Objective Toward the Speaker's Message. Because we have attitudes toward everything of significant meaning in our lives and because we listen-observe largely in terms of our previous language and life experiences, it would be unrealistic to urge you to abandon all prejudgments while attending to oral communication. However, you should recognize your prejudices and attempt to keep them in check. If carried to extremes, the hardening of the attitudes may be a disservice to your intellectual growth and to the well-being of your country.

In listening to a speaker on a controversial issue, attempt to (1) *React intellectually rather than emotionally.* Prejudices are emotional prejudgments. When a person's emotions become strongly stimulated, he is no longer a seeker of truth. Inevitably he assumes the role of a defender, an advocate of a previously accepted judgment. (2) *Listen accurately, without distorting the speaker's message.* Sometimes the will to believe is so strong that the listeners may not "hear" qualifying phrases, may subconsciously add material they wish the person had said, or may otherwise misconstrue the intention of the speaker. Sometimes, of course, inept phrasing by the speaker promotes deliberate or subconscious misinterpretations. (3) *Avoid constructing refutations during the presentation.* Do not deny the possibility of merit in another's proposals. After an intellectual evaluation of all the evidence offered, construct all the rebuttals you desire. (4) As is shown in the next section, *be analytical and evaluative but not hyper- or hypo-critical.*

BEING ANALYTICAL AND EVALUATIVE

Because of its power to inform and to mold opinion, effective speaking should be the goal of every student. However, a course in speech fundamentals should teach more than rhetorical techniques and practices. It should present an ethical philosophy for the beginning speaker and should provide the skills by which the student can analyze and evaluate the oral communication about him for his own protection and for the preservation of democratic liberties.

All of the elements of our socio-economic structure—education, industry, business, government, the courts, the family—depend upon the ethical use of effective language. Unfortunately, however, speakers are not always ethical or intelligent. Sometimes speech serves as the efficient servant of the fraudulent advertiser, the political shyster, and the demagogue. What was the most important single agent in the transformation of the National Socialist Movement from an idea into a dictatorial ruling power in Germany? According to Adolf Hitler, it was the power of the spoken word. In a series of illuminating studies, Ross Scanlan reports that "From the very beginning, from the summer of 1919 when Hitler joined the seven-man nucleus of the German Workers Party and took charge of its first efforts at propaganda, down to the latter part of World War II when the tremendous edifice of the Third Reich was about to crash in ruins, the speaker was the Party's chief propagandist." In his belief that public speaking represented the best channel to influence the popular mind, Hitler developed the most elaborate party speaker system in world history. Throughout the existence of Nazism, the official party speaker system "kept a central position in the Party's propaganda machinery." [1]

By the very nature of its democratic philosophy of free speech our society provides an avenue for its own possible destruction. The demagogue never states baldly and honestly, "I am an evil man with malicious motives who seeks to destroy democratic ideals." Instead, he employs the devious methods of character assassination, fabrication, and distortion of evidence. In addition to the demagogue, many other types of persuaders attempt to sell us "a bill of goods." Dishonest advocates and mouthpieces for unethical causes appear on public platforms, speak over the airwaves, and frequent stores, offices, courtrooms, and studios. At the time of this writing, many persons are purchasing filter cigarettes partly because of misleading advertising. They believe that filters may eliminate cancer-producing agents from the smoke. Scientific tests have demonstrated, however, that present filters fail to eliminate harmful ingredients. Furthermore, one of the most popular brands of filter cigarettes passes more nico-

---

[1] Ross Scanlan, "The Nazi Party Speaker System," *Speech Monographs*, August, 1949, pp. 82–97; "The Nazi Party Speaker System, II," *Speech Monographs*, June, 1950, pp. 134–148; "The Nazi Rhetorician," *The Quarterly Journal of Speech*, December, 1951, pp. 430–440; "Adolf Hitler and the Technique of Mass Brainwashing," *The Rhetorical Idiom* (Ithaca, N. Y.: Cornell University, 1958), Donald C. Bryant, ed.

tine into the mouth than do the standard filterless cigarettes. The effective listener-observer might adopt as a warning motto the Latin phrase *caveat emptor:* "Let the buyer beware." Apply intelligent caution in purchasing products and in accepting ideas and philosophies.

A. Analyze and Evaluate the Speaker. Preserving an open mind does not preclude an obligation to analyze and evaluate the speaker. Such an estimation may be essential to an accurate appraisal of his message. In assaying the worth and reliability of a speaker, first recognize that you tend to be more receptive to ideas advanced by persons whom you like and admire; conversely you tend to be more critical of proposals advanced by persons whom you dislike or distrust. Second, ask yourself such questions as: (1) *What is the source of the speaker's information?* Is he in a position to know first-hand about the subject, or is he interpreting the reports of others? Does his academic, professional, business, or other training make him an authority on the subject? (2) *What is the speaker's reputation for accuracy of judgment? Objectivity? Reliability?* To some extent, we can predict the value of what a speaker says today by what he has said and done in the past. (3) *Why is the speaker addressing me on this subject?* Can ulterior motives reasonably be attributed to him? If I act upon his suggestions, will he, his company, his political party, be benefited? Is he a paid advocate or spokesman such as the national chairman of a political party, a sales representative of a lumber supply company, a football coach, an attorney for an insurance company, or an official of the AFL-CIO, NAM, AMA, or the NEA? (4) *Does the speaker appear candid and sincere?* Careful listening-observing may detect subtle indications in the speaker's oral or physical delivery which belie his words. Observe especially whether he attempts to conceal weak points or adverse evidence and whether he answers questions in a straightforward manner. (5) *Does the speaker seem to be a person of good will?* Much can be judged by a speaker's attitudes toward himself, his audience, the occasion, his subject, and toward society. If he evidences vindictiveness and acrimony toward his opponents, perhaps his prejudices may impair his reliability. Especially in discussional or conversational situations, if a person fails to demonstrate respect for your ideas, perhaps such discourtesy indicates an opinionated, unreasoning mind. (6) *Does the speaker substitute the techniques of demagoguery* (discussed in the following section) *for logical evidence?*

B. Analyze and Evaluate the Speaker's Message. In listening to informative and persuasive speaking, follow these guides:

1. As a rule, attempt to acquire ideas rather than individual facts. Factual evidence is used to develop, clarify, or make persuasive a speaker's major ideas. Although you should evaluate all of the facts presented, do not concentrate upon them to the extent that you lose track of the important viewpoints.

2. Distinguish between the important and the less important. All of the information given will not be of equal signficance. In a well-constructed presentation, the speaker organizes his thinking into a few trenchant propositions, major topics, main steps, or essential arguments. Under these first-degree headings he groups his supporting ideas and evidence. Familiarity with the standard patterns of organization (see Chapters 12 and 18) will enable you to estimate more accurately the relative importance of the materials offered.

3. Analyze and evaluate the logical content of what is said. Recently the small town of Norwich, New York, witnessed an unusual trial. Arraigned in court, a World War II veteran pleaded innocent to a charge of drunken driving. As presented to the jury, the evidence against him seemed conclusive. The traffic officers testified that when he was arrested, "his eyes were glassy, his speech thick, and his walk unsure." Furthermore, at the police station he had failed the usual tests of sobriety. He had been unable to pick up a coin from the floor or to blow up a balloon. "Do you admit the accuracy of the officers' report?" the judge asked. Woods nodded his head affirmatively. Yet, within a few minutes the jury returned a verdict of "not guilty." Did this decision represent another failure of the jury system? No.

Weaving slightly and speaking with difficulty, Woods explained in his defense that during his war service in the South Pacific he had sustained twenty-seven injuries. Perhaps his eyes had looked glassy. One of them was an artificial substitute for an eye lost in battle. His speech was thick because wounds had left his throat partially paralyzed. He could not stoop to pick up the coin because a bone-graft operation had failed to restore full use of a shattered leg bone. He had failed to blow up the balloon because injuries had destroyed much of his lung capacity. Of course, this is an unusual case. Nevertheless it demonstrates the necessity for considering a problem from every angle and for examining all evidence carefully and fully before making up our minds. For an analysis of the appropriate use of reasoning and evidence, see Chapter 13.

4. Beware of specific techniques of propaganda. The propagandist and the demagogue distort factual evidence and substitute emotional appeals for logic. Frequently such an advocate so skillfully entwines propaganda and logic that an identification and analysis of factual content may become exceedingly difficult. As a critical listener-observer, beware of overt appeals to passions, feelings, and prejudices. Even when you agree with the speaker, refuse to be carried along on a purely emotional current. Apply the checks of logical thinking: What are the facts? Do the speaker's conclusions fit the facts? Am I letting my own prejudgments make me hypo- or hyper-critical?

Here are some of the more common tricks of the propagandists.

a. THE HALF-TRUTH AND THE BIG-LIE. In using the vicious technique of the half-truth, the unethical persuader (1) presents as completely true a statement (2) which is not true (3) but which contains enough elements of factual material (4) to make it seem plausible. The half-truth puts the victim on the defensive and forces him into sometimes involved explanations. Example: Rosemary and Betty were employed in the same office. Their friends knew that Betty rode to and from work every day in Rosemary's car. The two girls had a quarrel and Rosemary spread the story that Betty was a "moocher" who had never offered to pay for her transportation. When the report reached her, Betty was hurt and perplexed as to how she could defend herself. What were the facts? Betty had *not* offered to pay for her rides. To have done so, she thought, would have commercialized an act of friendship. However, she had more than repaid Rosemary by buying her lunches, taking her to the movies, and so forth. Unfortunately, when persons asked her, "Well, did you or did you not offer to pay Rosemary?" Betty could only answer, "No, but. . . ." Some persons listened only long enough to hear the "No." If the unscrupulous person offers a series of half-truths, the non-thinker may be induced to believe that "where there is smoke there must be fire." The half-truth device is a convenient method by which the trickster can manufacture wisps of smoke to blind the non-critical and those who have a will to believe.

The major difference between the half-truth and the big-lie is the relative magnitude of the fabrication. The big-lie is cut out of whole cloth. It is a complete falsehood. To the credulous the monstrous untruth holds a fascination. As Hitler pointed out, "in the size of the lie there is always contained a certain factor of credibility." One of his most enduring convictions was that "the great masses of a people . . . more easily fall victim to a great lie than to a small one." Unfortunately, the big-lie did not originate with Hitler, nor did it die with him.

b. Irrelevant Personal Attacks. A frequently used device to divert attention from a deficiency in logical proof is to abuse or ridicule an adversary. Nothing is too sacred or irrelevant for the demagogue. If his own honesty or reasoning is questioned, he may avoid answering the charge by attacking his critic's personality, physique, age, mentality, war record, experience, intestinal fortitude, religion, race, relatives, and so forth. The propagandist believes, and rightly so, that if he introduces enough diversionary charges he may succeed in muddling the entire controversy. Clearly the critical listener-observer should attempt to determine when a personal attack is relevant and when it is not. In any event, insist upon the speaker's offering evidence and logical reasoning.

c. NAME-CALLING. A close correlative of the previous point, name-calling is an attempt to discredit or ridicule a person by affixing to him an objectionable label. In calling an individual a left-winger, a reactionary, a fellow-traveler, a bureaucrat, an egg head, or a Park Avenue money-grubber, the speaker seeks to link his victim with something the audience will probably consider undesirable. Unless the speaker proves that his labeling is logical and accurate, he is appealing to the emotions rather than to the intellect.

d. SLANTED LANGUAGE. It is true that colorful words heighten interest, and that any persuasive exhortation involves slanted language. However, the use of highly emotional language should be tempered by a respect for adequate evidence and logical reasoning. The insidious effect of directive language is that listeners may be guided non-critically to the conclusion desired by the speaker. Learn to distinguish between slanted language and informative language. The latter is free from inferences and judgments; it consists exclusively of objective reports for the purpose of conveying information. This is an example of informative language: "The defendant turned slightly. His eyes moved from the district attorney to the revolver and returned to the attorney. His reply was a given in a quiet, slow manner." By substituting loaded words for objective ones, the material can be slanted against the defendant: "The once convicted murderer wilted. His eyes shifted uncertainly away from the State's attorney to the murder weapon and reluctantly slid back to the attorney. His reply came in a strained croak." Slanted in favor of the defendant, the passage becomes: "The tired old man leaned forward. His level gaze moved from the arrogant young prosecutor to the alleged weapon and returned to confront his tormentor. His reply was given in a quiet, deliberate manner."

e. BAND WAGON. As Wilfred Trotter points out in his *Instincts of the Herd in Peace and War,* we dislike physical or mental solitude and are more sensitive to the opinions of others than to any other single influence. To a considerable extent, our social, moral, and political concepts as well as our fashions in clothes, automobiles, and entertainment are determined by the unwillingness to be "different." Advertisers, politicians, and other advocates frequently seek to capitalize upon our herd instincts by creating the impression of universal support for their products or ideas. The persuadee is encouraged to feel that if he does not buy or accept he will be isolated as an outsider. The bandwagon technique substitutes for logical consideration the implied plea: "Come on, everybody is doing it. Get on the band wagon before it passes you by. Don't be left out."

f. TRANSFER. This trick attempts to create favorable attitudes by coupling an idea or product with emotional sources of prestige, reverence, or authority. A familiar practice is to urge the acceptance of an idea because of its previous endorsement by some distinguished forefather(s). The advocate does not admit that catastrophic changes in conditions might invalidate the advice of the past. Furthermore, persons who use this "argument from antiquity" frequently have an extremely hazy or distorted understanding of the historical reference. Most students will recall that until very recently isolationists and nationalists were still using (and perverting) Washington's warning against "entangling alliances." In another type of transfer, speakers may attempt an irrelevant or even illogical transference in linking their causes to famous people, the home, the church, the flag, the Bible, Americanism, military heroes, and so forth. Examples: Van Johnson smokes Luckies; La Comtesse Alain de la Falaise uses Pond's Cold Cream; politician "X" grew up on a farm; politician "Y" enjoys romping with his grandchildren; politician "Z" is a Rock of Gibraltar, a veritable Pillar of Hercules. Of course many attempts at transfer are ethically acceptable. However, those which are intended to circumvent logic should be recognized as such.

g. BEGGING THE QUESTION. When a person "begs the question," he assumes the point at issue instead of proving it. If a speaker argues that an expansion of the reciprocal-trade-agreements program should be avoided because it would represent a swing toward free trade, he should prove, not assume, two points: (1) the program is a movement toward free trade, and (2) such a movement is undesirable. Sometimes the reasoning of an advocate moves in a circle. He presents a series of unproved assertions which eventually return to the starting point and, in identical or synonymous form, affirm the original proposition. Example: an expansion of the reciprocal-trade-agreements program should be avoided because it would represent a swing toward free trade and because any policy that would reduce tariffs should be avoided.

h. SHIFTING THE BURDEN OF PROOF. A speaker who advances a contention must assume the burden of proof. He cannot logically shift to an opponent the task of disproof. The ignorance or inability of the persuadee to disprove an argument does not necessarily indicate that the proposition is valid. Examples: A psychology student asserted, "You should believe in extra-sensory perception."

His companion replied, "I don't know much about it, but it doesn't make sense to me."

"It doesn't, huh? Well, prove that there isn't such a thing as extra-sensory perception or admit that I'm right."

Obviously the psychology student failed to accept the responsibility for proving his assertion. In the law courts a man is assumed innocent until proved guilty. If an accountant proposes to his employer a method for cutting costs, he will be expected to prove the efficacy of his plan. As an effective listener-observer, remember that invariably he who originally proposes or denies must accept the responsibility of proof or disproof.

REMEMBERING WHAT YOU HAVE HEARD AND SEEN

When Dr. Roscoe Pound, a former Dean of the Harvard Law School, was complimented on possessing a marvelous natural memory, he replied: "Nonsense! I remember because I must. I worked to develop my memory." The ability to remember what one hears and sees is an important asset to students, teachers, executives, salesmen, lawyers, engineers, doctors, housewives—to everyone. However, unlike Dr. Pound, most persons have not cultivated their powers of retention.

Certainly the improvement of memory would be facilitated by an exact understanding of how the mind functions. Although interest in the subject probably predates the Grecian worship of Mnemosyne [2] as the goddess of memory, unfortunately science cannot yet explain the physiological processes of thought and recall. At the present time we are certain of relatively little more than this: thinking depends upon memories; memories are patterns of nerve cells in the brain; when the brain thinks, complicated electro-chemical changes take place.

According to some authorities, neural impulses follow along pathways or patterns of nerve cells which may be called neurograms. Some neurograms are thought to exist at birth and to be responsible for innate or inborn reactions having to do with vegetative processes and with basic emotions. Other neurograms are believed to be acquired through experience or learning. The more we learn, the more neural patterns we develop. Memory involves the retracing of previously acquired neurograms and is dependent upon the number and the firmness of the pathways. Forgetting results from the fading of neurograms.

What does this mean to the student who wishes to improve his ability to remember what he sees and hears? In a somewhat loose sense, memory may be considered the product of both physiological and psychological processes. Probably we can do nothing to improve the actual physiological workings of the brain. However, we can improve the psychological aspects of remembering (1) by developing our powers of observation and concentration; (2) by utilizing effective methods of review and repetition; (3) by

[2] It is perhaps indicative of the importance the Greeks accorded memory that their mythology also considered Mnemosyne to be the mother of the nine Muses— the goddesses of song, poetry, and the arts and sciences.

improving our techniques of analysis, classification, and association. Now let us put these general principles into specific application.

A. Remembering Names and Persons. Do you experience difficulty in remembering names when engaging in conversation, telephoning, interviewing, or in forum and parliamentary speaking? If so, try these suggestions. (1) In the case of introductions, make certain that you understand the name. Unfortunately many persons fail to enunciate clearly when performing introductions. Therefore, concentrate intently. If necessary, ask that the name be repeated. Once you have distinctly understood the name, say it immediately, as "How do you do, Mr. Powers?" Use the name several times during the conversation and in saying goodby, as "I enjoyed meeting you, Mr. Powers. I'll look forward to seeing you at the Lodge." (2) You may find helpful the practice of forming associations between the person's name and that of some *famous person* (Wilson, McCormick, Williams), *familiar object* (wood, car, head), *color* (gray, red, brown), *animal* (wolf, fox, deer), *season of the year* (winter, summer, fall), or *occupation* (tailor, fisherman, gardener). Also, this linkage system operates effectively for names of multi-syllables such as Halstead (hall), Mayflower (May-flower), Stringfellow (string-fellow), Fogarty (fog). (3) Carry with you a pocket-size notebook. When appropriate, as in telephoning and sometimes in parliamentary speaking, record immediately the name you wish to remember. In all other cases in which retention is important, record the name as soon as possible after the meeting. Recall will be facilitated by including pertinent details such as his title, place of employment, where and under what circumstances you met him, and identifying personal characteristics (see below). Periodically review the contents of the notebook.

Perhaps you have trouble in remembering persons whom you have seen in conferences or discussions, or whom you have met in social or business conversations. If so, experiment with these techniques of directed observation, association, and repetition: (1) Analyze his facial characteristics. For example, is the face round, square, rectangular, slender, or fat? Does he wear glasses? Is the nose broad, thin, pug, humped, or hooked? Is the forehead low, high, slanted, or marked by furrows? Are the ears unusually large or small? Do they flare out from the head or lie close to the skull? (2) Observe the person's hair. What is the color? Is the hair heavy, receding, or gone? Is it wavy or straight? Is it parted on the side, top, or not at all. (3) Notice the individual's skin color and complexion. (4) Analyze his general appearance. What is his approximate age? Is he exceptionally tall, short, stout, thin, or muscular? Is there anything unusual about his posture or his selection of clothes or jewelry? (4) Listen to the person's voice for unusual features of quality, pitch, flexibility, or pronunciation. (5) Attempt to associate the person with the circumstances of the meeting. (6) Record such pertinent data as you wish in the notebook mentioned previously.

B. Remembering Ideas and Factual Data. Retention of ideas and factual material is assisted by being co-operative with the speaker, by concentrating, by being objective, by being analytical and evaluative, and by making use of summaries and notes.

As was stated earlier, the speed of your thinking processes is several times the rate of vocal utterance. Therefore, you usually can make mental summaries during the presentation. Periodically review the major lines of argument and the most significant evidence presented up to that point. Be alert for transitional statements such as "The third step . . . ," "Another reason is . . . ," "Furthermore . . . ," and "On the other hand. . . ." Intimate familiarity with the standard methods of organization will enable you to review more effectively the course of a speech or a discussion. For example, in problem-solving situations apply the formulas discussed in Chapters 12 and 18: What has been said concerning the nature of the problem, its severity, extent, and causes? What are the proposed solutions? What are the strengths and weaknesses of each? What specific proof has been submitted that a given solution could solve the problem or could be put into effect?

At the conclusion of the oral presentation, promote retention by making a mental or written recapitulation. A minimum final summary answers such questions as: What was the speaker's primary purpose? What were his main ideas or arguments? Was any especially significant evidence presented? If so, how can I link this factual data to items or topics with which I am familiar? Should I verify certain evidence before accepting it? Should I re-examine my own thinking or do some reading on the subject? What meaning or value does the speech have for me?

If essential that you retain the information, take notes during the presentation. Judicious recordings can be of inestimable value; unskilled note-taking can be detrimental. The primary function of notes is to aid the listener-observer in reconstructing the oral communication immediately upon its conclusion. At that time he can review the entries and, if necessary, can reorganize and rewrite them. Observe these *"Don't's":* Do not write voluminous notes. Usually avoid reporting verbatim quotations. Do not try to arrange a detailed outline of what is being said. (Especially in group discussions, oral communication may not follow a precise pattern of thought.) Follow these *"Do's":* Record major ideas. Use abbreviations when possible. Take skeleton notes, which can be expanded following the presentation. Use key words or cue words, rather than complete sentences. Record essential thoughts rather than isolated facts. If recording statistics, round-off figures to approximate accuracy.

SUMMARY

In the cycle of communication, the listener-observer is co-equal in importance with the speaker. Although most of us have not sufficiently developed our capacity for effective listening-observing, we can improve by following these suggestions: (1) Be co-operative and courteous. (2) Concentrate. (3) Be objective. (4) Be analytical and evaluative. (5) Make a systematic attempt to remember what you have seen and heard. A conscientious application of these rules will bring rich personal rewards.

EXERCISES AND ASSIGNMENTS

1. Before attending a class which in the past has seemed especially dull try to develop an anticipation for hearing the lecture. Think of all the possible ways that the lecture could be meaningful to your career or to your personal development. Tell yourself that you are going to get the maximum benefit from the class period. During the lecture attempt to listen actively, to feel positive toward the instructor and the subject, and to be a sympathetic listener-observer. At the end of the period determine whether you received more from that lecture than from previous ones.

2. Deliberately engage in conversation with a person you dislike. Attempt to be friendly and to concentrate on what he says. In a short talk explain to the class whether your improved manner bettered your relations with this individual, whether you found him to be a worthwhile person, and whether you received a positive sense of satisfaction from the meeting.

3. Attend a debate, lecture, or forum where you will hear comments or speeches with which you may disagree. Follow the suggestions for promoting objectivity. Give to the class a three- or four-minute account of this experiment, including these points: (a) the speaker's central idea; (b) his chief arguments; (c) the most significant evidence presented in support of these arguments; (d) your evaluation of the speaker's evidence and reasoning.

4. Attend a public meeting and record all examples you see of poor listening-observing. Describe your observations to the class.

5. Spend an evening listening to commercials on radio or television. In a speech of about four minutes, present to the class examples of both ethical and unethical advertising. For each example give reasons for your classification.

6. Carry with you a notebook and record every misuse of reasoning or of evidence heard during an entire day. Offer your findings to the class in a short talk.

7. Select a person in public life who in your judgment personifies the highest ethical standards in the use of evidence and reasoning. In a four-minute speech explain the reasons for your selection.

8. Select a person in public life who you feel substitutes demagoguery for logical reasoning and evidence. In a four-minute speech, explain how this individual misuses language.

9 ❧❧ *The Audience and the Occasion*

Earlier chapters have stressed the importance of the receiver in the cycle of communication and have explained that the purpose of speaking is to effect some response in the listener, that is, to inform, entertain, or persuade him. This chapter analyzes in detail the psychological nature of the audience and of the environment in which oral communicaiton takes place.

THE AUDIENCE

Norman Thomas suggests that "successful speech requires a speaker to come to proper terms with his audience as well as his subject. Success or failure in this respect marks the difference between speaking as a satisfaction—sometimes almost an intoxication—and as a dull and dreary task." [1] How does one "come to proper terms" with one's listeners? By first understanding their intellectual and emotional needs and then adjusting one's message and presentation accordingly. At this point some students might wonder: "Is all that sort of thing really necessary? Why can't I just stand up on my hind legs and speak my piece?" For a reply, consider this statement penned in 1760 by John Lawson: "If our hearers were always serious, attentive, knowing, and unprejudiced, we should have nothing to do but to lay the truth before them in its own genuine shape; but as men actually are, we find it necessary, not only to show them what is right, but to make use of all the skill we have, to induce them steadfastly to behold it."

[1] Norman Thomas, "Random Reflections on Public Speaking," *The Quarterly Journal of Speech,* April, 1954, p. 148.

Unfortunately, you cannot glean a thorough understanding of human nature from this brief treatment, nor even from a full-length tome on the subject. To understand human nature is to understand life. You can accomplish that only through experiencing as many of life's facets as possible by means of personal observation and wide reading. The purpose of the following discussion is to point out several limitations of human nature as they pertain to the speaker-audience relationship and to help you analyze and draw inferences from the characteristics of your potential listeners.

A. Understanding the Limitations of Human Nature. It is no disparagement to admit that mankind is imperfect. To believe otherwise is to be unrealistic.

1. We should recognize that man possesses limited objectivity. Seneca's frequently used definition, "Man is a reasoning animal," should be amended to: "Man is a complex being whose behavior is characterized by varying degrees of rationality." The syndicated columnist, Sydney J. Harris, suggests that because man "resists thinking as much as possible . . . human life is a state of perpetual tension between our intellectual need to probe reality and our emotional desire to escape it." Perhaps it is belaboring the obvious to add that man tends to judge first and then to examine the evidence, that a higher correlation sometimes exists between belief and desire than between belief and evidence, and that wants, ambitions, prejudgments, and culture patterns often control reason, rather than the reverse. Too frequently our attitudes can be epitomized by the phrase, "These are the conclusions upon which I base my facts." Probably few if any of our decisions are based upon reasoning purged of *all* emotional coloring. Objective thinking is difficult and, because pure logic has no respect for custom patterns or beliefs, frequently is disturbing. Therefore, we tend to avoid analytical reasoning when emotional or habitual behavior can answer our needs. A paradoxical characteristic of human nature is that, despite our reluctance to use objective reasoning, everyone gives lip service to it. Everyone *wants* to be rational, and possibly even the most opinionated and illogical person believes that he *is* rational.

H. A. Overstreet was not original in stating that in most persons "reason lies dormant while something else, which is far from reason, takes over." Such concepts are as old as recorded history. To Demosthenes, only the Athenians were sufficiently mature to be freemen. Alexander Hamilton considered pure democracy to be the "real disease" of the country: "Take mankind for what they are, and what are they governed by? Their passions . . . turbulent and changing, they seldom judge or determine right." The founding fathers of our Constitution so distrusted the reasoning abilities of the great masses that they prohibited the direct election of the President and U.S. Senators. Woodrow Wilson wrote: "We speak of this as an age in which mind is monarch, but I take it for granted that, if that is true, mind is one of those modern monarchs who reign but do govern. As a matter of fact, the world is governed in every generation by a great House of Commons made up of the passions; and we can only be careful to see to it that the handsome passions are in the majority." In his presidential address to the American Historical Society, Merle Curti expressed the views of many modern educators when he said: "Americans have not been taught to understand what critical thinking is." [2]

It should be emphasized that limited objectivity is a characteristic of *all* men—not merely of the unlettered, the unthinking, or the unwise. Perhaps Demosthenes, Hamilton, Wilson, and Curti were being subjectively smug in their sweeping indictments of the rest of mankind.

Not only is man reluctant to think objectively, but he also often displays a strong desire to deny to others the freedom to speak, read, or write on various sensitive subjects. Let us briefly examine some of the results of a study which the editors of *Look* term "one of the most searching surveys of public opinion ever

---

[2] For an eloquent defense of popular judgment, see Adlai Stevenson's address opening his 1956 Persidential campaign, *Vital Speeches*, October 1, 1956, pp. 755–756.

conducted in the United States." This investigation was planned by several distinguished Americans and was managed by the National Opinion Research Center and the American Institute of Public Opinion (Gallup poll). Interviews, each of which lasted over an hour, were conducted with 6,500 carefully selected Americans. Among their findings, the researchers determined that only 58 per cent of the public would permit a person to advocate publicly the government ownership of railroads and major industries; 35 per cent believed that books favoring such government ownership should be removed from the public library (13 per cent had no opinion on this question); 54 per cent would not permit an advocate of such government ownership to teach in a college. The survey showed that 60 per cent of the public would not permit a person to speak publicly against churches and religion; 60 per cent favored the removal from the public library of a book against churches and religion; 84 per cent would refuse to permit an opponent of religion to teach in a college. Also, the researchers found that only 70 per cent of the public would accord the right of free speech to a person whose loyalty had been criticized but who had sworn under oath that he had never been a Communist.[3]

We can safely conclude that large numbers do not concur with publisher John S. Knight's paraphrase, "Ideas can be dangerous but the suppression of ideas is fatal," or with Thomas Jefferson's proclamation of intellectual freedom for the University of Virginia: "The University will be based upon the illimitable freedom of the human mind, for here we are not afraid to follow truth wherever it may lead, nor to tolerate any error as long as reason is left free to combat it."

In spite of man's emotionality and apparent intolerance, obviously he is not bereft of reason. If one dominant feature can be said to characterize human existence, it is the groping, but

[3] Samuel A. Stouffer, *Communism, Conformity, and Civil Liberties* (Garden City, New York: Doubleday & Company, Inc., 1955). Also, see Edgar F. Borgatta and Jeanne Hulquist, "A Reanalysis of Some Data from Stouffer's *Communism, Conformity, and Civil Liberties,*" *The Public Opinion Quarterly*, Winter, 1956–1957, pp. 631–650.

irresistible surge from superstition and dogmatic ignorance toward understanding and tolerance. This forward progress of the human race has been possible because man has the ability to use analytical reason in the solution of his problems. Man's intellectual capacity has brought us to the beginnings of a wonderful new scientific age in which research in atomic energy, electronics, and medicine promise unprecedented prosperity and health. At the same time, man's reluctance to utilize objective reasoning in the solving of the world's social and political problems has brought us close to the world destruction prophesied in Chapter 8 of The Revelation.

Application: Seated in the audience, the individual represents in microcosm both the capacity and the reluctance of mankind to use reason. Do not expect your listeners to be dispassionate reasoning machines, especially where basic culture patterns, wants, needs, and desires are involved. Perhaps our message can be epitomized by this statement of William Gladstone: "truth is not necessarily loved when seen," and "she is not necessarily seen when shown."

2. We should recognize that man's knowledge and intelligence are limited. General knowledge depends upon retentiveness of memory, intelligence, formal education, intellectual curiosity, energy, and the variety and extent of personal experiences. Viewed in respect to the totality of available information, the most learned of men are merely somewhat less ignorant than the rest of us. Although a well-informed citizenry is the mainstay of democratic government, personal observation and research polls demonstrate conclusively that most of us are poorly informed on current affairs, government, history, geography, and so forth. During the height of interest in the Army-McCarthy hearings when radio, television, and the press were deluging the country with coverage of the affair, the Stouffer pollsters found that 30 per cent of the people interviewed did not know the correct name of any of the senators or congressmen who were investigating Communism—they could not even identify Joseph R. McCarthy. George Gallup estimates that only four out of every ten voters have an "approximate idea" of the meaning of the term "electoral college." Even college students frequently display distressing gaps in general information. Many students and, if Gallup poll findings are accurate, a large majority of the American people cannot answer such questions as: What is the Bill of Rights? What is the difference between the length of the elected term served by U.S. Senators and that served by U.S. Representatives? What is the Bricker Amendment? Who made the statement "with malice toward none; with charity for all"? or "Speak softly and carry a big stick"?

Application: Keep materials easy to understand, especially when addressing an unselected audience. Norman Vincent Peale has pointed out that listeners "want to understand without excessive cerebration." To help his audience follow his message easily, Dr. Peale follows these three criteria in speech preparation: "keep it simple, interesting, and brief." [4] Do not conclude that because the material is clear to you it will therefore be understandable to your listeners. Auditors can absorb only limited amounts of new information during a short speech and they understand best when the speaker connects the unknown with the familiar. Follow the advice of Theodore Parker: "Think with the sage and saint, but talk with common men."

3. We should recognize that man's powers of attention are limited. Undoubtedly, you have already discovered that capturing and maintaining favorable attention is one of the most perplexing problems of speechmaking. Unless you can induce your hearers to give attention to what you are saying, you cannot inform, entertain, or persuade them.

Here are three significant facts about attention: (1) Because of the limitations of our neuromuscular system, we cannot respond to all the stimulation we receive at a given time. Our surroundings, our physical states of being, our memories, our psycho-

---

[4] Eugene E. White and Clair R. Henderlider, "What Norman Vincent Peale Told Us About His Speaking," *The Quarterly Journal of Speech*, December, 1954, pp. 407–416.

logical drives, etc., continuously compete for our attention. From the multiplicity of potential stimuli we must select, either consciously or unconsciously, the ones to which we shall respond. *Application:* One of your basic tasks as a speaker is to serve as a sort of "stimuli selector" for your listeners. Present your material in such a fashion that your auditors will respond to it rather than to the host of competing stimuli. (2) Absolute attention to an unchanging stimulus can be maintained for only a few seconds at a time. As an experiment, attempt to concentrate completely upon the page number at the top of this page. How long can you preserve undivided attention? One, two, or three seconds? If you believe that you have sustained unbroken attention for longer than that, other stimuli have probably intruded into your consciousness and then faded as your concentration upon the number returned. Try the test again. This time did you notice that your attention was not fixed but came in spurts? *Application:* The more your delivery and materials tend toward monotony, the harder it is for listeners to remain attentive. (3) We respond to stimuli in one of two ways, either by voluntary (willed) attention or by involuntary (effortless) attention. A sense of duty, a desire to co-operate, or respect for the speaker may encourage the listener to attempt to follow carefully a boring address. In such cases the task of concentration usually becomes too difficult: attention begins to wane, the good intentions lose their compulsiveness, and sometimes the well-meaning auditor sinks so deeply into sluggish languor that even the knob of a Colonial tithing man could not easily arouse him. Of course, when motivation is unusually high, as in the case of an apprehensive student listening to a pre-examination briefing, one may force oneself to give fairly close attention during an extended discourse. Nevertheless, evidence exists to prove that people learn most rapidly and are most receptive to persuasion when they are genuinely interested. *Application:* To rely upon the voluntary attention of your listeners is to invite somnolence. Make your presentation so interestingly vital that your audience will follow you eagerly, with a minimum of conscious effort.

Although the general limitations of human nature constitute barriers to successful oral communication, they are not insurmountable. You have already learned the importance and methods of adjusting language and vocal and physical delivery to the demands of the speaking situation. In future sections, you will learn how to answer the intellectual and emotional needs of your listeners by organizing and developing your ideas in the most effective logical and psychological manner.

B. Analyze Your Potential Audience. Now that we have examined certain general limitations of human nature as they apply to the speaker-audience relationship, let us look closely at your potential listeners. Perhaps the basic element in effective speaking is the correct analysis and evaluation of those to whom you will talk. Obviously, a speech which is well suited to one audience may be poorly adjusted to another. Recently a civic leader spoke to the P.T.A. organization of a junior high school. His address was so well received that the principal asked him to speak on the same subject to the school assembly. Unfortunately the speaker miscalculated the intellectual and emotional level of junior high school students. The results? His second speech was, in the language of one of the students, "a complete bust." Of course, the analysis of your listeners does not stop when you have prepared and rehearsed your presentation. During your speaking you should be alert to the overt and covert reactions emanating from the audience. As you acquire experience, you will recognize that by keeping your organizational structure elastic you can adjust materials and delivery to the exigencies of the situation. Admittedly, human reactions are sometimes inexplicable, and hidden road blocks to persuasion may frustrate your most careful plans. However, you have a much better chance of achieving your speaking purpose if you carefully estimate the listeners' knowledge of and attitudes toward you and your subject.

How much do the listeners know concerning you and what are their probable attitudes toward you? Do they regard you as an expert in the area covered in your speaking? Do they accept you as a person of good will who is sincerely interested in them and in their problems? Do they know you to be a person of sincerity, honesty, and modesty? If you have been brought in from another city or state to speak at a particular function, you possibly will enjoy somewhat higher prestige than would a local authority of comparable importance. As the grass on the other side of the fence seems greener, so the outside person may appear to be more impressive than a familiar individual. If you have been selected in advance of the speaking date and have received considerable publicity, you will perhaps have higher prestige than if you are a last-minute substitute. The speaker who enjoys high prestige and is well liked can usually accomplish much more with his speech than the speaker whose audience is unimpressed with his qualifications and is unfriendly toward him personally.[5]

How much do your listeners know concerning the subject and what are their probable attitudes toward it? How much background information do they require in order to follow your presentation easily? How much will you have to explain? Will they be eager to listen, uninspired, or disinterested? Will they be favorable to your recommendations? Neutral? Hostile? How much will they accept? How much will you have to prove? Your subject should be within the scope of the hearers' interests, desires, and understanding, and, when consistent with ethics, should be developed according to their capacities and attitudes. If you attempt to inform, your subject must not be too technical or too difficult for your listeners, nor should it to be a topic which is already well understood. Amplifying and clarifying materials must be gauged against the intellectual abilities and the

---

[5] Percy H. Tannenbaum, "Initial Attitude Toward Source and Concept as Factors in Attitude Change through Communication," *The Public Opinion Quarterly*, Summer, 1956, pp. 413–425; Stanley F. Paulson, "The Effects of the Prestige of the Speaker and Acknowledgement of Opposing Arguments on Audience Retention and Shift of Opinion," *Speech Monographs*, November, 1954, pp. 267–271; Franklyn S. Haiman, "An Experimental Study of the Effects of Ethos in Public Speaking," *Speech Monographs*, September, 1949, pp. 190–202; Harold B. Gerard, "The Anchorage of Opinions in Face-to-Face Groups," *Human Relations*, August, 1954, pp. 313–325.

interests of the hearers. What is necessary explanation for one audience may be interest-killing redundancy for another. If you wish to entertain, recognize that a performance which would be a delightful diversion to one group might be agonizing boredom to another. A women's missionary society might regard as obscene the same humor that might send a night club audience into hurricanes of laughter. A lively discourse ridiculing out-dated theories of field-crop production might be highly enter-taining to an agronomists' club but might be wearisome to an engineers' club or to a philosophers' club. If you hope to per-suade, your purpose in speaking should be one which you can reasonably expect to achieve with your listeners, and your major contentions should be selected and developed in light of the attitudes and capacities of the audience. For example, if you were addressing a Knights of Columbus meeting about the problems of India, you would not stress that country's "need" for population limitations.

You can acquire significant clues concerning the knowledge, wants, interests, needs, and attitudes of your listeners by ana-lyzing these audience characteristics: age, sex, size, educational backgrounds, and group affiliations. In the following discussion, the suggestions are intended to be indicative and not prescrip-tive. Obviously any generalizations concerning the intellectual and emotional properties of large groups of persons are subject to numerous exceptions.

1. Age. What range of ages will be represented in your audi-ence? What will be the dominant age group? Different age groups have different problems, desires, attitudes, and behavior characteristics. For the sake of convenience, we shall divide the ages into "young adults" (roughly between the years of seven-teen and thirty), "mature adults" (between thirty and fifty-five years) and "older persons" (over fifty-five years). Naturally, with-in each age group great variations and, not infrequently, contra-dictions occur in the thinking, predispositions, and behavior patterns. Furthermore, the identifying attributes become less sharply defined as one age group merges into another. Thus, the thoughts and actions of a man of twenty-eight may be closer to those of mature adults than to those of the typical young adult. Also, an individual of fifty-eight may exhibit fewer of the characteristics of older persons than those of mature adults.

a. YOUNG ADULTS. Perhaps the key to understanding the character of young adults is found in Aristotle's assertion that youths "have strong desires, and whatever they desire they are prone to do. . . . They are shifting and unsteady in their desires . . . for the longings of youth are keen rather than deep." On the one hand, we can accept as generally true this variation of Alexander Pope's expression, "Youth rushes in where angels fear to tread"; youth is the time for exuberance, enthusiasm, willingness to experiment, impulsive action, easy laughter, and loud applause. On the other hand, we know that to many persons youth is also the time for pronounced feelings of inadequacy, fear, and insecurity, and for the frustrating search for firm goals and anchors; to many, it is a period of introspection, moodiness, and unpredictable behavior. Because young people have had limited experience, they typically possess a smaller body of knowledge than their elders with equivalent formal education, and they tend to underestimate the difficulties and sacrifices entailed in attaining important goals. Since they possess high physical vitality and good health, young people are usually interested in competition, adventure, romance, sex, and sports. Looking forward to many years of zestful living, they are inclined to be more optimistic than older persons and to be less interested in matters of health. To them, the present and the future are more absorbing than the past. They respond well to obvious humor and appeals to pride, loyalty, and direct action.

In recent years much has been said about the alleged trend of American youth toward conservatism and non-critical conformity. Professor Franklyn Haiman says, "I notice . . . during student discussions in the college classroom, that some of the most naive and meaningless expressions of political, social, and religious dogma—comments that would have been carefully dissected by skeptical classmates prior to the Era of the New

Conservatism—are now received with hardly a raised eyebrow." [6] Professor Willis Moore protests that "Among students we discover . . . silence on controversial issues, a marked reluctance to join any but social clubs, neglect of humanitarian causes, and a shunning of classmates who speak or act 'liberal.' " [7] Perhaps critics are correct in their belief that since World War II liberalism and skepticism have gone out of fashion. If so, it is reasonable to assume that the new emphasis upon moderation may have influenced our young people. Various studies indicate that between 1936 and 1956 young adults grew progressively less inclined to vote Democratic in Presidential elections. In 1956, for the first time in at least a quarter-century these phenomena occurred: a majority of young adults voted for the Republican Presidential candidate; even more significantly, probably a higher percentage of young adults voted for Mr. Eisenhower than did mature adults. Of course, we should recognize that Mr. Eisenhower held an especial appeal to young persons and that since 1956 most young voters have returned to their Democratic allegiance.

Although youths may be growing more conservative, they evidence little increase, if any, in interest concerning politics. They seem to be less interested in political matters and to know less about them than their elders; when eligible, they vote less frequently. Today a higher proportion of young adults are church members than formerly, and more seem to be genuinely interested in religion and prayer. Nevertheless, they probably are less well informed and less interested in religion than their elders. Despite charges that youths are illiberal, research studies indicate that young people are more tolerant than older ones of unorthodox political, religious, and social beliefs and are less afflicted with authoritarian attitudes.

b. MATURE ADULTS. Mature adults are in their prime mentally but possess less physical vitality than do young adults. Because

[6] Franklyn S. Haiman, "A New Look at the New Conservatism," *AAUP Bulletin*, Autumn, 1955, p. 451.

[7] Willis Moore, "Causal Factors in the Current Attack on Education," *AAUP Bulletin*, Winter, 1955, p. 622.

they have shouldered responsibilities, they are more sober, more cautious, more analytical, and less trusting than they once were. They now are more interested in health, safety, and security. Their social, economic, political, and religious attitudes and their behavior habits are well established. They are much concerned with acquiring property and power and with maintaining and increasing social status. As Aristotle suggests, "To put it generally: all the valuable qualities which youth and age divide between them are joined in the 'mature adult' and between the respective excesses and defects of youth and age . . . strikes the fitting mean." Despite the basic validity of Aristotle's assertion, the middle years are not free from problems and anxieties. For instance, once over forty-five years of age, workers must increasingly fear the perils of unemployment. According to a 1958 study conducted by the New York Office Executives Association, by the time a man reaches fifty-five nearly 70 per cent of companies will refuse to hire him because of his age.

c. OLDER PERSONS.   Today the average life expectancy is about seventy years. Nearly one out of four Americans is fifty-five or older. For these persons physical processes have slowed considerably. In the past we have theorized that their mental ability also declined steadily after reaching a crest in their twenties. However, such an assumption may be erroneous. According to George K. Bennett, new methods of testing, which reduce the premium on speed, demonstrate that "the peak [of mental ability] may not be reached until sometime in a person's thirties and then may continue on a rather level line into his seventies." [8] Persuasive evidence of the high mental competence of older persons is found in the fact that in such fields as politics, education, medicine, law, business, and the military, a person does not often reach his highest competency until after the age of fifty-five.

[8] Associated Press release, March 30, 1956. Also, see Irving Lorge, "Intelligence and Learning in Aging," in *Aging A Current Appraisal* (Gainesville, Florida: University of Florida Press, 1956), Irving L. Webber, ed.; and M. W. Smith, "Evidences of Potentialities of Older Workers in a Manufacturing Company," *Personnel Psychology*, Spring, 1952, pp. 11–18.

The widely held belief that older persons are more conservative than younger ones is typified by such remarks as "With old age comes a hardening of the attitudes" and "By the age of fifty-five, one settles down into certain well-defined convictions, most of which are wrong." One social scientist, Robert S. Henshaw, has gone so far as to say that "conservatism of opinion varies directly with increasing age in contemporary America." [9] While possibly true as a general rule, such an assertion needs to be interpreted with some elasticity. Some older persons are considerably more liberal than the typical youth. Nevertheless, available evidence indicates that a greater degree of conservatism exists among older persons as a group. For example, between 1936 and 1956 a consistently higher percentage of older persons voted Republican in Presidential elections than did mature or young adults. Older persons probably tend to be more authoritarian in their attitudes than younger ones and to be less tolerant of non-conformists. Also, they tend more to direct their thinking into rigid categories of right and wrong, good and bad, etc. Older persons are more interested than younger ones in "conservative" concerns like religion, prayer, Bible reading, health, safety, and economic security. As the twilight of the sixties deepens into the shadows of the seventies, persons possibly grow less optimistic, laugh less frequently, and tend more and more to live in memories and to cherish traditions. They appear to exhibit lowered psychological plasticity and are inclined to resist changes, especially those which are unexpected, novel, or "radical." [10] In a capsule, new horizons offer somewhat less appeal to older persons than to younger ones; characteristically the

[9] Robert S. Henshaw, *The Relation of Attitudes and Opinions to Age* (Ph.D. Dissertation, Princeton University, 1944). Quoted in Hans Toch, "Attitudes of the 'Fifty Plus' Age Group: Preliminary Considerations Toward a Longitudinal Survey," *The Public Opinion Quarterly*, Fall, 1953, pp. 391–394.

[10] Stauffer, *op. cit.*, pp. 89–108; Jacob Tuckman and Irving Lorge, *Retirement and the Industrial Worker* (New York: Columbia University Press, 1953), pp. 33–89; Ruth S. Cavan, *et al.*, *Personal Adjustment in Old Age* (Chicago: Science Research Associates, 1949), pp. 40–61; Karl M. Bowman, "Personality Development in Aging Adults," *Geriatrics*, December, 1954, pp. 563–566.

elderly are more deeply concerned with preserving what they already possess.

2. Sex. The old ways when "men were men and women's place was the home" have yielded to new customs. As Laura Bergquist points out, fifty years ago life was easier for a woman in many ways: She "enjoyed a certain lifetime protection from husband, brother, or father. She did little agonizing about her place in the scheme of things. Her aims were fairly single-minded: to find a good spouse, marry, raise children. No need to switch from job to domesticity or vice versa. Her husband might wander, but he was firmly tethered to home and family." Although marriage is still a woman's main goal, such a union is much different from her grandmother's, or even her mother's. Her new position in marriage as a coequal or partner is more demanding and less secure.[11] Today husbands are more inclined to share their problems with their wives and to accept greater responsibilities in the running of the home. Marriage counselor David R. Mace states: "The American father today, aided by our present five-day-week working pattern, is taking an unprecedented interest in his children and his wife's problems. Fatherhood has been transformed into daddyhood. The formerly aloof husband now helps out with everything from diaper-changing to baby-sitting, dishwashing and even cooking." [12] Women still delight in their role of homemakers, as is evidenced by the fact that they marry younger than did their mothers and have more children. Although most women still maintain a central interest in domestic matters, they enjoy greater personal freedom than ever before to pursue activities outside the home. They attend college in greater numbers, travel more, get about more and are more active in schools, churches, and other organized community activities. Approximately 50 per cent more women are employed

[11] Nearly one out of every four U.S. marriages fail, making our divorce rate the highest in the Western World. Laura Bergquist, "A New Look at the American Woman," *Look,* October 16, 1956, p. 40.

[12] David R. Mace, "What Do You Want from Your Marriage Today?", *Woman's Home Companion,* April, 1956, p. 79.

outside of the home than fifteen years ago. The current total of more than twenty-one million working women represents perhaps one-third of the nation's labor force.

Despite these significant and continuing changes which reduce the dissimilarities between the sexes, various social, political, religious, and economic differences still exist. Women seem to be less interested in careers than in supplementing the family income. Few top-drawer, high-prestige positions are held by women. Out of the quarter of a million "real" executives in the U. S., only about five thousand are women.[13] Only 5 per cent of the biographees in the latest issue of *Who's Who in America* are women.[14] In contrast to women, men continue to know more about, and are more interested in, business, industry, economics, geography, natural and applied sciences, abstract principles, sports, the professions, and politics. Men are more inclined to favor Democratic candidates than are women, and a larger proportion of men vote. In general, women are still more interested in home management, family life, and children. Also, they are more concerned with morality, religion, prayer, and the opinion of others. Women tend to be more self-centered, more sensitive, more conservative, and more amenable to discipline. Men get around more, are more aggressive, and are more willing to take chances. Women are more interested in art, classical music, literature, drama, aesthetics, current best sellers, gardening, famous personalities, elite society, fashions, and personal appearances. According to Dr. Harold Wolff of the Cornell University Medical School, men have far better absenteeism records in industry, have fewer operations, complain much less, are far less emotional, but die younger. In all age groups and at all educational levels women seem to be less tolerant than men of religious and political nonconformists. Women in business and in the professions are less tolerant than men in the same occupation.

[13] Perrin Stryker, "Who Is an Executive," *Fortune*, December, 1955, pp. 107–109, and 228–232 *passim*.

[14] Cedric Larson, "In and Out of 'Who's Who,'" *The Saturday Review*, August 18, 1956, p. 8.

3. *Size of the audience.* The number of persons in your audience has great psychological significance. In the small audience, the listener basically retains his own individuality with his customary habits of thinking and behaving. In the large audience, crowd psychology tends to shape the individuals into a single mass unit. In-group feeling inclines the listeners to subordinate their individuality to the thinking and emotions of the group. Appeals for overt mass response are much more effective when directed to a large number of persons closely arranged together than when applied to a small, scattered audience. The excitement produced by the large numbers in close proximity helps bring emotions to the surface. When this happens, intellect and logic tend to be submerged: listeners are much more easily swayed by non-logical appeals; they are much less critical of the speaker's evidence and reasoning, particularly if he tells them what they want to hear; they are much less willing to reason logically and objectively; they are more suggestible and more inclined to accept desire as evidence. Since emotion (e-MOTION) tends to express itself in action, the large crowd is much easier to persuade to laugh, cheer, applaud, cry, donate money, sign pledges, volunteer services, buy bonds, and so on. When the members of the audience obviously agree with one another and with the speaker, a state of polarization is said to be present. A Nazi throng was an example of an extremely polarized audience. With their intellects turned off, the members of such an audience were easy victims for the demagogue and the charlatan.

Sometimes the size of the audience may influence the degree of prestige enjoyed by the speaker. If only a small number of persons attend an open meeting, the typical auditor may reason that the speaker and/or the occasion must not be very important. He may wonder: "Have I made a mistake in coming?" Conversely, if a large throng appears, the size of the assemblage may be interpreted as a tribute to the speaker. As we have previously indicated, the speaker with high prestige has a better chance of achieving his speaking purpose than does one with lower prestige. Also, the number of persons in relation to the size of the room will directly affect the speaker-audience relationship. An aggregation of two hundred listeners will seem larger in a hall designed for that number than in an auditorium large enough to seat a thousand. Crowd psychology has a better opportunity to function when a room is nearly filled or overflowing. When large patches of vacant seats exist, the spread of an in-group feeling is inhibited or prevented.

4. Educational background. One of your problems in speaking is to provide enough supplementary information and amplification so that all of your listeners can understand but, at the same time, to avoid supplying so much that the better informed will lose interest. A rough guide to the knowledge, intelligence, and behavior patterns of your listeners is their amount of *formal* education. Admittedly, numerous exceptions exist! However, in general terms we can say that the more formal education a person possesses, the better equipped he should be to understand your message. As a rule, better-educated persons read more books and quality magazines. Writing in *The Saturday Review*, Gordon Dupee says: "If we went to college, more than a quarter of us have not read a single book in the last year." But if "our formal training ended with high school, almost three-fifths of us have not cracked the binding of a book in the last year." [15] The better educated read newspaper editorials more frequently and listen to more of the serious programs on radio and television. The less well educated depend more upon radio and television as the exclusive source for their news. As the level of education rises, so in general does the individual's range of

---

[15] Gordon Dupee, "Can Johnny's Parents Read," *The Saturday Review*, June 2, 1956, p. 6. Dupee's estimation is substantiated by an earlier study conducted by the National Opinion Research Center. The NORC poll found that the proportion of adults who had read at least one book during the previous month included: 50 per cent of college graduates, 27 per cent of high school graduates, and only 11 per cent of persons whose formal education stopped after graduating from grammar school. Also, the study indicated that 86 per cent of college graduates read magazines regularly but that only 68 per cent of high school graduates and 41 per cent of grade school graduates did so. Wilbur Schram, ed., *The Process and Effects of Mass Communication* (Urbana, Ill.: University of Illinois Press, 1954), p. 70. Also, see *The Public Opinion Quarterly*, Summer, 1950, p. 374.

general information and his knowledge about current events. The better educated more frequently are in the higher income brackets; they are far more apt to appear in *Who's Who in America* (90 per cent of such listees attended college); they take a more active part in the running of their communities; they belong to more clubs and civic organizations; they listen to more speeches and give more of them. As the educational attainment increases, so does the general tendency to vote more frequently and, apparently, to endorse the Republican Party.[16] Despite the fact that the poorly educated are usually less well informed, read less, and take less interest in the running of their communities, they tend to be more authoritarian in their attitudes. Perhaps Ludwig Lewisohn was correct in saying: "Nothing is so sure of itself as ignorance." In all age categories, the better educated as a group are less inclined toward rigid categorization and are more tolerant of non-conformists. The Stouffer study indicates that "higher education, by and large, makes for greater tolerance of human differences, whether ideological, racial, or culture." In his *The Nature of Prejudice*, Gordon W. Allport asserts "that general education does to an appreciable degree help raise the level of tolerance, and that the gain apparently is passed along to the next generation." [17]

One important aspect of the educational backgrounds of your listeners is their specialization of skills and knowledge produced by *occupational education*. Today almost everyone is a specialist, even the salesman, the office worker, and the football player. Increasingly, lawyers, doctors, engineers, and academic scholars

---

[16] Angus Campbell, *et al.*, "Political Issues and the Vote: November, 1952," *American Political Science Review*, June, 1953, pp. 359–385; Campbell, *et al.*, *The Voter Decides* (Evanston, Ill.: Row, Peterson & Company, 1954), p. 72; *The Public Opinion Quarterly*, Spring, 1950, p. 184; American Institute of Public Opinion syndicated column (release dates: September 19, 1956, October 15, 1956, and November 4, 1956).

[17] Stouffer, *op. cit.*, pp. 89–108, and 119–121; Gordon W. Allport, *The Nature of Prejudice* (Cambridge, Mass.: Addison-Wesley Publishing Co., 1954), p. 434; Morris Janowitz and Dwaine Marvick, "Authoritarianism and Political Behavior," *The Public Opinion Quarterly*, Summer, 1953, pp. 192 and 193; also, see various American Institute of Public Opinion polls, such as the ones released on September 14, 1951 and on October 26, 1958.

concentrate on learning more and more about smaller and smaller areas in their already specialized fields. With the development of the second industrial revolution, loosely called automation, the trend toward job specialization is certain to be accelerated. In terms of speechmaking we should understand that minds which have been directed into definite channels will exhibit distinctive and frequently narrow interests and knowledge. Attempt to discover the specialized knowledge and skills possessed by your listeners and shape your speaking accordingly.

The amount and character of the *life education* of your listeners may be nearly impossible to ascertain. However, as previously pointed out, life experiences provide an exceptionally rich source of knowledge and understanding. A first mate of a freighter, a big-city reporter, a private detective, a test pilot, a manager for a touring dog act, an elementary school teacher, a marine salvage expert—all have had vivid and educational life experiences.

5. Group affiliations. If you can, discover the various special groups represented in your audience and the approximate proportion of hearers belonging to each group. "People are inherently social; they do their living in groups." Since persons usually subscribe to the objectives of their groups, their affiliations may tell something about their probable knowledge concerning your subject and their attitudes toward it. Of course, we cannot place too much reliance upon group identification. Persons frequently belong to groups which may ocasionally have conflicting interests. For example, a member of the American Medical Association may belong to the Young Democrats Club. His professional association is militantly opposed to state medicine, but his political organization advocates state medical insurance. Although imperfect indicators, the group memberships of your listeners may afford helpful clues.

a. RELIGIOUS GROUPS. A person's religious affiliation, or lack of it, offers some important intimations. Along with the ascendancy of the spirit of conservatism, now dominating the nation's thinking, has come a greater interest in religion. In 1956, with the highest proportion of our people in history—62 per cent—belonging to some religion, U.S. church members numbered more than 103 million.

Protestant, Catholic, and Jewish faiths differ on various social and religious issues. For instance, the Republican Party draws the bulk of its strength from Protestants, while a majority of Roman Catholics support the Democratic Party. Catholics seem to attend church with greater frequency than do Protestants and want more children than Protestants. (For both religious groups, parents who attend church regularly seem to want more children than those who attend sporadically.) [18] The Catholic Church is especially strong in large urban centers with heavy foreign colonies such as New York City, Boston, New Orleans, and Cleveland, and in states like Massachusetts and Maryland, and in various ones in the Southwest. The numerous Protestant churches defy brief analysis.[19] Perhaps we can illustrate their wide variance by mentioning that the Episcopal Church tends to attract its membership from persons of means and social position, that the Baptist Church tends to draw persons of average means and is especially strong in the South, and that some of the smaller evangelical denominations appeal chiefly to the unlettered and the highly emotional. Jews are members of a "historical community held together by common memories, religious traditions and external pressure." More than three-fourths of America's Jews live in sixteen large cities, with nearly one-half residing in New York City. Jews include among their numbers a higher proportion of business, professional, and white-collar workers than do Protestants or Catholics. In general, Jews have superior earning power and lower incidences of crime, divorce, delinquency, and alcoholism than the national average.

[18] *The Public Opinion Quarterly,* Winter, 1950–51, p. 816; American Institute of Public Opinion syndicated column (release date: December 24, 1957); Frank W. Notestein, "As the National Grows Younger," *The Atlantic Monthly,* October, 1957, pp. 131–136.

[19] A national survey, reported to the North American Conference of Faith and Order, indicated that there is "comparatively little relationship" between a Protestant's denominational affiliation and his doctrinal beliefs. United Press release, September 5, 1957

Although Jews rarely change to another faith or marry outside their religion, only about one in six or seven attends weekly services.[20] Since 1932, Jews have leaned strongly toward liberalism and the Democratic Party.

As a general rule, churchgoers seem less tolerant than non-churchgoers of "unorthodox" beliefs, including those beliefs outside the area of religion. Stouffer concludes: "There would appear to be something about people who go to church that makes fewer of them, as compared with non-churchgoers, willing to accord civil rights to nonconformists who might be Communists, suspected Communists, or merely Socialists."[21] Also, Protestants and Catholics seem to be less tolerant of nonconformists than do Jews.[22]

b. OCCUPATIONAL GROUPS. Inevitably a person's occupation exerts a significant effect upon him. One of our largest occupational groups—comprising 38.8 per cent of the national work force—is composed of blue collar workers. On the average, skilled or semi-skilled workers are more interested in and better informed on politics than unskilled workers; but, they are probably less well informed and less interested than the average persons belonging to the professional, managerial, or "general" white collar groups. If rated on their sense of civic duty, their membership in civic organizations, the probability of their being civic leaders, and the frequency with which they vote, the skilled or semi-skilled workers would rate higher than the un-

[20] William Attwood, "The Position of the Jews in America Today," *Look,* November 29, 1955, pp. 27–35; Lawrence H. Fuchs, "American Jews and the Presidential Vote," *American Political Science Review,* June, 1955, pp. 385–401; Fuchs, *The Political Behavior of American Jews* (Glencoe, Ill.: Free Press, 1956); American Institute of Public Opinion syndicated columns (release dates: October 12, 1956, November 4, 1956, January 24, 1957, and December 24, 1957); Campbell, *et al., The Voter Decides* (Evanston, Ill.: Row, Peterson, 1954), p. 7.

[21] Stouffer, *op. cit.,* pp. 140–155.

[22] Stouffer, *op. cit.,* pp. 140–155; William Attwood, "The Position of the Jews in America Today," *Look,* November 29, 1955, pp. 27–35; Maurice L. Farber, "The Communist Trial: College Student Opinions and Democratic Institutions," *The Public Opinion Quarterly,* Spring, 1950, pp. 89–92; Charles T. O'Reilly and Edward J. O'Reilly, "Religious Beliefs of Catholic College Students and Their Attiudes Toward Minorities," *The Journal of Abnormal and Social Psychology,* July, 1954, pp. 378–380.

skilled workers; but, they would score lower than the professional and managerial persons and possibly lower than the white collar workers.[23] Union members tend to vote more frequently than non-union workers. Both union and non-union workers are much more likely to vote for Democratic than Republican candidates, with union members leaning more strongly than non-union members toward the Democrats. As a group, manual workers seem to be somewhat more authoritarian in their attitudes than white collar workers.[24]

Today class lines are becoming increasingly blurred. The previous thirty years have witnessed a revolutionary change in the social, economic, and psychological conditions of blue-collar workers. Because of the improved comparative economic status of the worker and because more than one member of his family may be employed, the family income of even the unskilled worker may exceed that of many white-collar workers. In fact, Vance Packard states that "A clear majority of all families in the middle income ($4,000–$7,500) bracket now wear blue, not white collars." Writing in *The Atlantic*, Sumner H. Slichter points out that "one out of five families of skilled craftsmen has an income of more than $7,000 a year. But among professional and technical workers, the proportion is one out of six, and among sales and clerical workers, only one out of seven. About 72 per cent of the families of managers and non-farm business proprietors have incomes of less than $7,000. Hence one out of five skilled craftsmen and their families are able to live better

[23] For sample studies, see these articles published in the *American Sociological Review:* John M. Foskett, "Social Structure and Social Participation," August, 1955, pp. 431–438; Wendell Bell and Maryanne T. Force, "Urban Neighborhood Types and Participation in Formal Associations," February, 1956, pp. 25–34; Morris Axelrod, "Urban Structure and Social Participation," February, 1956, pp. 13–18.

[24] Campbell, *et al., The Voter Decides,* pp. 72, 191, and 197; George Belknap and Ralph Smuckler, "Political Power Relations in a Mid West City." *The Public Opinion Quarterly,* Spring, 1956, pp. 73–81; Jack Chernick, "The Political Role of Organized Labor," *Current History,* August, 1956, pp. 77–83; American Institute of Public Opinion syndicated column (release dates: October 27, 1955; October 7, November 2, and November 4, 1956; January 28, and June 20, 1957; and March 27, 1958).

than more than seven out of ten managers and business owners."
With workers' families receiving an increasingly large share of
the country's prosperity, it is inevitable that they should have a
growing sense of "belonging," that they should take more interest in civic affairs, and that they should increasingly adopt
conservative, middle class attitudes toward public issues.[25]

Space does not permit us to examine additional occupational
groups. However, as drill in audience analysis you may wish to
contrast an audience composed mainly of blue-collar workers
with audiences made up chiefly of farmers, or newspaper editors,
or physicians, or businessmen, or clergymen, or firemen.

   c. ECONOMIC AND SOCIAL POSITION GROUPS.   Although class
lines in the United States are increasingly becoming less clearly
defined, we can still generalize with some confidence. In comparison to the average person in the medium or low brackets, the
typical person of superior economic and social position tends
to be better educated; he seems to read more, listen to more of
the serious programs on radio and television, attend more plays
and symphonic programs, and so on; he is more apt to believe
that big business is good and that big unions are "out of hand";
he is more conservative politically. Naturally, when an individual achieves superior standards of living and of social prestige,
he is inclined to view the *status quo* with satisfaction. Most of
our leaders in politics, culture, and civic enterprise are persons
of superior economic and social position. In comparison to the
representative person in the high or middle income and social
position groups, the typical person of low income status is less
well educated. He seems to read fewer quality magazines and
books; he tends to be less well informed on current events,
history, geography, government, etc.; he tends to be more authoritarian in his attitudes and to be less tolerant of ideas
different from his own; he is more inclined to vote the Democratic ticket. Since he has more to gain, the person of low social

[25] Vance Packard, "How Does Your Income Compare with Others," *Collier's*
November 23, 1956, pp. 55–59 *passim; Time,* November 25, 1957; Seymour E.
Harris, "Who Gets Paid What," *The Atlantic,* May, 1958, pp. 35–38; Sumner H.
Slichter, "The Growth of Moderation," *The Atlantic,* October, 1956, pp. 61–64.

and economic status is usually responsive to social programs such as state medicine, better unemployment insurance and social security benefits, high taxes on corporations, federal aid to education, higher minimum wage laws, and so forth. (Similarly, many well-to-do persons oppose these measures because they believe that it is to their economic advantage to do so.) The middle income group falls between the upper and lower ones in most of its attitudes, needs, desires, and beliefs. The bulk of the persons in this category are individuals of average intellect, knowledge, education, ambition, and ability.[26]

d. Political Groups. The political affiliations of your listeners may help reveal their probable attitudes toward various social, economic, and political questions. To interpret the political reactions of party members, we need to look closely at the parties themselves. At the time of this writing, most differences between the Republican and Democratic parties are those of degree rather than of basic philosophies. James Reston points out that "both parties actually accept the same obligations in both the national and international fields. Both accept the obligations of the Federal Government to maintain full employment, minimum wages and controls over the nation's internal economy. Both accept the obligations of collective security in the field of foreign affairs. The main questions have to do with the means by which these objectives are to be achieved." [27] The

[26] Some representative studies relating to social and economic groups are Alfred C. Clarke, "The Use of Leisure and Its Relation to Levels of Occupational Prestige," *American Sociological Review,* June, 1956, pp. 301–307; Philip K. Hastings, "The Voter and the Non-Voter," *The American Journal of Sociology,* November, 1956, pp. 302–307; Charles R. Walker and Robert H. Guest, *The Man on the Assembly Line* (Cambridge, Mass.: Harvard University Press, 1952); Andrew R. Baggaley, "White Collar Employment and Republican Vote," *The Public Opinion Quarterly,* Summer, 1956, pp. 471–473; William J. MacKinnon and Richard Centers, "Authoritarianism and Urban Stratification," *The American Journal of Sociology,* May, 1956, pp. 610–620; Gerhard E. Lenski, "Social Participation and Status Crystallization," *American Sociological Review,* August, 1956, pp. 458–464; Elliott McGinnies and Willard Vaughan, "Some Biographical Determiners of Participation in Group Discussion," *Journal of Applied Psychology,* June, 1957, pp. 179–185; Gardner Cowles, "What the Public Thinks about Big Business," *Look,* February 8, 1955, pp. 19–21.

[27] James Reston, "Campaign of Extremes," *The New York Times,* October 5, 1956.

similarity in the political philosophies of the parties seems to be the result of a growing public demand for moderation. As Crawford H. Greenewalt, Du Pont president, points out: "Politically, we are becoming a nation of conservatives in the sense that more and more people have moved into an economic status where they have something to conserve." [28] With both parties swinging toward the middle, the voices of the far right and the far left have less influence than formerly, and some extreme conservatives like Dorothy Thompson have protested that "both parties are settled in the mold of leftish orthodoxy."

Of course, this does not imply that no substantive differences exist between the parties. As William Carleton points out: "When the attitudes of all the Democratic constituencies in the United States are added together, the Democrats ordinarily come out just a little left of center; when the attitudes of all the Republican constituencies are added together, the Republicans ordinarily come out just a little right of center." [29] Many, if not most, national issues such as farm supports, tidelands oil, public vs. private power, and federally financed low-rent housing projects, arise from conflicting interpretations of the proper function, size, and scope of the federal government.

In addition to understanding the national, regional, and local political cross currents, you should also understand the far-reaching realignments which now seem to be taking place in the voting strength of the parties. Seventy years ago, the arrangement of the parties was basically on geographical lines, with perhaps only a half-dozen genuinely two-party states. Since that time, particularly since 1932, Democratic strength has increased in the Republican area; conversely, Republican sentiment has developed in the Democratic strongholds. Despite problems concerning integration, some authorities believe that the two

[28] *Time,* November 26, 1956, p. 98–99. Also, consult references, such as: Slichter, *op. cit.;* William Carleton, "The Triumph of the Moderates," *Harper's,* April, 1955, pp. 31–37; American Institute of Public Opinion syndicated column (release date: November 17, 1955).
[29] William Carleton, "Our Congressional Elections In Defense of the Traditional System," *Political Science Quarterly,* September, 1955, pp. 341–357.

parties are probably becoming more national and less regional in character. Lubell suggests that "The sectional political differences of an earlier age are losing force as the nation's balloting tends to stratify more and more along lines of social and economic class." According to Elmo Roper, "the strongest forces in the country today are working to break down the old regional loyalties and sense of 'separate' problems. They will be with us a good while yet, but as the country becomes more alike, North and South, East and West, the really important differences are becoming those of class and occupation, which are intimately connected with whether one lives on a farm or in a city apartment or in the ever expanding suburbs." [30]

Some significant shifts (most of which we have noted earlier in this chapter) seem to be developing in the voting preference of various segments of the populace: (1) Young persons seem to be growing somewhat more conservative politically, and older voters seem to be retaining their political conservatism. (2) Jews and Negroes still lean strongly toward the Democratic party, although some Negroes seem to be shifting to the Republican. A majority of Roman Catholics and most of the members of nationality groups continue to prefer Democratic candidates, but this allegiance may be less strong than formerly. (3) Among occupational groups, business and professional people are most united in their support of the Republican party. A majority of farmers, blue-collar workers, and white-collar workers support the Democratic party. A higher proportion of union workers are Democrats than are non-union workers; skilled workers are probably less inclined to vote Democratic than are the unskilled; and in 1956 all types of workers were somewhat less likely to vote Democratic than during the 1930's and 1940's. (4) The inhabitants of small towns and suburbs are much more likely to be Republicans than those living in the large cities. (5) As in

[30] Elmo Roper, "The Candidates and the Voters," *The Saturday Review,* October, 1956, p. 20; Peter F. Drucker, "Eleven Coming Issues in Politics," *Harpers,* June, 1955, pp. 52–59; Heinz Eulau, "Perceptions of Class and Party in Voting Behavior: 1952," *American Political Science Review,* June, 1955, pp. 364–384; William S. White, "The Changing Map of American Politics," *Harper's,* August, 1959, pp. 77–80.

the past, a higher proportion of men vote Democratic than do women. (6) College-educated persons are still considerably more inclined to vote Republican than are high school graduates, who, in turn, continue to be more Republican in sentiment than are grade school graduates.[31]

Between 1940 and 1956, the percentage of Independents among the electorate remained fairly constant—between 20 and 23 per cent. George Gallup says that such voters "are found in all income and occupation groups and in all sections of the country, but the proportion runs highest among voters with the most education and among the young voters. Among people who have attended college, one in every four today claims to be an Independent. The proportion is the same among young voters and among business and professional men and women." [32] Although a majority of the Independent vote has gone to the Republicans only three times in national elections during the last two decades, Independents probably possess little emotional dedication to the Democrats. As a general rule, Independents seem to examine political issues with greater rationality than do partisans.

Strictly speaking, organizations like the American Legion, the NAACP, the NAM, and the AFL-CIO are not political groups. However, they are potent political forces. For example, if a number of Legionnaires are in your audience, you know that they will probably be interested in veterans' benefits, "Americanism," an aggressive foreign policy, investigation of subversives, and so on. Legionnaires are less tolerant of "unorthodox" views than veterans who are not members of a veterans organization, but are probably more tolerant than the general public.[33]

[31] Oscar Handlin, "The Changing Nature of the Republican Party," *Current History*, August, 1956, pp. 65–69; Norman Graebner, "The Changing Nature of the Democratic Party," *Current History*, August, 1956, pp. 70–76; American Institute of Public Opinion syndicated column (release dates: January 17, April 16, June 17, and June 23, 1957; February 3, May 19, May 25, October 5, October 12, and October 31, 1958).

[32] American Institute of Public Opinion syndicated column (release date: July 23, 1956).

[33] Stouffer, *op. cit.*, pp. 27, 234, and 235.

e. RACE AND NATIONALITY GROUPS. Although we are a nation of one people, our races and nationality groups sometimes present sharp variations of thoughts and attitudes. For years to come, race relations will probably be disturbed by the problems associated with integration and the influx of Southern Negroes and whites into Northern and Western cities. If races are mixed in an audience, delicate discernment and adroit diplomacy must be employed when dealing with racial issues. In the larger cities many of the nationality groups live in "colonies" and maintain vestiges of old world customs and attitudes. Recognize the influence of such habits and behavior patterns when addressing nationality groups.

THE OCCASION

Different social situations engender in the individual correspondingly different patterns of thought and behavior. One's deportment at a barn dance or at a Christmas office party contrasts sharply with that at a formal tea. Likewise, different speech occasions produce in the listener different psychological states of being. At a lodge meeting, the auditor usually experiences warm feelings of good fellowship and may anticipate hearing relatively light speeches laced with genial humor. At a meeting called to protest the alteration of the neighborhood building codes, the average auditor possibly is in a heightened emotional state; very likely he has already arrived at strong convictions and is ready for action; he may be inclined toward overt expression, such as waving his arms and shouting; and probably he has little patience with lengthy explanations, tedious disputation, or jocularity. At the inauguration of a university president, the listener usually is impressed by the dignified nature of the proceedings; he conducts himself with sedate propriety and looks forward to a formal, imposing ceremony. Like the social occasion, the speaking situation exerts a potent influence upon the individual.

To adjust successfully your speech purpose, content, and delivery to the demands of the occasion, analyze these four characteristics of the meeting: its basic nature, the time, the place, and the program.

A. What Is the Basic Nature of the Meeting? What reasons motivated the listeners to assemble at this time and place? Is the meeting one of those regularly scheduled by an established organization, such as the weekly luncheon of the Optimist Club, the monthly meeting of the ministerial association, or the bimonthly meeting of the university dramatic club? If it is a regular meeting, you can easily determine what will be expected of you as a speaker, that is, what conventions or customs will exist concerning appropriate subject matter, lightness or sobriety of speech materials, dress, delivery, and so forth. If the meeting has been scheduled for a special reason, your speaking must be suitably oriented to that purpose. Skillful adjustments are demanded of the speaker at special occasions, such as a political barbecue, a public report concerning the findings of the county grand jury, or a Phi Beta Kappa address at a university auditorium. In analyzing the basic nature of the occasion, attempt to determine what influence the purpose of the meeting will have upon the psychological set of the audience. How impressive is the occasion? How much publicity have you and the meeting received? How much prestige will you enjoy? Will the listeners be eager to be informed, to be entertained, or to hear your advocacy of a particular proposal? Or, will their initial mood be one of lethargy, protest, or disinterest? Will they expect a rollicking presentation or, perhaps, a well-reasoned discussion on a serious topic?

B. What Is the Time of the Meeting? The day and the hour of the meeting may influence the mood of the audience. Examples: If the meeting occurs immediately after a meal, the hearers probably will feel relaxed, comfortable, and pleasant, but may suffer from drowsiness. If the meeting comes just before lunch, some auditors may find that the thought of food is more compelling than your speaking. If the meeting is held late in the afternoon after the listeners have completed the day's work, they probably will be tired and may lack the patience to examine a topic logically for an extended period. To attend a mid-morning or mid-afternoon program, the hearers have had to leave their jobs or household tasks; they will expect your performance to compensate them for their efforts to attend. Although they may feel somewhat weary, the members of a nighttime audience probably will not suffer from the lethargy of the after-dinner audience, the hunger pains of the pre-lunch group, the tired irritability of the late afternoon audience, or the "I should be at work" feeling of the mid-morning or mid-afternoon assemblage. However, the auditors have made some personal sacrifices to attend: they have given up a restful evening at home or have forgone some other meeting or entertainment; perhaps they have incurred the expense of a babysitter. Night speech occasions seem to possess an added atmosphere of importance. As one person said, "When you go to a meeting at night, you feel more like you're going somewhere." Such situations tend to be somewhat more formal; speakers and listeners usually dress more carefully and more formally; and the audience may expect more from the speaker.

Also, the time of year may require adaptations by the speaker. Some recognition of the date may be advisable, or even mandatory, if your speech occurs during the Christmas season, at World Series time, on July 4th, on Memorial Day, and so on.

C. What Is the Place of the Meeting? The location and physical setting of the meeting directly affect both the speaker and the listeners. Frequently speeches are delivered out-of-doors, as at a political rally in the local bandshell, a ground-breaking ceremony for a university library, the dedication of a statue, an Easter sunrise service, a mass meeting of strikers. If the meeting is to be held outdoors, consider these questions: Does the location (such as a cemetery) produce a mood of respect and restraint? Or, does the location (such as a baseball park) stimulate a mood of exuberance and gaiety? Will seating be available for the listeners? Remember that a standing audience tires easily, tends to be restless, and is more likely to walk off. Will the listeners be protected from the sun, wind, and rain? If distractions (like traffic noise or smoke from nearby industries) seem probable, how can you cope with them? What other effects might the outdoor conditions have upon the composition and mood of the audience?

If the meeting is to be held indoors, consider whether any historical or sentimental significance is attached to the building or room in which you are to speak. If the room contains symbols (such as flags, bunting, blown-up photographs, trophies, etc.), will they aid or impede the accomplishment of your speech purpose? What is the size of the room? A large hall containing a lectern and an elevated platform offers a more formal speaking situation than a small room without podium or speaker's stand. Will the temperature be comfortable? The ventilation good? In a hot, stuffy atmosphere you will have more difficulty in maintaining the attention of the auditors. Will the chairs be comfortable? Will the appointments of the room be bare, adequate or luxurious? As an extreme example, think how an expensively furnished conference room would produce a different mood from that provided by a dingy, ill-furnished hiring hall. Are the acoustics satisfactory? If not, you may be forced to speak more slowly and with greater precision. Is the lighting adequate? Will you be able to see the facial expressions of the listeners? Will they be able to see you and your visual aids, if you should wish to use some?

By anticipating the influence which the physical conditions may exert upon the audience, you can plan adjustments in content and delivery—thus increasing the likelihood of your presenting a successful speech, discussion, or oral reading.

D. What Is the Program for the Meeting? What relationship does your performance have to the entire program? Will your presentation be the only event? Have the listeners assembled primarily to hear you? If so, why? Is it because of your professional or civic position, some particular experiences you have had, or because of curiosity? When the program includes other speakers, ascertain the subject and mood of each discourse.

Usually the speakers will be expected to present a reasonably well-integrated program. Are you the principal speaker? If you are a preliminary speaker, do not attempt to steal the spotlight from the featured performer. What is your position on the program? If the first speaker, you are in large measure responsible for setting the tone of the meeting. If one or more speakers precede you, keep your speech structure sufficiently fluid so that, if necessary, you will be able to adjust to their presentations. If your position is near the end of a long program, by the time your turn comes the audience may be surfeited from speaking. Therefore, plan perhaps to use more humor, to lighten the tenor of your remarks, and to employ more vigor in delivery. When your presentation is to be preceded by scheduled events, activities, or musical numbers, contemplate what effect they will have upon the psychological mood of the listeners. Will your appearance immediately precede the main speech of the program, an important ceremony, an election, or a social hour? Then, do not be chagrined if you discover that your listeners seem eager for you to conclude. How much time has been allotted to your speech? Your speaking purpose and methods of development will be influenced by the time limitations. Will you be expected to answer questions? If so, anticipate the queries most likely to be asked and prepare tentative replies.

SUMMARY

The nature of the audience and the occasion exerts a determining influence upon what you as a speaker should say and how you should say it. To adjust effectively to the requirements of the audience you should (1) Appreciate the limitations of human nature as they apply to the speaker-audience relationship. (2) Analyze the characteristics of your listeners (their age, sex, educational backgrounds, and group affiliations, and the number of persons present) to determine their probable knowledge concerning you and your subject and their probable attitudes toward you and your subject. To adjust effectively to the requirements of the occasion, you should analyze (1) the basic nature of the meeting; (2) the time; (3) the place; and (4) the program.

EXERCISES AND ASSIGNMENTS

1. By means of reading newspapers and current affairs magazines and by means of interviewing friends, neighbors, professors, and townspeople, attempt to determine the five most significant problems now facing your region of the United States.

2. To determine their attitudes on current social, economic, and political matters, interview one or more of these types of people: a farmer; an unskilled worker; a skilled worker; a clerk; a businessman; a professional person; a Protestant; a Jew; a Catholic; an American Legionnaire; a housewife; a college graduate; an adult with no more than grade school education, and one with no more than a high school education. Pool your findings with those of your classmates.

3. Study carefully the syndicated public opinion polls. Sometimes the polls record differences in beliefs among persons of different age groups, levels of education, types of employment, etc. In each case, try to reason why these people believe as they do.

4. For class presentation, prepare a four-minute speech in which you do one of the following:
   a. Explain why you agree or disagree with Samuel Lubell's assertion: "Most voting, I have learned, is emotional rather than rational." A "chain of emotions" governs "political feelings."
   b. Amplify this statement by Courtney Brown: "A . . . reason why business is broadening its interests in the liberal arts, it seems to me, is that it is becoming increasingly aware that the world of the specialist is a narrow world and tends to produce narrow human beings."
   c. Explain what Maurice Baring meant in these lines: "All theories of what a good play is, or how a good play should be written, are futile. A good play is a play which when acted upon the boards makes an audience interested and pleased. A play that fails in this is a bad play."
   d. Relate this quotation from Robert Browning to age as a factor in audience analysis:

   > What Youth deemed crystal,
   > Age finds out was dew
   > Moon set a-sparkle, but which
   > noon quick dried.

5. Here are some topics which might be suitable either for short speeches or for class discussions.

a. Common stereotypes
b. The prejudiced personality
c. The tolerant personality
d. The authoritarian personality
e. Leadership qualifications
f. In-group feelings
g. The will-to-believe
h. Nationality groups
i. Public opinion polls
j. Group cohesiveness

k. Women executives
l. The elderly worker
m. Problems of retirement
n. Unions in politics
o. Special interest groups
p. Liberalism—past, present, and future
q. Who reads? And what?
r. Motivation research
s. The normalcy of prejudgment

IV ❦❦ *Basic Forms of Oral Communication*

PUBLIC SPEAKING

ORAL READING

GROUP DISCUSSION

10 ❧❧ *Selecting the*

Speech Subject

Probably you are familiar with the television program "You Are There." If, in some similar manner, we could lift the heavy shroud of the past, we could experience dynamic situations in which public speakers have molded public judgment and influenced the course of human affairs. We could hear Moses exhorting the Hebrews to depart from Egypt and to seek the land of Canaan, Aristotle lecturing to his disciples at the Lyceum in Athens, and James Otis in Boston arguing the illegality of the Writs of Assistance. We could witness Daniel Webster and Robert Hayne debating unionism versus sectionalism in the U.S. Senate, and William Jennings Bryan nearly stampeding a Democratic national convention with his Cross of Gold address. We could be present at the East Front of the Capitol when Franklin D. Roosevelt calmed a distraught nation with his candor and eloquence.

Of course, we do not have to project into the past to witness public speaking at work shaping the major and minor affairs of society. More speeches are being given today than ever before. Furthermore, public speaking is exerting an unprecedented influence upon international, national, state, and community affairs.

As you will remember from Chapter 1, every speaking situation is composed of four interrelated components: the speaker, the speech, the audience, and the occasion. In this chapter we shall consider the process of selecting a suitable speech subject.

DETERMINING THE SUBJECT AREA
FOR YOUR SPEECH

Successful speaking is audience-centered: your reason for speaking is to effect some response in your listeners. To elicit an appropriate reaction, your subject must directly affect the hearers' desires, interests, and needs and must be within their capacity to understand.

A. Begin Your Search for a Subject by Utilizing the Suggestions in Chapter 9 to Analyze the Audience and the Speech Occasion. Of the guides offered in Chapter 9, perhaps only one requires further emphasis here: the scope of a speech must be carefully adjusted to the amount of time allotted for the presentation. Frequently inexperienced speakers select subjects which are entirely too broad to be discussed adequately within the time limits. In such cases, one of two evils inevitably result: either the topic is treated superficially, or the speaker exceeds his time boundaries. Do not attempt to cover too much in one talk. Avoid sweeping themes like socialism, medicine, transportation, the farm problem, history of naval vessels, or women's fashions. Narrow the scope of such blunderbuss topics until they represent a constricted area that can be discussed adequately within the assigned number of minutes. Example: a meaningful analysis of "current U.S. foreign policies" would probably necessitate a speech of several hours. However, five or ten minutes might suffice to present the essentials of "U.S. policy toward Spain."

B. After Analyzing the Audience and the Occasion, Analyze Yourself as the Speaker. In what subjects are you interested? On what topics have you earned the right to talk? As you already know, successful speaking requires an animated, dynamic presentation and the simulation of such enthusiasm is both difficult and hypocritic. Therefore, select only topics which interest you and which fall within the range of your direct or vicarious experiences. In real-life situations, invitations to speak are usually based upon the supposition that the person has acquired valuable knowledge or opinions from his occupation, personal experiences, civic responsibilities, hobbies, or training. Customarily, a banker is expected to talk about business or economic conditions, a state senator about local political matters, a scout master about the Boy Scout movement, and so on. Unfortunately, many college students do not have either a rich or a varied background of experiences. To them the selection of a suitable topic may represent the most frustrating phase of preparing a speech. Perhaps these suggestions may be helpful.

1. Select only those topics about which you already know something and on which you can find additional information. You risk acquiring an acute attack of mental indigestion if you select a speech subject at random and then attempt to "read-up" on it in a hurry. Furthermore, you have not earned the right to talk on this subject but are merely parroting, and very likely misinterpreting, the ideas of others. Under such circumstances you will sound superficial, possess less confidence, and will tend to experience awkward hesitations during presentation.

2. Capitalize upon your personal experiences. Out of your personal experiences might come the nuclei of several meaningful speeches. For example, perhaps you worked for several years in a tool and die factory before coming to college. If so, you have probably acquired opinions and some knowledge concerning questions such as the closed shop, guaranteed annual wage, minimum wage laws, safety regulations, and seniority.

3. Utilize the information gained in university or high school courses. Your speech class can serve as an unexcelled medium for the practical application of this store of knowledge. Example: a course in geography might provide the background necessary for an interesting description of the physical, economic, and societal nature of Israel.

4. Select a current events topic. With your background knowledge and with additional information gleaned from reading or from interviewing faculty members or townspeople, you can help your classmates to understand the importance of the occurrence and to place it in its proper frame of reference. Some possible topics are an impending strike, an international crisis, a mechanical invention, a scientific discovery, a Presidential veto, a national political convention, a major sports event, or a destructive flood.

5. Make use of your hobbies. Unusual hobbies like seeking fossils, collecting treasure maps, reworking antique furniture, making costume jewelry, or studying World War II naval battles might provide interesting subjects.

6. Select a controversial issue. The list of such potential topics is endless. A few are the adoption of free trade, jail sentences for drunken driving, equal rights and responsibilities for women, changes in the university grading system, admission of Red China to the U.N., construction of a state turnpike, and de-emphasis of extracurricular activities.

DETERMINING THE AUDIENCE REACTION DESIRED

Once you have selected the subject area, determine the reaction you wish to secure from your listeners. Decide which of the three general speech purposes is best suited to your subject, the audience, and to the occasion: (1) to inform, (2) to entertain, or (3) to persuade. Then, narrow this generalized purpose to the exact, restricted goal, the bull's-eye of the talk, which is the *Specific Speech Purpose.* Few elements in speechmaking are more significant to the beginning speaker than an adequate understanding of the Specific Speech Purpose. Briefly defined, the Specific Speech Purpose is a precise, succinct, definite statement of what you plan to accomplish in your talk. It should be a practical goal which you can reasonably expect to achieve within the allocated time limits. The main criterion of your effectiveness as a speaker is your degree of success in accomplishing the Specific Speech Purpose. Now let us examine each of the general purposes to see how the Specific Speech Purpose is conceived for each type.

A. Do You Want to Inform Your Listeners?   Probably most speeches are concerned primarily with the conveying of information and are designed as speeches to inform. Although almost every speech contains informative material in the form of definition, explanation, or interpretation, only the speech to inform has for its chief, if not sole, function the promoting of intellectual understanding and the increasing of knowledge. As an informative speaker you are not principally an entertainer or an advocate of a new policy of action. Your concern is to present meaningful information in a clear, concise, and interesting manner. Another distinguishing characteristic of the speech to inform is that its success depends upon whether the audience *retains* the instruction it has received. The entertaining speaker accomplishes his basic purpose if he affords his listeners a pleasant diversion; the persuasive speaker achieves his primary objective if his auditors believe, feel, or act in the desired manner; but the informative speaker has not successfully accomplished his goal of imparting knowledge unless his hearers remember the essence of what has been said.

Notice that the following Specific Speech Purposes for the speech to inform represent definite, limited targets:

To have my audience understand the process of photosynthesis
To have my audience understand how to conduct a business meeting
To have my audience understand how meat is koshered
To inform my audience about the educational program of the American Institute of Banking
To explain to my audience the dust cloud hypothesis
To describe to my audience the process by which steel cable is manufactured

B. Do You Want to Entertain Your Listeners?   Sometimes a speaker's paramount purpose may be neither to inform nor to persuade. Instead, he may wish primarily to divert his listeners from routine problems and obligations. Probably most effective speeches contain elements of entertainment. However, the speech to entertain is unique in that its basic function is to provide a pleasant diversion. Some entertaining speeches which are presented at stag dinners, fun nights, parties, and smokers, may be completely free from any serious purpose. Such speeches might have Specific Speech Purposes like the following:

To entertain my audience by describing some of the passengers one meets on a Lakewood Avenue bus

To entertain my audience by demonstrating some feats of magic

To amuse my audience by explaining how to lose juries and alienate judges

To amuse my audience by telling how not to build a silo

Usually, however, entertaining speeches have the secondary purpose of providing information. For instance, many talks (as well as quiz shows and some panel discussions) scheduled for recreational meetings are intended to serve as pleasant distractions, but may also contain considerable instruction. Some sample Specific Speech Purposes for this type of entertaining talks are:

To entertain my audience by reviewing the play *Caine Mutiny*

To entertain my audience by describing a trip to the moon in 1980

To entertain my audience by predicting the results of the pennant races in the major leagues

To entertain my audience by telling about my visit to Greece

C. Do You Wish to Persuade Your Listeners? The persuasive speech invariably contains information and frequently some elements of entertainment. However, its basic purpose is neither to inform nor to divert, but rather to influence belief, arouse emotions, or impel action. Persuasive speeches may be divided into three sub-types: to convince, to stimulate (reinforce or impress), and to actuate. In later chapters, we shall discuss the methodologies involved in organizing and developing each of these types. Our immediate discussion, however, is confined to identifying and analyzing the general purposes as such.

1. The general purpose TO CONVINCE. As is illustrated in the following diagram, on a controversial issue every person in the audience will be either extremely favorable toward your proposal, extremely opposed, or somewhere in between. The basic opinion of the audience, which you can frequently ascertain by a preliminary investigation, determines whether your general purpose is to convince or to stimulate (reinforce or impress). The audience which already is in moderate to extreme agreement cannot be convinced, because "convince" means to change the mind-set of others from an attitude of neutrality or

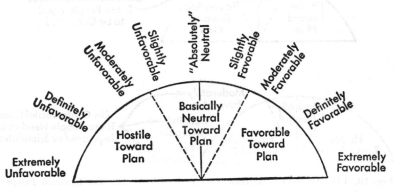

Fig. 9. Diagram of Audience Attitudes Toward Controversial Issues. *From Eugene E. White and Clair R. Henderlider,* Practical Public Speaking *(New York: Copyright by The Macmillan Company, 1954). Used by special permission of The Macmillan Company.*

opposition to one of agreement. Speeches to convince are directed toward audiences which are primarily neutral or opposed to the speaker's recommendations. The members of a basically neutral audience have not yet crystallized their judgments; hence, they probably will be receptive to a rational presentation of evidence and will be inclined to judge the speaker's arguments upon their logical merits. A far more difficult task of persuasion is presented by the audience which is composed of persons who are opposed to the speaker's position. Such persons are preconditioned against the proposals and usually will stoutly resist any attempts to change their thinking. When speaking on a genuinely significant topic, a speaker conceivably might win over some of the moderately opposed listeners but will have relatively little chance of convincing those who are definitely or extremely opposed. A realistic appraisal indicates that long established habits of thought and belief rarely can be uprooted by a single speech. Perhaps the most you can hope to accom-

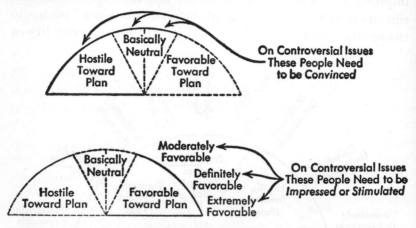

Fig. 10. The Audience Attitude Determines Whether the General Purpose Is to Convince or to Stimulate. *From Eugene E. White and Clair R. Henderlider,* Practical Public Speaking *(New York: Copyright by The Macmillan Company, 1954). Used by special permission of The Macmillan Company.*

plish when addressing actively hostile hearers is to soften or weaken their existing opposition.

Examples of Specific Speech Purposes: (1) If you are addressing an audience which is undecided about the desirability of a program of federal financial assistance to education, your Specific Speech Purpose might be: "To convince my audience that the nation's schools should be (or should not be) subsidized by the federal government." (2) If you are presenting your company's stand against the guaranteed annual wage to a group of plant workmen who favor the G.A.W., your Specific Speech

Purpose could be: "To convince as many as possible of the workers that the guaranteed annual wage is undesirable for both labor and management and to mollify those who cannot be convinced."

2. *The general purpose* **TO STIMULATE (REINFORCE OR IMPRESS).** On *controversial* issues, the speech to stimulate (reinforce or impress) can be successfully directed only toward those audiences which are basically in sympathy with the speaker's proposals. In such situations no conflict exists between speaker and audience; both agree. The speaker's task is to reinforce already existing beliefs, to intensify previously acquired attitudes, and to stimulate emotions. What is the psychological nature of the favorably disposed listeners? Extremely favorable auditors are completely sold on your proposal; their powerful will-to-believe renders them almost entirely non-critical. Definitely favorable listeners wish strongly to agree but, unlike the extreme supporters, have not forsaken all objectivity. Moderately favorable auditors are basically on your side; they are willing, though perhaps not eager, to agree but are more analytical than the more ardent partisans. Examples of Specific Speech Purposes: (1) If most of your listeners believe that Russia plans future warfare against the U.S., you cannot convince them on the matter. Instead, your Specific Speech Purpose might be "To stimulate my audience to feel more intensely that Russia plans war against the U.S."; or, "To reinforce my audience's belief that Russia intends to wage war against the U.S." (2) If addressing a regional convention of the lay leaders of your church, you know that the listeners are dedicated to the cause of religion but may need encouragement and stimulation. A suitable Specific Speech Purpose might be: "To impress upon my audience that the church exerts a great moral force on society."

An Adequate Understanding of the General Purposes to Convince and to Stimulate Requires an Examination of Three Additional Points.

a. *It is not always possible to determine in advance the knowl-*

edge and attitudes of your audience. By following the suggestions contained in Chapter 9, you usually should arrive at fairly reliable estimations of the knowledge your listeners have on your subject and of their attitudes toward it. But if a close investigation of the occasion and the potential listeners fails to reveal the attitudes you will probably encounter, assume that you will face a basically neutral group and plan a speech to convince. However, be prepared to make on-the-spot adaptations to the reactions of the listeners.

b. *Assuming that you are able to determine the probable knowledge and attitudes of your listeners, you may find that the audience cannot be categorized as being primarily sympathetic, undecided, uninformed, or opposed. Many groups resist such a facile identification.* When a preliminary inquiry discloses a fairly even distribution of attitudes from strong support to strong opposition, you usually should plan a logical, conciliatory speech. In such a case, you would have the exceedingly difficult task of convincing the neutrals, retaining the support of the partisans, and lessening the intensity of the opposition.

c. *The general purpose to stimulate (reinforce or impress) includes speeches designed to arouse enthusiasm or interest on non-controversial matters.* Such talks may be directed to the neutral or apathetic auditors as well as to the favorable. Indeed, speeches to interest are customarily concerned with exciting the lethargic and the unimpressed. Sample Specific Speech Purposes: to stimulate the audience to a greater appreciation of the importance of research in modern medicine; to stimulate the listeners to become interested in calypso music; to impress upon the audience the importance of family love; to inspire the audience with the story of Dr. Albert Schweitzer's contributions to humanity.

3. *The general purpose TO ACTUATE.* As you will remember, informative speeches attempt to provide understanding, entertaining ones seek to afford enjoyment, convincing ones try to secure mental and emotional agreement, and stimu-

lating ones wish to vitalize previously accepted beliefs. None of these types attempts primarily to motivate the listeners to action. Only the actuating speech has for its principal purpose the securing of direct, observable, specific, and relatively quick action. Some students may wonder: "Don't all speakers hope to influence the behavior of their hearers? If not, what's the purpose of speaking?" The speaker who attempts to inform, convince, or stimulate (reinforce or impress) *does* seek to alter the thinking and/or emotions of his listeners and, thereby, to exert an indirect influence upon their behavior patterns. However, if action does result, it might take place at any time in the future and might be expressed in any of countless unpredictable ways; potential action of this sort is vague, indefinite, and eventual. In contrast, the speech to actuate attempts to win more from an

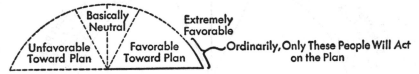

Fig. 11. Ordinarily Only Extremely Favorable Auditors Will Act Upon the Speaker's Recommendations. *From Eugene E. White and Clair R. Henderlider,* Practical Public Speaking (*New York: Copyright by The Macmillan Company, 1954*). Used by special permission of The Macmillan Company.

audience than intellectual agreement and emotional feelings, which might possibly produce some sort of action at some future occasion; it wishes to impel others to do something concrete in the near future, that is, to buy, join, give, sell, sign, vote, etc. For instance, a speaker might wish to *convince* his listeners that the direct popular vote would be a more democratic method of electing the President than the present electoral college system. If he persuades his hearers to agree, he has accomplished his purpose. Perhaps sometime later they may vote differently or speak differently as a result of his speech. However, he probably will never know whether they do or not. Now, let us assume that the speaker wishes to *actuate* his audience to sign a petition calling for the direct election of the President. This requested action is clear-cut and immediate. If he convinces his listeners that the direct vote is more democratic but fails to motivate them to sign the proposal, he has not accomplished his purpose.

Can the actuating speech be directed to listeners who are neutral or opposed to one's proposition? Theoretically, a speaker can attempt to move any audience to action. However, from the standpoint of practicality it is pointless to ask persons to do

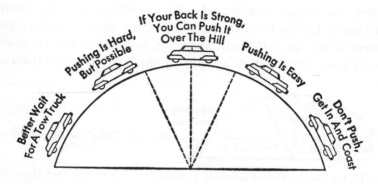

Fig. 12. Pushing an Automobile Is Like Winning an Audience. If Consistent with Ethics, Go in the Direction of Least Resistance. *From Eugene E. White and Clair R. Henderlider,* Practical Public Speaking *(New York: Copyright by The Macmillan Company, 1954). Used by special permission of The Macmillan Company.*

something they will not or cannot do. Usually, only those who are definitely or extremely favorable will act. This means that in speaking to a hostile group the speaker must convince them of the rightness of his cause and then stimulate them to the point that they are willing to act. If his hearers initially are favorable, he has a much better chance of motivating them to act. The above diagram demonstrates that, like pushing a car, persuasion is easier to accomplish when going in the direction of least resistance. (Of course. one should never violate ethics in order to please an audience.) Also, the action which the speaker requests should be within the capacity of the listeners to perform. It would be foolish to attempt to actuate an audience of middle-aged persons to devote their lives to the study of science. Such a topic would be far more suitable to a group of high school students.

Here are some sample Specific Speech Purposes for the speech to actuate.

> *To persuade my audience* to contribute to the Heart Fund
> *To persuade my audience* to buy P-E-P vitamin pills
> *To persuade my audience* to sign the petition denouncing Commissioner Kelly
> *To persuade the city council* to investigate possible corruption in the police department
> *To persuade the civil service board* to reinstate Charles Green
> *To persuade the city commission* to purchase an emergency rescue car
> *To persuade the women* to become cub scout leaders
> *To persuade the teachers* to join the National Education Association

SUMMARY

Your reason in speaking is to achieve an appropriate response from your listeners. To determine the subject area for your speech analyze the audience, the occasion, and yourself as the speaker. To determine the audience reaction desired decide which of the three general purposes (to inform, to entertain, or to persuade) is best suited to the subject, the audience, and the occasion; then narrow the general purpose to the exact, limited goal which is the Specific Speech Purpose.

EXERCISES AND ASSIGNMENTS

1. From a recent issue of a metropolitan newspaper, select perhaps twenty topics that would be appropriate for speeches of about four to five minutes in duration. Phrase a Specific Speech Purpose for each topic. Share your list with the class.

2. Examine recent issues of *Time, Newsweek, U.S. News and World Report, The Atlantic, Harper's, Current History, Look,* and *Life.* A quick survey should give you an idea of the topics which the editors of these magazines believe to be currently important.

3. Interview a classmate concerning his course of study, class in school, extracurricular activities, professional plans, club affiliations, hobbies, attitudes toward domestic and international problems, nature of his home town, high school experiences, favorite authors, and so on. Attempt to secure a reliable profile of his personality, background, interests, and attitudes. Present your analysis to the class in a short speech.

4. As a result of the speeches suggested in exercise 3, you should now have a better understanding of your classmates. Draw up a list of general areas in which you think the class will be especially interested. Phrase Specific Speech Purposes for several short talks in each area.

5. Analyze your own interests, ambitions, academic background, beliefs, needs, and personal experiences. As an outgrowth of this inventory, list five or six general areas in which you are especially competent and/or interested. Phrase Specific Speech Purposes for several short speeches within each general area.

6. Give to each class member copies of the list you prepared for exercises 4 and 5. Let each student rate the topics, including which subjects he considers most interesting and meaningful.

7. Attend a speaking situation off-campus. In a written report, state the speaker's general purpose and his Specific Speech Purpose. Also, explain how successfully the Specific Speech Purpose seemed to be adjusted to the audience, purpose of the meeting, time and place of the meeting, physical conditions present, time limitations for the address, and the speaker's background, personality, and prestige. If the speaker's purposes seemed unsuitable, suggest changes that might have increased his effectiveness.

8. Prepare a five-minute speech explaining a process. If you wish, select one of the following *How to Do It* topics.

Stop worrying	Refinish antiques
Stop bleeding by first aid	Reduce weight
Identify counterfeit money	Train a hunting dog
Prepare for a job interview	Make a home "accident-proof"
Apply stage or TV make-up	Break the smoking habit
Make fishing flies	Prepare creole gumbo
Take good baby pictures	Control common garden pests
Make simple plumbing repairs	Teach a child to swim

9. Prepare a five-minute speech explaining a *How it Operates, How It Is Done, How It Is Produced* type of process.

Public opinion surveys
Voice of America
New York Stock Exchange
Slot machines
Sense of smell
Lie detector
Water conservation system of the Saguaro cactus
Drapery aurora
Lightning
Human vision
Electronic vacuum tube
Sense of balance
Silicon extraction
Automated data processing
Fluorine in preventing tooth decay
Coaxial cable
Photo-electric eye

Bessemer process
Gulf stream
Bacterial "nitrogen fixers"
Octopus' jet propulsion
Elliptical orbits of our solar system
Sense of taste
Abacus
Electroshock treatment
Endocrine system
Broaching machine
Simulated flight tests
Fighter plane ejection seat
Fund for Adult Education
European Travel Commission
Syntopicon—literary invention of the publishers of *Encylopaedia Britannica*

10. Prepare a five-minute speech in which you describe the appearance of some physical thing. Here are some *How It Looks* topics.

Tobacco warehouse
Suez Canal
Brooklyn's Navy Yard
U.S.S. *Saratoga*
jai alai court
Alcatraz
Kitchen at Trader Vic's (or at The Statler Hilton, etc.)
Stockholm (or Amsterdam, etc.)
Ocean floor
Brontosaurus
Atlanta Cyclorama
Pandanus tree (or Mangrove tree, etc.)
Mohave Desert (or Sonoran Desert, etc.)
George Washington Bridge (or Golden Gate Bridge, etc.)
Cotton gin

Saw mill
French Quarter of New Orleans
House fly under magnifying glass
Black Canyon of the Gunnison River (or Royal Gorge, etc.)
Steel framework of a large building
Mont-St.-Michel (or Notre Dame Cathedral, etc.)
A window display
Moon through a telescope
Human brain
Molecular structure of gasoline
Cave dwellers' ruins in Mesa Verde
Gila monster
Stanton Hall (or Westover, or another famous historical home)
Church Street in Charleston (or State Street in Chicago, etc.)
Colonial Williamsburg, as restored

11 ❧❧ *Gathering Materials*

Several years ago, before adjourning for the late summer recess, the Senate gave Walter George, one of its members, a standing ovation. Although possessing mediocre talents of delivery, Senator George was one of the most persuasive speakers in Congress. Ralph McGill, editor of the *Atlanta Constitution,* explained George's effectiveness in this way:

> Sen. Walter George is not a genius. He has no unusual gifts. He is the living illustration of the fact that genius is 98 per cent sweat and work. He had to study hard and work hard to be ready for a lawsuit. But when it came, he was ready.
>
> That has been his history in the Senate. When Walter George speaks, the gallery fills up. His fellow senators remain to hear him. They know he will not be speaking just to get something into the record, or for political effect.
>
> The key to the man's position is that he works at a subject until he is prepared—ready to present it.

The truism that nothing worth-while is accomplished without genuine effort is pertinent to speechmaking. You will be disappointed if you expect a course or a textbook to reveal magic formulas which will insure brilliant speaking without exertion. The student who attempts to circumvent painstaking preparation courts failure. Accurate knowledge provides the only foundation upon which valid opinions and actions can be based. As the Reverend Mr. Joseph M. Dawson has said, "The only kind of 'speaking' to be countenanced is the one which flows from a full fountain." Emerson was even more explicit when he wrote:

> Eloquence must be grounded upon the plainest narrative. Afterwards, it may warm itself until it exhales symbols of every kind of color . . . but,

264

first and last, it must still be at bottom a . . . statement of fact. The orator is thereby an orator, that he keeps his feet ever on a fact. Thus only is he invincible. No gifts, no graces, no power of wit or learning or illustration will make any amends for want of this. All audiences are just to this point. Fame of voice or of rhetoric will carry people a few times to hear a speaker; but they soon begin to ask, "What is he driving at?" and if this man does not stand for anything, he will be deserted.

Henry Thoreau's statement "Nothing can be more useful to a man than the determination not to be hurried" applies directly to the process of speech development. Speeches mature slowly. To hasten either the fermenting of wine or the accretion of speech materials will produce inferior products. In your speech class, you will usually not have much time to compose your talks; therefore begin preparation as soon as you receive the assignments. Even if thoroughly grounded in your topic, you will want to secure additional information such as personal on-the-spot observations, statistics, opinions of others, illustrations, quotations, comparisons, and anecdotes. The following suggestions may help you to discover these materials.

ACQUIRING IDEAS BY THINKING

Inevitably the first stage in gathering materials is to ask yourself: What do I already know about the subject? What experiences have I had which concern it? What relevant ideas can I remember from previous reading or courses? (If you are already using the suggestion in Chapter 3 that you begin a permanent classified catalogue of ideas, stories, and quotations, you may find in the file significant and appropriate ideas.) This process of acquiring ideas by thinking takes time, because you are attempting to bring into awareness ideas which may have existed undisturbed for years in your subconscious. As a result of your probing, one recalled memory leads to the uncovering of a related one, and so on. After ascertaining what you already know about the subject, decide what other data you need to accomplish your Specific Speech Purpose. To get these facts, plan a program of observing, communicating, and reading.

ACQUIRING IDEAS BY OBSERVING

Why does Edward R. Murrow fly to England to observe a British election first hand? Why do sport columnists attend the baseball games they write about? Why do major newspapers and news magazines maintain correspondents in strategic areas around the world? Because in such cases there is no adequate substitute for personal experience. On-the-spot observation gives an atmosphere of authentic concreteness and colorful vividness to writing and speaking. Direct contact with the subject can also motivate a sincere and animated delivery. If you are speaking on a subject such as the existing conditions at the county detention home, the cost of operating the local charity hospital, the efficacy of treatment at the state alcoholic rehabilitation center, or the need for off-street parking facilities in the downtown area, arrange a visit to the institution or place involved.

Effective observation is planned, complete, objective, and accurate. To secure information which will be most valuable to your speech, carefully *plan* your visit. Under the existing circumstances, attempt to make your inspection trip as *complete* as your purpose demands. Be *objective* in your evaluations. Recognize that predetermined attitudes might cause you subconsciously to distort the evidence. Observation is usually unreliable in unexpected or startling circumstances. However, since your tour is planned, comprehensive, and objective, it therefore should be *accurate*. To aid in recall, take brief notes which you can expand immediately after the experience.

ACQUIRING IDEAS BY COMMUNICATING WITH OTHERS

Woodrow Wilson once said that he used not only all the brains he had, but all that he could borrow. Communicating with others affords one of the richest and most readily available sources of information. In our complex society, almost everyone possesses some specialized training or experience. You can easily discover experts on your topic at the university, the city hospital, the local branch of the state forestry service, the district office of the FBI, or at some other accessible source. In addition to giving you data which is not widely available, these authorities may suggest valuable sources of reading matter, other persons to interview, or situations to observe. Before the interview read and think intensively on the subject. Plan a series of definite, relevant questions which can be answered briefly. During the meeting, be concise, be polite, and listen carefully. If it seems inappropriate to take notes, make a determined effort to remember the salient facts; immediately after the interview record on paper all items which might prove helpful in composing your speech.

If diligent research fails to yield the needed information and if a personal interview is impossible, write a letter to the proper agency or authority. In asking for information, be clear, brief, and specific. Enclose a self-addressed and stamped envelope. Or, when the nature of the requested information permits, inclose an addressed postcard which contains on its back several questions answerable by brief statements or check marks.

In addition to interviewing or writing letters to experts, seek information from friends, fellow students, neighbors, and the "man in the street." Engage others in informal discussion of your speech topic. You will find this an excellent way to gain new viewpoints and to test the effectiveness of your thinking and reasoning.

ACQUIRING IDEAS BY READING

In Chapter 3, you were advised to initiate a long-range reading program for the purpose of improving your intrinsic worth as a speaker. Here you will find some recommendations for utilizing reading in the specific preparation of a particular speech.

A. How Much Should You Read? Sometimes you may secure ample materials for your talk by reviewing what you already know about the subject, by on-the-spot observations, and by conversing with others. Usually, however, you should do some reading research for a speech. The amount will depend upon your background, the complexity of the topic, the importance of the speech, and so forth. A good rule of thumb is to read at least four or five times as much on the subject as you can possibly use in your talk. In this way you can select discriminatingly from a large accumulation of data.

B. What Should You Read? Each speech presents a somewhat different problem in research. Skill in tapping the resources of a large library comes only with experience. However, the following listings of source materials may help you get started.[1]

1. General references. A concise yet comprehensive survey of almost any subject can be obtained by consulting one of the standard encyclopedias, such as: *Encyclopaedia Britannica, Encyclopedia Americana, New International Encyclopaedia, Collier's Encyclopedia, Macmillan Everyman Encyclopedia,* and *World Book Encyclopedia.* (Remember that some encyclopedias publish supplementary yearbooks.) Also contained in the open shelves of the reference room are specialized indexes like *Encyclopedia of Religion and Ethics, Encyclopaedia of the Social Sciences, Cyclopedia of American Government,* and *Cyclopedia of Education.*

2. Biographical references. For a rapid treatment of a prominent person's life and career, see one or more of the following: *Dictionary of American Biography, Dictionary of National Biography* (British Empire), *Webster's Biographical Dictionary, American Men of Science, Who's Who Among North American Authors, Who's Who* (English), *Who's Who in America,* and regional volumes such as *Who's Who in the South and Southwest.*

3. Books of quotations. Apt quotations may be secured from such references as: Bartlett's *Familiar Quotations,* Stevenson's

---

[1] For a more complete guide to the use of the library consult Ella V. Aldrich, *Using Books and Libraries* (New York: Prentice-Hall, Inc., 1951) , 3rd ed.

Home Book of Quotations, Oxford Dictionary of Quotations, Hoyt's New Cyclopedia of Practical Quotations, and Mencken's *A New Dictionary of Quotations.*

4. Statistical information. An almost unbelievable wealth of factual data is contained in each of these yearbooks: *World Almanac, Information Please Almanac, Statesman's Year-Book,* and *Statistical Abstract of the United States.*

5. Newspapers. In additional to serving as sources of information for current happenings, newspapers also provide excellent reference material for occurrences of the past. Many university libraries possess the *New York Times Index,* as well as microfilm recordings of back issues. Some libraries also have the index to the *London Times.*

6. Magazines and professional journals. More than one hundred popular periodicals are indexed by author, title, and subject matter in the *Reader's Guide to Periodical Literature.* Almost every profession, trade, industry and academic field has one or more journals, many of which have official indexes. Various specialized guides catalogue periodical and, in some cases, other types of publications within a given field. Examples: *Business Periodicals Index, Education Index, Engineering Index, Agricultural Index, Index to Legal Periodical Literature,* and *Public Affairs Information Service.*

7. Documents and pamphlets. Great quantities of materials are printed by the different levels of government. The publications of the bureaus and departments of the federal government are indexed in the *United States Government Publications Monthly Catalogue;* those of the states, territories, and possessions are listed in the *Monthly Check List of State Publications.* Numerous associations and special interest groups publish pamphlets, bulletins, newsletters, and booklets. To discover relevant pamphletlike material, see the *Vertical File Service Catalog* or consult your librarian. Frequently you can acquire additonal printed matter by writing to the national offices of various pressure groups. To secure the addresses of such organizations, refer to the *World Almanac.*

8. Books. Each book in the library is indexed in the card catalogue under its title, author, and subject. If a book is not listed in the card catalogue, consult the *Cumulative Book Index* which registers nearly every book published in this country. Once you have determined the exact title, author, and publisher, you can form an estimation of the book by reading the abbreviated reviews about it in the *Book Review Digest*. If the book seems important to your research, you can recheck the library card catalogue, seek the volume at another library, rent it from a commercial lending agency, purchase it from a local bookstore, or order it from the publisher.

C. How Can You Read Most Effectively? (1) Plan your reading so that you select those sources which seem to be most rewarding. (2) Adjust your reading methods to fit the material and your purpose. If seeking to determine the pertinence of the material or to acquire general impressions, read at a rapid rate. If searching for specific dates, statistics, illustrations, quotations, and so on, read slowly and analytically. (3) Be objective. Keep prejudices in check and examine all sides of the question. (4) Read critically. Refuse to be gullible. Accept what you read only after testing the author's motives, evidence, and reasoning.

D. How Can You Retain What You Have Read? What seems unforgettably etched in your mind may have faded beyond recall a few minutes later. Therefore, always take cards and a pen with you to the library and record the material which you wish to remember. Here are some suggestions for note taking: (1) Use cards of uniform size, preferably 3″ by 5″ or 4″ by 6″. (2) Put only one idea on each card. Later you will see that in organizing the speech the cards may need to be shuffled to different locations in the file. Such rearrangements would be impossible if the individual cards contained multiple ideas. (3) Some authorities suggest that you write on only one side of the paper. (4) Record all direct quotations with meticulous accuracy. (5) Use quotation marks to enclose direct quotations and three periods (. . .) to indicate each omission of words or letters. (6) At the bottom of each card, record the exact source of the information. For books give the author, title, edition, publisher, place and date of publication, and page number. For periodicals include the author, title of the article, name of the magazine, date, volume, and page number. (7) In the upper right corner, label each card as to general subject matter. (8) In the upper left corner, you may later wish to classify each card as to its location in your speech outline.

SUMMARY

When you have selected the Specific Speech Purpose, your next step is to acquire the materials with which to construct the speech. Speech materials may be discovered by four methods: (1) By *thinking*, determine what you already know concerning the subject and what additional information you will need to secure. (2) By *observing*, acquire on-the-spot information about your topic. Effective observation is planned, complete, objective, and accurate. (3) By *communicating* with others, gain ideas, interpretations, facts, as well as suggestions for your further research. (4) By discriminate *reading*, secure general concepts and/or specific information. Promote retention by recording pertinent data in a systematic manner.

EXERCISES AND ASSIGNMENTS

1. Examine several issues of each of the following news magazines: *Time, Newsweek, U.S. News and World Report, The Pathfinder,* and *The Reporter.* What similarities and differences do you discover in format, organization, and philosophy? Also, is there any apparent slanting in the selection or presentation of the news? Discuss your findings with the class.

2. Study several issues of each of these magazines: *The Atlantic, Reader's Digest, The Saturday Review, Fortune, The Nation, The New Republic,* and *The American Scholar.* In a written report, explain the similarities and differences in the type of reading audience toward which the magazine is directed; the general format and organization; the literary quality, objectivity, reliability, and type of material. Also, explain the types of speech topics which might logically draw source material from these magazines. (If you need assistance, consult your speech, English, or journalism instructor.)

3. Become better acquainted with the resources of your library by examining each of these (or similar) reference works: *World Book Encyclopedia; Cyclopedia of American Government; Dictionary of American Biography; Who's Who in America;* Bartlett's *Familiar Quotations; Statistical Abstract of the United States; New York Times Index; Reader's Guide to Periodical Literature; Education Index; Document Catalogue; Vertical File Service Catalog.* In a written or oral report, describe each of these references and explain how each might contribute valuable source materials for the public speaker.

4. Interview a prominent speaker in your community on his methods of gathering speech materials. Prepare a written or oral report on what you have learned.

5. After you have prepared the speech for exercise 7 and/or 8, write an essay telling what resources you tapped in gathering the materials. Describe fully and concretely your procedure in utilizing personal experiences, observation, interviews, and reading. Indicate the nature and the applicability of the materials you acquired.

6. (A correlative of exercise 5) Discover all of the relevant materials on your subject which are listed in the card catalogue and in the appropriate indexes. Arrange the titles of these references in a bibliography, indicating those items you read in preparing the talk and the extent to which each was helpful.

7. After careful research, prepare a five- to seven-minute speech on one of these *What It Is* subjects. In your talk, attempt to define and describe your topic clearly, concisely, interestingly, and in sufficient detail.

St. Elmo's fire	Heavy water reactor	Farthingale
Interposition—an old doctrine in modern dress	Isotope	Mesabi ore range
	Enzyme	Cathode ray
	Bacterial virus	Cochlea
Orinase	Medulla	Chromosome-doubling
Gresham's Law	Cortisone	North American Basin
World Bank	Army ant	Oligocene Period
Hedonism	Trusteeship Council	Electronic microscope
Code of Hammurabi	International Boxing Club	Electoral college
Nordic myth		Gothic arch
Electromagnetic spectrum	Phrenology	Central Intelligence Agency
Crystallography	Atomic Energy Commission	Lateen sail

8. Following special study (see exercises 5 and 6), prepare a five- to seven-minute talk on one of these *This Is the Story* biographical or historical subjects.

Frank Lloyd Wright—master architect
Henry L. Mencken—astringent critic
Billy Graham—world evangelist
Artur Rubinstein—magnetic Pole
Benedict Arnold—tragic villain
Jerry Simpson—sockless Socrates
Maximilian—puppet-emperor
Thomas A. Edison—"Wizard of Menlo"
Samuel Gompers—father of the AFL
The Medici—papal bankers
Humphrey Bogart—"Gentle tough guy"
Frederick Douglass—Negro orator

Joseph Pulitzer—sensational journalist
Thorstein Veblen—scholarly radical
Peter Abélard—master at Paris
Aristophanes—Greek dramatist
Simon Bolivar—South American patriot
John Q. Adams—shaper of Monroe Doctrine
Enrico Caruso—great lover
John S. Pillsbury—inventive miller
Paul Brown—"Coach of champions"
Nicholas Trist—a clerk who ended a war
George Gershwin—jazz composer

Assassination of Leon Trotsky
Trial of Warren Hastings
Gunpower plot
El Alamein
Dreyfus affair
Settlement of Pitcairn Island
Americans at Château-Thierry
Teapot Dome scandal
Molly Maguires
Knights of the White Camellia
Hamilton-Burr duel
Travels of Marco Polo
French Revolution
Black Friday
Last days of Hitler
Manhattan Project
Haymarket riot

Capture of Geronimo
Cripple Creek—converting ghosts into dollars
Comstock Lode
Anti-Saloon League
Salem witch hunt
Underground Railroad
Manifest destiny
Second Punic War
Trial and execution of Joan of Arc
Explorations of Henry Hudson
Discovery of vaccination
Marconi's invention of the wireless telegraph
Vigilante days in San Francisco
Constellation—"Hard-luck frigate"
Siege of Wake Island

12 ❧❧ *Organizing the Body*

Once you have selected the Specific Speech Purpose and have gathered appropriate ideas and information, your next steps are to organize and develop your material in the most effective logical and psychological manner.

Plato suggests that "every speech ought to be put together like a living creature, with a body of its own, so as to be neither without head, nor without feet, but to have both a middle and extremities, described proportionately to each other and to the whole." In somewhat simpler language, a speech should be composed of a beginning (Introduction), a middle (Body), and an ending (Conclusion). The Introduction, which typically constitutes about 10 per cent of the entire speech, serves to stimulate favorable attention and to prepare the audience for the Body. The Conclusion, usually comprising about 5 per cent of the total speech, summarizes what has been said, promotes the proper mood, and, if necessary, attempts to induce action. Although both the beginning and the closing are important, the main purpose of the address is accomplished in the Body. Most speech teachers agree that the Body should usually be prepared before the Introduction or the Conclusion.

To organize the Body requires a working knowledge of the fundamentals of outlining. Therefore, before analyzing specific techniques for discovering and arranging the main heads of the Body, we should turn first to general principles, that is, to the nature, purposes, and methods of developing the outline.

PREPARING AN OUTLINE: BASIC PRINCIPLES

What is an outline and what purposes does it serve? Nearly every speaker prepares some sort of outline on paper, because the outline is the most practical method of organizing and testing one's thinking, and because it is the only system of representing thought relationships on paper in an abbreviated manner. The preparation of an outline will enable you to estimate more accurately the length of the speech and to insure that your ideas possess unity, coherence, and emphasis. When completed, the outline is neither a summary nor a manuscript copy of the speech. It is an abridgment consisting of main heads and subheads which are arranged according to a meaningful code of symbols and indentations.

A. The Outline Should Clearly and Accurately Indicate Thought Relationships. By applying these suggestions you can insure that your outline possesses appropriate thought relationships.

1. Adopt and remain consistent in the use of some standard system of symbols and indentations, such as the one illustrated below.

Specific Speech Purpose: (Remember that this is the exact goal you wish to accomplish in your speech)

Body:

I. *Major idea No.* I *in direct support of the Specific Speech Purpose*
   A. *First main point supporting* I
      1. *Subhead supporting* A
         a. *Subpoint supporting* 1
           (1) *Subpoint supporting* a
           (2) *Subpoint supporting* a
         b. *Subpoint supporting* 1
         c. *Subpoint supporting* 1
      2. *Subhead supporting* A
      3. *Subhead supporting* A
   B. *Second main point supporting* I
II. *Major idea No.* II *in direct support of the Specific Speech Purpose*

When a point reinforces, amplifies, or clarifies another heading, it is called a *subordinate point* and is always indented to the right and placed under the heading it supports. This produces the descending staircase effect below.

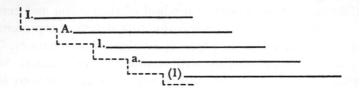

When points are independent of each other, are of approximately equal importance, and are logically subordinate to the same superior heading, they are termed *co-ordinate points*. Such points are placed in a perpendicular order.

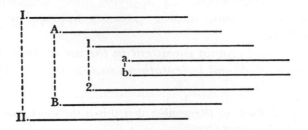

As can be seen readily, all headings possess both co-ordinate and subordinate relationships. The dotted lines in the following diagram demonstrate that the Roman numeral headings are co-ordinate to each other and subordinate to the Specific Speech Purpose, the first set of capital letter headings are co-ordinate to each other and subordinate to major heading I, the second set of capital letter headings are co-ordinate to each other and subordinate to major heading II, and so on.

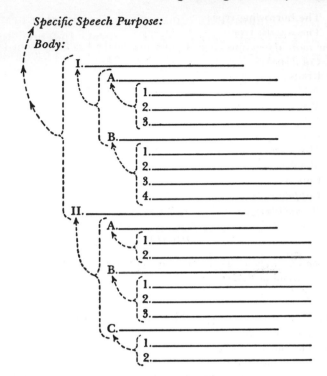

2. Subordinate points must logically develop, clarify, or "prove" the headings they are designed to support. To represent proper logical relationships, each subordinate point must be an integral part of its immediately superior heading; it cannot be co-ordinate in nature or in importance to that heading. In the outline below, the italicized headings are incorrectly used as subordinate points.

WRONG

Specific Speech Purpose: To inform my audience about the more common types of poisonous snakes

Body:

    I. The less dangerous type of poisonous snake has fixed back fangs
      A. The tree type

    B. The burrowing type
    C. The aquatic type
  II. The more dangerous type of poisonous snake has fixed front fangs
    A. Coral snakes
    B. Kraits
    C. *Adders*
    D. *Movable fang snakes*
    E. *Vipers*
    F. *Rattlesnakes*
    G. *Moccasins*
    H. Mambas
    I. Cobras
    J. *Copperheads*
    K. *Bushmasters*

RIGHT

Specific Speech Purpose: To inform my audience about the more common types of poisonous snakes

Body:

    I. The least dangerous type of poisonous snake has fixed back fangs
      A. The tree type
      B. The burrowing type
      C. The aquatic type
   II. An extremely venomous type of poisonous snake has movable fangs
      A. Those which are found in the United States
        1. Rattlesnakes
        2. Moccasins
        3. Copperheads
      B. Those which are not found in the United States
        1. Vipers
        2. Adders
        3. Bushmasters
  III. Perhaps the most deadly type of poisonous snake has fixed front fangs
      A. Coral snakes
      B. Kraits
      C. Mambas
      D. Cobras

3. Co-ordinate points must not overlap. In the following outline, main heads I and III overlap—they are not mutually exclusive. Heading III should be eliminated.

WRONG

Specific Speech Purpose: To convince my audience that the railroad industry should be given the same basic freedoms enjoyed by other businesses

Body:

I. The railroad industry does not have the same freedom of enterprise accorded other businesses
II. The railroad industry needs greater freedom from restrictions in order to serve America's expanding needs
III. *The automobile and steel industries, among others, can make decisions and put them into effect immediately*

4. Each heading should be phrased as a single idea. A heading should represent a single thought, not multiple points. In the next outline, heading II represents two separate reasons why the listeners should purchase the speaker's product. Each of the "reasons" should be given the status of first-degree headings.

WRONG

Specific Speech Purpose: To persuade my audience to buy Adolph's Meat Tenderizer

Body:

I. Adolph's Meat Tenderizer saves money
II. *Adolph's Meat Tenderizer saves cooking time and makes meat taste better*

5. Each division should result in two or more subheads. Every assertion of importance should be reinforced by supporting evidence. Typically the arranging of subordinate points under a heading represents a division of that topic—when something is divided, it is separated into more than one part. Sometimes, however, outlining is not a matter of divisions but one of amplification or proof. In such cases, a skilled speaker conceivably might explain or prove an assertion by means of a single supporting statistic, reference to authority, illustration, quotation, or reason.

6. Each major heading should be expressed concisely and accurately in a simple declarative sentence. Avoid long, rambling, complex sentences phrased in vague or ambiguous language. Also avoid the question form of heading, as well as the fragmentary, key-word type; although the experienced speaker can use both forms effectively, the beginner should write out each major heading as a simple, terse sentence.

7. Each set of co-ordinate points should be phrased in parallel structure. Parallel phrasing makes memorization of the outline easier for you, promotes understanding and retention for the audience, and verifies the coordinate relationships of the ideas. Contrast the effectiveness of the following outlines.

WRONG

Specific Speech Purpose: To convince my listeners that they can buy an OK used car from an authorized Chevrolet dealer with warranted confidence

Body:

    I. Is an OK used car thoroughly tested?

    II. There is no question but that you can count on its being thoroughly reconditioned

    III. Unlike many other used car dealers, the Chevrolet used car departments always describe every car honestly, even though that procedure may make it less easy to sell the automobile

    IV. Dealer warranty in writing

RIGHT

Specific Speech Purpose: To convince my listeners that they can buy an OK used car from an authorized Chevrolet dealer with warranted confidence

Body:

    I. OK used cars are thoroughly inspected

    II. OK used cars are thoroughly reconditioned

    III. OK used cars are honestly described

    IV. OK used cars are guaranteed in writing

B. An Outline of the Body Should Contain Between Two and Five Main Heads. Obviously an outline of the Body must contain at least two main headings; if only one first-degree heading is used, it represents merely a restatement—not a division—of the Specific Speech Purpose. The basic theme of every well-organized speech is developed by a few major ideas, points, arguments, or contentions. Although beginning speakers may think this statement strange, as a general rule long speeches do not have a larger number of main heads than do short ones. The longer address gives the speaker greater opportunity to make his main points clear, vividly interesting, or persuasive. Regardless of the length of the talk, the wise speaker rarely uses more than five first-degree headings. Some authorities recommend even fewer major heads. Harry Emerson Fosdick says that "audiences simply cannot grasp more than three at one sitting." When Norman Vincent Peale was asked how many heads he used in the Body of his speeches, he replied: "Never more than three. And if I can cover the ground under two headings, I try to do so. The more major points you present, the more complex the speech becomes." Furthermore, an excessive number of main heads usually indicates illogical and muddled thinking on the part of the speaker. Almost any subject can be divided into a few basic parts. If you find that the main headings number more than five, reexamine your speech structure and attempt to group your materials under as few major topics as possible (always having at least two, of course).

The following outlines demonstrate how the organization of the Body can be improved by reducing the number of main headings.

WRONG

Specific Speech Purpose: To inform my audience about the proper method of preparing mangoes for freezing

Body:
  I. Select firm, ripe fruit
 II. Wash the fruit
III. Peel the fruit
 IV. Slice or dice the fruit
  V. Place the fruit in a moisture- and vapor-proof container
 VI. Cover the fruit with limeade
VII. Seal the container carefully

RIGHT

Specific Speech Purpose: To inform my audience about the proper method of preparing mangoes for freezing

Body:
    I. Select firm, ripe fruit
   II. Prepare the fruit for packing
      A. Wash the fruit
      B. Peel the fruit
      C. Slice or dice the fruit
 III. Pack the fruit
      A. Place the fruit in a moisture- and vapor-proof container
      B. Cover the fruit with limeade
      C. Seal the container carefully

C. The Outline of the Body Should Cover the Subject Adequately. Although you probably could not completely exhaust every facet of even a simple topic, you should always cover all of the elements necessary to accomplish your Specific Speech Purpose. If this is impossible within the allotted time limits, constrict your purpose. If you leave out basic points, you may find it impossible to achieve your goal of informing or persuading. For example, consider the outline on page 280, concerning OK used cars. If the speaker neglected to include main heading IV (OK used cars are guaranteed in writing), his talk would have lost much of its credibility.

DISCOVERING THE MAIN HEADS OF THE BODY

In organizing the Body, first select the major points which you wish to present, then group supporting materials under these main headings. Always determine all of the Roman numeral heads before attempting to arrange the supporting subheads. Unfortunately, the discovery of the main headings causes many beginning students considerable difficulty. Perhaps, if you follow these suggestions, you will find this task somewhat simplified.

A. Prepare an Analysis List Containing the Points You Might Wish to Present in Your Talk. This step can be taken in conjunction with that of gathering materials, or can be done afterwards. In compiling Analysis Lists, Dr. Fosdick utilizes the "free association" technique.[1]

I sit down with pen and paper and practice what the psychologists call free association of ideas. That is, I jot down haphazardly any idea that comes into my mind, which directly or indirectly bears upon the matter in hand. At this stage I do not consider how the sermon will begin or end, or what its structure may turn out to be. I give free gangway to my mind, and let it pick up anything, within the scope of the sermon's object and subject, which it may chance to light upon. If an idea is only a vague intimation with no development or application evident, I do not labor it. If an idea branches out into consecutive suggestions, I briefly note them. I observe no logical continuity in accepting any suggestion that may come, but jot it down. This process may go on for hours—one idea awakening another, and all of them an unorganized jumble and potpourri, without order or logical connection; but not infrequently, when this stage is finished, I have the basic material, the loose bricks, with which the sermon will be built.

Although the experienced speaker may sometimes prepare the Analysis List in his mind, you should put your ideas on paper. Give full release to your imagination; try to record everything that you might want to use in your talk. If you have gathered material on cards, arrange them on the table in front of you and enter the topic of each card in the Analysis List.

B. Evolve from the Analysis List the Main Heads of the Body. At first impression, the completed Analysis List may appear to be merely a hodge podge of disjointed scraps of material. However, as you study this medley, a few ideas begin to emerge as being of fundamental importance to the accomplishment of the Specific Speech Purpose, others as being of less importance, and still others as being irrelevant. Now prepare a tentative list of two to five major ideas to serve as the basic framework of the Body. Revise your selections until you can answer these four questions affirmatively: (1) Is each main heading a direct division of the Specific Speech Purpose? (2) Does each possess relatively the same importance as the others? (3) Is each

---

[1] Charles A. McGlon, "How I Prepare My Sermons: A Symposium," *The Quarterly Journal of Speech*, February, 1954, p. 50.

a separate and independent thought unit, capable of standing on its own feet? (4) Do strong ties of logical association link together the main headings? That is, do these headings follow a natural sequence of thought that will carry the listener progressively point by point to the acceptance or understanding of the speaker's purpose? The main divisions of the Body can be arranged according to a Time order, a Topical series, or a Problem-Solution arrangement. The following section will help you to judge which of the three standard patterns will best fit your materials and your purpose.

ARRANGING THE MAIN HEADS OF THE BODY

If your general speech purpose is to inform, the material contained in the Analysis List may fall naturally into a Time order; it may group itself around a few major topics; or, occasionally, it may suggest a Problem-Solution pattern. If your general purpose is to entertain, the major headings will probably present a Time or Topical arrangement. If your general purpose is to persuade, the basic contentions will require a Topical succession or a Problem-Solution sequence.[2]

A. Time Order. In applying the Time pattern, let each main head represent a unit or period of time. The first head indicates the initial period; the others form a temporal sequence, moving either forward or backward from the starting period.

1. How to organize the Body of the informative speech according to the Time Order. The chronological order is the natural plan for informative speeches which relate a personal experience, give directions, explain a process, describe the historical development of an idea or an institution, or which

---

[2] For the sake of simplicity, this discussion has been confined to three basic patterns. If the student masters their use, he will have little difficulty in organizing any type of speech. Other patterns, such as Spatial, Cause and Effect, the Proposition of "Fact," are primarily variations of the three analyzed here. See Eugene E. White and Clair R. Henderlider, *Practical Public Speaking* (New York: The Macmillan Company, 1954), Chapter 5.

trace the life of an individual. Here are some sample Specific Speech Purposes for informative speeches which might be organized according to a Time Order.

To inform my audience about (1) the discovery of the miracle chemical—hydrazine; (2) the construction of the St. Lawrence Seaway; (3) the history of the N.A.A.C.P.; (4) the development of the first interplanetary space station; (5) how to lay a hardwood floor; (6) how to plan a wedding.

Now we turn to two abbreviated outlines which demonstrate how the main headings are disposed according to a Time Order.

(1) *Specific Speech Purpose:* To have my audience understand the physical processes by which a manuscript is made into a book

   Body:
      I. The first stage is the composition
     II. The second stage is the printing
    III. The third stage is the binding

(2) *Specific Speech Purpose:* To have my audience become better acquainted with the political career of David Lloyd George

   Body:
      I. Lloyd George established the beginnings of his great career as a member of Parliament (1890–1906)
     II. Lloyd George become a major political figure as a cabinet minister (1906–1916)
    III. Lloyd George achieved greatness as Prime Minister (1916–1922)
     IV. Lloyd George gradually lost influence during his years as a member of the opposition (1923–1945)

2. How to organize the Body of the entertaining speech according to the Time Order. The chronological sequence is a convenient method of organizing the entertaining speech which is based upon a real or fictitious narrative, a personal experience, or a light treatment of some historical development. Sample Specific Speech Purposes:

To entertain or (divert) my audience by (1) telling how the back scratcher was invented; (2) explaining how not to conduct a time and motion study; (3) tracing my military career; (4) telling about my first appearance on television; (5) describing my tour through Disneyland; (6) discussing some of the adventures I experienced while driving over the Alcan highway.

Here is a sample outline:

Specific Speech Purpose: To amuse my audience by describing my camping trip in the Sierra mountains

Body:
    I. My experiences during the first day
   II. My experiences during the second day
  III. My experiences during the third day

B. Topical Order. Frequently an Analysis List divides itself naturally into a few main topics or parts. Often these categories represent conventional or traditional divisions such as: plants and animals; National and American Leagues; youth, middle age, and old age; Democrats, Republicans, and Independents; cause and effect; effect and cause; labor, management, and the public; political, economic, and social. Sometimes these major topics represent basic functions, purposes, defects, attributes, or structural parts of some agency, institution, or thing. In other cases, the main categories are "reasons why" something is good or bad, "reasons for" the adoption or rejection of some program, or "objections against" the acceptance of some idea or course of action.

1. How to organize the Body of the informative speech according to the Topical Order. If the Analysis List for an informative speech does not arrange itself into a Time pattern, it usually can be divided into two to five natural or convenient categories. As a general rule, the most important or most interesting topics should be placed first and last, with the less interesting or less important ones in the middle. However, when speaking on a technical or complicated subject, apply the order of understandability by proceeding from the simplest topic to the most complex.

Sample Specific Speech Purposes for speeches to inform which could be organized according to the Topical Order:

To inform my audience about (1) the methods employed by the U.S. Department of Forestry to combat tree diseases; (2) some propaganda techniques used by politicians; (3) the distinctive contributions to society rendered by the Rotary Clubs; (4) the attributes of a successful teacher;

(5) the organizational structure of the UN; (6) the scientific contributions of Harold C. Urey; (7) the major types of pronunciation errors.

The following outlines demonstrate the Topical Order.

(1) *Specific Speech Purpose:* To have my audience understand the requirements for effective listening

   Body:
   I. The effective listener is cooperative
   II. The effective listener is attentive
   III. The effective listener is objective
   IV. The effective listener is analytical
   V. The effective listener is retentive

(2) *Specific Speech Purpose:* To have my audience understand the basic organization of the federal government

   Body:
   I. The legislative powers of the federal government are vested in the Congress
   II. The executive powers of the federal government are vested in the President
   III. The judicial powers of the federal government are vested in the Supreme Court and in inferior courts

2. How to organize the Body of the entertaining speech according to the Topical Order. Almost without exception, if the Analysis List does not contain an obvious Time Order, the speech to entertain can be structured by means of a series of topics or categories. These Specific Speech Purposes would probably be developed by a Topical sequence:

To entertain (or divert) my audience by (1) describing various types of professors; (2) telling about several interviews I had as a reporter for the school paper; (3) analyzing the attributes and deficiencies of the modern girl; (4) describing several interesting customs of the Eskimos; (5) describing the outstanding attractions of Rocky Mountains National Park; (6) telling the three lies which won highest ratings in the National Liars' Club contest.

Sample outline using the Topical Order:

Specific Speech Purpose: To amuse my listeners by describing various types of speakers

Body:

    I. The "perpetual motion" type
   II. The "statue" type
  III. The "mugger" type
  IV. The "limp bag" type
   V. The "orator" type

3. How to organize the Body of the persuasive speech according to the Topical Order. As has been suggested previously, when you wish to persuade an audience that a particular belief, opinion, or proposition is true or false, good or bad, workable or unworkable, you can ordinarily arrange your material under two to five compelling "reasons why" headings; when you are advocating the acceptance or rejection of some policy, the first degree coordinates can be "reasons for" adoption or "basic objections against" adoption. In addition to the familiar rules for the phrasing of coordinates, the main points of a persuasive speech should be expressed in vital, impelling language, that is, they should appeal as directly as possible to the wants, interests, and needs of the listeners. Sample Specific Speech Purposes for persuasive speeches which might be developed according to the Topical Order:

To persuade the members of my audience that (1) German nationalism constitutes a threat to world peace; (2) socialism in England has been [has not been] a failure; (3) cigarette smoking causes cancer; (4) the public school system should adopt a twelve-month school year; (5) atomic reactors should be [should not be] exported from the U.S. to "unfriendly" nations; (6) one should purchase war bonds.

To emphasize the logical relationships in each of the following outlines, linking conjunctions or phrases have been inserted.

(1) *Specific Speech Purpose:* To persuade my listeners that they should consider teaching as a career

    Body:

        I. (*Because:*) Teaching offers you security—(*and, because:*)
       II. Teaching offers you prestige—(*and, because:*)
     III. Teaching offers you pleasant working conditions—(*and, because:*)
    IV. Teaching offers you an unexcelled opportunity for service

(2) *Specific Speech Purpose:* To persuade my audience to buy State Farm Mutual Automobile Insurance

Body:

    I. *(Because:)* State Farm Mutual offers you maximum protection—*(and, because:)*

    II. State Farm Mutual offers you prompt, fair service—*(and, because:)*

    III. State Farm Mutual offers you the lowest possible rates

C. Problem-Solution Order. From diaper to shroud we are continually confronted with problem-solving situations. Think of the perplexities that you encounter during a typical day. In the morning, even before you rub the sleep out of your eyes, the problems begin to multiply. What to wear? How to get that spot off your coat sleeve? What happened to the theme you wrote last night? Should you skip the first period lecture in economics in order to study for the test in history scheduled for the second period? And so on through the day. Sometimes even when you retire for the night problems still intrude upon your consciousness: How to stop worrying about meeting the car payments? Or, how to persuade the couple next door to stop their loud arguing, so that you can get to sleep? Not only is the individual person beset with problems, so are all social, economic, political, and religious groups. As a public speaker, you may wish to inform your listeners about a problem and its solution, or to persuade them that a particular program should be initiated in order to remedy an undesirable situation.

1. How to organize the Body of the informative speech according to the Problem-Solution Order. The speech to inform may use the Problem-Solution Order to (1) explain how a problem was solved, or (2) present objectively one or more possible solutions to an existing problem.

Use Format No. 1 to explain how a problem was solved

Here are some Specific Speech Purposes for speeches which might be developed according to this format.

To inform my audience how (1) the economic problems of the free world were alleviated by the Marshall Plan; (2) the menace of gangsterism was conquered in my community; (3) the need for a tough, heat-resistant alloy was answered by the Pratt & Whitney engineers; (4) the problem of controlling color in TV tubes was solved by the American Brass Company; (5) the problem of keeping human tissue fresh in storage was solved by the Navy; (6) the problem of producing multiple photocopies from a single negative was solved by Remington Rand.

Outline for Basic Format No. I

Body:

I. This was the problem

   A. The problem was important

   (Explain the significance of the problem; what might have happened if the problem had not been solved; who were the persons directly and indirectly affected; what relationship the topic has to the members of the audience. *Note:* As we shall see in Chapter 14, this heading probably should be placed in the *Introduction* as a part of the *Favorable Attention Step*. It is included here to illustrate the complete thought process.)

   B. This was the nature of the problem

   (Explain clearly the character of the problem. What were the major aspects or phases of the situation which necessitated remedial action?)

   C. These were the causes of the problem

   (You may need to explain what causative factors produced the problem.)

II. This program solved the problem

   A. This is the nature of the program which solved the problem

   (Explain the essential characteristics of the solution.)

   B. This is how the program solved the problem

   (Explain how the program was able to remedy the various aspects of the problem.)

   C. This is an estimation of the total results of the program

   (For some speeches, you may wish to present a brief objective analysis, balancing both the good and the bad results of the solution. Did it cause any negative results? If so, did they outweigh the positive effects? Viewed in perspective, did the solution have a salutary effect? *Note:* This point probably belongs in the *Conclusion,* but it is included here to emphasize the total thought sequence.)

Application of Basic Format No. I

To illustrate the functioning of this basic format, the following outline is presented in a form suitable for a speech of about five to seven minutes.

Specific Speech Purpose: To have my audience understand how the American forces won the battle for Iwo Jima

Body:

I. *(Problem Step:)* The occupation of Iwo Jima by the Japanese represented a major obstacle to the successful culmination of the War in the Pacific
   A. *(Importance of Problem:)* Because of its strategic location 750 miles south of Tokyo, Iwo's conquest was vital to the war effort
      1. The conquest of Iwo was the key to the air war against Japan
      2. The conquest of Iwo would open the way for the assault on Okinawa, 362 miles southwest of the main Japanese island of Kyushu
   B. *(Nature of Problem:)* Iwo Jima was a strongly defended island bastion
      1. The Japanese commander, Lieut. General Tadamichi Kuribayashi, had about 23,000 men under his authority
      2. General Kuribayashi had skillfully planned his island defenses to withstand bombardment and direct assault
      3. The physical characteristics of the island also made a successful assault more difficult

II. *(Solution Step:)* The conquest of Iwo Jima by American forces represented a costly victory
   A. *(Nature of Program:)* The battle plans were carefully drawn
      1. In October, 1944, the Joint Chiefs of Staff directed Admiral Chester Nimitz to take Iwo
      2. D day was originally set for January 20, 1945, but unforeseen events caused a postponement until February 3, and then to February 19
      3. The plans called for close coordination of air, sea, and land forces
   B. *(How Program Solved the Problem:)* The conquest of Iwo required an extended and bitterly fought campaign
      1. The pre-invasion bombardment failed to destroy the island's defenses

2. The actual invasion required a month of heavy fighting
3. Final mopping up extended into April
C. (*Estimation of Results:*) In perspective, we would have to assess the Iwo Jima campaign as a successful and necessary military venture, but one tragically costly in human life and suffering
1. The victory helped make inevitable our triumph over Japan
2. However, it proved to be the bloodiest engagement yet encountered by the Marines
3. The Japanese lost an island outpost, General Kuribayashi, and an entire garrison

Use a modification of Format No. I to explain possible solutions for an existing problem

If you wish to inform an audience about the various programs which have been proposed to remedy a current problem, you might follow this sequence. (1) Point out the areas of agreement and disagreement concerning the significance of the problem, its extent and severity, and possibly the factors which produced the alleged undesirable conditions. (2) Then present objectively the several possible solutions. Taking up each proposal individually, explain its basic nature; point out its strengths as claimed by its adherents and its weaknesses as claimed by its detractors; show in what particulars it differs from the other plans. Here are some Specific Speech Purposes which might be developed according to this formula.

To inform my audience about (1) the measures now before the Armed Services Committee to curtail waste in the services; (2) the plans which have been proposed to improve fishing in Lake Tanneycoma; (3) the recommendations now before the Student Council for improving school spirit; (4) the proposals which have been offered to end the strike at the Brighton Mills; (5) the major plans which have been proposed to solve the farm surplus problem; (6) the methods which have been suggested to entice Northern industries to relocate in the South.

2. How to organize the Body of the persuasive speech according to the Problem-Solution Order. Any speech which attempts to persuade an audience to accept a new policy or course of action can be organized according to a Problem-Solution sequence.

*Use Format No. II to advocate the adoption of a particular
solution for a problem*

Study these sample Specific Speech Purposes:

To persuade my audience that (1) the voting age should be lowered to
eighteen; (2) rigid curfew hours for young people under eighteen should
be instituted in the community; (3) an honor system should be instituted at
the university; (4) the federal government should launch a full-scale investigation of professional boxing; (5) a Public Defender system should be
adopted in the community; (6) discount houses should be declared illegal.

The following format will serve as the basis for any talk which
advocates a particular plan or program as the solution to an
existing problem. In individual cases, some modification of the
formula may be necessary because of the character of the available evidence, because of time limitations, or because of the
attitudes and knowledge of the listeners.

Outline for Basic Format No. II

Body:
  I. This is the problem
     A. The problem is important
        (Demonstrate that the problem has significant import for the mem-
        bers of the audience and for society. Explain the harmful effects
        which might result if the problem is not solved satisfactorily.
        Note: As was mentioned in Basic Format No. I, this heading prob-
        ably belongs in the *Favorable Attention Step* of the *Introduction.*
        It is included here to illustrate better the complete sequence.)
     B. This is the nature of the problem
        (Prove that there is a *need* to change from the present system, or
        status quo. [If no compelling need exists, why should a new policy
        be instituted?] Divide the problem into its major topics, aspects,
        or phases. Show concretely the ways in which the present situation
        is unsatisfactory.)
     C. These are the causes of the problem
        (At times, the causes of a problem may be obvious, or may be cov-
        ered indirectly under heading B. In such instances, do not assign
        a separate heading for the analysis of the causative factors. Usually,

however, you should attempt to prove that the problem has been produced by certain faults or weaknesses which are inherent under the existing circumstances. If you can convince your listeners that the present situation is unsatisfactory, that a genuine and serious problem exists, and that it has been caused by defects inherent in the system itself, they have no logical course except to agree that the present program should be changed, if possible.)

II. This program should be adopted
    A. This is the nature of the program
       (Explain clearly, concisely, and adequately the essential characteristics of the plan you are advocating. Unless the listeners understand the nature of your proposals, the remainder of your arguments may fall upon deaf ears.)
    B. This program will solve the problem
       (Prove that your plan will remedy the undesirable aspects of the present situation.)
       (Sometimes, you must also prove that your plan is thoroughly practical and can be put into effect. To show that your proposals are feasible, you perhaps should demonstrate that sufficient monies can be acquired, that the public will cooperate, that engineering skill is available, that the appropriate land can be secured, that sufficient time exists, and so on.)
    C. This program is the best one available
       (It would be psychologically unwise to use this heading if your listeners are emotionally conditioned in favor of another plan, if they are not likely to think of competing ideas, or if your policy is not obviously superior to others. To prove that your program is the best one available, take up the other plans one at a time and show specifically how each fails to solve the problem as effectively as does yours.)
    D. This program will not create additional problems which are as bad or worse than the original
       (As in the case of heading C, you should carefully consider whether or not to include this topic. A claim that your plan will not create serious new problems may stimulate negative thinking on the part of the audience. Sometimes, however, you must prove that the adoption of your suggestions will not cause harmful results. Example: if a speaker advocates the passage of a law prohibiting the discussion of socialism or communism in universities, he must establish that such a law would not produce witch hunts, nor deprive students of necessary knowledge, nor abridge the right of free speech.)

Application of Basic Format No. II

The following outline illustrates how this basic format might be used to develop a persuasive speech of perhaps five to seven minutes' duration.

Specific Speech Purpose: To persuade the members of the Delta Kappa fraternity that all members and pledges whose mid-term grade averages are below a "C" should be suspended immediately.

Body:

I. (*Problem Step:*) The University officials have threatened to cancel our local charter
   A. (*Importance of Problem:*) Such an action would have immediate, heart-breaking effects upon each of us
   B. (*Nature of Problem:*) The University has good reason to threaten our chapter
      1. According to university regulations, any fraternity which is on academic probation for three straight semesters will lose its campus charter
      2. Our chapter has been on academic probation for two consecutive semesters
   C. (*Causes of Problem:*) The causes for our poor grades are obvious
      1. We have overemphasized non-academic activities
      2. We have underestimated the importance of study

II. (*Solution Step:*) If we are to survive as a fraternity, we must adopt a practicable plan to improve our academic standing
   A. (*Nature of Program:*) I propose that all members and pledges whose mid-term grades average below a "C" be suspended immediately from the fraternity
   B. (*Program Will Solve Problem:*) My proposal will save our charter
      1. It will raise our chapter average to the necessary "C" level or better, because it will motivate each man to greater effort
      2. It can be put into effect by a majority vote of the members now present
   C. (*Program Is Best Available Plan:*) My policy is the only feasible method to raise grades
      1. Two semesters ago we tried unsuccessfully an honor plan
      2. Last semester we tried unsuccessfully a complicated study program
      3. There is no reason to believe that either of these systems, or any similar system, would work this semester

4. My plan will work because it offers a positive program with a powerful compulsive force but without negative, restrictive features

D. *(Program Will Not Create New Severe Problems:)* My proposal will have no adverse effect upon the chapter but will save it from disaster

1. Because each person will feel motivated to do his best, few, if any, men would be suspended

2. However, even if some individuals should be suspended, that course would be greatly preferable to the destruction of the chapter itself

SUMMARY

After selecting the Specific Speech Purpose and accumulating suitable ideas and information, you should then discover the main headings of the Body and arrange them in the most effective logical and psychological order.

To organize the Body requires an understanding of the basic principles of outlining. (1) Your outline will clearly and accurately indicate thought relationships if you follow these guides: (a) Adopt and remain consistent in the use of a standard system of symbols and indentations. (b) A subordinate point must be an integral part of its immediately superior heading. (c) Co-ordinate points should be mutually exclusive, that is, they should not overlap. (d) A heading should represent a single idea, rather than compound ideas. (e) Usually every division should result in two or more headings. (f) Major headings should be expressed in simple declarative sentences. (g) Co-ordinate points should be phrased in parallel structure. (2) Your outline should contain at least two first-degree heads, but not more than five. (3) Your outline should cover adequately the subject as delimited by the Specific Speech Purpose.

Two steps are involved in discovering the main heads of the Body: (1) Prepare an Analysis List containing the points you might want to present in your talk. (2) Then, evolve from the Analysis List the chief categories. These major headings, being co-ordinate points, must be determined before supporting materials are placed under any particular head.

The primary divisions of the Body should be arranged according to one of the three basic patterns: Time, Topical, or Problem-Solution. If your general purpose is to inform or to entertain, the material contained in the Analysis List will usually suggest either a Time or Topical sequence, although in informative speaking the Problem-Solution pattern is also sometimes appropriate. If your purpose is to persuade, the Body should be developed according to either a Topical or Problem-Solution sequence. Once you have determined the first-degree captions, you can group under them the appropriate supporting materials.

EXERCISES AND ASSIGNMENTS

1. Select at random about twenty-five of the speech topics listed at the end of Chapters 10 and 11. For each, determine which basic pattern (Time, Topical, or Problem-Solution) would seem most appropriate as a means of organizing the main heads of the Body.

2. Read three addresses in Baird's *Representative American Speeches,* or in some other collection. For each, identify the Specific Speech Purpose and list the main contentions or points of the body.

3. Listen to a speech on radio, on television, or at some meeting. In a written report, answer these questions:

    a. What was the speaker's general purpose? Specific Purpose? Did the speaker state his purpose as such, or did you understand his objectives from the general nature of his material? Do you think that his purpose was apparent to his listeners?

    b. Did the Body of the speech contain definite main heads? If so, what where they? Did they follow a logical pattern of development? Explain. If the speech had no apparent framework, did the clarity and persuasiveness suffer? Explain.

    c. Although we have not yet studied the Introduction and Conclusion, estimate whether the speaker's opening and closing seemed appropriate. Explain.

4. As practice in outlining and as an excellent study aid, immediately after each of your classes reorganize your lecture notes into outline form. The process of analysis and synthesis will help make clear formerly obscure thought relationships and will promote retention.

5. Rearrange the following main and subordinate headings in proper outline form.

Specific Speech Purpose: To have my audience understand the procedure by which the people of the United States elect their President

Body:

I. The presidential candidates and their parties campaign for office
   A. The nature of the party system
      1. Presidential candidates are nominated by party conventions
   B. Procedures followed by conventions in nominating a President
      1. The convention system rests largely upon customs
         a. The size of a convention
      2. Selection of convention delegates
   C. Party machinery must be organized

II. The campaign must be financed
   A. Strategy must be determined
      1. How the members of the electoral college are selected
         a. The electoral college elects the President
      2. How the electoral college elects the President

6. Prepare a four- to five-minute entertaining speech on one of these topics (or on some similar topic):

Is modern art really art?
How to keep bad habits
Let's abolish money
If George Washington should return today
How not to get along with your wife (husband)
If the automobile had not been invented
Modest Texans and no taxation
Co-ed jargon
Soap operas—opiate of the masses
Chewing gum—a national menace
The bobbysoxer—our most civilized savage
How to be an old maid
Five ways to be a fool
If I were President
Political spell-binders I wish I hadn't heard
Human nature as interpreted by a waitress
Adventures in a wax museum
Palmistry—a handy art

7. After making a special study of one of the problems listed in exercise 9, page 514, determine what in your judgment is a workable, feasible, and desirable solution. In a speech of five to seven minutes, urge the class to accept your program. Organize the Body of your talk according to the Problem-Solution pattern.

8. Prepare a five- to seven-minute persuasive speech for class presentation. Organize the main headings of the Body according to a Topical pattern. If you wish, use one of the following subjects.

Television should (not) be admitted to the courtroom.
The police of our community warrant our gratitude for their services.

More rigorous pure food and drug laws should (not) be enacted.

Each industrial worker should (not) receive a guaranteed annual wage.

Relief rolls should (not) be made public.

The divorce laws of this state are antiquated.

Sex education should (not) be taught in the public schools.

A dangerous spirit of anti-intellectualism exists (does not exist) in America.

An international police force should be established as a permanent part of the UN.

The student activity fee should be increased (decreased, abandoned).

A national system of pay-as-you-see television should (not) be established.

Foreign movies are on the whole superior (inferior) to American ones.

Lobbying helps (hinders) the legislative process.

Better highways in the sky are needed.

Marriage counseling can cut the divorce rate.

Trading stamps are (not) a bogus bonus.

Flexible price supports are (not) the answer to the farm problem.

Current high taxes restrict (do not restrict) freedom.

The open stock law of the state should (not) be repealed.

Advertising is (not) an essential element in the capitalistic system.

The immigration laws of the United States should (not) be made more restrictive.

Our national economy is (not) threatened by an unofficial alliance between big business and big labor unions.

9. Prepare a five- to seven-minute actuating speech on a topic, such as one of the following.

Convert your personal liabilities into assets

Get your free chest X-ray

Enlarge your vocabulary

Enroll in an elementary course in accounting

Attend the pep rally tonight

Contribute to the campus charity fund

Vote for _____ for student body president

Join the square-dance club

Enroll in the Red Cross first aid course

Attend the Wednesday evening lecture at the observatory

Engage actively in extra-curricular activities

Stop smoking

Give a pint of blood to the University blood bank

Take up leather working as a hobby

Visit the special display at the art gallery

Drive more carefully

Help keep the campus free from trash

Buy copies of the campus literary magazine

Help solicit toys for the firemen's Christian toy project

Buy personal liability insurance

13 ❦❦ *Developing the Body*

Napoleon's military genius has been attributed to his minute and pervasive attention to details of logistics and strategy. Somewhat like the planning of a successful military campaign, the effective speaker must marshal supporting details to buttress his major contentions. The first and second degree headings of an outline are general assertions, representing the basic thought framework. Lacking concreteness, impressiveness, and persuasiveness, they must be reinforced by means of compelling evidence and reasoning. Only in this way can the listener understand the full meaning and significance of the speaker's fundamental ideas or arguments. Only in this way can the skeptic be convinced, the sluggard stimulated, or the procrastinator moved to action.

USING THE FORMS OF SUPPORT

To clarify, amplify, or to prove his major headings, a speaker may utilize various types of materials, such as: illustrations, quotations, statistics, comparisons, reiteration, explanations, and visual aids. (Inevitably, in any such list some overlapping exists. For instance, a quotation might contain a comparison, statistics, or an illustration.) The standard method in using the forms of support is to state the point under discussion, present the developing materials, and then show the application of the data to the topic. In somewhat unusual cases, the experienced speaker may prefer to use the method of implication, that is, to present the supporting matter before stating the idea or contention which it develops.

In the following pages each form of support will be analyzed in terms of its strengths and weaknesses, its uses and limitations, and its application to speeches of basic types.

A. The Illustration or Example. Most speech teachers would agree with Lincoln, who said that the average person is "more easily influenced and informed by illustrations than in any other way," with Henry Ward Beecher, who characterized the illustration as "a window in an argument," and with Norman Vincent Peale, who stated that "The true example is the finest method I know of to make an idea clear, interesting, and persuasive." If you wish to become a truly effective speaker, master the use of the example.

The illustration is a narrative. It is a report of an event or occurrence for the purpose of developing the heading under consideration. Now, let us take up the three types of illustrations: the detailed factual, the undeveloped factual, and the hypothetical.

1. The detailed factual illustration. This kind of example relates in detail some true-to-fact happening or incident. In the following passage, notice how Dr. Peale develops a true narrative in such a manner as to achieve maximum inspirational effect.[1]

Statement of the Main Point	If you want true and permanent peace of mind, you have to get close to God. Get Him into your life, let His spirit drive deeply into your personality.
Detailed Factual Illustration	A friend of mine who operates *The American Surgical Trade Association Journal* sent me a story . . . of a hardpressed surgeon in one of the hospitals of our city. He had grown irritated from over-work, and came to perform an operation in an irascible mood. All was in readiness in the operating room when they wheeled in a beautiful girl who had been badly injured in an accident. She did not know she was considered a hopeless case. The nurse who was to give the anaesthetic said, kindness in her voice, "Relax and breathe deeply." The girl looked up at the nurse and asked, "Would

[1] This excerpt comes from the sermon "Peace for the Troubled Heart," delivered at the Marble Collegiate Church, New York City. Used by special permission of Dr. Peale.

you mind very much if I repeated something my mother taught me when I was a child? I would like to say the twenty-third Psalm."

The nurse looked at the doctor and he nodded. The girl started: "The Lord is my shepherd: I shall not want."

The surgeon listened as he washed his hands. The attendants were very quiet. They had heard this Psalm in churches and cathedrals, but here it seemed to have a deeper meaning. ". . . though I walk through the valley of the shadow of death, I will fear no evil: for Thou art with me . . ."

The nurse started to give the anaesthetic, but the doctor said, "Hold it. Let her finish." Then he said to the patient, "Go on, honey, say it to the end. Say it for me, too."

As she finished the doctor looked down on her. He was at peace, relaxed. His skillful hands were ready now, and peace was in his heart. The operation was a success.

Application to the Main Point

Queer, isn't it, how peaceful all of us have become. What have we done? Nothing but call attention to some of the most familiar words we know. And these are just a few of the words out of the Book which drive deeply to the essence of human nature with its therapy.

Do you want peace? Get near to God—that is the answer. . . . All basic and lasting peace is from God.

In using detailed factual illustrations, ask yourself: Is each one obviously *relevant? Fair? Clear? Vivid? Accurate?* And, have I used a sufficient *number* of them? (1) To insure that the listeners recognize the relevancy of the example, make a direct application of the example to the argument it supports. (2) Use only those examples which are fair representatives of the great mass of evidence. Do not pass off an exceptional case as the norm. (3) Since the purpose of the example is to present a series of word pictures, prepare each illustration in a plausible, adequately developed fashion. Give sufficient background material in the proper order so that your auditors can formulate the desired sequence of mental images. Overloading the example with unnecessary or irrelevant details blurs its focus and dulls its trenchant qualities. (4) The effective illustration tells a story so graphically that the listeners are carried along without conscious effort on their part. By means of empathy, they experience vicariously, or "live in," the happening which the speaker is relating. Achieve maximum appeal to the intellect and to the emotions by utilizing the Factors of Interest discussed later in this chapter. (5) A factual illustration is true to fact. This means that you are a reporter of an event or occurrence which has actually happened. Therefore, all details of your narration should be accurate and consistent with the real occurrence. (6) As we have already learned, the typical audience represents a wide latitude of wants, interests, attitudes, and experiences. Unless its selection is unusually felicitous, a single illustration may not prove to be sufficient clarification or amplification for an important point. The use of more than one example fosters understanding and attention by utilizing additional fields of interest, and it promotes belief by providing a more comprehensive coverage.

2. The undeveloped factual illustration. Unlike the detailed example, the undeveloped one contains only the barest essentials. Because it affords only a partially developed picture, a condensed example may be inferior to the extended narration in its appeal to the intellect or to the emotions. On the other hand, several condensed illustrations can be presented within the span required for a single full-length example; this permits the speaker to exploit additional areas of interest and to document his point with evidence drawn from a variety of sources.

When employed skillfully, the short illustration can add strength and comprehensiveness to your ideas. (1) As a rule, avoid using one or two undeveloped examples as the sole means of developing an idea. (2) Instead, present a series of three or more short illustrations, or offer one or more condensed examples in conjunction with some other form of support such as a detailed factual illustration.

B. Brewster Jennings, Socony Mobile Oil Company execu‚ tive, used a series of specific instances to vitalize an otherwise abstract idea.[2]

Statement and Explanation of the Main Point

Man's greatest discovery is not fire, or the wheel, or the internal combustion engine, or atomic energy, or anything in the material world. It is in the world of ideas. Man's greatest discovery is teamwork by agreement. . . .

Series of Short Factual Illustrations

Every step of the way on the long road of human progress has increased the need for teamwork. A man can transport himself and his goods by walking or even riding a horse if he can catch himself a horse. That requires little or no teamwork. A wagon or stagecoach provides better transportation, but requires more teamwork. And, of course, an immensely greater amount of teamwork is needed to move us and our goods by auto, truck, bus, train, ship, or airplane.

A few men with a few tens of thousands of dollars of savings can drill a shallow oil well in settled country. It takes a much bigger organization to build a steel-legged island in the Gulf of Mexico or in the Pacific Ocean, and from it drill a well reaching down miles below the waves.

Similarly the costs and risks involved in searching for oil in underdeveloped countries across the ocean are of an entirely different dimension from those in this country. It is necessary to build docks and roads and water systems and complete towns, to bring in vast stores of equipment, and skilled people to train the nationals for a variety of jobs. On top of all that, facilities for transporting, refining and marketing the oil have to be created, sometimes from scratch.

No major oil development in the Middle East is now the undertaking of a single company, even though the leading companies in the oil industry are of substantial size. . . . Iranian oil formerly produced wholly by the Anglo-Iranian Oil Company today is being handled by a consortium of oil companies from England, France, the Netherlands and the United States.

[2] *Vital Speeches*, October 1, 1956, p. 758. Reprinted by permission of the editors of *Vital Speeches*.

The history of the development of foreign sources of iron ore has paralleled oil. One or two of the biggest steel companies have ventured abroad alone, but their smaller competitors have banded together in joint ventures to share the enormous costs and risks both in foreign operations and in working low grade ores in this country.

Perhaps the most spectacular of the recent examples of the ever increasing need for more and bigger teamwork was the discovery and release of atomic energy by a gigantic wartime consortium under government auspices in an effort far too big for any single company—even the biggest. . . .

Application to the Main Point

The farther mankind pushes out the frontiers of knowledge the larger must be the safari organized to take the next scientific explorer into the unknown. . . .

As I have indicated, teamwork by agreement takes many forms, but its essence is that men join together to accomplish what they could not do at all, or as easily, or as well, by themselves.

3. *The hypothetical illustration.*   Because it is a narration of an imaginary rather than a true incident or happening, the hypothetical illustration is usually less persuasive than a factual example. However, since it does not purport to be an accurate, true-to-fact report, it possesses an extraordinary flexibility. Despite diligent searching, the speaker sometimes cannot find a suitable factual example. In such cases he can invent a situation, weaving the narrative to fit the particular needs of his listeners, the occasion, and his point. Also, a speaker can use the hypothetical illustration to predict future events and to clarify and vitalize abstract ideas or complicated processes. Of course, when using a fictitious example never attempt to disguise its imaginary nature.

In speaking to a group of Butler University students, Dr. James T. Perry employed this humorous hypothetical narrative.[3]

Statement and Explanation of the Main Point

The point I am pressing as essential to our well-being is that you try to keep open the channels of communication within the family group, in your community life,

[3] *Phi Kappa Phi Journal*, Fall, 1956, pp. 12 and 13. Used by special permission.

and in your business and professional relationships. Differences will remain, but a difference is nothing to be afraid of if you know what it is and why.

Both intellectual and physical differences are the materials on which natural selection works. They are the best guarantee for the nation's health and vigor. . . . That so many organizations and well-intentioned persons are devoting themselves to the task of leveling down and eliminating such differences is for me a disturbing fact of life. That many of them believe their efforts are serving the ends of freedom is even distressing.

Some time ago I heard a distinguished editor tell a story which I must share with you. It obviously is not factually true, but it is philosophically sound.

Hypothetical Illustration

You probably know something of the Doukhobors, that strange sect that came to western Canada from Russia in the latter part of the nineteenth century. About this time of year, as part of their religious rites, they follow a practice which is always startling to persons outside the faith. They remove all their clothing and follow their usual pursuits in a complete state of nudity. As the story has it, one fine spring day a young male Doukhobor accordingly appeared in his original state in the market place of the town. A policeman tried to apprehend him in the interest of the community's morals and sensibilities. The Doukhobor, not wishing to be incarcerated, started to run. Fleet of foot and traveling light, he outdistanced his pursuer. The heavily accoutered officer peeled off his jacket and shirt but without improving his position. He kicked off his shoes in order to run faster. Later he shed his trousers and then other pieces of apparel. Happily for the morals of the community, he finally caught the Doukhobor, but by that time, nobody could tell which was the policeman and which was the Doukhobor.

Application to the Main Point

As I read the newpapers, I am often equally confused as to who are the friends and who are the foes of our fundamental liberties. . . . We can never close the chasms between us, but we can span them. We can override the differences and find common values in the free exchange of culture and ideas.

B. Testimony. Emerson wrote in his *Letters and Social Aims,* "By necessity, by proclivity,—and by delight, we all quote." Certainly most effective speakers make liberal use of direct quotations and paraphrases. Why should you use testimony? For one reason, listeners may hesitate to accept an opinion or course of action merely upon your unsupported assertion. However, they perhaps will be impressed if you can show that prominent experts or public opinion endorses your position. For instance, if you were to assert that winters are not as cold as they were when you were a small child, would your word be accepted? Undoubtedly not. Your point would be far more persuasive if you were to quote the release which the International News Service attributed to Francis W. Reichelderfer, Chief of the U. S. Weather Bureau: "There are indications that the temperatures throughout the world are one or two or three degrees warmer than they were ten or twenty years ago. At least we suspect that's true although we don't have complete records for all parts of the earth. . . . It means that winters are not as cold as they once were." In addition to promoting persuasion, testimony also helps to make ideas clear and interesting. Almost every important topic has been written about or spoken about by others. Frequently such expressions offer a lucidity and a vividness which we, ourselves, would find difficult to equal. Furthermore, involuntary attention will be encouraged if the source of the quotation is a well-known personality, a person of high prestige or of interesting experiences, or a famous historical figure.

A student speaker used these quotations from Abraham Lincoln to add vivid support to a contention.

Statement and Explanation of the Main Point	Everyone is at least partially imprisoned by the mores and beliefs of his times. For instance, even Abraham Lincoln, whom I regard as the greatest of all Americans, could not completely divorce himself from the stultifying influence of mass opinion. Living as we do in 1958, we are inclined to forget that our liberal attitudes concerning race relations are far advanced from those held

First Quotation

Second Quotation

*Application to
the Main Point*

in 1858 by even as great a humanitarian as Lincoln. We know that Lincoln loved all men, regardless of color or creed. But, what were his beliefs on social and political equality? In his debate with Stephen A. Douglas at Charleston, Illinois, September 18, 1858, Lincoln stated: "I will say then that I am not, nor ever have been in favor of bringing about in any way the social and political equality of the white and black races, that I am not nor ever have been in favor of making voters or jurors of negroes, nor of qualifying them to hold office, nor to intermarry with white people; and I will say in addition to this that there is a physical difference between the white and black races which I believe will forever forbid the two races living together on terms of social and political equality. And inasmuch as they cannot so live, while they do remain together there must be the position of superior and inferior, and I as much as any other man am in favor of having the superior position assigned to the white race." Somewhat later in the same debate, Lincoln asserted: "Judge Douglas has said to you that he has not been able to get from me an answer to the question whether I am in favor of negro-citizenship. . . . He shall have no occasion to ever ask it again, for I tell him very frankly that I am not in favor of negro citizenship." My purpose in using Lincoln's words on this subject is not to detract from the memory of that noble man. I have endeavored to demonstrate that even the greatest of men are at least partially imprisoned within the envelope of their environment.

Here are some suggestions for the effective use of testimony: (1) When you imply that you are using a direct quotation, give a verbatim report. Do not distort the meaning by additions, by deletions, or by lifting the statement out of context in a prejudicial manner. When paraphrasing, indicate by words or manner that you are using your own expressions and not those of the source. Furthermore, conscientiously endeavor to reproduce both the spirit and intent of the original statement. (2) Unless imperative that the listeners know exactly which words are being quoted, avoid using the words "quote" and "unquote."

Let a change in tempo, pitch, or emphasis indicate the beginning and closing of a quotation. (3) Avoid triteness in introducing a quotation. Instead of using a worn out phrase like, "I have a quotation here I should like to read," say something like this: "Last night on NBC's "Meet the Press" television program, Senator Stuart Symington said. . . ." (4) Keep quotations short. Usually several pithy references are more attention compelling than a single long quotation. (5) Do not use out-dated quotations on controversial issues to represent the current thinking of a person. Changing conditons may have persuaded him to alter his opinions. (6) Use testimony of only unquestionable credibility and appropriateness. The source should be intellectually and emotionally acceptable to the listeners. A thinking audience will reject testimony which appears to be influenced by prejudice or self-interest; it will insist that the source be a competent authority in the field and that he have had the opportunity for first-hand observation of the particular subject. If the source is not well known to your listeners, perhaps show that his opinions possess significant value by giving his title, or by briefly mentioning some of his achievements or experiences. (7) If the testimony is of critical importance to your argument, you may wish to explain when and under what circumstances the statement was made, what agency recorded it, and how it can be verified.

C. Statistics. Statistics are figures which the speaker employs to develop an idea or to prove an assertion. Although perhaps the most frequently misused form of support, statistics can be both interesting and impressive. The statement, "The heart is a strong, tough, and durable organ," is a sterile abstraction. Specificity and vividness could be given the concept by saying something like this:

> How much do you know about nature's most perfect pump? I'm speaking about the terrific power plant that is your heart. If your car were as efficient as your heart, you could drive 1,000,000 miles without going to a garage for a motor overhaul. In a single minute, the heart beats about 72 times and produces enough energy to lift a 78-pound dumbbell a foot off the floor. In an average lifetime, the heart beats nearly 3,000,000,000 times and generates enough energy to lift the "U.S.S. Missouri" out of the water.

As you probably know, the blood supplies the body with vital nutrition, carries away wastes, regulates the water balance, equalizes the body temperature, distributes various glandular secretions, and aids in the defence against disease. To accomplish these functions the heart must push a continuous flow of blood through a complex network of tubes. If the heart falters for even a moment, unconsciousness ensues. If it stops for more than a few minutes, you die. How much blood do you think your heart must pump each minute even when you are resting? Two pints? Maybe three? The answer is five quarts. During my five-minute speech your heart has pumped over six gallons of blood. If you are normally active today, your heart will pump about 5,000 gallons. If you live an average life span, your heart will pump a total of nearly 130,000,000 gallons. How long do you believe it takes for the blood to make a complete circuit from heart-to-arteries-to-capillaries-to-veins and back to the heart? Fifteen minutes? An hour? The answer is a little over a minute. May I suggest that the next time you are in a reflective mood you might give thanks for the strong, sturdy heart which labors so durably in your behalf.

In applying statistics, observe these rules: (1) Avoid the overuse of numerical data. No other form of support loses its interest value more quickly than do statistics, and none places greater strain upon the understanding and retentive powers of the listeners. (2) Make your figures only as precise as the circumstances warrant. The rounding off of figures will promote understanding and retention, usually without impairing accuracy. As an example, ordinarily you would be sufficiently precise to say "73 billion dollars" rather than "72,986,318,479 dollars and 51 cents." And, your listeners would have only two digits to remember instead of a confusing total of thirteen. (3) Make statistics vivid and meaningful by explaining their significance and by interpreting them in terms which are familiar and interesting to the listeners. For instance, a University of Miami student used this method to make more meaningful the number of registered motor vehicles in Dade County, Florida:

If the 450,000 cars and trucks registered in Dade County were parked bumper to bumper, the lead cars would rest in New Hampshire. If the line were headed for Cleveland, many of the cars would be submerged in Lake Erie. If the file curved around the Gulf of Mexico, it would stretch from Miami, through New Orleans and Houston, and nearly to the Mexican border at Laredo.

(4) The sayings, "Figures don't lie, but girdles condense the truth" and "There are lies, damned lies, and statistics," typify the almost universal skepticism of statistics. Audiences are more inclined to accept data which have been gathered and interpreted by some reliable source, such as the U.S. Department of the Interior, the American Institute of Public Research, or the American Education Association. When speaking on a controversial topic, if figures are essential to your case, you should usually identify the source and explain specifically where the data may be inspected, that is, *"Statistical Abstract of the United States,* 1959 edition, page 127," or "the April 17, 1959, issue of *U.S. News and World Report."* If the data have been prepared by a source which is unknown to the hearers, you may wish to explain the methods used to compile and interpret the information. (5) In using the term "average," you usually should specify which kind of average you mean—median, mean, or mode. "Median" designates in a series the mid-point at which half of the individuals or numbers are on one side and half on the other. "Mean" refers to the simple arithmetical average which is determined by adding the quantities involved and dividing by their number. "Mode" indicates the figure which appears most frequently. Thus, if seven students have test scores of 40, 40, 45, 50, 55, 65, and 150, the median score is 50, the mean is 63.6, and the mode is 40. Obviously, the use of only one type of average may fail to present a reliable understanding of the range or the deviations within the series. (6) Avoid using obsolete statistics. Especially in some fields the validity of numerical data decreases rapidly with the passage of time. As an illustration, the Nielsen estimate of the number of persons who watch a particular TV program might be accurate at the time the survey is made, but the same figures might be deceptively inaccurate after a lapse of one or more weeks.

D. Comparison or Analogy. The analogy notes the similarities between objects, ideas, or institutions and draws inferences from those resemblances. By connecting a known, understood, or accepted idea with one which is unknown, misunderstood, or unaccepted, a *literal* comparison may advance both conviction and clarification. As one would judge from its name, the literal analogy compares things of the same class, as automobiles to automobiles, bridges to bridges, paintings to paintings, politicians to politicians, and so on. To form an effective literal comparison, the two items involved should be alike in as many essential details as possible. Furthermore, the basis for comparison should be well known and accepted by the listeners, that is, one of the halves of the analogy should be familiar and approved. To compare two unknown items or two unacceptable things would not encourage understanding or persuasion.

Louis Waldman, President of the Brooklyn Bar Association, used this extended literal comparison to develop his argument for containment (rather than coexistence or liberation) of Communism: [4]

Statement of the Main Point

What then is the alternative to an agreement with the Kremlin for peaceful coexistence? Here I again appeal to the valuable lessons of history. It would be well for our people and our statesmen to restudy the history of the 20-year period preceding our own Civil War. Three choices were then presented to the American people. One was a policy of containment—the Missouri Compromise. Another was a policy of liberation—the doctrine of the Abolitionists. The third was the policy of peaceful coexistence—the program of . . . Stephen Douglas. . . . Those three principles were presented with great ardor and conviction before the American people. Stephen Douglas, in one of his great speeches, presented the doctrine of peaceful coexistence, although not by that name:

First Half of the Analogy

"Let each state mind its own business and let its neighbors alone. . . . If we stand by that principle, then Mr. Lincoln will find that this republic can exist forever divided into free and slave states. . . ."

As you can clearly see, that was the philosophy of coexistence. The Abolitionists, demanding liberation, obviously did not agree. Lincoln, who stood somewhere

[4] *Vital Speeches*, June 15, 1955, pp. 1293–1294. Reprinted by permission of the editors of *Vital Speeches*.

between the ardent Abolitionists and the apostles of peaceful coexistence, answered Douglas thusly:

"You say it (slavery) is wrong; but don't you constantly . . . argue that this is not the right place to oppose it? You say it must not be opposed in the free states, because slavery is not here; it must not be opposed in the slave states, because it is there; it must not be opposed in the pulpit, because it is not religion. Then where is the place to oppose it? There is no suitable place to oppose it."

As you know, throughout his term of office, the Great Emancipator did not wish to fight the Civil War. But neither did he favor the philosophy of peaceful coexistence with slavery. He did favor containment as a policy dictated by necessity and liberation as an ideal toward which the Nation would aspire. . . .

Qualifications of the Analogy

I know that there are some differences between the situation that existed in our country in 1861 and the situation that exists in the world today. We were one nation under a single constitution, whereas the world consists of independent, sovereign nations. Actually, however, separate countries are far more interdependent at the present time than were the states in the 1858–61 period. Supersonic airplanes, speedy ships, radio, and television have all shrunk the world into a unit more compact than the pre-Civil War United States.

Lincoln . . . saw the difference between a vital interest of a nation and the ideal of a nation. . . . Lincoln felt that containment would have meant ultimately a slave United States. . . . But although he set up containment as the absolute minimum, he nevertheless held aloft for the Nation and its people the ideal of liberation, never giving moral sanction to slavery in the slave states and never giving moral sanction to slavery in the free states. . . . And yet he would not resort to war to fight for the ideal. . . . He felt that if we could only keep the peace, time would solve the slavery problem.

Second Half of the Analogy

These precepts of Abraham Lincoln could well be applied by the statesmen of our time. . . . Our security depends upon a policy of containment. Much as we hate war, we have got to serve notice that when it comes to the extension of the slave police state of Communism to the free western world, we will have to take a stand

> against it as affecting our own safety and security.
> Liberation of these people who are now in the Com-
> munist empire should be maintained as an ideal. . . .
> Yet it must be made clear . . . that we are not ready
> to throw the world into a bloody horror to accomplish
> liberation by war.

By pointing out unique relationships between two ideas which appear to be completely different (such as a smile to sunshine, or Communism to a disease), a *figurative* analogy can make a point impressive and stimulatingly vivid. Examples: (1) In 1920, when he was appointed to the newly created position of Director of the Budget, Charles G. Dawes urged that President Harding call a special briefing session for the Cabinet. In the course of explaining the functions of his office to the Cabinet members, Dawes used this figurative analogy:

> A cabinet officer, as I see him, is on the bridge with the President, advising him on the direction in which the ship shall sail. He will not properly serve the captain of the ship or its passengers, the public, if he resents the call of the Director of the Budget from the stokehole, put there by the captain to see that coal is not wasted. . . . The way coal is handled and conserved determines how far in a given direction the ship will sail.

(2) Perhaps the outstanding contemporary master of the figurative analogy was Winston Churchill. In a speech to the House of Commons, August 20, 1940, he made this typically Churchillian comparison: "The British Empire and the United States will have to be somewhat mixed up together in some of their affairs for the mutual and general advantage. For my own part, looking out upon the future, I do not view the process with any misgivings. I could not stop it if I wished; no one can stop it. Like the Mississippi, it just keeps rolling along. Let it roll. Let it roll on full flood, inexorable, irresistible, benignant, to broader lands and better days." (3) In speaking to the Second Annual New Product Introduction Seminar, New York City, Wendell B. Barnes (Administrator, Small Business Administration) used these figurative analogies: [5]

[5] *Vital Speeches*, April 1, 1955, pp. 1149–1150. Reprinted by permission of the editors of *Vital Speeches*.

<table>
<tr><td>*Statement of
the Main Point*</td><td>While there are disadvantages, small business has a few inherent advantages of its own [over big business].</td></tr>
</table>

*Statement of
the Main Point*

While there are disadvantages, small business has a few inherent advantages of its own [over big business].

Did you ever see a race between a rabbit and a greyhound? I mean a *real* race, not one where there is an electric rabbit running against the dogs at a dog-track.

*Figurative
Analogy No. I*

If the rabbit just keeps on, straight-away, the greyhound will soon overtake him.

But that isn't the rabbit's game. *His* game is to make a short dodge and double back. And he will gain twenty yards every time he does. The secret is that the rabbit is short-coupled. The greyhound has more length of body and can't turn or maneuver as well.

*Figurative
Analogy No. II*

The Spanish Armada sailed up the English channel in its might to sink the pitiably small British fleet under Drake. Anybody looking at this immense task force, with ships four times the size of Drake's vessels and at least ten times the number, would have thought the Spaniards would win, hands down. And yet Drake had what the Spaniards lacked—great maneuverability. And that is what turned the tide for Britain.

*Application of
Analogy to the
Main Point*

This lesson should be easily applied. Maneuvering is comparatively easy for a small company with few executives. They can make up their minds much faster than a company with a long chain of command. If they decide to quit making a product, it doesn't take six months to "phase out" that product.

Big policy decisions should take a long time, but in large corporations, the policy decisions seem to take an inordinate amount of time. Things get too highly specialized, agreement can't be had between the various types of specialists and policy makers. Some companies must even use committees to make policy and you know how long it usually takes a committee to reach a decision.

Figurative analogies should be brief, credible, and striking. Unless a figurative comparison is particularly vivid and impressive, do not let it stretch more than thirty seconds. Your linkage of the two dissimilar halves of the analogy must be conceivable; absurd relationships would impede rather than facilitate comprehension. A final caution: since the items being compared represent different classes, the figurative analogy usually represents a weak form of logical proof; its primary purpose is to vivify and to clarify, rather than to serve as factual evidence.

E. Restatement and Repetition. The teacher, the safety engineer, the politician—everyone who speaks frequently in public—learns that few listeners understand either the nature or the significance of an idea upon a single exposure. Reiteration helps provide the concentration and duration of focus which is necessary for comprehension and appreciation. Broadly speaking, reiteration can refer to any material which develops an assertion made by the speaker. However, the term is used here in the much more restricted sense of *restatement* (saying the same thing over again in different words) and *repetition* (repeating a statement in identical phrasing). An example of repetition is provided in Bishop G. Bromley Oxnam's sermon at the initial service of the Second Assembly of the World Council of Churches, Evanston, Illinois. Wishing to emphasize the necessity for religious unity among the member churches, Oxnam repeated the phrase *"We intend to stay together"* nearly a dozen times during the course of his address. In his charge to the British people, June 4, 1940, Churchill employed restatement by saying: "Victory at all costs, victory in spite of all terror, victory however long and hard the road may be; for without victory there is no survival." The following passage from one of Franklin D. Roosevelt's most controversial fireside chats presents a skillful blending of both restatement and repetition as well as a striking figurative analogy.[6]

The American people have learned from the depression. For in the last three national elections an overwhelming majority of them voted a mandate that the Congress and the President begin the task of providing . . . protection [against another depression]—not after long years of debate, but now.

The courts, however, have cast doubts on the ability of the elected Congress to protect us against catastrophe by meeting squarely our modern social and economic conditions.

[6] *Vital Speeches,* March 15, 1937, p. 349. Reprinted by permission of the editors of *Vital Speeches.*

We are at a crisis in our ability to proceed with that protection. It is a quiet crisis. There are no lines of depositors outside closed banks. But to the far-sighted it is far-reaching in its possibilities of injury to America.

I want to talk with you very simply about the need for present acton in this crisis—the need to meet the unanswered challenge of one-third of a Nation ill-nourished, ill-clad, ill-housed.

Last Thursday I described the American form of Government as a three horse team provided by the Constitution to the American people so that their field might be plowed. The three horses are, of course, the three branches of government—the Congress, the Executive, and the Courts. Two of the horses are pulling in unison today; the third is not. Those who have intimated that the President of the United States is trying to drive that team, overlook the simple fact that the President, as Chief Executive, is himself one of the three horses.

It is the American people themselves who are in the driver's seat.

It is the American people themselves who want the furrow plowed.

It is the American people themselves who expect the third horse to pull in unison with the other two.

Here are a few suggestions for the use of reiteration: (1) Although it may exert a persuasive appeal, reiteration should not be substituted for logical proof. Since it merely says the same thing over again, it offers no new support to an idea. (2) Adjust the amount of reiteration to fit the requirements of the audience and the subject: too little will not provide adequate reinforcement; too much will be tedious and redundant. Heed the admonition in St. Matthew vi, 7: "Use not vain repetitions, as the heathen do; for they think that they shall be heard for their much speaking." (3) Repeat all significant ideas twice or more, and important or unusual names, dates, prices, etc., at least once. (4) Remember that rhetorical and direct questions may serve as effective reiteration (review Chapter 4). Presently we shall consider the efficacy of visual aids as reiteration and amplification. of the subject.)

F. Explanation. As a form of support, explanation refers to those descriptions and definitions which are employed to make a heading clear and understandable. Descriptions promote clarity by depicting what a thing is, how it looks, what it thinks, how it feels, what it does, and so forth. In speaking to a group of teachers, Andrew T. Weaver presented this concrete explanation of the meaning of speech.[7]

Statement of *Main Point*	Speech is man's greatest discovery and invention.
	In that dim and misty age, before the dawn of history, speech was on man's tongue and in his ears when he was but an infant on the earth. Speech was with him when he lived in caves and carved crude symbols on the
Explanation	walls, striving to picture it in visible form. Through speech, man's traditions were preserved and passed along from generation to generation. Through speech, men learned to live together in families and to cooperate for the promotion of the common welfare.

Speech forms that inner stream of awareness which we call mind. Speech molds us in its own image. Speech teaches us to know and to sympathize with one another. Speech enables us to think clearly, feel truly, judge justly, and act wisely.

Were speech to fail, our intelligence would lapse to the level of the beasts, each individual would dwell apart from his fellows, the structure of society would crumble, the very fabric of life itself would disintegrate, and all the vital processes of civilization would grind to a faltering stop.

Speech reflects the history of all that is past and prophesies all that is yet to be. Of speech Confucius said, "What man requires to administer government is that in his words there be nothing incorrect." Dante sang, "It must be done by speech or not at all." And mindful of the power of speech, Mentor Graham, humble teacher of the immortal Lincoln, charged his pupil never to forget that "the right words will guide the world."

Restatement of *Main Point*	Speech is man's greatest achievement and his crowning glory.

If you are to speak with clarity, you must explain unfamiliar, complex, or technical terms (for example, words like "feed back," "infield fly rule," "perihelion," and "group dynamics"

---

[7] A. Craig Baird, W. Norwood Brigance, Wayland M. Parrish, and Andrew T. Weaver, "What Is Speech? A Symposium," *The Quarterly Journal of Speech*, April, 1955, pp. 145–153.

are not widely understood) as well as those terms which are familiar, but are confusing because of various possible interpretations (such as "progressive education," "free enterprise," "socialism," and "intellectual"). The basic method of defining is to place the word or idea in its logical general classification or category and then to show how it differs from other members of that order. For instance, we might define a "panel" in this way.

Basic Category	*Differentiating Characteristics*
A panel discussion is a form of group speaking which:	(1) is conducted in the presence of an audience.
	(2) It has a chairman and
	(3) three to six discussants
	(4) who sit in a semicircle
	(5) facing each other and the audience.
	(6) The group utilizes give-and-take conversation
	(7) which is systematically organized
	(8) and relatively objective
	(9) to discuss a meaningful question.

Although this definition is more detailed than most dictionary explanations, amplification in the form of further explication, examples, comparisons, etc., would make clearer the nature, purposes, and uses of the panel. (You might be interested in glancing ahead to Chapter 19 to see the full-length treatment of the subject.)

Consider these three suggestions: (1) Keep explanations simple. Complicated, technical, abstract, or obtuse exposition not only fails to clarify but is guaranteed to anesthetize your audience. Use simple, concrete, and accurate language to make your material instantly intelligible. (2) Keep explanations brief and germaine. Long-winded, rambling explication stultifies interest. (3) Consider explanation as the initial step in making an idea clear and meaningful. Definitions and descriptions usually require reinforcement by other forms of support such as illustrations, statistics, analogies, and so on.

G. Visual Aids. Up to the present, we have considered only audible forms of support, those presented verbally by the speaker. Now we turn to an analysis of visual aids, one of the most stimulating and persuasive types of supporting materials. Both experimental studies and practical experience demonstrate that man learns faster and is impressed more readily if both the senses of sight and hearing are stimulated. Seeing *is* sometimes worth "a thousand words." When prepared carefully and presented skillfully, visual aids are unexcelled in promoting clarity, capturing involuntary attention, stimulating the feelings, encouraging belief, and in impelling action. The validity of this statement is proved by television commercials and programming, teaching, military training, platform speaking, and by the sales of magazines like *Life, Look,* and *American Heritage.* Whenever possible, incorporate into your speaking such visual material as actual objects or specimens, full-sized or scaled models, moving pictures, slides, film strips, maps, diagrams, charts, graphs, globes, cartoons, photographs, and blackboard diagrams.

In using visual aids: (1) Always consider the knowledge, background, and interests of the listeners, the physical conditions under which you will speak, and the amount of time required for the demonstration. An exhibit which might be well adjusted to a textbook or to a specialized or highly motivated group might be too complicated for the general audience. Aids should possess sufficient size and distinctness of detail to be seen easily and clearly by everyone in the audience. Since visual material should be almost instantly intelligible, avoid crowding too many details into a chart or graph. In general, a visual aid should contain a single primary idea. If you wish to present several basic ideas, prepare additional exhibits. Keep labels and printed descriptive matter as short as possible. Often a chart does not require a title, because the accompanying oral continuity explains its purpose. Before determining to use visual materials always weigh the probable benefits against the amount of time required for execution. Minutes seem to assume jet speed when you attempt to put a machine into operation, control a monkey for an inoculation, or record a table on the blackboard. (2) By careful planning and rehearsing, save precious seconds, perhaps minutes, in presentation and add a professional polish and smoothness to your performance. If you are personally to operate equipment such as a projector, a mechanical model, or a machine, practice until you are able to maintain good eye contact and an easily flowing oral commentary. If an assistant is to help with the visual aid, brief him thoroughly; drill him until he is prepared to do an expert job. Check all relevant physical elements beforehand, such as the location and size of the screen, the placement of the wall outlets, the lighting in the room, the presence of a sturdy stand for the displaying of large diagrams or charts (or tape for the attaching of smaller exhibits to a wall or panel), the proper working order of all mechanical parts, and so on. Remember: a few extra minutes spent in planning the demonstration may save you costly mistakes and grim embarrassment. (3) General suggestions: Before your talk remove any objects on or near the platform which might distract from your visual material. Usually do not display the aid until you are ready to discuss it in your speech; when you have concluded talking about it, put it out of sight. Direct your gaze and discourse to the listeners with only an occasional glance at the material you are demonstrating. As was mentioned in Chapter 5, if you wish to direct attention to a specific part of the display, stand to one side and employ a pointer. Do not turn your back to the listeners unless absolutely necessary and do not stand directly between them and the aid.

USING THE FACTORS OF INTEREST

You already know that to be an effective speaker you must capture and maintain the favorable attention of the listeners. Every form of support used in a speech should be selected and developed in terms of its appeal to one or more of the various factors of interest: proximity, significance, vivid concreteness, variety, and humor.

A. Proximity. The planets of the solar system move in elliptical orbits around their common center of gravitation, the sun. Although the analogy is imperfect, we can consider that the wants, desires, needs, dreams, ambitions, and frustrations of our personal world revolve around their gravitational center, our own selves. It is natural that our lives should be primarily concerned with the direct cares of ourselves and our families. Is not the answer to each of the following questions, "You"? When you suffer an attack of intestinal flu, who runs a fever? When you forget to study for an examination, who fails? When you are called upon to deliver a speech, who experiences butterflies in the stomach? When you swim too far from the shore, who must struggle for survival? Throughout life, your only contact with the world is by means of your neuromuscular system. Education, experiences, love, and a learned concern for humanity undoubtedly increase your areas of sensitivities and feelings of social responsibilities. Nevertheless, because of biological, logical, and psychological needs, your own self is the gravitational center around which the rest of the world revolves.

Now let us apply this principle to the speaker-audience relationship. The closer you direct your materials to the immediate wants and interests of the listeners, usually the greater will be your appeal to their involuntary attention. Examples: Students ordinarily will be more interested in a fatal accident that happened recently on the campus than in a similar tragedy which occurred several years ago in another part of the country. Young men are more concerned with their own imminent problem of securing good jobs than in the similar need of unemployed elderly workers. Young mothers are more concerned about the care and raising of infants than about the preparation of the junior Miss for high school or college. A class in public speaking is more interested in the struggles of Walter Reuther to become an orator than in the corresponding efforts of Cotton Mather, the colonial minister. Also, because of each person's interest in his immediate surroundings, an audience may give involuntary attention when a speaker refers to some object or happening in the room, comments on a previous remark by the chairman or another speaker, or mentions by name someone in the audience.

B. Significance. In applying this factor of interest, consider both general significance and the basic human wants (the desire for physical, psychological, and economic security; the desire for companionship, loyalty, reverence, affection, and sexual expression; the desire for personal freedom; and the desire for excitement, adventure, and change).

1. Appeal to general significance. By selecting speech subjects and supporting materials which possess general significance, you appeal to the involuntary attention of your listeners.

Consider these major news features which, at the time of their occurrence, captured the attention of much of the world.

On an April afternoon, Sir Winston Churchill emerged from Buckingham Palace and climbed heavily into the back seat of his car. Tightly packed crowds pressed close to catch a glimpse of the old man with the big cigar and the black frock coat. As the limousine passed down narrow Downing Street, the crowd cried "Good Old Winnie." Before he disappeared through the historic black door numbered "10," the former Prime Minister smiled and waved his fingers in the victory salute. Within an hour, Buckingham Palace issued this announcement which was soon speeded around the globe: "The Right Honorable Sir Winston Churchill had an audience with the Queen this evening and tendered his resignation as Prime Minister and First Lord of the Treasury, which Her Majesty was graciously pleased to accept." Why was this episode of absorbing interest to so many people? Because it possessed great historic significance. It marked both the end of an era and the close of an unparalleled career. It made a difference in the lives, the thinking, and the emotions of millions of persons from Chartwell, England, to Sydney, Australia.

A week after Churchill resigned, Dr. Thomas Francis, Jr., stepped to a microphone and addressed an audience of distinguished scientists assembled in the University of Michigan's

Rackham Building. Although an hour earlier the press and radio had prematurely released the gist of his message, millions of persons awaited his official pronouncements concerning the safety and efficiency of the Salk vaccine. Why were persons interested? Because the vaccine promised the end of the killing and crippling disease, poliomyelitis.

Admittedly, a reference especially rich in, let us say, vivid imagery or humor might be more stimulating than one of general significance. However, an audience will usually be more interested in a World Series baseball game than in a pre-season practice game, in a Presidential election than in a high school election, in a hurricane than in a gale, in a U.S. Supreme Court decision concerning a major topic such as desegregation in intra-state transportation than in a judgment of a small claims court, in a famous television star than in an obscure stand-in, and so forth.

2. Appeal to significant human wants. To make your ideas interesting and persuasive, appeal to the basic human motives. Psychologists tell us that human behavior is basically goal seeking behavior. According to *Business Week:* [8]

People . . . don't seem to be inherently reasonable. They often don't know why they do the things they do; what they do often has little logical connection with the situation they are in; their actions are almost never the result of rational evaluation of profit and loss. But people do act with purpose. Their behavior makes sense if you think about it in terms of its goals, of people's needs, of their motives. That seems to be the secret of understanding or manipulating people.

For genuine effectiveness, an appeal to reason should also constitute an appeal to a want. Listeners usually respond with alacrity if you base your evidence and reasoning upon their fundamental needs and cultural patterns. With somewhat less readiness, they are also attentive to references concerning the influence of vital drives in the lives of others.

On the following pages the categorizing of the impelling

---

[8] "Behavior Research: To Get Answers, Ask the People," *Business Week*, August 21, 1954, pp. 130–143 *passim.*

human wants and desires is meant to be suggestive rather than arbitrary. Since any such catalogue is potentially misleading, we should recognize that the expression of all drives is strongly conditioned by social consciousness, that they "wax and wane in intensity as they undergo periods of deprivation and as they achieve gratification," [9] and that several might operate simultaneously, frequently in conflict. For instance, after a long afternoon spent in working tedious laboratory experiments, you might experience a strong impulse to speed while driving back to the dormitory. Probably, however, you would refuse to yield to this urge for excitement because you fear that an accident might result in costly damage to the car, physical injury, or social disapproval.

Although Justice Holmes believed that "Security is an illusion," *one of our most imperative desires is to be physically, psychologically, and economically secure and comfortable.* (1) Without a deeply ingrained instinct of self-preservation, a species would soon become extinct. Our preoccupation with the preservation of our physical well-being is evidenced by our buying a half-billion dollars' worth of drugs each year, paying the nation's physicians an average annual salary of over $15,000, and directing unprecedented sums into medical research. To promote our physical comfort we carefully select innerspring mattresses for restful sleep, choice steaks for pleasurable eating, sparkling beverages for smooth drinking, cathartics for regularity, well-constructed shoes for easy walking, mild cigars for a non-irritating smoke, and so on. (2) Competition has produced an America of tremendous economic and industrial development; competition has also produced widespread psychological insecurity. Unlike those societies where a caste system or tradition relegates the individual to a certain status, Americans, generally speaking, have the opportunity to develop as far as their initiative and abilities permit. The resultant competition for material treasure and for individual and group

[9] Bert R. Sappenfield, *Personality Dynamics* (New York: Alfred A. Knopf, Inc., 1954), p. 54.

status tends to produce tensions and anxieties. In addition, psychological frustrations are produced by threats of war, automation, conflicts inherent in our political system, and so on.

According to Bishop Gerald Kennedy our emotional tensions have produced a national "lust for security." In addressing the National Convocation of Methodist Youth at Purdue University, he stated: "We are afraid of Communists, or ideas, or change, or controversy, or analysis, or facts. Too many people seem to be saying by their attitude: 'I have made up my mind. Do not confuse me with the facts.' We want to tie things down and make everything quiet, safe, and dead." Perhaps critics like Bishop Kennedy exaggerate our feelings of tension, doubt, guilt, hostility, and insecurity. Nevertheless, statistics say that we Americans swallow 20 million tablets each night to induce sleep, that we take 15 tons of aspirin every day to ease headaches, largely the result of nervous tension, that we spend perhaps $150 million a year for tranquillizing pills, and that possibly one out of ten Americans has sought mental security in the reading of Joshua Loth Liebman's *Peace of Mind*, Fulton J. Sheen's *Peace of Soul*, or Norman Vincent Peale's *The Power of Positive Thinking*. One of the most potent methods of promoting psychological security is to demonstrate to the listener how he can protect and increase his social prestige, power, and influence. Also, you appeal to a basic motive when you show that your proposals are based upon the stable, the known, and the familiar. (3) Everyone desires economic security. We want protection from job insecurity, inflation, national depressions, property devaluation, law-suits, fire, accidents, theft, economic hazards of old age, loss of income through illness, and so on. Only time will answer whether Americans swing further toward the British concept of the welfare state or back toward the concept of individual initiative and responsibility. We do know, however, that men will always be greatly interested in economic security.

Another impelling motive is our universal and pervasive interest in companionship, loyalty, reverence, affection, and sex. As John Donne wrote, "No man is an island." One of the most terrifying punishments in penal institutions is to place a person in solitary confinement. Most of us prefer company when walking to class or attending a movie or ball game. We are a gregarious people, a nation of joiners. (In Miami there is even a club devoted to the preservation of the African violet!) Furthermore, we feel bonds of loyalty, even devotion, toward our clubs, universities, communities, states, athletic teams, nation, family, church, and God. Sometimes our feelings of loyalty are so intense that we are willing to fight, kill, and be killed.

Freud believed that the sex drive was the wellspring actuating all human behavior. It is unnecessary to accept Freud's extreme views to recognize the omnipresence of the sex impulse. The parade of cheesecake pictures in the newspapers is endless. Perfumes feature names like "My Sin," "Ecstasy," "Surrender," "Escapade," and "Indiscreet." Romantic love is the primary theme of modern songs, folk ballads, and many novels. It vies with crime as the main staple for dramatic shows on radio, television, and movie screens. Furthermore, sex provides the source of much of our humor. Apparently almost no one is too old or too infirm to maintain an interest in sex.

Also, we possess a deep-rooted desire to experience as much personal freedom as possible. We realize that some external restraint over our freedom is necessary to provide an efficiently regulated society. We work at our jobs 40 or more hours a week mainly because of desire for security and because of feelings of loyalty for our families. In times of crisis, we submit to rigid restrictions because of patriotism, fear of social disapproval, etc. Nevertheless, we frequently chaff at controls and, when they impinge too strongly upon our desire for freedom, we rebel. We modern Americans possess the same independent spirit which motivated our forefathers to dump tea, to tar and feather stamp collectors, and to circumvent the hat act, the wool act, the sugar act, and other repressive measures of our parent country, England. We wish to live where we please, eat and drink what we choose, go to bed and get up when we desire, read what we want, say what we please, work at a job of our own selection, and belong to any religious faith we wish, or none at all if so inclined. Everyone wishes to preserve and increase the area of his personal freedom and is interested in the attempts of others to do likewise.

Because most of us live fairly routine, humdrum lives, we desire excitement, adventure, and change. The skin diver, the hot rod racer, and the hunter are responding to the need for escape from the monotony of daily living. Usually the fear of injury, economic factors, and family responsibilities keep us within our normal, safe orbit. However, we enjoy experiencing vicariously the adventures of others. Comfortably seated in our chairs, we can listen spellbound as a speaker demonstrates how to force-feed a cobra, tells how it feels to be shot out of a cannon, or depicts his gun battle with a couple of thugs on the waterfront.

C. Vivid Concreteness. Make your material attractive and instantly intelligible by employing vivid concreteness. In Chapter 4, the symbolic nature of language was discussed and specific guides were offered for the effective use of language in speaking. Perhaps it would be wise to re-emphasize here that words are not things, but are vocal symbols. Since they are not things, words cannot be transferred from one person to another in the simple fashion of a grocery clerk handing a can of sardines to a housewife. Words have accurate symbolic values only if both the speaker and the listener have attached relatively similar meanings to the words. And words are most effective in stirring up meanings in others when they are specific and graphic. Despite his ability to pursue extremely abstract and philosophical trains of thought, man thinks in images. The more abstract a speaker's language becomes, the more difficulty his auditors will experience in attempting to follow, and the weaker becomes his appeal to involuntary attention. To be vivid, you must first think in terms of specific reality and then must phrase your ideas in clear, graphic, specific language.

Inexperienced speakers tend to underestimate the value of imagery. By means of carefully selected words you can verbally create scenes, events, and happenings, thus enabling listeners to experience vivid sensory impressions. For example, in recounting one of his experiences as a Marine trainee, a student invoked all of the types of imagery. He stimulated *auditory* imagery by mentioning the chatter of machine guns as they fired live ammunition a yard above his head, by recounting the rustle among the leaves as he crawled around a log, and by describing the sudden violent warning of a snake's rattles. He used *visual* imagery by telling how the snake slithered off the log and coiled menacingly, with head drawn back and jaws opened. He appealed to *motor* or *kinaesthetic* imagery by picturing the evident tension in the snake's body, by relating how his own body had temporarily "frozen," and by recounting how he began to inch backward out of striking range. He employed *tactile* imagery by describing the feel of the mucid, slippery humus against his face and hands. He utilized *olfactory* imagery by mentioning the sour, fetid odor of the rotted vegetation. He even invoked *gustatory* imagery by telling how satisfying a chocolate bar had tasted following his exhausting experience.

D. Variety.   As we have already seen, wearisome sameness in speech content or delivery makes difficult, if not impossible, the effective appeal to involuntary attention. (1) In developing your ideas, use as many as possible of the factors of interest. Do not appeal exclusively to a single type of motivation, but attempt to stimulate several of the impelling drives. Draw your evidence and reasoning from a variety of fields which should be interesting and meaningful to the listeners, and use an appealing selection of the various forms of support: examples, statistics, comparisons, explanations, repetition, and so on. When possible, supplement oral communication with visual aids, such as pictures, charts, and objects. Improve the clarity and attractiveness of your ideas by employing a variety of the types of imagery. When using illustrations and humor, attempt to utilize the techniques of surprise, suspense, and climax. (2) Vary your style of utterance by employing figures of speech, such as similes, metaphors, and personification. Also, make occasional use of rhetorical and direct questions, exclamatory and imperative sentences, and bits of conversational dialogue. (3) In vocal delivery, avoid monotony in pitch, rate of speaking, vocal quality, loudness, and intensity. Let your voice reflect the natural flexibility you experience in animated social conversation. (4) In physical delivery, attempt to avoid the wooden stiffness of a totem pole or the mechanical, repetitive movements of a robot. If you apply the principles in Chapter 5, and if you possess a strong wish to communicate, your physical presentation probably will not be handicapped by inflexibility.

E. Humor. Frank M. Colby observes, "Men will confess to treason, murder, arson, false teeth, or a wig. How many of them will own up to a lack of humor?" Humor plays a significant part in the lives of nearly everyone. Perhaps, as William Rose Benét suggested, man is "born to laughter." Certainly humor is unexcelled for capturing involuntary attention and for stimulating a congenial feeling of rapport between the speaker and his audience. In basically serious presentations, the judicious application of humor provides an enjoyable change in pace. Audiences welcome occasional relief from the effort of concentrating upon earnest explanation and evocation. Furthermore, humor can make ideas strikingly vivid, thereby promoting understanding, persuasion, and retention.

Despite its importance and wide occurrence in our daily living, humor is a complex psychological phenomenon, resisting easy understanding. Perhaps the most helpful concise explanation of the nature of humor is offered by Oliver and Cortright: "Humor arises from a sudden perception of incongruity accompanied by a sense of well-being." [10] Let us examine this definition more closely. "Sudden" means that humor usually must contain the element of surprise. It must strike home its point with a swift, unexpected, sharp thrust. When a slowness or clumsiness in its development causes the listeners to anticipate the results, humor usually loses its trenchant qualities. The fol-

[10] Robert T. Oliver and Rupert L. Cortright, *New Training for Effective Speech* (New York: The Dryden Press, Inc., 1951), rev. ed., p. 481.

lowing attempts at humor derive most of their punch from unexpected twists in thought.

The remarkable thing about college reunions is that your classmates have gotten so stout and bald they hardly recognize you.

A small town is a place where everybody not only knows which men beat their wives, but also which wives need beating.

Psychiatrist: "What did you say?"
Patient: "I said that for some strange reason people don't like me. . . . Pay attention, fathead!"

"Incongruity" refers to an unfamiliar, incompatible, or unreasonable combination of familiar elements. Thus, these quotations attempt to divert the listener, primarily by unique relationships or situations.

Two camels trudged along side by side in a caravan crossing the burning desert. Finally one of them looked around furtively and spoke: "I don't care what anybody says," he whispered. "I'm thirsty."

At a party a woman leaned over to a friend and confided: "I'm miserable. I've got on my sitting-down shoes and my standing-up girdle."

Humor should promote a "sense of well-being" on the part of the listeners. To provide pleasure, the incongruity must be painless. Humor involves a spirit of enjoyable play which is shared by both the speaker and the audience. An attempt at humor is not amusing if it evokes in the listener the unpleasant emotions of pity, sorrow, anger, embarrassment, jealousy, alarm, and so on. Furthermore, a "sense of well-being" usually should be present in the audience *before* the humor is presented. If the hearers are disturbed, very serious, or tired, the introduction of humor may be ill-advised.

Despite the complex nature of humor, it can be safely asserted that successful humor is relevant, appropriate, and fresh, and usually is planned. Humor is *relevant* if it possesses a direct application to the subject, audience, or occasion. Such humor develops naturally out of the speaker's thinking. It reinforces and makes stimulatingly graphic the point the speaker is attempting to establish. The attention provoked by irrelevant humor will not compensate for its distracting influence from the topic under consideration.

Humor is *appropriate* if it fits the audience, the occasion, your purpose in speaking, and yourself as the speaker. As general rules: avoid off-color remarks; refrain from embarrassing individuals or minority groups in the audience; regard humor as a spice and use it sparingly—if overused, it may impair or destroy the basically serious mood of the informative or persuasive communication; do not lose your poise or sense of propriety in seeking to get laughs.

Humor is *fresh* if it is new to the members of the audience. Make your witticisms as original as possible. Achieve freshness by drawing humor from the nature of the occasion, the physical surroundings, previous remarks by other speakers, or from appropriate banter with the chairman. Also, original humor can be successfully derived from hyperbole or understatements, trenchant irony or burlesque, clever turns of phrases, novel twists of familiar statements or poems, ludicrous comparisons and contrasts, mimicry, and pointed dialogue. Perhaps somewhat less effective, as a general rule, are original puns, jokes, and funny stories. When borrowing humor from others, adapt the details to the needs of your speech and the speaking situation, thus providing some sparkle of originality.

Humor is *planned* if the speaker has analyzed the potential receptivity of the audience and the influence of the occasion; insured the pertinence of the humor to the unfolding of his ideas; prepared his material so that it appears to be spontaneous and so that it proceeds crisply, smoothly, and effortlessly to a sudden disclosure of its incongruent ending; rehearsed his vocal and physical delivery so that he is able to get maximum mileage from the humor. Practice can vastly improve the timing and emphasis which are so important in putting humor across. In case you are wondering whether impromptu humor has any place in platform speaking, it should be added that undoubtedly brilliant flashes of humor sometimes occur to speakers in the course

of their addresses. However, much of what seems to be impromptu wit has been carefully prepared by the speaker and held
in readiness for the appropriate opportunity. Off-the-cuff humor
usually lacks neatness and dispatch in the telling and, particularly in the case of satire, may be inappropriate. Our advice is
to use impromptu wit with caution.

SUMMARY

The first- and second-degree headings represent merely the
basic thought framework of the speech. To make these headings
clear, interesting, and persuasive, the speaker should utilize the
various types of supporting materials: detailed and undeveloped
factual illustrations, hypothetical illustrations, testimony, statistics, literal and figurative comparisons, restatement and repetition, explanation, and visual aids. All supporting material
should be selected and developed in terms of its appeal to one
or more of the factors of interest: proximity, significance, vivid
concreteness, variety, and humor.

EXERCISES AND ASSIGNMENTS

1. Prepare a brief speech describing some event or happening which you
have witnessed. Use as many of the various types of imagery as possible.

2. In a short speech, explain which forms of support provide the strongest
logical proof and which offer the weakest. Support your contentions.

3. Prepare a five- to six-minute talk involving the use of some visual aid.
Many of the topics listed at the end of Chapters 10, 11, and 12 will prove
suitable subjects. Here are some additional ones.

Building a hi-fi set
Treating a snake bite
Administering artificial respiration
Giving a blood transfusion
Drawing animated cartoons
The muscular system of a human
being
Simple electrical repairs
How sonar operates

Pruning fruit trees
Reupholstering a chair
How glasscutters make the Cape
Cod glassware
Diving for sponges
Bulldogging a steer
Relining automobile brakes
Installing a room air conditioning
system

The Battle of Gettysburg
Preparing film strips
How the colonists made bayberry
  candles
Simple feats of magic

Aligning and balancing wheels
How Coast Guard helicopters effect
  rescues at sea
Operating marionettes
Cutting diamonds

4. During your reading of newspapers, books, and magazines, observe any unusually effective usage of the forms of support. Here are two examples.

(1) In this excerpt, Francis and Katherine Drake use statistics to prove that a significant share of our defense costs are caused by the training of officers to replace those who have resigned.

> Most jet pilots, for instance, come from college ROTCs. They are committed to serve for three years. It takes two of these years and $200,000 to train them combat-ready, which leaves them one year of their hitch to serve. Then if they quit (70 per cent do) we have to start training new men. Over a ten-year period this means training ten pilots, at a total cost of two million dollars, to keep one cockpit combat-ready. And we have 10,000 combat planes in the Air Force and 8,000 in the Navy! There goes 36 billion dollars!
>
> "How We Could Have Better National Defense—for Less Money," *Reader's Digest,* February, 1957, p. 75.

(2) In this passage, Joseph Wechsberg uses two illustrations to dramatize the fate which awaits refugees from the Iron Curtain countries who return home.

> A Czech refugee who had been in one of Germany's refugee camps, before going back home, promised his fellow inmates to write to them how things were in Czechoslovakia. It was agreed that if his letter was truthful he would sign it "sincerely." If, however, he was forced to write lies, he would sign the letter "very sincerely." When the letter arrived weeks later, describing the wonderful life in Czechoslovakia, it was signed, "Yours very, very sincerely." And a Lithuanian who recently returned from Buenos Aires to his Baltic homeland wrote to his friends in Argentina, "It's marvelous here. You should all come back. Don't forget to buy a good trunk at Lazaro Costa's store." The "trunks" which Costa sells are—coffins.
>
> "Aliens in a Free World," *The Atlantic,* January, 1957, pp. 39–43.

5. Analyze a news broadcast by some prominent radio or television commentator to discover the forms of support and the factors of interest used.

6. From the written text of an address in *Vital Speeches* (or in some other collection of speeches), pick out each form of support and each factor of interest. Also, note the speaker's appeals to the basic drives and his use of imagery.

14 ❧❧ *Developing the Introduction and the Conclusion*

As we have seen earlier, the main function of the speech is accomplished in the Body. Nevertheless, both the Introduction and the Conclusion are of great importance to the achievement of the speaker's purpose and should be closely integrated with each other and with the Body. Although the analogy is somewhat stretched, in some ways a speech may be compared to a rocket: the first stage (Introduction) gets the speech underway by stimulating favorable attention and by orienting the audience to the Body; the second stage (Body) takes the speech most of the way by applying information, logical reasoning, and emotional appeals to the subject; the third stage (Conclusion) concludes the course of the speech by summarizing the thought, promoting the proper mood, and, if necessary, by attempting to impel action.

DEVELOPING THE INTRODUCTION

Your opening remarks should be carefully planned to meet the anticipated initial reaction of the listeners, the nature of the occasion, and the demands of your subject. Because special adaptations are required for each speech situation and each speech purpose, no fixed length can be given to the Introduction. If the audience is favorably impressed with the speaker and is interested in his message, and if the speech theme is uncomplicated, a very brief Introduction may be sufficient. On the other hand, if the speaker must stimulate a lethargic group, relieve hostility toward himself or his proposals, or give considerable background explanation, an extended Introduction may be necessary. However, as has been mentioned before, the typical Introduction probably runs about 10 per cent of the total speech length.

The functions of the Introduction can be achieved by means of a Favorable Attention Step and a Clarification Step.

A. Promote a Receptive Attitude on the Part of the Listeners by Means of a Favorable Attention Step. As a speaker, you will find that most audiences will give fairly close attention for the first minute or two; however, unless you establish a friendly, animated mood, attention soon wanes and may be difficult to recapture. It is during the first few minutes that you establish proper rapport with your listeners, set the mood, and point out the direction of the speech. To encourage a receptive attitude on the part of the listeners, demonstrate at the outset that you are an alert, animated speaker with an interesting, meaningful message. Here are the basic methods of promoting attention and good will in the Introduction.

1. Point out the significance of your subject. One of the most effective methods of securing favorable interest in the Introduction is to explain to your listeners how important your subject is *to them* and to society. In beginning an address before a convention of the National Education Association, Earl James McGrath (President, University of Kansas City) attempted to secure sympathetic attention by stressing the importance of his topic.[1]

Text

No one can any longer be accused of being hysterical, unduly dramatic or inflammatory when he says that today American education faces problems more serious than at any time in our history. The most obvious justification of this statement is to be found in the growing shortage of teachers and schoolhouses. But there are a host of others of lesser magnitude related to the organization and administration of the schools, the content of instruction, methods of teaching, the education of children of workers,

[1] *Vital Speeches,* September 15, 1955, pp. 1479–1480.

instruction for exceptional children, expanded library service in rural areas, and many others which need not be elaborated for this audience.

Readily available facts prove that these problems are getting worse rather than better. Paradoxically, at the same time, informed Americans agree that our individual well-being, our prosperity as a people, and our national strength are in large part the result of the educational opportunities made increasingly available to our citizens. If the present situation is to be improved, all thoughtful Americans must consider what steps can be taken toward this objective; but such a responsibility devolves especially upon us, the members of the educational fraternity.

Outline

Introduction:

I. *Favorable Attention Step* [2]
   A. American education faces problems more serious than at any time in our history
      1. The most obvious justification of this statement is to be found in the growing shortage of teachers and schoolhouses
      2. There are other justifications of lesser magnitude
   B. These problems are getting worse rather than better
   C. Informed persons agree on the vital importance of public education
   D. The responsibility for resolving the problem falls upon all Americans, but especially upon the professional educators

2. Use pleasantry, wit, and humor. If prolonged, in poor taste, trite, or irrelevant, the use of humorous material can easily be detrimental. However, good-natured banter or repartee with the chairman, witty anecdotes, clever play on words, novel comparisons and contrasts, and amusing references to the speech situation or the audience can get your speech off to a sparkling beginning. Benjamin F. Fairless (then Chairman, United States Steel Corporation) used this light, friendly passage to open an address before the Economic Club of Detroit.[3]

That was a wonderful build-up that Harlow Curtice has just given me, and I would be the last man in the world to dispute a single word of it. But just for the sake of his future reputation, I hope that you gentlemen will remember that toastmasters are not expected to stick too closely to the

---

[2] Because of their specialized functions, the Introduction and Conclusion do not necessitate a slavish adherence to the general guide that each division should result in two or more sub-heads.

[3] Used by special permission of Mr. Fairless.

awful truth. They are merely supposed to make their victim feel as happy as possible before he is fed to the lions. And in my case, that has never been done more successfully!

There was one part of his remarks, however, that I liked even more than the others; and that was when he referred to a statement of mine as "Detroit talk." Now, in my book, that is a very great compliment indeed, for it has always seemed to me that whenever Detroit talks, it speaks the economic language of a growing, dynamic America—the kind of America that has confidence in itself and a boundless faith in its future. That is the kind of America I believe in; and it is the kind of talk that I believe in, too.

You see, the automobile industry and I were born at the same time, so I've watched it grow from a pup; and while I've never been a direct part of it, it has taught me a great deal about the true meaning of the word *enterprise*. In fact, you people in Detroit remind me a lot of the old Swedish prospector who went out to California and struck it very, very rich. Every time he disappeared into the hills he came up with a new vein of ore that was even bigger and better than the last one; and his envious companions were trying desperately to learn his secret. Finally, one day, he broke down and told them how he did it:

"Boys," he said, "I yoost keep digging holes."

And that's how it is with you fellows. Come hell or high water, you yoost keep making cars!

3. *Use an illustrative story, comparison, or quotation.* An example, an analogy, or a quotation may serve as an interesting springboard into your speech. Such materials may be drawn from your personal experience, imaginary occurrence, history, or literature. Robert T. Oliver began an extended address on "The Top Communist Weapon—the Spoken Word," with several illustrations and quotations.[4]

The Sunday New York *Times* [recently] carried a striking story of two Americans, a man and a woman, who had been released by the Chinese Communists after three and a half years of imprisonment, and returned home insisting that they had deserved their imprisonment on charges of spying, that they had been well treated, and that the Communist system is so much superior to free enterprise that it will inevitably be adopted around the world.

During that same week there appeared on the newsstands an issue of

[4] *Vital Speeches*, May 1, 1955, pp. 1200 and 1201. Reprinted by permission of the editors of *Vital Speeches*.

Look containing an article, "Inside Red China," by William Stevenson, in which the author relates how he was escorted through Communist China with flowing assurances that everything was wonderful in the "workers' paradise." After enjoying the opera in Shanghai he went backstage to congratulate the singer-actors, and then, suddenly, "saw the naked reality behind the Bamboo Curtain." There on a prominent blackboard was written an abject "confession" of error by one of the actors. As Stevenson wrote, "He had uttered some criticism of the government. The Communist cell in the theater called a discussion meeting. His fellow thespians recited his weaknesses and sins. Now it was all there on the blackboard retold by the miserable wretch himself. . . ."

My own major experience with the effects of the discussion meetings held by the Communist came in Korea, where I interviewed scores of north Korean refugees who had fled into south Korea. They all related stories of enforced attendance at weekly discussions. . . . [They] suffered deeply inflicted mental wounds and twisted thinking, all the more insidious because it had been imposed upon them from within their own misdirected brains.

Gradually it has become apparent that the weapons of Communism are not alone guns and bombs, nor torture and slavery, but even worse: tortured ideas and a lethal misuse of facts.

We are so accustomed to thinking of public speaking, discussion and debate as essential instruments of democracy that it may shock many people to learn they also are shrewdly utilized as indispensable weapons of Communist tyranny.

In speaking to an American Legion meeting in Florence, South Carolina, the Reverend Mr. Feltham James introduced his plea for military preparedness with this analogy.[5]

The men of many wars lie silent. Victims of a terrible disease. . . . The battles they fought made history, yet to many of them the glory of the victory was theirs on history's pages only, for we have not stamped out the disease. In spite of the achievements of science, in spite of the development of the wonder drugs . . . in spite of the discoveries that have rid mankind of deathly plagues, America is still infected with a disease that has claimed uncounted thousands. It is America's perpetual disease. The tragic results of that disease are visible in every cemetery where lie the remains of our soldier dead; in every hospital where the maimed and the sick are suffering from battle-caused inflictions; and even on our streets where the crippled and handicapped depict the casualties of war.

[5] *Vital Speeches,* June 15, 1955, p. 1307.

America's perpetual disease is . . . the result of the failure of the supreme legislative bodies of our country to fulfill their obligation laid down
in the Constitution. . . . Except in times of extreme emergencies Congress
has not made provision for the protection of the Nation.

*4. Make a stimulating statement or ask a provocative ques-
tion.* To capture favorable attention, a statement or question
should be intriguing, relevant, and in good taste. Avoid striving
awkwardly to be shocking or sensational. Also, avoid being
crude or insulting. One student alienated his listeners at the
outset of his speech by asking, "When was the last time you
cheated on an examination?" Another irritated his auditors by
beginning with this question: "Do you falsify your income tax
returns?" Perhaps the following examples will illustrate the use
of the stimulating statement and the provocative question.
Robert G. Ingersoll introduced his famous lecture "The Liberty
of Man, Woman, and Child" with these sentences: "There is
no slavery but ignorance. Liberty is the child of intelligence."
A student used these questions to begin a talk on first aid.

What would you do if, on your way home from this meeting, an accident occurred and your arm was cut badly? Would you panic and struggle
hysterically? Or, would you have the knowledge and skill to stop the bleed-
ing and perhaps save your life? If you were playing golf and one of your
companions suffered a sunstroke, would you be able to apply emergency
treatment and perhaps save his life? If a fish bone or a toy should become
lodged in your child's throat, would you be able to remove the object and
restore breathing—and save that previous life? You could successfully cope
with each of these crises and many others if you enroll for the American
Red Cross first aid course which begins next Monday at Central High
School.

5. Mention common bonds. A commonly used method of
fostering favorable attention is to refer briefly to relationships,
beliefs, interests, and feelings which the speaker shares with the
audience. To arrive quickly on common ground with one's
listeners is sometimes of critical importance in speeches of persuasion. The following excerpt shows how U Nu (Prime Minister of Burma) attempted to establish common bonds with his

listeners in beginning a speech to the National Press Club of
Washington, D.C.: [6]

Mr. President, distinguished guests, and members of the National Press
Club, this is a very happy event for me. I do not feel that I am a total
stranger here. I suppose that this is partly because I, too, am a writer. In a
certain sense, I am even a reporter. Therefore, we have a common interest
and a common love for truth and the expression of truth.

Furthermore, I feel that I know you. How could anyone in public life
these days fail to know the American press? You are everywhere, at all
times, and under all circumstances. In fact, having seen so many of you
recently in so many parts of the world, I wonder that so many of you
could be here today. In any event, I am very pleased to join the long list of
guests who have appeared before you and which has included so many
distinguished names.

When I accepted your invitation, I did so with a certain feeling of responsibility not to waste your time with generalities and platitudes—a
responsibility to speak frankly what is in my mind on the subjects that are
important to all of us. I believe that this is in the tradition of the National
Press Club.

6. Refer to the occasion or purpose of the meeting. If you
are a visitor addressing a regular meeting of an established
organization, or if you are speaking at a special meeting called
for a particular purpose, you may wish to make appropriate references to the occasion or purpose of the meeting. In a Fourth of
July address at Faneuil Hall, Boston, Clare Boothe Luce immediately related the purpose of the meeting to her speech.[7]

Today in this historic Faneuil Hall, revered by all American patriots
but especially beloved by Bostonians, we come together to commemorate
the 179th anniversary of the signing of the Declaration of Independence.

You may guess with what emotion, with what a mingled sense of pride
and humbleness I speak to you today, in this place, known throughout
America as the cradle of liberty.

I remember that well over two centuries ago, Peter Faneuil, a Huguenot
refugee from the political and religious intolerance of an old world king
fled to Boston, that he prospered and was happy here, and that in gratitude
he gave this hall to his townfolk for a marketplace. Before the last brick
had been laid, Peter Faneuil died. His eulogy was delivered at the first

[6] *Vital Speeches*, August 15, 1955, p. 1417.

[7] *Vital Speeches*, August 15, 1955, p. 1415. Reprinted by permission of the
editors of *Vital Speeches*.

annual town meeting by the master of the Boston Latin School, John Lovell. In concluding, Lovell said, "What now remains, but my ardent wishes . . . that this hall may be ever sacred to the interests of truth, of justice, of loyalty, of honor, of liberty. . . . May liberty always spread its joyful wings over this place. Liberty that opens men's hearts to beneficence and gives the relish of those who enjoy the effects of it."

And so it has been. Since that far off day, the walls of Faneuil Hall have echoed to the eloquent voices and the heroic footsteps of the greatest patriots in our history—Washington and Lafayette, Daniel Webster, Charles Sumner, Wendell Phillips . . . are but a few.

I, a daughter of New England, and a child of Connecticut, presume to share this hour here with you only because I know that it behooves your speaker to say nothing original, nothing startling, nothing new. Yet I feel that a moment of beauty, ever old and ever new, is achieved whenever we make a reaffirmation of our dedication to John Lovell's ideals—truth, justice, loyalty, honor, liberty. Indeed, this reaffirmation is the prime duty of the glorious Fourth.

7. Pay the audience a sincere compliment.   Everyone appreciates honest approbation. Likewise, everyone resents obvious flattery. In this regard, as in all others, you should voice only sincere expressions. As a rule, audiences detect guile and chicanery. Here are several examples of situations which would afford you the opportunity to pay your audience genuine compliments: if you are the guest of an organization, such as a university, and have been treated generously; if you are an outsider speaking in a community or state noted for its scenery, industry, culture, or its historic significance; if the organization you are addressing possesses a distinguished tradition or is currently engaged in some worthwhile public service; if the audience has greeted you in an especially hospitable manner. When John L. Lewis addressed the Chicago Executives' Club, he faced an audience of prominent business leaders, among whom were some of his strongest critics. To establish a positive, friendly atmosphere, Lewis was conciliatory and complimentary in his Introduction: [8]

I suppose I have been a long time coming here. But it is generally known that I was detained either by an industrialist or a federal judge. And as I

[8] Used by special permission of Mr. Lewis.

look back on those numerous detentions through the years I am not right now clear as to how they all came out. At least, however, I am happy that time and circumstances have permitted me to be your guest at this magnificent meeting of your great club. The Executives' Club of Chicago is one of the nation's great forums and has been made so by its interest in public and national affairs, by the vigor and ability of its members, their mobility of thought, and their desires constantly to break new ground in the affairs of the nation and of the world. So I come here today by invitation and with gratification that circumstances have permitted me to come on this occasion. I am delighted with your hospitality. I shall speak to you merely as a fellow American.

I am particularly happy to see present here today so many of the towering figures of one of our great basic industries—the coal industry—whom I have valued as friends and adversaries, wise counselors and earnest men. . . . As I look upon them here today and greet them, I am happy to think that they have honored me with their attendance at this luncheon to join with us in any discussion that may ensue affecting those problems that are so important to every American.

B. Orient the Audience to the Body by Means of a Clarification Step. Sometimes the speaker's efforts to secure favorable attention will also serve to orient the listeners to the subject matter of the talk; in such a case, there may be no necessity for a separate Clarification Step. Occasionally the speaker may wish to begin his speech by delimiting its scope, or by otherwise orienting the listeners; in such a case, he would place first the Clarification Step and then the Favorable Attention Step. Nevertheless, the novice usually should use both a Favorable Attention Step and a Clarification Step, with the Favorable Attention Step coming first.

To enable the auditors to understand the Body with greater ease, your Clarification Step should include one or more of the following: an explicit statement of the purpose of the speech, an explanation of how you plan to treat the subject, and a presentation of necessary background information.

1. State the POINT or purpose of your speech. Until you acquire experience, follow the Favorable Attention Step with a simple, precise statement of the POINT of your talk. In this way, at the outset you enable the hearers to grasp the essential point or concept that you will develop later. To telescope the intent of your speech, merely paraphrase the Specific Speech Purpose. Of course, avoid stating the POINT in such a bald fashion as "My Specific Speech Purpose is to inform you about methods by which manufacturing can be stimulated in this state." Instead, you might say "This morning I should like to explain several methods by which manufacturing can be stimulated in our state." (In speaking to a hostile audience on a controversial issue it may be unwise to state your purpose in the opening. However, your early speeches in class will probably be informative rather than persuasive.) Ezra Taft Benson began a talk on "Farm Surpluses and the Soil Bank" with a brief Favorable Attention Step and a statement of his POINT: [9]

Text

I am highly honored indeed, and feel deeply my responsibilities in meeting with so many of you today—both you in this hall, and those I am privileged to reach by radio in their homes throughout the land.

Yesterday President Eisenhower sent to the Congress his special message on agriculture. It is the recommendations in that message that I wish principally to discuss with you today.

Outline

Introduction:
  I. *Favorable Attention Step*
    A. I am highly honored and feel deeply my responsibilities in this situation
  II. *Clarification Step*
    A. I wish principally to discuss the recommendations contained in President's Eisenhower's message to Congress on agriculture

Adlai Stevenson opened a campaign address with a statement of his speech purpose: "I want to talk with you about the most serious failure of the Republican Administration. I mean its failure in conducting our foreign policy. For although its failures have been serious here at home, in serving the cause of peace they are far more serious." [10]

---

[9] A. Craig Baird, *Representative American Speeches: 1955–1956* (New York: The H. W. Wilson Company, 1956), p. 91.

[10] *Vital Speeches,* November 1, 1956, p. 36.

2. Explain how you plan to develop the topic. By explaining in advance the procedure you will use to develop the Body, you prepare your listeners to follow the course of the speech with greater ease. In introducing a complex subject like UNESCO, you might say: "During the next few minutes, I shall attempt to explain what UNESCO is, what it does, and how it works." Thus in terse fashion you have stated the three main ideas or headings of the Body and, thereby, have provided a helpful preview of the ensuing information. Warning: Although a splendid clarifier, this method has scant attention-commanding qualities and sometimes may lend a stilted, academic flavor to the Introduction. Here is the Clarification Step which Ernest V. Hollis (Chief of College Administration, U.S. Office of Education) used in a commencement address at the University of Nevada: [11]

In order to stay within the time allotted for radio, it has been necessary for me to jettison all my jokes and to otherwise forgo embellishing my prosaic paper. This limits my remarks to three ideas that should have a common core of interest for the graduating class and their parents, for educators, and for the public generally. The first concerns the educational implications of the rising tide of students; the second concerns the impact of our world position on college and university programs; and the third concerns the educational impact of a new industrial revolution that labor and management call *automation.*

Learned Hand (formerly Judge of the United States Circuit Court) used these preliminary statements in the Introduction of a speech before the Eighty-sixth Convocation of the University of the State of New York: [12]

What I have to say will be directed toward . . . the preparation of citizens for their political duties. I shall argue that the "humanities," instead of being regarded only as a solace, a refuge, and an enrichment of the individual—as indeed they are—are also an essential factor in training him to perform his duties in a democratic society.

[11] *Vital Speeches,* September 15, 1955, p. 1494.
[12] *American Association of University Professors Bulletin,* Winter, 1952–1953, p. 520.

3. Provide necessary preliminary definitions and explanations. Some speakers, particularly high school and college debaters, belabor the obvious by defining and explaining that which is already understood. However, some topics require preliminary interpretations. In the Introduction of a lecture on "The Pseudo-Conservative Revolt," delivered at Barnard College, Professor Richard Hofstadter used an extended definition: [13]

Twenty years ago the dynamic force in American political life came from the side of liberal dissent, from the impulse to reform the inequities of our economic and social system. . . . Today the dynamic force in our political life no longer comes from the liberals who made the New Deal possible. . . .

There is, however, . . . dissent in America today. Representing no more than a modest fraction of the electorate, it is not so powerful as the liberal dissent of the New Deal era, but it is powerful enough to set the tone of our political life and to establish throughout the country a kind of punitive reaction. The new dissent is certainly not radical—there are hardly any radicals of any sort left—nor is it precisely conservative. Unlike most of the liberal dissent of the past, the new dissent not only has no respect for non-conformism, but is based upon a relentless demand for conformity. It can most accurately be called pseudo-conservative . . . because its exponents, although they believe themselves to be conservatives . . . show signs of a serious and restless dissatisfaction with American life, traditions and institutions. They have little in common with . . . the dominant practical conservatism of the moment as it is represented by the Eisenhower Administration. Their political reactions express rather a profound if largely unconscious hatred of our society and its ways—a hatred which one would hesitate to impute to them if one did not have suggestive clinical evidence.

DEVELOPING THE CONCLUSION

The Conclusion, which represents your last chance to accomplish the Specific Speech Purpose, must wind up the speech smoothly, strongly, and on a high point of interest. A dull, apologetic, long-winded, anti-climactic, or irrelevant closing will impair or nullify the rapport previously established with your audience. As you know, the Conclusion of the average talk

[13] *The American Scholar*, Winter, 1954–1955, pp. 9–10.

probably represents about 5 per cent of the total length. However, the nature of the desired emotional or intellectual response, the degree of complexity of the materials presented, and the attitude of the audience may suggest either an abridged closing or an extended appeal. Only experience will enable you to determine how long the Conclusion should be for a particular talk.

The function of the Conclusion can be accomplished by a *Summary Step* and, when the speech is designed to actuate, by an *Action Step*.

A. Promote Comprehension, Retention, and the Proper Mood by Means of a Summary Step. The four basic ways of summarizing a speech are: restate the POINT or purpose of the talk; list formally in a "one," "two," "three" order the major ideas presented; review informally the main thoughts; use a quotation(s), comparison, or illustration to summarize indirectly. Frequently a Conclusion may require the use of more than one of these types of reiteration.

1. Restate the POINT. A trenchant method of directing final attention to the fundamental purpose of the speech is to restate the POINT in a sentence or two. Although such a procedure promotes clarity, additional recapitulation is usually needed. George Meany (President, AFL-CIO) used a restatement of his POINT to close an address on the "Attitude of Labor Toward World Peace": [14]

> If we learned one lesson from this last ten years, it is the lesson that we must be strong, that the only way we can defeat aggression is to be strong enough to deter and defeat aggression. That is the policy we should follow if we want to preserve this way of life to which we are all committed.

Ezra Taft Benson concluded an address before the Farm Equipment Institute in New Orleans with this reiteration of his speech purpose: [15]

> I know that you of the equipment industry would prefer to see farmers doing better from an economic point of view than they are, just as I

[14] *Vital Speeches,* August 1, 1955, p. 1395.
[15] *Vital Speeches,* October 15, 1955, p. 29.

would. And I assure you everything that is sound, right and fair will be done to assist them through this point of adjustment.

We must continue to push forward a prosperous, expanding and free agriculture. I know that, with the help of God, this objective will be attained.

2. List formally the major ideas of the Body. When essential that the audience remember important directions, the steps in a process, or the prime contentions of an argument, itemize them in a formal "one," "two," "three" list. While this method is unexcelled for fixing specific points in the mind, it should be used with caution: it may easily appear stilted, too obvious, and too monotonous.

Here is the Conclusion of a speech by C. E. McCarthy (President, Allied Stores Corporation) to the Annual Boston Conference on Distribution. Notice that it illustrates both the clarity and the relative flatness of the formal listing type of summary.[16]

Formal
Listing

Here in brief summary is the picture as I see it:

1. There is a substantial college graduate market available to retailing.

2. Surveys indicate that there is no major prejudice on the part of the college graduate toward retailing. . . .

3. Inertia with respect to the recruitment of the college graduate seems to be a common ailment of far too many retailers.

4. Retailers generally are downright derelict in publicizing the virtues of this business. There's too much breastbeating and not enough hard selling.

Restatement of
the POINT

If we believe that a continuous inflow of good young people is an essential for continuing success, then let us make at least as strong an effort to sell the benefits of a career in retailing as we do to sell the merchandise we buy for the customer.

3. Review informally the main thoughts of the Body. The informal review is probably the most frequently used system to crystallize the thought and to promote the appropriate feelings. It possesses greater interest appeal than does the restatement of the POINT or the formal listing, and it provides a more

[16] *Vital Speeches,* November 15, 1956, p. 96.

effective method of tying up loose ends and reinforcing the basic contentions. The emphasize his thesis that the Democratic Party is the party of humanitarianism and idealism, Adlai Stevenson closed his 1956 acceptance address with this informal review: [17]

Text

It is time to listen again to our hearts, to speak again our ideals, to be again our own great selves.

There is a spiritual hunger in the world today and it cannot be satisfied by material things alone. Our forbears came here to worship God. We must not let our aspirations so diminish that our worship becomes rather of bigness—bigness of material achievement.

For a century and a half the Democratic party has been the party of respect for people, of reverence for life, of hope for each child's future, of belief that "the highest revelation is that God is in every man."

Once we were not ashamed in this country to be idealists. Once we were proud to confess that an American is a man who wants peace and believes in a better future and loves his fellow man. We must reclaim these great Christian and humane ideas. We must dare to say again that the American cause is the cause of all mankind.

If we are to make honest citizens of our hearts we must unite them again to the ideals in which they have always believed and give those ideals the courage of our tongues.

Standing as we do here tonight at this great fork of history, may we never be silenced, may we never lose our faith in freedom and the better destiny of man.

Outline

Conclusion:

I. *Summary Step*
  A. It is time to listen again to our hearts, to speak again our ideals, to be again our own great selves
     1. Spiritual hunger cannot be satisfied by material things alone
     2. For a century and a half the Democratic party has been the party of idealism and humanitarianism
     3. We must return to our former idealism
     4. We must give voice to our ideals
  B. Standing as we do here tonight at this great fork of history, may we never be silenced, may we never lose our faith in freedom and the better destiny of man

[17] *Vital Speeches*, September 1, 1956, p. 681.

4. Use a quotation(s), comparison, or illustration to summarize indirectly. Unlike the previously discussed methods, the indirect summary recapitulates in an oblique manner. When applying this technique, a speaker selects one or more quotations, a comparison, or an example which closely and vividly illustrates the basic theme of the talk. Although it may impart a sparkle and verve to the Conclusion, the indirect summary is rarely strong enough to serve as the sole means of reiteration. Customarily it is integrated into an informal review, or is placed after the restatement of the POINT or after a formal listing. Of the three methods of summarizing indirectly, the quotation is the easiest to employ and is the most frequently used.

By weaving several quotations into an informal review, President Eisenhower hoped that his Conclusion would direct favorable attention to the theme of his 1956 acceptance address—"The Republican Party Is the Party of the Future": [18]

My fellow Americans, the kind of era I have described is possible. But it will not be attained by revolution. It will not be attained by the sordid politics of pitting group against group. It will be brought about by the ambitions and judgments and inspirations and darings of 168,000,000 free Americans working together and with friends abroad toward a common ideal in a peaceful world.

Lincoln, speaking to a Republican state convention in 1858, began with the biblical quotation: "A house divided against itself cannot stand."

Today the world is a house divided.

But—as is sometimes forgotten—Lincoln followed this quotation with a note of hope for his troubled country:

"I do not expect the house to fall," he said, "but I do expect it will cease to be divided."

A century later, we too must have the vision, the fighting spirit, and the deep religious faith in our Creator's destiny for us, to sound a similar note of promise for our divided world; that out of our time there can, with incessant work and with God's help, emerge a new era of good life, good will and good hope for all men.

One American put it this way: "Every tomorrow has two handles. We can take hold of it with the handle of anxiety or the handle of faith."

My friends, in firm faith, and in the conviction that the Republican

---

[18] *Vital Speeches,* September 1, 1956, p. 689. Reprinted by permission of the editors of *Vital Speeches.*

purposes and principles are "in league" with this kind of future, the nomination that you have tendered me for the Presidency of the United States I now—humbly but confidently—accept.

The following excerpt illustrates how a student ended a talk on automobile insurance by restating his POINT, citing an example, and then briefly applying the example to the POINT:

In summation, let me urge you once again to carry adequate liability insurance for your car. Don't run the risk of becoming another William Howell. Bill is my cousin. Until two months ago he didn't believe in liability insurance. He was a careful driver and believed that careful drivers don't have accidents. Well, one rainy night Bill's car skidded into a street-car safety zone and struck three persons. Despite his record of having driven fifteen years without a previous accident, and despite the extenuating circumstances of the case, a jury awarded claims totaling $20,000 against him. Bill lost his home and his farm. However, he was fortunate in the sense that claims for such accidents are frequently much higher. Please remember, ladies and gentlemen, accidents sometimes happen to the most careful of drivers. Why take the chance of becoming another Bill Howell, when liability rates are so low?

B. Promote Action by Means of an Action Step. Although its composition will depend upon the nature of the Body, the type of action desired, and the reactions of the audience, the Conclusion of the *actuating speech* should usually consist of a Summary Step and an Action Step. (As you will remember, only the actuating speech has as its primary purpose the moving of listeners to definite, observable, and relatively quick activity. Therefore, it is the only type of address requiring an Action Step.) Admittedly, in some instances motivational appeals may be so interwoven with the summation that the two steps are fused into one. More frequently, however, the Summary Step should recapitulate the materials previously discussed, while the Action Step should make a direct plea for action. Ordinarily the Summary Step should contain a restatement of the POINT and either an informal review or a formal listing; also, it may include an appropriate quotation(s), comparison, or example. In attempting to impel overt response, the Action Step should constitute a sincere, suitable appeal to the emotions as well as to the intellect and, if appropriate, should state specifically the nature of the action requested, how it is to be accomplished, and the time and place of its execution. Here is the way a student closed a talk soliciting subscriptions to *Time* magazine:

Summary Step In the ten minutes allotted me I have attempted to explain why *Time* is the finest news magazine in the world today. I have pointed out that *Time* is unexcelled for its clear and graphic style, for its accurate, up-to-the-minute reporting, and for its comprehensive yet concise analysis of the important news events of the day. Regardless of the narrowness or breadth of your interests in current affairs, *Time* will meet your needs. Each big issue presents in vivid fashion what is really news in national and international affairs, in art, books, movies, theater, music, business, education, science, journalism, religion, and in sports. Truly, *Time* is the world's outstanding news magazine.

Action Step Let me urge you to *keep up with the times by reading Time!* As educated men and as future leaders we bear a moral obligation to understand the vital forces swirling about us.

Save time by reading Time! Capitalize upon this amazing shortcut to knowledge. Only an hour or two a week in reading *Time* is sufficient to keep you abreast of the important developments in our complex, rapidly moving world.

Save money by subscribing to Time! Fortunately, as students we are eligible for a special educational discount. Sign the business reply card I have put in your hands. Start *Time* coming to you each week for an entire year at the bargain price of $4.00. This is $2.50 below the regular subscription price and $6.40 less than the newsstand price. A cup of coffee with cream costs 8¢ at the snack bar. At the special educational rates, an issue of *Time* costs only 7½¢. I have several extra pens here if you need one. *Sign your card now!* Mail it after class or give it to me. I will be glad to mail it for you. Your signature will starting interesting, provocative *Time* coming to your home for 52 exciting weeks.

SUMMARY

The Introduction should be planned to meet the anticipated reactions of the listeners, the nature of the occasion, and the demands of the subject. The typical Introduction constitutes about 10 per cent of the total length of the speech and serves two important functions: to encourage a receptive attitude on the part of the listeners and to orient them to the Body of the speech. The Favorable Attention Step can be accomplished by (1) pointing out the significance of the subject; (2) using pleasantry, wit, and humor; (3) applying an illustrative story, comparison, or quotation; (4) making a stimulating statement or asking a provocative question; (5) mentioning common bonds; (6) referring to the occasion or purpose of the meeting; and (7) paying the audience a sincere compliment. The Clarification Step prepares the audience for the Body by (1) stating the POINT of the speech; (2) explaining how the speaker plans to develop the topic; and (3) providing necessary preliminary definitions and explanations.

The Conclusion is, of course, the speaker's final opportunity to accomplish his Specific Speech Purpose. Usually it constitutes about 5 per cent of the total speech length. In preparing a Conclusion, the speaker should consider his purpose, the nature of the preceding materials, and the attitudes of the listeners. The basic elements of the Conclusion are the Summary Step and the Action Step. The function of the Summary Step (to promote comprehension, retention, and the proper mood) may be achieved by (1) restating the POINT; (2) listing formally the major ideas of the Body; (3) reviewing informally; and (4) using a quotation(s), comparison, or illustration to summarize indirectly. When the speaker wishes to actuate his listeners, the Conclusion should include an Action Step. Such a passage should constitute an effective appeal to the emotions as well as to the intellect and, if appropriate, should state specifically the nature of the performance requested, how it is to be accomplished, and the time and place of its execution.

EXERCISES AND ASSIGNMENTS

1. Study the Introductions and Conclusions of three written speeches. (Use speeches which you have read in preparing assignments for earlier chapters or, if you prefer, select others.) Read whatever material is available to you concerning the speaker, the occasion, and the audience. Then, prepare a written report in which you do the following:

a. Rate each Introduction and Conclusion as good, poor, or average. Explain the reasons for your rankings.
b. Record the method(s) used in each Introduction to stimulate favorable attention and to orient the audience to the subject. If either the Favorable Attention Step or the Clarification Step is omitted, explain whether the omission seems warranted. In what ways do you think the Introduction could be improved? Be specific.
c. Record the method(s) used in each Conclusion to recapitulate the thought and to promote the proper mood. Notice whether an Action Step is present. Can you suggest ways in which the Conclusion could be made more effective?

2. By consulting one or more collections of speeches, discover an example of each of the different ways of securing favorable attention and of preparing the audience for the Body. Also, discover an example of an Action Step and of each of the ways of summarizing a speech.

3. For one of the persuasive speeches you have presented, or will give later, prepare in verbatim and in outline form *five* different Introductions. Each of the Introductions should be designed to meet the requirements of a different one of the following audiences: (1) an audience favorably disposed toward you and your subject; (2) an audience neutral toward your subject and unacquainted with you; (3) an audience hostile to your arguments and unacquainted with you; (4) an audience uninformed about either you or your subject; (5) an audience indifferent toward you and your subject. Within these restrictions, make any assumptions you wish concerning the specific nature of the different audiences and occasions.

After explaining to the class the suppositions you have made about the audiences and occasions, read each Introduction orally.

4. For the same speech used in exercise 3, prepare in manuscript and in outline form three different Conclusions: (1) one of these should be designed for an audience which is opposed to your arguments; (2) one should be adapted for an audience which is strongly sympathetic to your case; (3) one should be planned to motivate the listeners to action. As for exercise 3, make any other assumptions you wish concerning the various audiences and occasions; explain these assumptions to the class and read the Conclusions orally.

5. Analyze the methods used by various news commentators to begin radio casts or telecasts. Notice that frequently a program begins with the reporter's listing the main items of news; then, following a commercial, he discusses each of the items in detail. In such cases would the original listing serve as a Favorable Attention Step as well as a Clarification Step? Why, or why not?

6. Attend a sermon by a minister who is recognized as being an outstanding speaker. What does he do to get your attention at the outset? If a text is read, observe how it serves as a partial Clarification Step. Can you think of any way in which his Introduction could be improved? How does he conclude the sermon? Does he grow more emotional near the close? If so, why? If the Conclusion occupies more than 5 per cent of the total speech length, suggest reasons why.

7. During the next round of speeches in class, determine the best and poorest Introductions and Conclusions. In a brief essay, explain the reasons for your choices.

15 ❧❧ *Delivering the Speech*

Occasionally a student will ask, "Is it possible to teach speech delivery?" Such a query is basically a variation of the old saw, "Orators are born and not made." Skill in speech presentation is not a trait contained in the germ plasm and transmitted from one generation to another. Only potentialities for development are inherited, not specific abilities. The importance of practice and training in the acquiring of oral skills is attested by classroom experience, by the observation of speakers in public life, and by the history of public address. Demosthenes, Cotton Mather, John Adams, Daniel Webster, Abraham Lincoln, Winston Churchill, Norman Vincent Peale, Aneurin Bevan, and many other eminent speakers experienced difficulty in learning to speak to audiences. With concentrated effort, any average person can achieve effective speech delivery. Those students who possess exceptional native ability will require less training than their colleagues. However, just as few baseball players reach the majors without previous training in the bush leagues and few golfers can earn a living on the professional circuits without long practice as amateurs, so even the talented individual needs protracted practice and guidance before he can realize maximum oral effectiveness.

SELECTING THE MODE OF EXPRESSION
BEST ADAPTED TO YOUR ABILITIES
AND TO THE SITUATION

In delivering a speech, you may speak impromptu, memorize, read from a manuscript, or extemporize. The following section

357

presents some of the advantages and disadvantages of each method.

A. Speak Impromptu Only When Preparation Is Impossible. In using the impromptu mode, a person composes his speech on the spur of the moment. Perhaps you have already encountered situations in which you have been unexpectedly asked "to say a few words." If the preceding discussion was stimulating and the subject matter familiar, you may have been pleasantly surprised at your spontaneity and fluency. Usually, however, impromptu speaking is characterized by rambling, redundant, ungrammatical, and ambiguous utterance, which lacks unity, coherence, and emphasis. Develop your ability to speak impromptu, but reserve this mode for emergencies.

B. Avoid Memorizing an Entire Talk. The opposite extreme from impromptu speaking is the "memoriter" method, in which the speaker writes his address and commits it to word-for-word memory. Because memoriter speaking promotes exactness of expression and organization, successful speakers of the past like Daniel Webster, Edward Everett, and Wendell Phillips frequently memorized complete orations. However, this method is less widely used today. In our supersonic era, probably most speakers cannot spare the time for verbatim memorization. Although you may wish to experiment later with the memoriter mode, for the following reasons you probably should avoid memorizing your early speeches: (1) Except for seasoned veterans, verbatim memorization is dangerous and unreliable. The terror of forgetting stalks the speaker from the beginning to the end of his address. One unremembered word may disrupt the entire chain of associations. (2) Only the highly skilled performer can speak directly in the conversational manner while attempting to recall word-for-word the manuscript hidden in his coat pocket or left in a desk drawer at home. Instead of concentrating upon reaching his listeners, the speaker tends to worry about keeping his mental needle in the groove. Too often the recalling of the next sentence becomes the focus of his attention rather than the interpreting of the reactions of his listeners. (3) If you memorize your first speeches, you may experience difficulty later in developing adequate skills in extempore expression.

C. Read from Manuscript Only When the Situation Is Formal and When a Premium Is Placed on Exactness of Language, Felicity of Expression, and Careful Timing. When using the mansucript mode, the speaker writes out his remarks in verbatim form and reads orally from the text. This method is frequently used in radio and television, at formal gatherings, and on important professional, political, educational, or business occasions. As we shall see in Chapter 17, "Common Types of Oral Reading," the skilled practitioner may use this mode effectively. However, the novice typically writes an essay instead of a speech and usually reads in a stilted, unnatural manner. Until you develop an animated sense of communication, avoid employing the manuscript style of presentation.

D. For Most Situations, Including Your Speech Class, Speak Extemporaneously. Unlike the "memoriter" and manuscript methods, in extempore speaking the language is, for the most part, coined at the moment of utterance. When carefully planned and rehearsed, the extemporaneous address is the most effective mode for most speakers in most situations. It can be as well organized and nearly as polished as the manuscript or memorized speech and, for the typical individual, it affords a far more flexible, dynamic, and spontaneous manner of delivery.

According to strict interpretation, the extempore speaker writes only an outline and memorizes only this organizational structure. However, two variations from this procedure might be noted: (1) Although the memorization of an entire speech is usually not desirable, the extempore speaker might commit to exact recall a few sentences at the beginning or end of his talk, or perhaps an illustration, a bit of poetry, a joke, some statistics, or some other important passage in which precise phrasing is essential. Limited memorization of this type minimizes the negative features which usually characterize the attempt to remember long stretches of continuity. (2) Some extempore speakers follow the practice of writing out a complete draft of a speech as an aid in organizing and testing their materials. Rabbi Joseph Raugh, who speaks only extemporaneously, says, "I find that the mere writing of a sermon is of great help to me. It makes me careful in marshalling my material and guards me from carelessness in expression. . . . Frequently I think I am clear on this or that point only to find when I put it down on paper that I need more information, or more precise judgment, or both." [1] Once the written draft has served its function as a preliminary check on the suitability of the speaker's organization and the validity of his evidence, it should be put aside. From here on, the extempore speaker should work basically from the outline.

In extemporizing you may speak with or without notes. The absence of notes requires that you memorize perfectly the sequence of the ideas you wish to present. The presence of notes minimizes the danger of forgetting but may constitute a barrier to communication. In your beginning speeches you probably should refrain from using notes. Otherwise, you may develop an unnecessary dependency upon them. After you have acquired the ability to extemporize fluently, feel free to take a few written reminders to the platform. The kind and amount of such aids is immaterial, so long as they promote recall without interfering with spontaneity. The variety of methods used by speakers to spark flagging memories is endless: some employ only copies of important quotations or statistical data; others rely upon a brief list of key words; others use detailed outlines containing nearly every item they will mention; still others devise original systems involving such aids as capital letters for the cardinal ideas and small letters for points of less consequence, underscorings, red-colored type, stars, dashes, arrows, etc. After some experimentation you will probably devise a procedure that meets your individual needs. Here are some suggestions which you might find helpful: (1) Put notes on small (3″ by 5″, or 4″ by 6″) cards. (2) Type, print, or write clearly, using only one side of each card.

[1] Charles A. McGlon, "How I Prepare My Sermons: A Symposium," *The Quarterly Journal of Speech*, February, 1954, pp. 57 and 58.

(3) Number each card. (4) Use as few notes as possible. (5) Phrase the entries concisely, usually substituting key words for complete sentences. (6) Refer to notes only when really necessary—do not permit them to become crutches. If you are thoroughly prepared, an occasional glance at the cards should suffice. (7) Avoid awkward hesitations by anticipating the need to refer to the notes. As you are completing one idea, glance at the cards to secure the next point. (8) Place the cards on a lectern or hold them in your hand; notes put on a table or low stand will require your bending over to read them. (9) Unless you are confident that you will not forget, take the cards with you when you move away from the stand; otherwise, any necessary reference to notes will be delayed and obvious.

USING PHYSICAL DELIVERY EFFECTIVELY

As you know, the most important functions of physical delivery are to add interest, meaning, and emphasis to the spoken language. If your bodily action appears mechanical, artificial, or labored, it will attract unfavorable attention, thereby impairing the communication of ideas and the stimulation of appropriate emotions. To be effective, your physical presentation must be spontaneous, closely integrated with vocal delivery, and appropriate to the audience, the occasion, and yourself as the speaker.

Like any physical skill, proficiency in the use of the visible code usually does not come easily, but is acquired gradually by means of training and experience. Embark on a program of systematic practice based upon the advice contained in Chapter 5. Such a program, in conjunction with a conscientious application of your instructor's suggestions, should enable you to eliminate undesirable elements from your presentation and to develop habit patterns of appropriate bodily action.

USING VOCAL DELIVERY EFFECTIVELY

In previous sections, it has been emphasized that the sounds produced by the speaker convey much more than the denotative meanings of language. The voice can add connotative values ranging from obvious implications to subtle nuances. The voice can give vitality, interest appeal, clarity, and emphasis to language by indicating how you feel about your message, that is, by showing you are determined, excited, confident, irritated, angry, devoted, fearful, happy, indecisive, or sad. Also, the voice suggests much about your character, personality, familiarity with the subject, and your attitudes toward the hearers, the speaking situation, and yourself. Manifestly, successful public speaking depends upon the effective use of the audible code. To improve your use of the voice, review carefully Chapters 6 and 7.

USING LANGUAGE EFFECTIVELY

As you will remember from Chapter 4, to use language skillfully you must know precisely what you wish to communicate, select the proper words to reflect closely your thoughts and feelings, and utilize the visual and auditory codes efficiently. Although in extempore speaking you do not plan the wording of your ideas prior to the speaking engagement, you should know exactly what concepts you wish to present. Fuzzy or muddled thinking will result in obtuse utterance. By means of painstaking composition and rehearsal, the thought framework of your talk should become clearly etched in your mind. You should visualize distinctly each idea and its relationship to the entire speech. Few writers can delineate ideas lucidly and trenchantly in a first draft—likewise, few speakers can express themselves concisely and accurately the first time they deliver a thought orally. Therefore, apply the suggestions for rehearsal which appear in the ensuing section.

FOLLOWING A SUITABLE PROGRAM OF REHEARSAL

Preparation for a speaking engagement requires more than the organization and development of ideas. You must also condition yourself to deliver the speech with greatest efficiency. Athletes, dramatists, musicians, TV commentators, and public speakers— all must rehearse to insure a successful performance. The initial presentation of even a carefully composed speech is usually disappointing: instead of speaking fluently, dynamically, and precisely to the point, the average performer tends to ramble, to commit minor errors of syntax, to hesitate, and to phrase ideas awkwardly and redundantly. In addition to reducing to a minimum the possibility of forgetting during delivery, adequate rehearsal can smooth out disturbing breaks in the flow of language, improve poise and assurance, and can put real power into your speaking.

A. Where to Rehearse. Speakers have utilized almost every conceivable type of place for rehearsing. One student practices as he delivers the morning papers, another as he drives to and from school, and still another as he goes about his chores as a dormitory janitor. A young minister rehearses his sermons each Saturday afternoon on the isolated upper deck of a ferry, while the boat cruises back and forth across the bay. A newscaster runs over his lines in a dry run before the TV cameras. A politician practices in his office before several trusted advisers. The most suitable place for your practice, however, is probably a quiet room at home or at school, where you can work undisturbed. Also, if possible, arrange at least one rehearsal period in the room where the speech is to be given, or in a similar location. In this way, you can accustom yourself to the physical surroundings, test the acoustics, and determine the amount of volume necessary to reach the back rows.

B. When to Rehearse. The rehearsal period should not begin until you have selected all of the speech materials and have finished the outline. The optimum length of the practice span varies with different individuals. In general, however, plan to complete a short speech for class at least a day before presentation; a longer speech for a more important occasion should be finished a minimum of two days in advance. Such an interval will permit the speech to "jell" in your mind and will enable you to memorize the sequence of ideas and to polish the delivery. Of course, avoid concluding the speech so far in advance that you lose your warmth and enthusiasm. Ordinarily, you should complete all practice before the beginning of the meeting at which you are to speak. Last minute practice is unnecessary— if you have prepared properly—and may be harmful. Instead of encouraging nervous tension by running over your speech, concentrate on the program activities and attempt to enter into the spirit of the occasion.

C. How to Rehearse. Perhaps the following suggestions will constitute the nucleus of a realistic program for you to follow.

1. The purpose of the preliminary phase of rehearsal is to fix the speech in your mind. Aside from the exceptions mentioned earlier in this chapter, the extempore speaker memorizes only the sequence of the ideas he wishes to present. Such memorization should cause little difficulty, provided your outline adheres to the rules for the logical partitioning of materials and provided you follow the ensuing recommendations. (1) Several times read silently straight through the entire outline. THINK while you read. (2) Several times read orally through the entire outline, without stopping or back-tracking. (3) Attempt to give the entire speech aloud, without interruptions or reference to notes. If you should forget at any point, struggle on as best you can. (4) Repeat the sequence of silent reading, oral reading, and extemporization until you have the outline firmly in mind. Important: during this stage of rehearsal, seek mastery of the *total sequence* of the speech. Until you have memorized perfectly the entire outline, do not interrupt the course of a presentation and do not concern yourself with techniques of delivery.

2. The purpose of the second phase of rehearsal is to polish the delivery of the speech. When you have learned the complete structure of the talk, work systematically to improve both vocal and physical delivery. (1) Divide this phase of rehearsal into several periods. A given amount of time will prove more beneficial when distributed over four or five sessions than when concentrated into one or two protracted periods. (2) If possible, arrange for a friend in whom you have confidence to sit in on at least one rehearsal. When working alone, you might place several chairs in a row and imagine that persons are seated in the chairs. During your practicing, take into consideration the probable size and composition of the audience, and the physical circumstances of the room in which the speech is to be given. And, as suggested previously, try to give at least one trial run of the speech in the place assigned for the meeting, or in a similar location. (3) Rehearse your speech an optimum number of times. Because of the variable elements involved, we cannot recommend an arbitrary and magical number of complete presentations that you should perform. However, the average student probably should rehearse between four and ten times a five-minute speech to be given in a public speaking class. If the talk is longer or the situation more demanding, the number of repetitions may be increased. *Warning:* in your eagerness to polish delivery, do not over-practice so that enthusiasm or spontaneity is impaired. (4) Possibly devote some time to practicing before a full-length mirror. Such a procedure can be helpful in checking on posture, stance, gestures, facial expression, and the general effectiveness of physical delivery. However, if seeing your reflection proves distracting, avoid this form of rehearsing. (5) Attempt to secure the use of a tape recorder. Listen critically to the playbacks. At the appropriate places on the outline make marginal notations for needed polish. Do not erase the tape, but estimate improvement by replaying the various recordings. (6) Reflect on the previous criticisms by your instructor and conscientiously try to improve. If your presentation has lacked sufficient animation and vitality in the past, try to force yourself to be more enthusiastic and dynamic. Put greater intensity into the voice, use more volume, drive home important points with greater emphasis, make some gestures, loosen the facial muscles, move about occasionally, and so on. If your general appearance has been unsatisfactory, check your posture and stance in a mirror. Try to get the "feel" of an attractive, comfortable carriage. If your vocal delivery has been monotonous, work for increased flexibility of the voice. Seek to develop greater variations of pitch, rate, force, and vocal quality. If your language or grammar has been faulty, the use of a tape recorder can be especially helpful. With the help of a competent critic play back the trial presentations, listening for possible errors of sentence structure or grammar, and noting where your language tends to be wordy, redundant, vague, inaccurate, dull, trite, or ambiguous. If you have been criticized for inadequate volume, slurred or muffled utterance, distracting hesitations, or for speaking too rapidly or too slowly, try to correct these faults. (7) Since you mastered the total sequence of the speech in the first stage of rehearsal, do not feel compelled to continue to practice the entire talk as a unit. Instead, devote particular attention to those portions which give you difficulty. Probably you should rehearse especially carefully the Introduction, Conclusion, transitions from one main point to another, and the use of visual aids. (8) Remember that your purpose in rehearsing is to improve your ability to communicate ideas and feelings to your listeners. Do not permit your delivery to become stilted, mechanical, or artificial.

EMPLOYING APPROPRIATE PLATFORM ETIQUETTE

In addition to applying the suggestions given earlier for appropriate vocal and physical delivery, dress, and grooming, consider the following recommendations concerning suitable platform conduct.

Under typical formal conditions, when several persons are to speak, the main speaker should lead the procession to the platform and the chairman should be last. While you are approaching the platform, realize that the audience is sizing you up. Walk in a brisk yet unhurried manner, avoiding both the nervous rapid stride and the reluctant dragging step. When you arrive at your appointed chair, sit down as gracefully as possible. As you wait your turn to speak, try to look at ease without adopting an excessively informal manner. On very dignified occasions, avoid crossing your legs; on most occasions, avoid relaxing to the extent that the body assumes an obvious slump; and on all occasions, try to avoid excessive stiffness, fidgety movements, or preoccupation with your notes. Instead of mentally reviewing your speech, attempt to be an ideal listener. Follow the program with evident interest; enter into the mood of the situation; engage in such group activities as singing or applauding the performances of a speaker. If you evidence proper decorum and seem glad to be present, the audience will be inclined to accept you as a cooperative, poised person; the other speakers will appreciate your moral support; and, as you turn your attention away from yourself and toward the proceedings, you may find that apprehension over speaking has begun to decline in intensity. If you are inclined to build up tension, breath deeply and slowly—particularly just before you are introduced.

After the chairman introduces you, rise and move easily and firmly to the speaker's stand. If no lectern is present, come to a stop midway from either side of the platform and near the front. If neither a lectern nor a platform is present, take a station within a few feet of the front row, standing as close as possible without appearing to press upon the audience. Pause for a moment and look directly at your listeners. Customarily, after you have their quiet attention, you should turn slightly toward the chairman and acknowledge his presence by saying "Mr. Chairman"; face the listeners and address them by saying "Ladies and Gentlemen"; then move smoothly into your opening sentences. Observe these special cautions in beginning your speech: (1) Do not engage in distracting bodily action. Make any necessary adjustments—such as wiping spectacles, straightening your tie, clearing your throat, buttoning or unbuttoning your coat, or arranging your notes—at your seat before rising to speak. (2) Do not begin to speak before you have settled into position and have ascertained that the audience is prepared to listen. Otherwise, you may give the impression of being unpoised, or some listeners may miss your initial sentences. (3) Do not shy away from establishing immediate eye contact with the hearers. You must demonstrate from the outset that you are sincerely eager to share your ideas and feelings. (4) As we have mentioned before, do not begin by announcing your subject in a fragmentary sentence, as "How to develop your personality," or by stating baldly your intent, as "My Specific Speech Purpose is to convince you that the United States should drastically curtail its program of foreign aid."

Throughout your address, concentrate on the process of communication. Think of the intellectual concepts and the emotional feelings you wish to stimulate in your hearers; be alert to the signals which indicate how they are responding and attempt to adjust both your content and manner accordingly. Feel confident and assured because you are well-prepared and because you have earned the right to talk on your subject. Feel sincere because you believe in what you are saying. Feel modest and unassuming because you recognize your own limitations and because you recognize the intrinsic worth of your hearers. Seek to establish the kind of rapport with your audience that Woodrow Wilson upon occasion secured with his. One former critic of Wilson, after hearing him for the first time, exclaimed: "Professor Wilson is a man of the people. You never saw anything like it. When he speaks to you, you feel like he was going to put his finger on your nose." [2]

When you conclude, pause momentarily as you look the audience in the eye. Perhaps give a nod of recognition to the applause, pick up your notes, and walk deliberately to your seat. Unless you have requested the speech appearance, there is no necessity to thank the audience for listening. Give courteous, cooperative attention to the remainder of the program.

[2] Hardin Craig, "Woodrow Wilson as an Orator," *The Quarterly Journal of Speech,* April, 1952, pp. 145–148.

SUMMARY

In delivering a speech follow these six guides: (1) Select the mode of expression best adapted to your abilities and to the situation (speak impromptu only in an emergency; avoid memorizing an entire talk; read from a manuscript only when the situation is formal, and when a premium is placed on exactness of language, felicity of expression, and careful timing; for most situations, including your speech class, speak extemporaneously). (2) Attempt to make effective use of posture, movement, gestures, eye-contact, and facial expression. (3) Work for audibility, pleasant voice quality, fluency, flexibility of the voice, and clear and appropriate pronunciation. (4) Strive to develop an oral style that is clear, direct and conversational, appropriate, vivid, and impressive. (5) Follow a program of rehearsal which provides for a suitable location and time for practice as well as a feasible method for fixing the speech in the mind and for polishing delivery. (6) Dress and conduct yourself suitably.

EXERCISES AND ASSIGNMENTS

1. In conjunction with your classmates, try this experiment involving the impromptu and extempore modes.
   a. Your instructor will assign to you (and each of your colleagues) an impromptu speech topic which should be appropriate to your background of knowledge. This speech will be recorded.
   b. Carefully compose and rehearse an extempore speech on the same subject and deliver it in class. This speech will also be recorded.
   c. Play back both recordings. Compare their relative effectiveness.

2. Attend several speaking engagements by a successful public speaker. Examples: a lawyer arguing a case in court; a preacher speaking in the pulpit or at civic gatherings; a professor lecturing to classes or addressing community meetings. If possible, select audiences and occasions which differ considerably among themselves. Observe the characteristics of the speaker's delivery and the manner in which he adjusts his presentation to meet the requirements of his particular audiences. Give a short oral report in class concerning your findings.

3. Follow exactly the same procedure as for exercise 2, with this exception: instead of selecting a skilled speaker, choose an unusually poor one. In a short talk to the class (without identifying the speaker), discuss the inadequacies of his manner of presentation.

4. To provide practice in maintaining poise under adverse circumstances, your instructor may assign a round of heckling speeches. In that event, prepare your talk carefully and anticipate a barrage of interruptions. In answering questions, attempt to maintain your decorum and sense of humor. Parry any unreasonable questions; answer others with candor and courtesy; and attempt to keep your speech moving toward its goal. In asking questions of the speaker in this exercise, both you and your classmates should restrict your queries to the speaker's evidence and reasoning. Avoid asking insulting or puerile questions and do not permit the session to degenerate into hilarious tumult.

5. Spend a portion of an evening watching television with the sound turned off. Concentrate your attention on the announcers, commentators, panelists, moderators, and speech makers. Observe their facial expressions, gestures, gross bodily movements, eye contact, and their presentation of visual aids. Attempt to estimate the extent to which their physical delivery aids in communicating their message. To follow the gist of their remarks, occasionally turn up the volume.

6. Beginning speakers are often urged to "just be natural" in delivering a talk. In a short speech to the class, explain how meaningful this advice would be to the following: the inordinately shy person; the sloucher; the awkward, rustic individual; the person who normally has a monotonous voice, poker face, muddy pronunciation, and/or obvious dialect.

7. In a short speech to the class, explain the meaning of this statement: "an effective gesture involves the use of the entire body."

16 ❧❧ Basic Principles of
Oral Reading

Is facility in reading aloud a practical tool? It is indeed. Oral reading is not a "cultural" subject to be placed on an intellectual shelf at the completion of the course. Almost everyone encounters the necessity of reading orally to others: many public speakers prefer to read from manuscript; nearly all radio speaking is read; businessmen read reports and statements to board meetings; teachers read assignments and announcements to classes; lawyers read excerpts from previous cases to juries; ministers read passages from the Scriptures to congregations; club women read cuttings of novels to literary teas; secretaries of organizations read the minutes of previous meetings; treasurers read financial reports; army officers read instructions and citations; TV commentators, announcers, and entertainers read from manuscripts and teleprompters; husbands read excerpts from newspapers to their wives; parents read bedtime stories to their children.

In addition to helping one to develop the specific skills involved in oral reading, a supervised program of reading aloud provides an unexcelled means of developing the attributes (such as projection, vocal phrasing, and clarity of articulation) common to all types of speaking.

Is oral reading practically the same as silent reading? No. Vital differences in nature and function exist between the two. (1) The core or hub from which all differences arise is almost too obvious to mention. In the silent mode, the reader is the only recipient of the message. His own comprehension, retention, and enjoyment provide the sole objectives for the act of reading. In the oral mode, the basic purpose of the reader is not to acquire meanings for himself, but to convey meanings to others.

(2) Since nothing passes between a speaker and his listeners except waves of sound and light, the oral reader cannot physically transfer the printed words to the cerebrum of his auditors. Suitable intellectual perceptions and emotional feelings can be communicated only by stirring up in the mind of the listener concepts closely similar to those "inherent" in the printed symbols. Obviously, the process of reading to others is more complicated than that of silent reading. Basically, silent reading requires a single step: to translate the language symbols in one's own mind. Oral reading necessitates three additional steps: (a) The speaker must retranslate his thinking into language symbols. (b) Following this, he must activate nerves and muscles to convert the language symbols into appropriate sounds and bodily action. (c) The listener then must correctly translate the speaker's use of the audible and visual codes. If inaccuracies or inadequacies occur in any of the four steps in the oral reading process, the inevitable results will be distortion, confusion, or a complete breakdown in communication.

(3) In the silent mode, the reader's own needs and interests determine the speed and method of reading. He may proceed as rapidly as he can translate the printed symbols into mental understanding. If he encounters a complicated concept, an unusual word, or involved syntax, he can slow down, stop for reflection, or retrace a sentence or several paragraphs. In the oral mode, the reader must realize that his listeners can neither stop for contemplation nor "replay" previously delivered material. They must follow as best they can at the rate he sets. As discussed before, oral communication must provide for instant intelligibility. Therefore, instead of tripping along at a silent reading rate of three hundred, four hundred, or perhaps five hundred words a minute, the oral reader must adjust his pace to the absorption powers of his listeners as well as to the other factors in the speaking situation.

(4) In the silent method, punctuation marks help the reader to understand the meaning of the written text. In the oral method, the speaker's vocal and physical delivery must provide the "punctuation guides" for the listeners.

(5) In both the silent and oral styles, the eyes of the reader move in a series of jumps from the beginning to the end of each line. During the movements, the eyes do not focus. Perception of the printed symbols occurs only during the brief pause or fixation between jumps. The number of words that can be "absorbed" during a stop is called the *eye-span*. The eye-span of the poor silent reader is limited, frequently encompassing only one or two words; furthermore, the eyes of the poor reader may make frequent backward jumps, or regressions. Conversely, the wide eye-span of the good reader enables him to reduce the number of fixation pauses to perhaps three or four for a line similar to those in this text; also, his eyes move smoothly, swiftly, and regularly along each line, and from the end of one line to the beginning of the next.

The importance of eye-span in oral reading may be seen easily: the speaker's voice must follow his sight reading. An adequate eye-voice interval is essential for smoothly flowing and expressive oral reading. By becoming thoroughly familiar with his materials, the poor silent reader can partially compensate for his limited eye-voice interval. However, his ability in impromptu oral reading will probably remain ineffective until he receives remedial training in a reading clinic.

Although different situations require specific adaptations (see Chapter 17, "Common Types of Oral Reading"), *certain basic principles are common to all forms of reading aloud.*

MAINTAINING A KEEN SENSE OF COMMUNICATION

Like the extempore speaker, the oral reader has a practical purpose. He wishes to effect some change in his listeners. He wants to give information, provide a pleasant diversion, influence belief, stimulate emotions, or impel others to action. The chairman of a Congressional investigating committee may request the official recorder to read excerpts of previous testimony by a witness—the purpose of the recorder in reading aloud is to supply information. At a library club meeting, a renowned poet may read selections from his latest book—possibly his purpose is to entertain or divert his listeners. A vote-seeking politician may speak from a manuscript to a mass audience—his purpose is to persuade others that he is the best qualified candidate.

To achieve any of the general purposes of oral reading, you must focus your attention on the process of conveying intellectual perceptions and emotional feelings to your auditors. Oral reading should be *audience-centered* rather than page-centered. Your task is to make the printed words come alive in the form of animated, stimulating vocal and physical presentation. The effect you exert upon the listeners furnishes the ultimate criterion of how well you have performed. Did you, or didn't you, accomplish your general purpose is reading?

If you possess a keen, lively sense of communication, your oral reading will not be dull and lifeless, devoid of vitality. It will not be a mere vocalization of words, monotonously strung together in a meaningless procession. It will not be a mubled soliloquy or a breathless dash through a jumble of nouns, verbs, and gerunds. A genuine sense of communication will enable you to establish between yourself and the audience that close feeling of rapport which is the essence of all effective speaking. A genuine sense of communication will provide that fine discrimination of balance, timing, and touch which, as you know, is fundamental to the skillful use of the techniques of vocal and physical delivery.

Also, a keen sense of communication will motivate you to be as direct and conversational as the written materials and the speaking situation permit. When delivering a manuscript speech, attempt to maintain the spontaneity and immediate contact of extemporaneous delivery. When interpreting novels, short stories, plays, and poems, you may not be able to speak in the intimate, direct manner of conversation. The listeners recognize that you are not speaking to them in the form of public address, but are attempting to portray the moods and feelings intrinsic in the selection. Nevertheless, do not deviate further from the direct speaker-to-audience mode than the particular writing warrants. Never adopt the complete characterization of acting; such a presentation belongs in the category of the theater, not oral reading.

Of course, to possess a keen sense of communication, you must thoroughly understand the nature of the materials you are to read.

UNDERSTANDING THE MATERIALS YOU ARE TO READ

If you have written the copy, you probably comprehend its meanings well. However, if reading from a text prepared by someone else, you should carefully analyze it before attempting to present it orally. Ascertain the central thought of the entire selection and of each passage; differentiate essential concepts from those of lesser importance; determine the progression of thought, the transition from one point to another, the shifts of setting, and the changes of characters; note the differences in style as the material unfolds; study the variations in sentence structure; consult a dictionary to determine the denotations and the pronunciations of all unfamiliar words; be certain that you know the textual meaning of each word. In addition to analyzing the intellectual content, study the emotional components. Recognize that even simple, informative prose may contain a variety of moods and feelings. What is the dominant emotional tone of the selection? Does this mood remain constant? Does it blend into other moods? Or, does it occasionally change abruptly into contrasting emotions? Only after you have mastered the intellectual and emotional content of the materials can you adjust physical and vocal delivery effectively. (For suggestions on understanding literary works, see Chapter 17.)

USING THE VISIBLE CODE APPROPRIATELY

As we have seen previously, in face-to-face occasions all speakers employ the visible code, effectively or ineffectively. Since the auditors see the speaker, they inevitably receive visual impressions from the directness of his gaze, and from his facial expressions, dress, stance, posture, gestures, bodily activity, and so on. To be a skillful reader, work for suitable physical delivery.

A. Maintain Adequate Eye Contact with the Listeners. You will recall that, except for occasional references to notes or to visual aids, the extempore speaker attempts to maintain constant eye contact with his listeners. Obviously, since he must refer to his written text, the oral reader cannot look continuously at the auditors. Furthermore, the type of material and the reader's purpose will influence the degree of eye contact. In delivering a manuscript address, a speaker should look at his listeners at least 80 per cent of the time. Although he has a manuscript before him, he should still give the impression of speaking directly from his mind and heart. The text is merely an aid in phrasing and in organization. If he concentrates his gaze upon the pages, the mansucript becomes a barrier to communication. The public speaker must *speak to,* not *read at* his auditors. In giving a statistical report or in presenting the minutes of a previous meeting, the reader performs a function somewhat different from that of the public speaker. Usually, a less intimate rapport exists between such a reader and his audience. Unlike the public speaker who always is identified intellectually and emotionally with his materials, the reporter typically does not editorialize; he merely reads necessary factual information, perhaps written by someone else. Because of his different role, the reporter will maintain adequate eye contact if he looks at his hearers about half of the time. Still further removed from the degree of eye contact requisite for public speaking is that which is possibly appropriate for the interpretation of literature. Some authorities believe that frequent glances at the audience might defeat the interpreter's purpose of creating a psychological mood or unfolding a dramatic plot. A few extremists contend that, instead of looking at the listeners, the reader should direct his gaze just over their heads, or at the copy. However, other authorities consider that occasional, or even nearly continuous, eye contact will foster rather than impair the interpreter's effectiveness.

A safe rule to follow would be to look at your listeners as much as the nature of your materials and your general purpose permits. Remember that the beginner usually does not secure adequate eye contact with his audience.

B. Use Appropriate Facial Expression. Like all other forms of oral communication, reading aloud requires suitable facial expression. Except when attempting to create an illusion (such as an impression of gloom, pessimism, indecision, indolence, or weakness) your countenance should express warmth, sincerity, and vitality; a wooden or glum aspect will impair your efforts to put across your personality and your message. Cautions: (a) Most novices should not plan specific facial expressions for incorporation into the reading at certain places. (b) Even in dramatic readings, be careful not to overdo facial expressiveness.

C. Use Appropriate Stance, Posture, and Movement. Because of the variety of types of oral reading, few universally applicable guides can be suggested for stance, posture, and movement. Basically, the suggestions made in Chapter 5 hold true for the reader. (1) *Guides for the use of the lectern.* Frequently no lectern is available to the speaker in those situations which call for the reading of committee reports, minutes of meetings, and so on. On the other hand, a stand is usually present at those occasions involving the delivery of a manuscript address or the presentation of a program of dramatic readings. When a lectern is present, place the book or manuscript on it; of course, occasionally you might wish to pick up the copy and temporarily move away from the desk. Since many beginning oral readers are guilty of flagrant misuse of the lectern, these familiar cautions should be emphasized: Although resting one or both hands for short periods upon the stand is acceptable, do not lean obviously or continuously. Avoid draping the upper half of your body over the lectern and do not grasp it as though goblins were attempting to wrest it from you. Do not slump in the belief that the lectern will conceal your posture, and do not rest a foot on the side of the stand as though you are about to climb upwards. (2) *Guides for the handling of materials in the event no lectern is present or in case you prefer to hold the written copy*. Unless impossible to do otherwise, avoid reading from heavy, bulky volumes. Such books are difficult to handle, and your efforts to control them may attract negative attention. Hold the copy high enough to permit easy reading of the print but not so high that your face is partially hidden. If you hold your elbows close to your sides, they find secure resting places along the ribs, making it easier to hold the materials steady. Do not hold the book or manuscript in exactly the same position throughout the entire presentation. Occasional slight changes will help you to avoid giving a stiff, unnatural appearance.

D. Use Appropriate Gestures.   Here again it is difficult to be prescriptive. In general, follow the advice given earlier. When speaking from a manuscript, you should experience approximately the same freedom to gesture that you do in extempore delivery. When reading reports or factual data, you may feel little, if any, impulse to gesture. When interpreting literature, you may wish to express characterization or moods by movements of the head, shoulders, or hands. Naturally, all gestures should be appropriate, well-timed, definite, and spontaneous. If they gestured more, most beginners would improve their readings; however, an insufficient amount of gesticulation seems somewhat less undesirable in oral reading than in extempore speaking. Occasionally a novice, usually when reading dramatic literature, will gesture excessively; such immoderation attracts negative attention and may even appear ludicrous.

USING THE AUDIBLE CODE
APPROPRIATELY

Your degree of success in conveying to others the meanings and concepts inherent in a written text will depend largely upon your skill in vocal delivery.

A. Your Reading Should Be Audible. Muffled, inaudible utterance appears to be more characteristic of reading aloud than of other forms of oral communication. The average person bends his neck, thereby "pinching" his larynx, and reads somewhat indistinctly into his book or manuscript. In addition to applying the suggestions in Chapter 6 for improving volume and projection, practice the accompanying exercises in this way: stand comfortably erect; hold the head up; open the mouth wide enough to permit easy exit of the sound waves; vigorously contract the muscles of exhalation, thereby forcing a strong column of air up and out the throat; read loudly enough to be heard fifty feet away; as a possible test, adjust your radio or television set to nearly full volume and then attempt to make yourself heard.

(*Ring Announcer:*) Ladies and gentlemen, your attention please. The main event of the evening. Two falls out of three, with no time limit, for the heavyweight championship of the world. Introducing, in this corner, weighing 263 pounds, wearing green trunks, from Dublin, Ireland, the present champion of the world—Mike Maroney.

(*Fire Chief:*) All right, boys, get the hose out in a hurry. Joe, put the ladder up to the second floor window. Hey, you guys on the roof! Are you waiting for a rain to come along and put out the fire? Get a hole in the roof. Mike, bust in the back door and see if anyone is trapped on the first floor. Hurry things up, men. There's 50,000 gallons of linseed oil in the warehouse across the street. If the fire gets over there, we'll be here a week.

> Think you a little din can daunt mine ears?
> Have I not in my time heard lions roar?
> Have I not heard the sea, puffed up with winds,
> Rage like an angry boar, chafed with sweat?
> Have I not heard great ordnance in the field,

And heaven's artillery thunder in the skies?
And do you tell me of a woman's tongue,
That gives not half so great a blow to ear,
As will a chestnut in a farmer's fire?

The Taming of the Shrew, Act I, Sc ii—Shakespeare

B. Your Reading Voice Should Be Pleasant. Except for character depiction, your voice should possess an agreeable, non-irritating tone or timbre. In oral reading, as in other types of speaking, an unpleasant voice will detract from your effectiveness. Try to relax the speech mechanism while you read. Work for sufficient breath support to insure firm, full tones. If you have some vocal problem such as nasality, thinness, or hoarseness, study especially carefully the pertinent sections in Chapter 6 and work diligently on the recommended exercises. Even if your voice is adequately pleasant, you may be able to improve its richness and clarity by practicing exercises like the following. For each selection read slowly; hold on to the vowels, semi-vowels, and consonants; and concentrate on developing good resonance and purity of tone.

The sea is calm to-night.
The tide is full, the moon lies fair
Upon the straits;—on the French coast the light
Gleams and is gone; the cliffs of England stand,
Glimmering and vast, out in the tranquil bay.
Come to the window, sweet is the night-air!
Only, from the long line of spray
Where the sea meets the moon-blanch'd sand,
Listen! you hear the grating roar
Of pebbles which the waves draw back, and fling,
At their return, up the high strand,
Begin, and cease; and then again begin,
With tremulous cadence slow; and bring
The eternal note of sadness in.

Dover Beach—Matthew Arnold

To-morrow, and to-morrow, and to-morrow
Creeps in this petty pace from day to day
To the last syllable of recorded time;
And all our yesterdays have lighted fools

The way to dusty death. Out, out, brief candle!
Life's but a walking shadow, a poor player
That struts and frets his hour upon the stage
And then is heard no more; it is a tale
Told by an idiot, full of sound and fury,
Signifying nothing.

Macbeth, Act V, Sc v—Shakespeare

C. Your Reading Should Be Animated. The process of speaking from the written page seems to exert a stultifying influence upon most persons—and the resulting presentation is far from stimulating. To be communicative, oral reading must possess vitality, vigor, alertness, and enthusiasm. (Even in the interpretation of literature when representing a debilitated character or establishing a depressed mood, the reader, himself, is vibrantly alive—even though he deliberately and artfully conveys a different impression to the audience.) Perhaps we should add this warning: In your efforts to give life to your reading, do not indulge in exaggerated or artificial vocal release. Such animation usually appears distractingly synthetic and forced. Effective animation arises from (a) a thorough knowledge and appreciation of what you are reading and (b) a genuine desire to communicate that material to your listeners.

If your oral reading tends to be spiritless, practice selections like the following. In each case, study the passage first, and then try to read it with the proper intensity. Shed your inhibitions and let yourself go.

(Nagging wife at the breakfast table:) Come on, Henry, you'll be late for the office. What would you like to have for breakfast? Oh, I wish you had told me that before; I've already fried your eggs. You certain have a grouchy look about you. Why can't you ever look cheerful in the morning? You look like you hated to see a new day. Put the paper down and act like you're glad to be eating a breakfast I've slaved over. What do you mean the coffee's cold? If you didn't put a half a pint of cream in it, it wouldn't be cold. Now, listen to me, Henry, you know you like a lot of cream in your coffee— and you don't put it in to kill the taste. The very idea! My mother warned me about you. I should have listened to her. Henry, put that paper down. I have a lot to say to you. What do you mean, you have to get to the office early? Henry, come back and finish your breakfast. Henry . . . Henry . . .

(Use a direct, conversational manner in reading the first stanza of "The Cataract of Lodore." Read the remainder with heightened animation to suggest the "hurrying and scurrying" and the "thundering and floundering" of the cataract.)

"How does the water
Come down at Lodore?"
My little boy asked me;
And moreover he tasked me
To tell him in rhyme.

The cataract strong
Then plunges along,
Striking and raging
As if a war waging
Its caverns and rocks among;
Rising and leaping,
Sinking and creeping,
Swelling and sweeping,
Showering and springing,
Flying and flinging,
Writhing and whisking,
Spouting and frisking,
Turning and twisting,
Around and around . . .
Collecting, projecting,
Receding and speeding. . . .
And rushing and flushing and brushing and gushing,
And flapping and rapping and clapping and slapping,
And curling and whirling and purling and twirling,
And thumping and plumping and bumping and jumping;
And dashing and flashing and splashing and clashing;
And so never ending, but always descending,
Sounds and motion forever are blending,
All at once and all over, with a mighty uproar,
And this way the water comes down at Lodore.

The Cataract of Lodore—Robert Southey

D. Your Reading Should Be Flexible. In your reading performances your voice may possess a monotonous sameness that is less noticeable, or even non-existent, in your extempore delivery. If so, the following section may help you to improve vocal flexibility when reading aloud.

As you know, variations in pitch, rate, force, and quality furnish the primary vocal tools for maintaining the attention of your listeners and for attaching meaning to the spoken words.

1. Pitch. Frequently the beginning reader employs either an unpliant pitch level or inflexible pitch patterns which are repeated monotonously. Written materials change continually in thought content and in sentence structure; also, they usually represent a variety of moods and feelings. Obviously, variegated sequences of meanings and emotions cannot be represented adequately by monopitch or by arbitrary, set pitch patterns. To translate the written symbols accurately into vocal symbols, the variations in pitch must correspond closely to the changing composition of the text. Only then will your voice convey to the listeners the full intrinsic meaning. With the aid of your instructor and recordings of your voice, determine whether your oral reading is characterized by inflexibility of pitch. If this seems to be the case, practice reading exercises like those on the following pages until you develop appropriate expressiveness.

a. *As you will recall, modulation of pitch is achieved by moving upwards or downwards on the musical scale by means of slides or steps.* The reader's mood, the ideational and emotional content of the material, the nature of the audience and the occasion—the totality of the reading environment influences the type and extent of pitch change. The contour patterns of language are extremely complicated and cannot be reduced to a few simple formulas. This treatment would be overly simplified if it passed along to you the elocutionary clichés that upward slides indicate uncertainty, hesitation, doubt, and surprise, that downward slides signify conviction, decision, determination, and defiance, and that circumflexes express double meanings and covert attitudes. In reading orally the accompanying exercises, try to develop the appropriate attitudes required by the material; then try to convey your feelings in your voice. Do not be concerned whether you use slides or steps or whether the pitch rises or falls in particular words. Instead, work for suppleness of pitch and for the projection of your thoughts and feelings. (In the first two exercises, the material within the brackets serves to indicate the thought processes of the speaker and, therefore, should not be read orally.)

Uncertainty or Hesitation:

Is that you, John?—[Should I open the door? I wonder if it really is John.]

I suppose.—[But, I haven't completely made up my mind.]

Well.—[I like the dress, but I'm not sure that I want to buy it.]

I might.—[But, I might not. Five o'clock seems mighty early to get up, even to go fishing.]

Maybe it's a good idea.—[I can't think of a valid objection, but I don't like to be high-pressured.]

Surprise:

What?—[That would never have occurred to me.]

He did?—[I'm shocked that Henry would do that.]

It's good?—[I thought he would give me a "D" on that paper.]

The package came this morning?—[I didn't expect it before next week.]

It's Pat?—[I thought he was in Chicago.]

Determination:

I have tried this experiment three times and have failed each time. Nevertheless, I am convinced that this time I will succeed.

To keep that man out of the governor's mansion, I would stump the state in my bare feet.

I know that your brother didn't do it. I'll keep working on the case until I prove he is innocent.

Defiance:

They can bring an eviction notice and a bulldozer if they want. But I'll not move from this house.

I refuse to be intimidated. I will not resign.

I will not be silenced. I will speak despite your boos and cat-calls.

Double Meanings:

You are a gentleman.

Your plan is interesting.

I wouldn't say that you are skinny.

Well, I suppose so.

She is a nice girl.

Now, now, Mr. Grayson, you don't mean that.

Really, you don't say.

Sara is such a charming person.

Your painting is a bit unusual.

Are you sure?

She couldn't come. She had a terrible headache.

b. *The character of the reading material influences the range and the "sharpness" of the pitch changes.* When the written matter contains lusty, energetic emotions like feverish excitement, alarm, sudden violent anger, and strong exhortations, let your voice respond with vigorous strides and slides in pitch. In reading this passage from *Native Son,* give free rein to your voice.

"There he is again, Bigger!" the woman screamed, and the tiny one-room apartment galvanized into violent action. A chair toppled as the woman, half-dressed and in her stocking feet, scrambled breathlessly upon the bed. Her two sons, barefoot, stood tense and motionless, their eyes searching anxiously under the bed and chairs. The girl ran into a corner, half-stooped and gathered the hem of her slip into both of her hands and held it tightly over her knees.

"Oh! Oh!" she wailed.

"There he goes!"

The woman pointed a shaking finger. Her eyes were round with fascinated horror.

"Where?"

"I don't see 'im!"

"Bigger, he's behind the trunk!" the girl whimpered.

"Vera!" the woman screamed. "Get up here on the bed! Don't let that thing *bite* you!"

Frantically, Vera climbed upon the bed and the woman caught hold of her. With their arms entwined about each other, the black mother and the brown daughter gazed open-mouthed at the trunk in the corner.

Bigger looked round the room wildly, then darted to a curtain and swept it aside and grabbed two heavy iron skillets from a wall above a gas stove. . . . "There he is!" the mother screamed again.

A huge black rat squealed and leaped at Bigger's trouser-leg. . . . Bigger dodged and the rat landed against a table leg. With clenched teeth, Bigger held the skillet; he was afraid to hurl it, fearing that he might miss. The rat squeaked and turned and ran in a narrow circle, looking for a place to hide; it leaped again past Bigger and scurried on dry rasping feet to one side of the box and then to the other, searching for the hole. Then it turned and reared upon its hind legs.

"Hit 'im, Bigger!" Buddy shouted.

"Kill 'im!" the woman screamed.

The rat's belly pulsed with fear. Bigger advanced a step and the rat emitted a long thin song of defiance, its black beady eyes glittering, its tiny forefeet pawing the air restlessly. . . .

Bigger aimed and let the skillet fly with a heavy grunt. There was a shattering of wood as the box caved in. The woman screamed and hid her face in her hands. Bigger tiptoed forward and peered.

"I got 'im," he muttered, his clenched teeth bared in a smile. "By God, I got 'im." [1]

When reading explanatory materials, factual data, and other writings containing mild emotions, your pitch changes probably should be somewhat less extreme than when interpreting materials embodying vigorous emotions. Notice that the "normal" moods of the following quotation require the "normal" pitch changes of animated extempore speaking.

My new assignment as Director of Community Affairs makes it necessary for me to ask for the cooperation of the faculty, staff, and administration in several ways. I have the responsibility of making the community aware of the considerable impact which the faculty and staff can have on the community as a result of participation in civic activities, church work, and club life. I have also the responsibility of administering the University Lecture Bureau which will bring faculty members before organizations in this area. I wish to assure you that I shall seek to distribute the burden of speaking in such a way that it will not fall heavily on anyone. I shall also seek, wherever possible, to see that the clubs which can pay a speaker will do so.

When portraying repressed moods (such as, physical inertia, gloom, sadness, reverence, devotion, or other types of quiet but intense feeling) you probably should use a limited range and narrow pitch changes. Study the following selection and then read it aloud. If you are thoroughly in sympathy with the meaning, your voice possibly will restrict itself to a limited pitch range and to relatively narrow steps and slides.

> Break, break, break,
>   On thy cold gray stones, O Sea!
> And I would that my tongue could utter
>   The thoughts that arise in me. . . .

---

[1] Richard Wright, *Native Son* (New York: Harper & Brothers, 1940), pp. 4–6. Copyright by Richard Wright. Used by special permission.

Break, break, break,
At the foot of thy crags, O Sea!
But the tender grace of a day that is dead
Will never come back to me.
Break, Break, Break—Alfred, Lord Tennyson

2. Time. In discussing time or rate as the second variable element of the voice, we shall consider these three somewhat overlapping topics: flexibility of general rate, vocal pauses, and duration of sounds.

a. FLEXIBILITY OF GENERAL RATE. As you know, in addition to considering the characteristics of the audience and the occa· sion, the oral reader should adjust his general speed of utterance to fit the complexity, the relative importance, and the mood of the materials. Examples: Background explanations and descriptions ordinarily can be read more rapidly than can statistical data or intricate patterns of thought development. Since transitional sentences link together the major ideas of a selection and may indicate shifts in setting or in mood, you should usually call attention to such bridges by being more deliberate in your rate. Because lead sentences introduce the essential theme of a paragraph or section, you will facilitate the ease of comprehension for the listener if you decidedly alter the pace, typically by speaking more slowly. Also, passages which contain light, effervescent, exciting, fiery, irritable, hysterical, violent, or enthusiastic moods require a more rapid utterance, while a slower rate would be appropriate for heavy, dignified, pompous, languid, sad, or grave moods.

b. VOCAL PAUSES. Most beginning readers experience an overpowering compulsion to maintain a constant rush of words, without permitting the pauses necessary for emphasis and easy comprehension. Do not fear silence. Pauses rarely seem as long to the listener as they do to the reader. Recognize that a distinguishing characteristic of the superior oral reader is his ability to show thought relationships by means of pauses. Don't you make extensive use of pauses in conversation and in extempore public speaking? Of course. Except for some forms of literary interpretation, maintain the normal pauses of oral communication.

The basic unit of meaning in oral communication is the "word group," or the vocal phrase. Occasionally a single word or a short simple sentence will serve as a "word group." Usually, however, we do not talk, nor should we read orally, in single words or in sentences. Within all but the simplest and shortest sentences we should combine the words into individual thought units, according to meaning. Words which represent a particular idea should be grouped together and should be separated from other words representing different thoughts. For instance, in a given sentence one "word group" might contain the basic concept, while an additional "word group(s)" might serve as modification or amplification. Read this statement: "The coach said the football player is a poor sport." Notice how a change in the word grouping may alter the meaning: "The coach," said the football player, "is a poor sport." Although we should perceive that inflections, sharp increases or decreases in force, and variations in voice quality are important aids, the primary method of setting apart thought phrases is the pause. In much the same manner that punctuation symbols separate written sentences into thought elements, pauses of varying length divide oral sentences into thought units.

What reactions would a person experience in reading an essay which lacked punctuation marks and capitalization? Confusion! Frustration! As an experiment, read silently the following exercise. Then, read it rapidly to a friend or to the class, pausing *only* when necessary to take a breath. After this venture, probably you will agree that a lack of pauses in oral reading is as detrimental as a lack of punctuation in written language.

not long ago another professor and i walked into an eating establishment just off the campus and sat down in a booth near the door we soon became aware of a minor uproar in the booth next to ours where strident voices were vigorously berating someone obviously a professor so we sat there chuckling while we wondered who the hapless instructor might be the brainless hayseed someone snapped he hasn't enough intellect to be a fourth class ditch digger another contributed if he was a private in the army and I was his sergeant i'd sure know what to do with him a third voice a slightly nasal baritone boomed even a half-baked moron wouldn't give a test like that

Haphazard word grouping is as detrimental to oral reading as would be a similar injudicious usage of commas, semi-colons, colons, and periods in written communication. As proof, read orally these lines, pausing *only* when a slanted line appears.

Suddenly I/ noticed my/ colleague was/ no/ longer enjoying the/ tirade; a/ dull flush was/ stealing over/ his face and edging/ up into/ his sparse/ hair. He/ had recognized one/ of the/ voices. These/ students were/ talking about/ him. As/ soon as we/ had gulped our/ coffee we/ slipped out, leaving/ the students still/ maligning the poor/ man's ancestry and/ his/ mental and/ moral/ qualities.

At this point, some students may assume that grammatical punctuation and vocal pauses bear an absolute relationship to each other. This is not true. Although punctuation marks provide helpful clues in oral reading, do not rely uncritically upon them. Only in somewhat unusual circumstances will the oral phrasing follow exactly the punctuation marks throughout an extended passage. In the following brief excerpt, probably you should pause for every comma and period, but nowhere else.

Here, gentlemen, is the enemy. Here is the army. The interest, the happiness of all America, is centered in this half-ruined spot. Come and help us. Here are laurels, come and share them. Here are Tories, come and help us to expel them. Here are Whigs that will make you welcome, and enemies that dread your coming.

The Crisis—Thomas Paine

Sometimes the oral reader should not pause where punctuation marks occur. For instance, five commas appear in this sentence: "Thomas Wade, III, was born May 4, 1952, in St. Joseph, Louisiana." Since it is short and contains a single, uncomplicated idea, the sentence might be read without pauses. Upon other occasions, the oral reader will wish to pause where no punctuation symbols appear. In this passage, you could focalize the thought by pausing for each slanted line:

He went into Main Street/ and sat on the curbing before Wracker's Tobacco Store./ For an hour he lingered about/ listening to the talk of men,/ but it did not interest him much/ and he slipped away.

Winesburg, Ohio—Sherwood Anderson [2]

Of course, not all vocal pauses are of the same duration. Variations in the length of the pauses aid in conveying thoughts and emphasis. In demonstration, read this exercise, allowing a short pause for each single slanted line and longer pauses for the double lines.

Have you ever stood on a downtown street corner/ and noticed, in the faces of the passing crowd,/ an expression of unrest,/ anxiety,/ and fatigue?// Each person, as he presses along,/ seems to be preoccupied with thoughts of late appointments,/ a missed bus,/ or a petty quarrel.// Everyone is caught in the hurry and bustle of life.//

Can it be that man has not learned how to be happy?// Aiken once said,/ "The sunshine of life is made up of very little beams/ that are bright all the time."// We set our eyes on the dazzling sun/ which we think to be our ultimate goal of happiness;// and, in working toward it,/ we are so blinded by its brightness/ that we cannot see the "little beams"//— the common things/ that are with us on all sides/ and that constitute our true happiness.

"The Little Beams"—Ruth Ferris, student at Oregon State College

The circumstances which necessitate a reduction in general rate call for lengthening the pauses and/or for shortening the extent of the thought to be expressed as a thought unit. Conversely, those conditions which require an increase in general rate suggest the shortening of the pauses and/or the lengthening of the thought units. For instance, if speaking to a small, informal audience which has gathered in a room possessing good acoustics, you might phrase the following passage in this way: "Mr. Chairman, Ladies and Gentlemen.// I am pleased that, despite the snowstorm,/ our entire panel of speakers is present.// Also, in view of the weather,/ I am delighted with the

[2] Sherwood Anderson, *Winesburg, Ohio* (New York: Boni and Liveright, 1919). Reprinted by permission of the copyright holders, The Viking Press, Inc.

attendance.// You have proved that a desire for culture is not dead on our campus." However, if speaking to a large audience, at an impressive occasion, or under poor acoustical conditions, you might use this method of phrasing: "Mr. Chairman,// Ladies/ and Gentlemen./// I am pleased/ that, despite the the snowstorm,// our entire panel of speakers/ is present./// Also,/ in view of the weather,// I am delighted/ with the attendance./// You have proved// that a desire for culture/ is not dead/ on our campus."

In addition to the preceding general factors, the shade of meaning which the reader wishes to express will influence the number and length of his pauses. Examples: a stop before and/ or after an important word or phrase will emphasize the "thought-center" so isolated; a stop just before the key line in a joke will add punch; a stop before the climactic sentence in a story will add suspense; and so on. To illustrate that skilled readers may interpret differently the nuances of meaning in a given passage and, hence, will read the passage with a somewhat different method of phrasing, study the following renditions of Hamlet's soliloquy.[3]

JOHN GIELGUD'S SYSTEM OF PAUSING

> To be,// or not to be:// that is the question://
> Whether 'tis nobler in the mind/ to suffer
> The slings and arrows of outrageous fortune,/
> Or to take arms against a sea of troubles,
> And by opposing end them?// To die:// to sleep;//
> No more;// and by a sleep to say we end
> The heart-ache and the thousand natural shocks
> That flesh is heir to,/ 'tis a consummation
> Devoutly to be wish'd.// To die, to sleep;//
> To sleep: perchance to dream: ay, there's the rub;//
> For in that sleep of death, what dreams may come
> When we have shuffled off this mortal coil,/
> Must give us pause:

---

[3] These transcriptions were prepared from recordings made by the three famous actors. See Otis J. Aggertt and Elbert R. Bowen, *Communicative Reading* (New York: Copyright by The Macmillan Company, 1956), pp. 212–214. Used by special permission.

MAURICE EVANS' SYSTEM OF PAUSING

To be, or not to be:// that is the question://
Whether 'tis nobler in the mind to suffer
The slings and arrows of outrageous fortune,/
Or to take arms against a sea of troubles,
And by opposing/ end them?// To die:// to sleep;/
No more;// and by a sleep to say we end
The heart-ache and the thousand natural shocks
That flesh is heir to,// 'tis a consummation
Devoutly to be wish'd.// To die,// to sleep;//
To sleep:/ perchance to dream:// ay, there's the rub;/
 For in that sleep of death what dreams may come
When we have shuffled off this mortal coil,/
Must give us pause:

LAURENCE OLIVIER'S SYSTEM OF PAUSING

To be,// or not to be:// that is the question:///
Whether 'tis nobler in the mind/ to suffer
The slings and arrows of outrageous fortune,/
Or to take arms against a sea of troubles,//
And by opposing// end them?// To die:/ to sleep;
No more;/ and by a sleep to say we end
The heart-ache/ and the thousand natural shocks
That flesh is heir to,// 'tis a consummation
Devoutly to be wish'd./ To die,/ to sleep;//
To sleep:// perchance to dream:// ay, there's the rub;//
 For in that sleep of death what dreams may come
When we have shuffled off this mortal coil,/
Must give us pause:

c. DURATION OF SOUND.   As you will remember, duration of sound refers to the amount of time consumed in producing the sounds of language, particularly the vowels, diphthongs, and semi-vowels. The length of the sounds should vary according to the intellectual and emotional meanings of the material. Solemn, reverential, ceremonious, sorrowful, gloomy, or depressing selections require a prolonging of the vowels, diphthongs, and semi-vowels, to accompany the generally slower rate. Light, sparkling, buoyant, cheerful, or frivolous material necessitates a shortening of the sounds, in conjunction with the more rapid general rate. In the next two selections, contrast the duration of sound requisite to reveal the appropriate meaning. For the first one, attempt to produce a bright, airy effect—by shortening the sounds and by maintaining a fairly rapid pace.

> There was a little turtle.
> He lived in a box.
> He swam in a puddle.
> He climbed on the rocks.
>
> He snapped at a mosquito.
> He snapped at a flea.
> He snapped at a minnow.
> And he snapped at me.
>
> He caught the mosquito.
> He caught the flea.
> He caught the minnow.
> But he didn't catch me.
>
> *The Little Turtle*—Vachel Lindsay [4]

In this passage, suggest the solemnity of the mood by lengthening the sounds and by speaking slowly:

> My friends: I know how vain it is to gild a grief with words, and yet I wish to take from every grave its fear. Here in this world, where life and death are equal kings, all should be brave enough to meet what all the dead have met. . . . From the wondrous tree of life the buds and blossoms fall with ripened fruit, and in the common bed of earth, patriarchs and babes sleep side by side. . . . They who stand with breaking hearts around this little grave, need have no fear. The larger and nobler faith in all that is, and is to be, tells us that death, even at its worst, is only perfect rest.
>
> *At a Child's Grave*—Robert G. Ingersoll

3. Force. The third variable element in the voice is force (intensity and loudness). Although less useful than changes in pitch and rate for indicating delicate shades of intellectual meaning, variations in force provide an excellent means for indicating emotional tones and attitudes. Only when seeking a particular dramatic effect should your degree of force remain constant for extended stretches.

[4] From Vachel Lindsay's *Collected Poems* (New York: Copyright by The Macmillan Company, 1923). Used by special permission.

a. Mild Emotions May Be Indicated By Using a Mild Degree of Force with Moderate, Not Abrupt, Changes in the Degree of Intensity and Loudness. For instance, the poem "'Flower in the Crannied Wall" represents a gentle, meditative mood and should be so indicated by the appropriate degree of stress in the voice.

> Flower in the crannied wall,
> I pluck you out of the crannies,
> I hold you here, root and all, in my hand,
> Little flower—but *if* I could understand
> What you are, root and all, and all in all,
> I should know what God and man is.
> *Flower in the Crannied Wall*—Alfred, Lord Tennyson

If you were to read the poem with loud, explosive force, wouldn't your presentation be most unsuitable? Your listeners would probably feel that instead of picking a small flower from a crevice you were attempting to pry loose a small tree.

b. Deeply Felt Emotions of the Repressed Type May Be Revealed by Using Considerable Vocal Intensity. *This intensity is usually characterized by a relatively steady expulsion of force.* In demonstration, read orally these stanzas from "The Death of the Flowers."

The melancholy days are come, the saddest of the year,
Of wailing winds, and naked woods, and meadows brown and sere.
Heaped in the hollows of the grove, the autumn leaves lie dead;
They rustle to the eddying gust, and to the rabbit's tread.
The robin and the wren are flown, and from the shrubs the jay,
And from the wood-top calls the crow through all the gloomy day. . . .

And then I think of one who in her youthful beauty died,
The fair meek blossom that grew up and faded by my side.
In the cold moist earth we laid her, when the forests cast the leaf,
And we wept that one so lovely should have a life so brief;
Yet not unmeet it was that one like that young friend of ours,
So gentle and so beautful, should perish with the flowers.
The Death of the Flowers—William Cullen Bryant

c. Strong, Vigorous Emotions May Be Indicated by Using Considerable Vocal Intensity. *Often this intensity is char-*

acterized by abrupt, staccato explosions and by sharp, striking variations in loudness. Re-read the selection from *Native Son,* pages 385–386. Assuming that you have thoroughly sensitized yourself to the emotional contents, in expressing the terrified screams of the mother and the violent ejaculations of Bigger, your voice will assume great intensity and will tend to explode various words and syllables in sharp bursts of energy and loudness. In the following drills, read the capitalized words with much greater intensity and loudness.

I don't care what you do, but I'M NOT GOING.
This program is not a good one. IT SIMPLY WON'T WORK.
WATCH OUT! You almost spilled that acid on my dress.
Mary TOLD you I would be late.
Run along now, but BE CAREFUL.
I asked you to leave. Please go. GET OUT OF HERE.

(*Mother to small child:*) Come on sweetie pie, eat your Pablum. That's a sweet boy. OH, HANK! SWALLOW IT. . . . HANK, DON'T YOU DARE SPIT OUT ANY MORE. IT'S ALL OVER ME. Well, you're just a little boy, aren't you, sweetheart? Here's another spoonful. Yum, yum, it's so good. I wish I could have some of it. Oh, there's the telephone. Now, Hank, I'll just be a minute. I'll put the bowl on the table out of your reach. Now, just be still for a minute. Mommy's going to be right back. . . . OH, HANK! ALL OVER THE FLOOR, AND I JUST SCRUBBED IT. . . . IT'S NOT A HAT, HANK. TAKE THE BOWL OFF YOUR HEAD.

d. Special Attention Should Be Directed to the Importance of Force in Achieving Climaxes. As you know, many manuscript speeches and literary selections are so constructed that they gradually build up to a highest point of concentration or climax. In fact, within a given selection several passages may develop peaks of attention. To indicate a heightening of emotional feeling, the reader may increase steadily his vocal intensity, frequently in conjunction with corresponding increases in loudness. (Also, he may quicken his rate of utterance and raise his pitch level.) As practice, study and then read orally the next selection. It begins with a story, which should be read with an animated, but conversational degree of force; it concludes with an application, which might be presented with steadily increasing intensity—the final two sentences, containing the important ideas of the selection, may be driven home by means of considerable intensity and volume.

In our friendly neighbor city of St. Augustine great flocks of sea gulls are starving amid plenty. Fishing is still good, but the gulls don't know how to fish. For generations they have depended on the shrimp fleet to toss them scraps from the nets. Now the fleet has moved to Key West.

The shrimpers had created a Welfare State for the St. Augustine sea gulls. The big birds never bothered to learn how to fish for themselves and they never taught their children to fish. Instead they led their little ones to the shrimp nets.

Now the sea gulls, the fine free birds that almost symbolize liberty itself, are starving to death because they gave in to the "something for nothing" lure! They sacrificed their independence for a handout.

A lot of people are like that, too. They see nothing wrong in picking delectable scraps from the tax nets of the U.S. Government's "shrimp fleet." But what about our children of generations to come?

Let's not be gullible gulls. We Americans must preserve our talents of self-sufficiency, our genius for creating things for ourselves, our sense of thrift and our true love of independence.

> *Advertisement published by the*
> *Barnett National Bank of*
> *Jacksonville, Florida*

4. The fourth variable element of the voice is its quality or timbre. (For definition and explanation of quality, refer to Chapter 6.) Of the four vocal components, timbre is perhaps the least flexible and the least valuable for conveying intellectual concepts; however, variations in quality are valuable for reproducing dialogue and for indicating emotional meanings.

In the next exercise, utilize changes in voice quality to indicate narration and dialogue. (Of course, also employ variations of pitch, rate, and force.) Do not overdo characterization, but give a suggestion of different personalities.

"Good morning, Mr. Harris," said the gas-station attendant as I drove up for a tankful. "Have you had your car Winterized yet?"

"No," I said apologetically, "I'm afraid it's still Summerized."

"We'll take care of it," he assured me briskly. "How's the oil?"

"I guess I could use a change," I ventured.

"Very good," he nodded. "We'll put the car in the Lubridome."

"In the what?" I asked.

"The Lubridome. That's where we do lubrication jobs."

"Oh," I said, "You mean the grease rack."

He ignored this. "With cold weather coming on, you might want an Integrated Engine Analysis."

"What's that?" I asked.

"Well, we check the spark-plugs and the timing and adjust the mechanism generally."

"I see. It's a tune-up, in other words."

"You could call it that," he shrugged.

"Could I have it washed by noon?"

"Certainly," he smiled. "It only takes a few minutes in the Automatic Cleanse-O-Port."

"Fine," I said, and walked off, leaving my car there, and thinking dark thoughts.

When I returned to pick it up that afternoon, I hailed the attendant with, "Sam, have you taken care of all my vehicular therapeutics?"

"Huh?" he asked.

"Is the car all ready?"

"Yes," he said. "It's all set."

"Good. Have you injected a sufficiency of volatile hydro-carbon mixture?"

"I don't get you, Mr. Harris."

"Is the tank full of gas?"

"Oh, yes."

"Fine. What about the dermatic ablutions?"

"The what?"

"Is the outside of the car washed?"

"Sure, sure—everything's all set, like I told you."

As I climbed behind the wheel and drove away, I heard him mutter to a co-worker: "Those writers—they sure use funny words."

Syndicated column by Sydney J. Harris [5]

To secure a better feel for appropriate vocal variation, read the following exercises. The first one, "Jazz Fantasia," requires wide changes in timbre. (Also, an effective reading of this selection necessitates striking alterations in (1) general rate and duration of sound; (2) degree of intensity and loudness; and (3)

[5] Used by special permission of Mr. Harris and General Features Corporation, 250 Park Avenue, New York City.

form of vocal release, ranging from a smooth even flow to an explosive staccato.)

Drum on your drums, batter on your banjoes, sob on your long cool wind-
    ing saxophones,
Go to it, O jazzmen!
Sling your knuckles on the bottoms of the happy tin pans;
Let your trombones ooze, and go hush-a-hush on the slippery sand paper.
Moan like an autumn wind high in the lonesome tree-tops;
Moan soft like you wanted somebody terrible.
Cry like a racing car slipping away from a motorcycle cop!
Bang, bang, you jazzmen! Bang all together, drums, traps, banjoes, horns,
    tin-cans!
Make two people fight on the top of a stairway and scratch each other's
    eyes in a clinch tumbling down the stairs.
Can the rough stuff!
Now a Mississippi steamboat pushes up the night river, with a hoo-hoo-hoo,
And the green lanterns calling to the high soft stars;
A red moon rides on the humps of the low river hills;
Go to it, O Jazzmen! [6]

Unlike "Jazz Fantasia," the next selection requires only moderate variations in timbre. Although somber and "overcast" in
its total impression, this passage contains several important
shifts in mood. Let your voice quality reflect the somewhat
lighter mood of explanation in the initial lines, the doom of the
approaching battle, the excitement of the engagement, the tragic
toll of casualties, and the solemnity of the closing thoughts.

. . . I was a lad in my teens, but I fired a Federal cannon from Cemetery
Ridge. Three days we had been fighting—General Lee, General Meade, and
me,—and the whole Union and Southern armies. Each army had a ridge
and in between a valley stretched on down to Gettysburg, a valley now
of death. For from the wooded crest a mile across the way two lines of
infantry came down to meet their fate. With Pickett in the lead they crossed
the road and passed the orchard on the left. On they came. Their eyes alight,
they could not see death's shadow waiting on our slope. And then our cannon belched with flames, and our rifles spit like serpents. Yet some rushed on
and climbed our wall before they fell dismembered. We died by the score on

[6] From *Smoke and Steel* by Carl Sandburg, copyright, 1920, by Harcourt, Brace
and Company, Inc.; renewed, 1948, by Carl Sandburg and reprinted by permission
of the publishers.

Cemetery Ridge, but our lines held firm and would not bend. For the enemy fought for slavery, and slavery had to end. And when the smoke was finally gone, seven thousand men and me would fight no more. But there on the gentle slopes of Gettysburg we struck the shackles from men's feet and let their souls be free. No more could pigment in the skin make slaves of men. And then, a man of peace, a lean, stooped man, with awkward limbs and tired face, came to our graves and spoke to us and to posterity. He said that ours was a "nation conceived in liberty, and dedicated to the proposition that all men are created equal." Equal, he said, not master and slave! There on that ridge at Gettysburg we pushed back the sea and opened men's eyes to liberty. . . .

"Open Men's Eyes"—Eugene E. White

In contrast to the wide changes in quality necessary for "Jazz Fantasia" and the moderate changes for "Open Men's Eyes," only slight variations in voice tone are required in reading the following announcement. Since this exercise consists of factual instructions, with little emotional coloring, its meaning may be conveyed chiefly by variations in pitch and rate.

I shall attempt to explain how each activity of registration fits into the total procedure. The actual process of registration will begin in either one of two rooms, Windsor 310 or 315. On Wednesday, February 8, at 9:00 A.M., registration materials will be given out in Windsor 310. Fifteen minutes later materials will be given out in Windsor 315, and so on at 30 minute intervals throughout the day. The last group will start at 2:45. New students begin registering on Friday, February 10. Seniors register first, followed by Juniors, Sophomores, and then Freshmen.

E. Your Reading Should Be Fluent. In addition to audibility, pleasant vocal quality, animation, and flexibility, an appropriate use of the audible code requires that oral reading be fluent.[7] Naturally, since the ideas have already been converted into language, fluency constitutes much less of a problem for the oral reader than for the extempore public speaker. When stumblings or hesitations do occur, the most common causes are excessive speed, nervousness, poor eye-voice interval, inadequate preparation, and losing one's place. (1) *If your rate tends to be too fast,* practice on exercises requiring deliberate, slow utter-

---

[7] Of course, in literary interpretation the reader may deliberately use hesitant speech to reproduce dialogue or to achieve dramatic effect.

ance. Resolve to keep a tight rein on your speed. And, watch your listeners for clues as to the suitability of your rate. Perhaps you might even try this technique which helped one person to conquer the habit of reading his manuscript speeches too rapidly: at the top of each sheet he typed in red capitals, "DANGER-SLOW." (2) *If you experience excessive tension when reading to a group,* review the suggestions in Chapter 2 for conquering nervousness. Select only material which is interesting and meaningful to you and which you genuinely wish to convey to others. Study carefully the intellectual and emotional content; then lose yourself in the process of communication. Think of yourself as a projector of ideas and emotions; think of the listeners as being likable, potentially receptive persons who hope you will carry off your reading successfully. Try to divert nervous energy into the positive outlets of increased vocal and bodily animation. Have faith in yourself. Do your best and refuse to worry about the results. (3) *If you have poor eye-voice interval,* become as well acquainted with your material as you can. Practice reading the selection orally a number of times. In speaking to the audience, resist becoming disconcerted by a few hesitations. Also, seek help from the university's reading counselor. (4) *When inadequate preparation causes you to stumble,* you have only yourself to blame. In addition to studying thoroughly the passage, you should read it aloud at least four times before presenting it in public. (5) *To avoid losing your place,* follow these suggestions: (a) Of greatest importance, become sufficiently acquainted with the sequence of the selection. (b) Familiarize yourself with the physical copy itself. By using the same copy during rehearsal as during the presentation, you will become accustomed to the physical appearance of each page. (c) Use the suggestions on pages 401–402 to insure that the written copy possesses suitable physical characteristics. (d) Ascertain beforehand that the amount of light is sufficient for easy reading. (e) Although the practice is unnecessary for the well-prepared reader, the running of a forefinger along the margin will help you to keep your place. *If you should lose your place and a rapid search fails to relocate it,* you might do one of several things: (a) Attempt to continue the thought by impromptu speaking until you regain the place. (b) Summarize what you have been reading with the expectation that you will recover the place before completing the recapitulation. (c) Offer a transition to the idea starting on the last paragraph on the page and begin reading there. (d) Above all, do not become flustered. In the case of the manuscript speech, the audience probably will not realize that you have lost your place. Even in literary interpretation, the listeners may believe that your impromptu insertion was deliberate.

F. Your Reading Should Use Clear and Correct Pronunciation. Except for some dialogue materials, your pronunciation should always be clear and correct. Check in a dictionary the pronunciation of any unusual word. As a phase of your rehearsal, try to record each reading. Listen critically in order to determine whether your utterance seems slurred, muffled, or mushy. Of course, do not go to the extreme of becoming overprecise; such would be as bad as the original problem of indistinctness. As we have suggested before, when facing the audience do not worry unduly about pronunciation. Instead, concentrate upon reaching your listeners. If you have developed correct habits, they will serve you efficiently during the presentation.

INSURING THE SUITABLE APPEARANCE OF THE COPY

Unless your handwriting or printing is unusually legible, do not read from such copy and, except in emergencies, do not read from the handwriting of another person. Books and magazines are suitable only if the print is sufficiently large and distinct, if adequate space occurs between the lines, and if ample margins exist. To prepare appropriate typewritten copy, follow these guides: (1) Use 16- or 20-pound bond paper, preferably the latter. Although some speakers prefer a colored paper to reduce glare, most use a standard white sheet. Cards may also be used;

however, if a number of them must be employed, the thickness of the cards may produce a cumbersome pile. (2) The paper should be of proper size. The 8½″ by 11″ sheet is somewhat too large to be handled easily. Therefore, you might prefer to use a smaller size of about 6″ by 8½″. (An easy way of securing such sheets is to fold and cut into halves the standard sized page, 8½″ by 11″.) (3) Use only one side of each sheet. (4) Number each page. Probably the most suitable place for the numbers is the upper right corner. (5) Depending upon your choice, use either the customary system of capitalization or convert all letters to capitals. The exclusive use of capitals will facilitate easier viewing; on the other hand, some persons find that the continuous appearance of capitals makes more difficult the recognition of sentence structure, proper nouns, statistics, and so on. (6) Do not crowd the copy. Double or triple spacing is necessary to guarantee easy reading. Also, allow ample space for all margins. (7) Read only from "clean" copy. Retype pages which contain erasures, crossed out passages, or insertions between the lines or in the margins. (8) If you find the practice helpful, mark the mansucript to indicate pauses, emphasis, and so forth. However, do not permit the overuse of such symbols to clutter the copy.

SUMMARY

Specialized training in reading aloud is important because oral reading is a practical tool for almost everyone, because skill in extempore delivery is not necessarily reflected in superior attainments in oral reading, because oral reading differs in nature and function from silent reading, and because oral reading provides an excellent avenue for developing attributes of effective vocal and physical delivery. In reading to others, follow these basic principles: (1) Maintain a keen sense of communication. (2) Understand the materials you are to read. (3) Use the visible code effectively by maintaining adequate eye contact and by using appropriate facial expression, stance, posture, movement, and gestures. (4) Use the audible code effectively by insuring that your voice is audible, pleasant, animated, and flexible, that your reading is fluent, and that your pronunciation is clear and appropriate. (5) Determine that the written copy possesses suitable physical characteristics.

17 ❦❦ *Common Forms of Oral Reading*

In Chapter 16, we considered unique characteristics of the oral reading process and basic principles applicable to all forms of reading aloud. In this chapter, we turn to the specialized adjustments required by the oral reading of manuscript speeches, quoted materials during the extempore speech, minutes and financial reports, and literature.

THE MANUSCRIPT SPEECH

As you already know, manuscript speaking is frequently used in radio and television, at formal gatherings, and on important professional, political, educational, and business occasions.

A. Advantages and Liabilities of Manuscript Speaking. Speaking from a manuscript has several advantages. It enables those who lack training or experience in extempore delivery to meet the needs of a speaking situation. It helps relieve nervous tension because the speaker realizes that memory and the finding of words is not a problem. It can insure the presentation of a polished, closely knit, exactly phrased, and precisely timed address. Also, it affords an immediately available written record of what was said. Some persons are extremely effective when reading a prepared speech. Harry Emerson Fosdick says: [1]

Speaking from an outline has been my most common practice. But in recent years I have found that one can have the full manuscript in front

---

[1] Charles A. McGlon, "How I Prepare My Sermons: A Symposium," *The Quarterly Journal of Speech*, February, 1954, p. 52.

of him, and can read it as though he were not reading but talking, with just as much freedom, spontaneity, colloquial directness and person-to-person impact as though no manuscript were on the pulpit. Just as one can *write* for listeners, so can one *read* for listeners, combining the advantage of a manuscript's careful preparation with the freedom of face-to-face address.

Unfortunately, most manuscript speakers fall disappointingly short of Dr. Fosdick's ideal characterization. Instead of being a speech, the manuscript too often turns out to be an essay, better adapted to the eye than to the ear; instead of rehearsing carefully, the average speaker relies upon a preparatory scanning of the copy; instead of speaking with a lively sense of communication, he usually reads in a stilted, hurried, and unnatural manner; instead of looking at his audience, he is inclined to study his manuscript; instead of feeling free to gesture or to move about the platform, he typically remains rooted to the lectern and raises his hands only to turn the pages; instead of adjusting the speech to the reactions of his hearers, he experiences difficulty in altering his language, organization, and content. Furthermore, listeners have heard so much poor reading that they groan inwardly when a speaker approaches the platform with a sheaf of papers in his hands. Doubtless you will observe that the foregoing complaints do not constitute an indictment of manuscript speaking as a mode of presentation, but rather a protest against the ineffectual practitioners of the method.

B. Preparing the Manuscript Speech. As you acquire experience, undoubtedly you will evolve a methodology which seems most appropriate for your particular needs. However, for the present probably you should follow this procedure:

1. Develop the outline. Although some experienced speakers minimize the use of the outline when preparing for manuscript speaking, the novice should prepare a complete, detailed outline. In developing the outline, follow exactly the same system that you used for your extemporaneous talks.

2. Write the initial draft. With the completed outline

before you, prepare a rough verbatim copy of what you wish to say. Try to write in the same mode that you talk. Do not prepare an essay! Remember that your language should be as direct and conversational as the mood of the occasion, the size of the audience, and the nature of your speech permit. Through imagination, try to see and hear yourself delivering the sentences to your particular audience. Perhaps you will find that your draft retains more of the qualities of oral communication if you dictate to a friend who takes shorthand. At this stage, do not worry excessively about smoothness or polish. Even if you recognize that you are phrasing an idea clumsily, struggle on as best you can. To stop and ponder for extended periods at each difficult point will inhibit the flow of thought.

3. Revise the initial and subsequent drafts. A critical analysis of the initial drafts may be somewhat discouraging. However, you may find comfort in the realization that almost all successful manuscript speeches go through several revisions. For example, even with the aid of skilled advisers, prominent speakers like Truman, Stevenson, Nixon, and Eisenhower sometimes must revise an address as many as a dozen times. Many speakers consider their first drafts so inadequate that they destroy them and begin anew. The number of revisions your speech will require depends upon its nature and importance and upon your skill as a writer. However, at least three drafts are usually necessary to obtain a maximum degree of polish, accuracy, and forcefulness of expression.

Warning: In your revisions, do not permit the talk to lose its spontaneity and freshness. Do not let it become emotionally sterile, stilted, indirect, or unnecessarily formal. Your manuscript should read like a speech and not a term report. As Quintilian pointed out many years ago, an address should be the product of conscientious effort but should not obviously smell of midnight oil.

In each revision ask yourself questions like these: Are my grammar and syntax correct? (In extempore speaking substandard colloquialisms and inaccurate sentence structure might be forgiven as inadvertent slips of the tongue; however, in a manuscript speech they might seem glaringly inappropriate.) Have I expressed my ideas as simply and precisely as possible? Do my sentences average about ten to twelve words in length? Have I varied their length sufficiently so as to avoid a choppy effect? Are they predominately simple in structure, rather than complex, compound, or compound-complex? Have I maintained the direct approach by means of personal pronouns, contractions, and appropriate idioms? Have I made maximum appeal to vivid concreteness and the various types of imagery? Do I get extra mileage from my illustrations, quotations, statistics, and so on?

One of the functions served by the revisions is to adjust the speech length to the time limits. As you probably know, if the talk is to be radio cast or telecast, its length must be gauged to within a half-minute of the prescribed limits. If you run overtime, you will be cut off the air; if you close too soon, the station must fill the interval with music or commercials. Although less need exists for precise timing in face-to-face speaking, your talk should not vary significantly from the time allotted. By carefully considering the time element during the composition of each revision, only minor adjustments will be required following the completion of the "final" copy. A trial reading of the "finished" manuscript at the same pace that you expect to use during the actual presentation should enable you to estimate accurately the length of time necessary for delivery. Be sure to make allowances for anticipated audience applause or laughter and for the tendency to speed up somewhat under the tension of the occasion. As a safeguard, some speakers arrange an optional paragraph near the end which they can include or omit depending upon the amount of time remaining. Naturally, such a detachable passage should not be vital to the speech.

C. Rehearsing the Manuscript Speech. Although the program of rehearsing the manuscript is basically similar to that for the extemporaneous speech, you should consider these additional recommendations.

1. Do not rehearse the speech until you have completed the final revision; then practice only from the copy which you plan to use in the actual presentation, or from an exact duplicate. Become familiar not only with the sequence of ideas but also with the physical way they appear on the typed page. Even minor alterations in the physical arrangement of the script to which you are accustomed may cause hesitations and uncertainties during the actual presentation.

2. Read the speech several times, first silently and then orally. By reading straight through the manuscript a number of times you can establish in your mind a firm grasp of the total sequence.

3. Study the script meticulously. Analyze the meaning and the structure of each sentence; ascertain the changes in mood and thought; identify the transitions and summaries; determine the ideas and contentions you wish to emphasize; locate the possible high points of interest. As you study each passage, consider how you can utilize vocal and physical delivery to secure greatest effectiveness from your presentation.

4. If you find the methodology beneficial, mark your copy to indicate emphasis, pauses, and vocal phrasing. Caution: The use of such symbols may cause you to become excessively conscious of techniques, thus impairing spontaneity. During rehearsal you might experiment with script markings. If you find your delivery becoming mechanical or stilted, immediately abandon further trials. Should you decide to use markings, follow the system introduced in Chapter 16: underline words to receive special stress; indicate a short pause by means of a diagonal line (/) and an extended pause by a double line (//).

5. Work to polish delivery. Once you have acquired a "feel" of the total sequence and have studied carefully the intellectual and emotional components of each passage, strive to improve your use of the audible and visible codes. As you practice, try to visualize yourself delivering the speech to your particular audience.

a. IMPROVING VOCAL PRESENTATION. If possible, record one or more trial rehearsals. Listen critically to the playback(s) and on the margin of the carbon copy of the manuscript record suggestions for needed improvement. Ask yourself questions like these: Do I seem to be talking, or am I obviously reading? Do I seem sincere and forceful? Do I maintain an animated sense of communication? Does my voice possess sufficient flexibility? Am I reading too rapidly? Have I retained the inflections, pauses, and other characteristics of normal oral communication? Does my personality come across in my voice? Do I achieve appropriate climaxes? Is my pronunciation clear and correct?

b. IMPROVING EYE CONTACT. Concentrate on reducing your reliance upon the manuscript. Become so well acquainted with the script that you can maintain eye contact with your listeners at least 80 per cent of the time. By conscientious effort you can increase your recognition span until you can grasp one or more sentences in a rapid glance. Naturally, you should not seek verbatim memory. If you take a manuscript to the stand, you should read from it rather than recite the entire address from memory.

c. IMPROVING PHYSICAL ADJUSTMENT TO THE MANUSCRIPT. Should you attempt to conceal the fact that you are reading from a manuscript? No, but make your use of the script unobtrusive. Learn beforehand if a speaker's stand will be present; if so, practice the use of a lectern during rehearsals. Place the manuscript upon the lectern; as you near the end of a page, slide it down perhaps an inch so that the top lines of the next sheet are revealed; then, move the page easily to the side—do not turn the discarded page over and do not insert it under the pile. If you have ascertained that no lectern will be available at the meeting, rehearse by holding the manuscript in your hands. Hold the sheets at the proper level and do not obviously bend your neck so that you attract undue attention to the copy or so that your voice becomes muffled. When you have completed the reading of a page, place it on the bottom of the sheaf of papers. In situations where you are compelled to hold the manuscript, the size of the sheets becomes signally important. The smaller

6″ by 8½″ pages are easier to handle and are much less conspicuous than the standard-sized 8½″ by 11″.

d. IMPROVING BODILY ACTION. During rehearsal, attempt to keep your body loose and animated. Do not let the process of reading cause you to become wooden or stilted. Experiment with gesturing and gross physical movement. Check your stance and posture in a full-length mirror. In general, work for smooth, forceful physical presentation.

D. Delivering the Manuscript Speech. Although we have already covered the basic principles of delivery, these points need additional emphasis: (1) Maintain a lively sense of communication. Converse with your listeners. Rethink and recreate the speech as you talk. Lose yourself in the process of conveying to the listeners the intellectual and emotional meanings of your message. (2) Keep a tight rein on your rate. If you visualize what you are saying at the moment of expression, you will experience less compulsion to increase the pace. To help monitor their rate, some speakers insert in the margin a large "5" to indicate the place where they should be after five minutes of reading; they add another marker at the 10 minute point, and so on. Probably this practice is most feasible in broadcast situations where usually a large wall clock affords easy reference. (3) Until you acquire experience in speaking from a script, you should follow the copy closely. Gradually you will develop the skill necessary to make successful impromptu adjustments to the reactions of the listeners. Only then will your manuscript delivery possess the flexibility necessary for greatest effectiveness.

QUOTED MATERIAL DURING THE EXTEMPORE SPEECH

In speaking extemporaneously, you probably will wish to give from memory the quoted material which is brief and uncomplicated. However, if a series of figures or an extended quotation must be presented, and if exact accuracy must be maintained, you usually should plan to read the statements.

A. Suggestions for the Preparation of Such Materials. (1) The intellectual and emotional content of the quoted matter should be well-adjusted to the remainder of the speech and to the total speaking situation. (2) If possible, avoid long or involved citations. (3) If speaking from notes on 3″ by 5″ or 4″ by 6″ cards, you may enter the quoted material at the appropriate place in the notes. Should you find that such insertions destroy the outline effect of the notes, place the excerpts on larger sheets of paper 6″ by 8½″ or even on standard-sized sheets 8½″ by 11″. For additional advice in preparing the physical copy, see the suggestions given in Chapter 16.

B. Suggestions for the Presentation of Such Material. (1) During the speech anticipate the need to refer to the quotations. In this way you can have them immediately at hand, thereby avoiding any awkward searching among your notes. (2) Avoid trite introductions such as: "I have some statistics here" or "I want to read something to you." Instead, say something like "Yesterday in Fort Worth, Senator Fulbright made this startling statement about our military preparedness," or "Here is documentary evidence that the City Commission is guilty of wasteful spending." (3) Do not attempt to conceal the copy while you are reading. Usually the audience will appreciate your desire to insure accurate reporting. (4) Your reading should possess the same spontaneity and vitality which characterize your extempore speaking. Do not permit the act of reading to impair your feeling of rapport with the audience. Maintain eye contact with the listeners at least 80 per cent of the time. Use adequate volume and projection. Try to avoid monotonous inflexibility of rate, pitch, force, and voice quality. Feel free to move and to gesture as you believe appropriate.

MINUTES AND FINANCIAL REPORTS

Customarily the reading of minutes and financial reports is singularly inept. The typical speaker seems to feel little, if any, desire to communicate: he mumbles rapidly and monotonously, violating most of the basic principles of appropriate delivery. In reading minutes or reports, your purpose is to share information and to facilitate understanding. Obviously, when the auditors fail to grasp the factual data, your attempt at communication has been unsuccessful. If you look at your listeners at least half the time and speak directly to them in an audible, animated manner, you will probably be regarded as an uncommonly successful reporter. To promote effective delivery, practice reading the material several times before presenting it in public. In addition to considering vocal and physical presentation, you should also prepare the data in conformity with high standards of organization and composition. Compose minutes or a financial report with the same care that you would devote to an extempore speech of the same length.

FAMILY READING

As the novelist John Hersey urges, "parents should create in the home an atmosphere that is conducive to reading. They should have good books and magazines at hand. Parents should read to children. They should try to entertain them with reading and to make reading a pleasure as television is a pleasure. If school is where *learning* to read belongs, home is where *happiness* in reading belongs." Oral reading in the home can be fun! It can provide keen pleasure for adults and high adventure for youngsters. Furthermore, it is a shared experience which draws together the members of the family. Johnny will want to learn to read if he is repeatedly immersed in the warm, friendly atmosphere of family reading.

Here are some suggestions to help make experiments in family reading more successful. Make "enjoyment" your goal, rather than "education." Choose selections that everyone wants to hear. Occasionally you might read a work merely to improve your literary IQ. However, a steady diet of "uplifting" classics will soon thin the ranks of the listeners. At first, read for only a half-hour or so. Stop when one or more members become weary. Also, take turns with the reading. Give even eight-year-old Karen her chance. Stress informality in listening. Instead of demanding continuous, concentrated attention, let Aunt Martha knit, Mother darn socks, Junior play with his Erector set, and let Grandpa listen awhile, snooze awhile, and listen awhile. Perhaps your family circle will enjoy a discussion period after each reading session. This pooling of impressions will enrich the communal spirit produced by oral reading.

INTERPRETATION OF LITERATURE

In definition: Interpretation is the process of communicating to an audience a literary work, from the printed page. The term "literary work" encompasses a wide gamut from essays through short stories, plays, and novels to poetry. Naturally not all examples of such works possess sufficient beauty of expression and universality of appeal to be considered "literary." We assume that the student will exercise sufficient discrimination to select materials possessing aesthetic merit.

A. Why Study Interpretation? An undergraduate once startled a class in interpretation by asking, "What benefits will I get out of this subject?" When she had recovered her aplomb, the instructor replied in a voice which seemed to come directly from a Minnesota blizzard: "Young man, do you wish to remain a barbarian the remainder of your life?" Contrary to the opinion of this instructor an indifference to interpretation will not categorize you as a savage. However, the study of interpretation will improve your personality and will make you a better-rounded, more sensitive human being. It will broaden and deepen your appreciation, knowledge, and understanding of literature. Surely no defense of literature is necessary. Every college student realizes that the magic of language enables him to harness his power of imagination to the printed symbols and thereby to experience vicariously all of the thoughts, adventures, and emotions possible to man. To appreciate fully much of literature, particularly the poetic and the dramatic, you must either read it aloud or listen to a skilled rendition by someone else. A supple, expressive voice can add depth, crispness, and clarity to the mental images inherent in a literary work. Even more important, since literature can exert a galvanic appeal to the feelings, the voice can bring a poignancy, an electrifying violence, or a throbbing gentleness to the emotions occasioned by the writing.

In order for you as an interpreter to *re-create* the moods, the characterization, and the dramatic effect of a literary work, you must determine what the author intended to *create*. This involves taking the selection apart piece by piece and analyzing each part in terms of the relevant information you have acquired concerning the nature and motives of the author, the times in which he lived, and the situation about which he was writing. Then, you must put the pieces together in your thinking so that you have a unified, complete impression. This process of analysis and synthesis serves the immediate function of ascertaining the structure, style, and background of a worth-while literary work. In addition, it sharpens the mind and widens the areas of sensitivity.

The skills of vocal and physical delivery which you develop in interpretation do have carry-over values to public address, debate, discussion, and conversation. Naturally, the reading aloud of a piece of literature is a far less direct type of communication than extempore speaking. However, the interpreter develops a poise and a disciplined control of body and voice which will serve him well in all other forms of oral communication.

The ensuing brief treatment can serve only as an introduction to the procedure of preparing and presenting interpretative readings. For a more complete discussion consult any standard text on interpretation. Your speech teacher or librarian will be glad to supply you with a list of such works.

B. Selecting the Material. Some literary works are better adapted to oral presentation than others. Particularly in the case of essays, some writing seems designed almost exclusively for the eye and cannot be easily converted into spoken language. In general, avoid selecting writing which contains a high proportion of long, complicated sentences or which deals primarily with abstract or abstruse thought. Instead, seek material which possesses a living, vital concreteness, a compelling sweep of thought and feeling, and a rhythm, beauty and clarity of language.

Recognize that your listeners respond to literature in terms of their own interests, psychological needs, and vicarious and real-life experiences. Few, if any, literary works possess such universality of appeal that they will fit equally well all audiences. Try to find a common denominator of interest and experience among your potential auditors by analyzing their age, sex, educational background, and their group affiliations. Also, consider the size of the group. To determine the psychological influence exerted by the reading occasion upon the listeners' receptivity and concentration, consider the nature of the meeting; its time and place; the remainder of the program; and the time limits assigned to you. Concerning time limitations, this caution should be added: many an inexperienced reader chooses a selection which is much too long and then relies upon cutting to reduce it to proper length. However, in many cases excessive pruning weakens the coherence and emphasis of a work.

In our study of public speaking, we learned that a subject which is appropriate to the audience and to the occasion may be unsuited to the speaker. This principle is equally applicable to interpretation. Unless you are genuinely interested in and sympathetic to your selection, you probably will be unable to project yourself unreservedly into the reading. In respect to your particular talents, pick the sort of selection which you can present most effectively. Do you read best those writings which are loud, forceful, and perhaps belligerent? Or, those which are subdued, philosophical, or sad? Do your abilities restrict you basically to selections which retain the same mood throughout, requiring a minimum of versatility? Or, do you possess sufficient vocal suppleness to read well those works which change frequently and sharply in their style, mood, and characterization? (Of course, for training purposes you should practice reading all types of selections.) Finally, a suitable oral reading of some selections requires only a cursory preliminary examination by the reader while others demand concentrated analysis and considerable background knowledge. If considering a selection that falls in the latter classification, are you willing to undergo the effort necessary to understand it?

Now, a few words about the source of materials. Any anthology or standard text on interpretation will offer numerous selections. Not only is the entire range of prose, poetry, and drama available in anthologies, but also many collections give helpful biographical information about the author and the circumstances under which he wrote. In addition, some offer critical notes or study guides for the selections themselves, indicating the thesis, scope, and style. Naturally, once you become interested and skilled in interpretation, you may range as widely in your search of materials as your time and energy permit.

C. Understanding the Intent of the Author. Let us assume that you have now chosen a selection which has some literary merit, which is appropriate for oral presentation, and which is well suited to the audience, the occasion, and to yourself as the reader. Your next step is to determine as accurately as possible what the author intended to say. Only in this way can you reveal with fidelity the intent and feelings which are inherent in the selection.

1. Become adequately acquainted with the author, his motives, his purposes in writing the selection, and his attitudes as revealed in the writing. Also, become adequately familiar with the historical context within which the plot takes place. Clearly, some selections require little or no background knowledge of this type. However, such would not be true if, at a program commemorating the birthday of Abraham Lincoln, you decided to read his First Inaugural Address. Much of Lincoln's message has immediate application to the America of today. Interposition, extra-legal efforts at nullification, and sectional animosity over the race question are once again matters of national concern. A successful reading of the address requires an understanding of the similarities and differences which exist between 1861 and today. In addition, you should understand Lincoln's genuine sympathy for the position of the South and his sorrowful apprehension concerning the impending conflict. Be sensitive to the tactful understanding with which his speech attempted to bridge the widening schism. Recognize the inflexible firmness with which he declared that secession was unconstitutional and that federal authorities would continue the collection of customs and the maintenance of U.S. forts in the South. Also perceive Lincoln's skill as a practical statesman in so constructing his message that the odium for secession would fall upon the withdrawing states and not upon him or the North. And consider the nature of both the immediate and the unseen audiences which Lincoln wished to reach. Perhaps now you appreciate more fully the degree of background research and thinking which sometimes must enter into the interpretation of literature.

2. Discover the intellectual and emotional meanings and the qualities of literary craftsmanship.   In the following explanation of the techniques involved in studying a literary work, the ancient ballad "Lord Randal" will be used as an illustrative sample. Admittedly, many selections are more difficult to analyze than "Lord Randal." However, because it is brief, compact, and familiar, it will serve our purposes well.

"Oh where ha'e ye been, Lord Randal, my son?
O where ha'e ye been, my handsome young man?"—
     "I ha'e been to the wild wood; mother, make my bed soon,
     For I'm weary with hunting, and fain would lie down."

"Who gave ye your dinner, Lord Randal, my son?
Who gave ye your dinner, my handsome young man?"—
     "I dined with my true-love; mother, make my bed soon,
     For I'm weary with hunting, and fain would lie down."

"What had ye for dinner, Lord Randal, my son?
What had ye for dinner, my handsome young man?"—

"I had eels broiled in broo (broth); mother, make my bed soon,
For I'm weary with hunting, and fain would lie down."

"And where are your bloodhounds, Lord Randal, my son?
And where are your bloodhounds, my handsome young man?"—
"O they swelled and they died; mother, make my bed soon,
For I'm weary with hunting, and fain would lie down."

"O I fear ye are poisoned, Lord Randal my son!
O I fear ye are poisoned, my handsome young man!"—
"O yes! I am poisoned; mother, make my bed soon,
For I'm sick at heart, and I fain would lie down."

a. ASCERTAIN THE BASIC THOUGHT AND MOOD. All selections
have a primary thesis, thought, or message, and most possess a
predominant mood or atmosphere. "Lord Randal" is a dramatic story of horror and treachery. However, the unknown
author, like all ballad-poets, maintains the impersonal, objective
quality of a reporter.

b. DISCOVER THE METHODS OF DEVELOPMENT. Most dramatic
works contain a beginning, an unfoldment, a climax, and an
ending. (Consider the similarity between this organizational
structure and that of a speech: Introduction, Body, and Conclusion.) The beginning may capture attention, introduce the main
characters, and/or indicate the theme or mood. The unfoldment
may carry the plot forward in a steadily rising level of action
until it reaches the inevitable turning point, or climax. Or, the
unfoldment may provide the background for a sudden or unexpected turn of events and then may rapidly build up to a high
point of concentration, or climax. The climax is the focal point
of a selection and usually represents the highest peak of emotional intensity. Following the climax typically comes a brief
period of falling action, or ending. The first stanza of "Lord
Randal," ignoring any preliminaries, gets the poem off to a fast
start by introducing the story and the two speakers. The unfoldment moves swiftly, without digressions, in a continuously rising
degree of tension until the tragic climax: "Oh yes! I am
poisoned." The final line and a half represents the declining
action: "mother, make my bed soon, For I'm sick at the heart,

and I fain would lie down." The ending includes no summation, no application of the thought, no moral, and no "afterthoughts."

c. ANALYZE THE STYLE AND MOOD OF THE WRITING. How does the author order the parts of the selection so that they merge into a single dominant channel of thought? Does he accomplish this primarily through the movements and activities of a main character, by the use of a single setting, by continuous changes in locale, by a temporal sequence of events, or by the words of a narrator? How does he achieve coherence and emphasis? Does the selection offer variety and contrast? If so, in what manner? If the work lacks frequent changes of pace, does it successfully compensate by providing an overpowering mood, catchy rhythm, and so on? If characterization is employed, ask yourself such questions as: What is the author's attitude toward the characters? How does he reveal them? What kind of people are they? What dominant personality traits does each possess? What manner of speech do they employ? Determine the methodologies the writer uses to develop suspense. Analyze the appeals he makes to sensory imagery, that is, sight, hearing, smell, taste, muscle movement and tension, and touch. Ascertain the stylistic devices the author employs to highlight the important thoughts and attitudes and to submerge others. Does he extensively use alliteration, personification, repetition, simile, metaphor, and/or balanced or periodic sentences? Does the word choice stress melody and rhythm, or does it deliberately produce a harsh, jangling, cacophonic effect? If so, why? Identify each change of setting and of mood; ascertain the purpose in the shifts; determine how the author prepared the reader for the changes. Now, to apply briefly these concepts to "Lord Randal": In true ballad form, the narrative is extremely condensed. The facts are given concisely and the picture develops decisively and rapidly. The entire poem is carried in the dialogue which is direct, terse, sharp, and tense. Although the characters are not described, their personalities emerge into clear delineation. We visualize the anxious mother and the weary youth. We glean a revulsive, if shadowy, impression of the treacherous sweetheart who, while professing love, served poisoned broth. The ballad secures dramatic effect by repetition, suggestion, and by the sharp contrast between the mother's mounting apprehension and the boy's deathly weariness. The unfoldment utilizes the mother's questions to heighten steadily the suspense until the tragedy is revealed in Randal's first reply.

D. Developing Appropriate Attitudes. As you will recall, the extempore speaker must possess appropriate attitudes toward the audience, the occasion, the message, and himself. Otherwise his presentation will lack the poise, animation, and keen sense of communication necessary for maximum effectiveness. Undoubtedly you have already realized that this canon is equally true for the interpreter. You must consider the listeners as being animate, responsive beings—not wooden posts or upholstered furniture. You must have a genuine desire to stimulate them in such a way that they experience empathically the thoughts and emotions in the selection. Also, you must be sensitive to the conditioning effects of the occasion. If the psychological mood of the meeting fosters appropriate responses from the listeners, capitalize upon it. If the reverse is true, attempt to overcome this disadvantage by your introductory comments (apply the techniques you studied in Chapter 14 for securing favorable attention in the Introduction of the public speech) and by your style of delivery.

Perhaps even more important than your feelings toward the audience and the occasion are your attitudes toward your materials and toward yourself as the interpreter. You already recognize that literature exerts a combined appeal to the emotions and intellect through the motor power of imagination. But do you appreciate fully the necessity for your entering freely, without emotional road blocks, into the mood of the writing? Only in this way can you become a successful medium for arousing the desired responses in the audience. Synthetic emotions usually will appear factitious to analytical observers. Unless for the time being you can accept without question the philosophy and the emotions inherent in the materials, probably you cannot project them successfully to others. Examples: If you believe Abraham Lincoln was an unscrupulous politician who conceived his First Inaugural as a fulcrum to pry the South loose from her constitutional moorings, if you believe Lincoln wished to instigate war, or if you believe in nullification or interposition, you should not attempt to read his address. Probably you would be unable to appreciate its beauty of language, its predominate mood of moderation, and its undercurrent of sadness. Furthermore, since most audiences consider Lincoln to have been a man of peace, gentleness, and humility, very likely you would be out of step with your listeners. In the case of "Lord Randal," you should be able to appreciate the warmth and love of the mother as she gradually realizes in terror that her son has been doomed by his malevolent sweetheart. If you should lack such sympathy, or if you dislike the dialect or the obvious emotional pull, you should look elsewhere for a selection.

Furthermore, you must be both willing and able to subordinate your personality and character to the literature itself. This does not mean that you completely lose your individuality. Manifestly, in re-creating the emotions and thought of the author, you must draw upon your own background of experiences and attitudes. Nevertheless, you are a "spokesman" for the author. Your primary function is to serve as a skilled translator, converting the printed symbols of a text into vocal and physical delivery which will stimulate the listeners, through their power of imagination, to experience the feelings and concepts intended by the author.

E. Using the Visible and Audible Codes. The following cautions will supplement the previous treatments of vocal and physical delivery.

1. Beware of artificiality and exhibitionism. Such negative characteristics are impossible if the reader possesses a genuine sympathy and understanding for the materials and proper attitudes toward the process of interpretation. Nevertheless, artificiality and exhibitionism occur with such disturbing frequency that you should be warned specifically against them.

2. Work for naturalness and spontaneity. Your presentation should not sound as if it is being read. Instead it should seem to spring directly from your mind and heart. Although you may have studied each sentence with critical intensity and have rehearsed your delivery accordingly, your reading must never seem studied and calculated. The highest form of artistic expression is that which seems effortless, fresh, and spontaneous.

3. Read to your listeners. *Do not impersonate or act.* In terms of the nature of his function, the extempore speaker and the actor are at opposite poles, with the interpreter and the impersonator somewhere in between. The speaker delivers his own thoughts directly to the audience. He is completely himself. He uses his own words, his own personality, and his own natural style of speaking. Conversely, the actor theoretically has no personal contact with the listeners. He gives not outward evidence of being aware of their presence. Instead of being himself, he assumes the role of another person. To persuade the audience to accept him *as* that person, he employs all the techniques and equipment of the theater; he memorizes a script which has been written by someone else; and he walks, talks, and gestures in accord with his characterization.

The unique function of the interpreter may be seen easily. The interpreter asks the audience to accept him as an agent of the author. He uses no props, scenery, costume, make-up, and so on. Through his reading he attempts to stimulate his listeners so that they will visualize the setting and the physical and psychological nature of the characters. He does not limit himself exclusively to the lines of one role as does the actor, but reads all parts in addition to the passages of description and explanation. He does not walk about the stage, drink tea, or hang pictures on the wall, as an actor might do. Furthermore, although the interpreter may memorize part or all of his presentation, he carries the script with him to the stand and appears to read. His degree of direct contact with the audience is mid-way between the complete rapport of the extempore speaker and the theoretically complete absence of contact of the actor. The interpreter maintains occasional-to-frequent eye contact with his listeners and reads to them. In brief, he attempts to reveal the meaning of literature by means of suggestion rather than by complete acting.

Impersonation is much closer to acting than is interpretation. Frequently the impersonator selects material involving only one character or one locale. He may employ stage properties and costuming. He enters much more thoroughly into characterization than does the interpreter. Whereas the interpreter might indicate the role of an old woman by minor changes in vocal delivery and by moderate alterations in facial expression and bodily tonus, the impersonator might bend over as though rheumatic and hobble around the stage. The interpreter suggests the physical and psychological qualities of a character; the impersonator assumes them. Because he is less an agent of the author and much more of an actor, the impersonator experiences far less direct contact with his listeners than does the interpreter.

Acting, impersonation, and interpretation all have their rightful outlets as forms of dramatic art. However, the interpretative mode is the most suitable for most types of literature and most oral reading situations. Only a discriminating judgment can suggest how far toward impersonation your materials and your audience will permit you to go.

SUMMARY

This chapter has covered the specialized requirements of the common types of oral reading: the manuscript speech; quoted materials during an extemporaneous speech; minutes and financial reports; family reading; and interpretation of literature.

18 ❧❧ Basic Principles of
Group Discussion

When confronted with an important problem or decision-making situation, most of us seek out the counsel of others. Of course, we make many personal decisions independently—whether to study or go swimming, whether to walk to the store or take the car, whether to get a haircut today or put it off. But when the problem becomes more consequential or more complicated, we usually supplement our own experiences and judgments with advice from respected friends and associates. "Should I take a part-time job in the post office?" "Should we marry now or wait until graduation?" "What career offers me the greatest chance for success and happiness?" Although you might "solve" such problems by yourself, the strong probability is that by drawing upon the intellectual resources of others the quality of your conclusions or courses of action will be improved.

In addition to personal problems growing out of the process of daily living, perplexing problems arise at all other levels of society—from the cultivating of tung nuts to the cracking of petroleum, from the promotion of a boxing match to the editing of a literary magazine, and from the supervising of a Sunday school class to the managing of the armed services. For their solution such problems require the concerted and cooperative efforts of the persons directly concerned. What are some of these problems? A foreman in the shipping department of a furniture factory calls a conference of his workers to determine why so many articles are being damaged in transit. A student council appoints a committee to recommend methods of improving relations between the faculty and students. A school board holds public sessions to determine the most feasible location of a new high school.

Obviously, discussion may take place whenever and wherever a problem occurs—at the breakfast table, at the cashier's register in a supermarket, in the choir director's office of a church, in the office of the president of a giant corporation, and so on. Since all of us make frequent use of the discussion process, can we conclude that as a result of such practice most persons have become skilled discussants? Unfortunately, no. Much of what passes for group deliberation can be more accurately described as a time-wasteful pooling of undigested, illogical, and emotionalized prejudgments. In view of the extreme importance and widespread use of discussion, we owe an obligation to ourselves and to society to become skilled in this form of oral communication.

THE NATURE OF DISCUSSION

Before analyzing the specific characteristics of effective group deliberation, we should consider these questions: What is discussion? How does it differ from other forms of oral discourse? What are its basic functions? values? limitations? and variations?

A. What Is Discussion?   As the term is used here, discussion is not "just plain talk" which is unplanned and undisciplined, nor is it argumentation or persuasion. Rather it is the *systematic, objective sharing and evaluating of ideas and information by two or more persons for the purpose of investigating and solving a problem.*

1. By using this definition as our basis for reference, *we can distinguish group deliberation from related types of group speaking.*

Because social conversation is desultory and non-purposive, it cannot be considered discussion. Conversation functions solely for the satisfaction and enjoyment of the participants; no serious problems are resolved as the flow of talk courses from one topic of interest to another. Of course, a conversation can develop into group deliberation if it centralizes upon a problem of common concern and attempts seriously to understand the difficulty or to discover feasible solutions.

Because zealous advocacy is a concerted attempt to persuade others, its spirit and intent preclude an "objective sharing of ideas and information for the purpose of investigating and solving a problem." Therefore, neither persuasive speaking nor debating constitute group discussion. The ideal discussant is a seeker. Although his interpretations and judgments are not rudderless, he anticipates that his thinking may be influenced by the common pooling of evidence, opinions, and evaluations. He welcomes diverse ideas, recognizing that their expression is essential to democratic group functioning and to the process of determining the most satisfactory group consensus. In contrast, the advocate is a *salesman*. His searching for answers has been completed; his hypotheses have matured into convictions; and now he seeks to convert others. Instead of being an objective deliberator who is eager to share in the common development of thought, the advocate is basically a subjective competitor who is determined to win the acceptance of his beliefs.

Although zealous advocacy has no legitimate place in group deliberation, we should recognize that a limited recourse to persuasion is probably inevitable and should not be repressed. During a discussion when matters arise on which you have definite opinions, you would be dishonest to yourself and to the group if you failed to present your ideas candidly and effectively. However, when disagreeing with others maintain a tactful, courteous, and conciliatory manner. Consistently emphasize the common areas of agreement and attempt to narrow the distance between your beliefs and those of others.

Because propagandizing and acquiescing groups make no legitimate attempts to understand or solve problems, they do not constitute true discussion. As an example of propaganda passing as discussion, a public relations firm might arrange for several experts to appear on TV for a supposedly impartial analysis of a controversial issue; but instead of an objective presentation, the agency might have cleverly slanted the program to favor a particular conclusion. As an illustration of order-giving masquerading as discussion, an executive might convene his assistants for the ostensible purpose of helping him determine policy; but in reality he expects them to "rubber stamp" decisions he has already made.

2. *Our definition of discussion emphasizes that group deliberation has two basic functions:* (a) *To facilitate learning and promote understanding.* An audience might assemble to hear a panel discuss "How foreign affairs affect us here in Duluth." Another group might gather under the auspices of the Great Books Program to exchange ideas and interpretations concerning Spengler's *Decline of the West* or Bacon's *Novum Organum.* Both of these groups hope to acquire a better understanding of and a deeper insight into the discussion subject. (b) *To discover appropriate courses of action.* A committee might be appointed by the city commission to investigate the existing zoning ordinances and make recommendations concerning possible revisions. The officers of a fraternity might meet to determine methods for reducing the hazards of "hell week." The purpose of both of these groups is to determine the most effective answer to an existing problem.

B. What Are the Values of Discussion? The value of group deliberation is demonstrated by its extensive application in business and industry. The profit and loss system under which the American economy operates compels business concerns to gear themselves to the most efficient operation possible. In view of this emphasis upon dollar-and-cents practicality, it may seem incongruent that perhaps 85 per cent of major companies agree that training in conference leadership is needed by the employees of their organization, that nearly 75 per cent of such concerns administer some kind of discussion program, and that the typical executive spends at least one-fourth of his working hours in conferences. According to management analyst William H. Whyte, Jr.,[1]

Now that "committee management" has become so much the rule, the average executive spends roughly six of his eight office hours talking with other executives in meetings and conferences, and he would be considered an odd bird indeed if he went out to lunch by himself. The other two hours are not spent in solitary contemplation; they are no more than the sum of a few minutes here and there between meetings and the ringing of the telephone. The executive, as one puts it, is never alone. Never physically, at any rate.

Why does Board Chairman Frederick C. Crawford of Thompson Products, Inc. assert: "Conferences have become increasingly important to us"? What are the values of discussion that make the time investment pay greater dividends to a company than the same amount of time spent by the same employees at the drafting table, the dictating machine, or in plant inspection? For answers let us look first at the following case study.

In the Marion, Virginia, pajama factory of the Harwood Manufacturing Corporation, a crew of eighteen hand pressers were summoned to a meeting. They were told by their supervisor that beginning immediately they were to follow a slight change in work methods designed to improve their productivity. Instead of stacking the finished articles on a flat piece of cardboard, they were to put them in a box the same size as the cardboard and placed in the same position. Because they had not been consulted concerning the necessity for the change, the women felt that they were being bossed around. In their resentment they deliberately slowed production, quarrelled with the supervisor and the methods engineer, protested to the union grievance committee, and five quit because the work had become "so much more difficult." After a month the group had not improved its efficiency, so it was disbanded and the thirteen remaining pressers assigned to new jobs in divers parts of the plant. Disturbed by this failure in human relations, the management

[1] William H. Whyte, Jr., "How Hard Do Executives Work?" *Fortune*, January, 1954, pp. 108–111, 148–152.

decided to experiment with group deliberation. After a "cooling off period" of two-and-a-half months, the same women were called to a conference. The supervisor explained that they were being assigned to a new pressing job (one which had been carefully selected as comparable in difficulty to the first one) and requested their help concerning possible improvements in work routine. By such a sharing of the problem the management demonstrated that it valued the intrinsic worth of the workers. Because they now felt appreciated, the women worked cooperatively to find answers to the production problems. Instead of feeling hostile toward their work and the management, they became interested in boosting their output and within a few weeks had exceeded all previous production efforts.

Although numerous similar case studies might be cited, we should recognize that the discussion method does not always produce such happy results. If it did, most of our problems of interpersonal relations could be speedily dissipated. Nevertheless, group deliberation possesses certain values which make it an extremely useful method of oral communication. (1) No better way exists to persuade an individual to feel an integral part of an organization than to give him the opportunity to participate actively in the setting of goals and the methods for achieving these goals. The Senior Vice-President of Boeing Airplane Company, Wellwood E. Beall, agrees that conferences are "good for morale and give an increased sense of participation in policy making." Persons who share in the making of a decision are more apt to feel that the judgment is a good one and usually will give more enthusiastic and enduring support. (2) If an individual participates actively in the discussion of a topic, he probably will understand it better and will retain more information for a longer period than if he receives instruction through passive listening. (3) Often group judgments are better than individual decisions. Admittedly no conclusive evidence exists that in a particular situation several persons can come to a better answer than a single person. If an individual is much better informed, more objective, or superior intellectually to his potential conferees, he very likely will arrive at better decisions than would the group. At the Standard Oil Company of California, authority for making group decisions is limited to the board of directors and the executive committee; all other conference groups report to the appropriate executive who makes the decision and assumes the responsibility. Similarly, at the Pacific Gas and Electric Company, conference groups are urged to offer recommendations, but actual decision-making is vested in the individual executives. Nevertheless, it is generally true that several intelligent, well-informed persons working co-operatively can do a better job of analysis and decision-making than can a single individual of comparable talents. An important point to consider is that, even though a particular group decision may be *logically* inferior to an individual decision, it may still be "better." If this seems ambiguous, recall that people tend to accept more readily and to cooperate more actively with policies they have helped formulate. (4) Discussion, along with debate, is the *sine qua non* of the democratic process. Although individuals vary greatly in knowledge and ability, each has the right and the obligation to share in the making of civic decisions which affect him and society.

C. What Are the Causes of Discussional Breakdowns? Because discussants are subject to the customary human limitations of knowledge, wisdom, objectivity, and power of attention, the discussion method itself is subject to limitations. It is not a curative guaranteed to resolve social ills. Rather, it is a methodology capable of producing desirable results under appropriate conditions. When group deliberation fails to accomplish its purpose, the cause is usually rooted in one or more of these somewhat overlapping factors: insufficient time, inadequate information, faulty evaluation of ideas and evidence, unsystematic development, subjectivity, group pressure, poor interpersonal relations, and deliberate sabotage.

1. Insufficient time. The give and take of group deliberation is time consuming. If swiftness in formulating a decision is an urgent consideration, perhaps the problem should be turned over to an individual. For the discussion method to work most effectively, all participants should feel free to speak as often as they believe they have relevant, worth-while contributions. When insufficient time exists for adequate discussion, either the group will fail to arrive at a decision or its solution will be based on ill-digested ideas and evidence. Typically when a group is acutely pressed for time, the chairman tends to exert greater control over the development of thought; the participants feel hurried and perhaps frustrated; and the spirit of "let's talk this thing over" is virtually impossible to maintain.

2. Inadequate information. Recently a friend of the author pleaded a prior engagement when invited to talk to a public meeting. However, when he realized that he was being asked to be a member of a panel discussion, he "rechecked" his appointment calendar and "discovered" that he was available. Later he complained, "Why didn't that fellow tell me straight off that it was to be a panel? I don't have time to whip up enough stuff for a speech, but I can take the time to go over there if all I have to do is talk." This man displayed a gross misconception of the nature and function of group deliberation. The exploring of a topic or the evolving of a policy demands the highest type of reflective thinking. And the basic tools of reflective thinking are *facts*. Without an adequate understanding of the relevant evidence, meaningful discussion is impossible.

3. Faulty evaluation of ideas and evidence. To constitute deliberation, more is necessary than the presentation of facts and opinions: this information must be evaluated as to its validity, relevance, and importance. On the basis of such examinations, particular items may be rejected, accepted as partially true, subjected to extensive probing, or may be integrated unchanged into the development of thought. Unfortunately, many groups make no systematic attempt to evaluate the individual contributions. Listeners tend to concentrate on what they plan to say rather than on what someone else is saying at the moment. Some persons seem unable to separate fact from opinion and uncritically accept subjective beliefs as actualities. Furthermore, discussants may lack skill in detecting irrelevancies or fallacies in reasoning. An absence of evaluations, or faulty evaluations of the shared information, may result in misunderstanding or in infeasible decisions.

4. Unsystematic development. A pernicious and frequently occurring fault is for a discussion group to set sail for nowhere and to bob about first in one direction and then in another as the running tide of conversation sweeps it into a blind cove, into a whirlpool, or vaguely outward onto the limitless expanse of unknown sea. Effective discussion is purposeful. It tries to resolve a felt need, and it moves systematically and relatively straightaway toward the realization of its goal.

5. Subjectivity. As we learned in Chapter 9, complete objectivity is an idealized state in which the mind is absolute master and emotions are non-existent. Although lip service is given to such an ideal, most thinking persons realize that true objectivity is impossible when one is confronted with problems of significant personal import. Usually the more important the problem and the greater the extent of personal involvement, the stronger becomes the influence of the emotions. Once a significant decision is reached, it is incorporated into the individual's philosophy. By sending out tendrils of logical and emotional associations, the new belief becomes more securely intwined with other accepted "truths" until the coalescence may become virtually indissoluble. And on this matter the individual may develop a closed mind. Edward R. Murrow advises that in speaking to others on controversial issues the most one can hope to do is "to know one's own prejudices and try to do the best one can to be fair." Unfortunately, because many discussants are unaware of the directing influences which prejudgments exert upon their behavior, they may not be fair to other participants and hence to the discussion method.

Although he may be unaware of their presence, the discussant-propagandist is motivated by strong emotional drives. Instead of welcoming different ideas as a means of evolving the best collective judgment, he experiences the urge to repress, bypass,

or tear down different opinions. Instead of trying sympathetically to understand the reasons why others believe and feel as
they do, he feels the need to attack their fundamental premises
and perhaps even their motives. Instead of being willing to
compromise or modify points of view if logic so directs, he is
inclined to refuse change and may even experience a strengthening of his views. Instead of applying to himself the same critical
scrutiny to which he subjects the evidence, reasoning, and
motives of others, he tends either to be oblivious to his own
limitations or to condone them. It should be emphasized that
we are considering the decidedly subjective discussant. Experimental evidence seems to indicate that the typical participant
has a fairly accurate concept of his merits as a group deliberator.

6. Group pressure. Another limitation of the discussion
method is the susceptibility of many persons to the influence of
group pressure. Although some individuals staunchly withstand
the impulse to "get in step" with majority opinions, most feel
a strong urge to conform. Some are so anxious to "go along"
with preponderant views that they tend to conceal genuine
differences of opinion by a misleading silence or by a verbalizing
of views which they do not accept. A few even alter, consciously
or unconsciously, their recollections of the facts. Naturally a
group does not actually deliberate if its members sacrifice the
expression of their ideas to the easy end of bogus "group
harmony."

A correlative of the willingness to conform is the inclination
of many persons, when members of the majority, to exert overt
or covert pressure upon dissenters. Those who may be considered authoritarians (perhaps 25 per cent of the population)
are especially likely to apply this form of coercion. True discussion cannot function if group pressure forces members into
pseudo-agreement or causes them to hesitate to offer ideas because of fear of group disapproval.

7. Poor interpersonal relationships. Although something of
a catch-all term, "poor interpersonal relationships" is a major
cause of discussion breakdown. As you know, efficient delib-

eration requires a congenial climate in which individuals appreciate the intrinsic worth of each other and afford a fair, if analytical, consideration of all relevant interpretations. However, the cultivation of such a permissive atmosphere demands more understanding and skill than some persons possess. What are the basic requirements for the smooth, non-frictional, meshing of different personalities?

a. Keen perception and tolerance of the non-rational aspects of human behavior

b. Sensitivity to one's own limitations and motivations

c. Warm sympathy for others in their efforts to grapple successfully with a significant problem

d. Determination to grasp and appreciate the "why's" of another's opinions

e. Eagerness to seek common bonds of understanding and agreement

f. Ability to criticize the ideas and evidence of others without attacking them personally

g. Willingness to present candidly and tactfully one's own ideas

h. Considerable skill in analytical listening and in conciliatory vocal and physical delivery

i. Willingness to accept criticism of one's ideas without becoming emotionally disturbed

Obviously this is a big order to fill—even for the well-integrated personality. And it is more than can be expected from the immature, the exhibitionistic, and dogmatic, the loquacious, the argumentative, the ignorant, and the malicious.

8. Sabotage. Discussional sabotage is any deliberate attempt to sacrifice the rational development of group thought for the purpose of increasing one's own status, injuring the prestige or influence of other participants, or of protecting and promoting hidden interests. *Mr. Egotism* is not uncommon. He is more desirous of attracting favorable attention to himself than in furthering the activities of the group. Frequently suave and ingratiating, he speaks often, forcefully, and perhaps a little louder than necessary. In his efforts to impress others, he may flaunt his knowledge, refer frequently to his associations with well-known persons, or usurp the duties of the chairman even though that person is performing adequately. Fortunately, *Mr. Duplicity* and *Mr. Subversion* are less frequently encountered. Nevertheless, they ruin many discussions. *Mr. Duplicity* is ostensibly a dispassionate, co-operative inquirer. In reality, he systematically attempts to undermine the prestige and influence of another discussant whom he dislikes. Under a pleasant, bland manner he conducts a running inquisition of the contributions of his victims. Eventually fixing upon an alleged weakness in reasoning or evidence, he exploits it to the maximum— even though the item might be inconsequential. If without scruples, *Mr. Duplicity* may subtly misrepresent the statements of his prey, attribute to him undesirable motives, or link him to unpopular philosophies or causes. For one reason or another, *Mr. Subversion* wishes to prevent the group from arriving at a decision. So, he attempts to divert the group to fruitless controversy over minutiae or irrelevancies, tries to spark conflicts among the members, demands documentation and clarification of obvious points, attacks the motives of participants, and engages in other tactics of delay and confusion.

D. What Are the Basic Types of Discussion? The various forms of discussion may be divided conveniently into two groups: those occurring without an audience and those occurring in the presence of an audience. The basic types within the two groups are identified in the following section and analyzed in detail in Chapter 19.

1. Discussion may occur without an audience. In most discussional situations there are no spectators; each person is expected to take an active part in the deliberation.

a. INFORMAL GROUP DISCUSSION. Since all discussion is relatively informal, this term is ambiguous. We use it for lack of a better label. In this form of discussion, a group of twenty, or fewer, persons talk over a subject of common interest customarily under the leadership of one of the members. Typically there are no set speeches. Usually the purpose of informal group discussion is to share information and opinions. Such a purpose motivates the music club when it estimates the influence of Jean

Sibelius on modern music and the garden club when it compares the effectiveness of new insecticides.

b. CONFERENCE. This form of discussion includes committee, staff, and instructional meetings. (1) *Committees* are small groups appointed by a parent organization to perform a specific task. Sometimes the purpose is to discover facts. Such is the function of a committee appointed by a labor union to investigate and report on the standards of safety existing in a particular plant. More frequently, the purpose is to recommend courses of action. Such is the purpose of the committee which is charged with studying the constitution of its parent organization and recommending any needed changes. (2) *Staff conferences.* This type of discussion is used extensively in business, government, education, and so on. It involves the pooling of ideas and opinions by a supervising official and his staff of subordinates. Frequently, several items may be on the agenda. For instance, a particular staff meeting might seek a better understanding of a new company policy, a solution for a departmental problem, and perhaps a policy recommendation to be submitted to the appropriate executive officer. (3) While the staff conference may or may not be leader-centered according to the circumstances, the *training conference* is typically dominated by the leader. A member of the supervisory or managerial force calls a meeting of the appropriate personnel to instruct them concerning policies or to train them to do a particular job. For example, a police captain might assemble the men on his special detail for briefing purposes before sending them out to raid a bookie establishment. Even in such a meeting there usually is opportunity for questions and answers and for some sharing of ideas and interpretations.

2. Discussion may occur in the presence of an audience. Such discussions are held in public for the benefit of the listeners. Rather than to enrich the thinking of the participants or to determine a course of action, the primary purpose of a public discussion is to interest, stimulate, and inform the audience. Such a program has achieved its purpose if it has sensitized the listeners to the various aspects of a problem, stirred them to reflective thinking, and awakened in them the desire to secure more information.

a. PANEL. In this form, a small group (customarily between three and six persons) converses systematically and purposefully about a topic under the guidance of a leader. No set speeches are given.

b. SYMPOSIUM. Between three and six speakers deliver prepared, uninterrupted speeches on different aspects of a common general topic. A chairman introduces the symposium program and each speaker. Unlike the panel, the symposium employs public speaking as its mode of communication.

c. LECTURE-FORUM. The lecture-forum is included because it is used with great frequency. However, the only discussional aspect of this type of program is the forum, or audience-participation period, following the speech.

d. BROADCAST DISCUSSION. Rather than a specific type, broadcast discussions usually represent an adaptation of either the panel or the symposium. The media of television and radio impose some modifications upon the discussion method; nevertheless, the basic principles remain the same.

THE CHARACTERISTICS OF GOOD DISCUSSION

Although the different kinds of discussion require specific adaptations of method and execution, the basic principles apply to all group deliberation. Effective discussion is characterized by an appropriate subject which is phrased suitably, reflective thinking, systematic organization, effective language, and qualified leadership and participation.

A. Good Discussion Deals with an Appropriate Subject Which Is Phrased Suitably. Outside of the classroom, most discussions grow out of a felt need. Examples: An automobile dealer assembles his salesmen to discover ways of increasing sales; a university president appoints a combined student-faculty committee to recommend methods of reducing accidents on the campus; the head of a testing laboratory assembles his staff of scientists to determine the reasons for the failure of an important experiment. Nevertheless, the selection of discussion topics is of crucial importance to institutions which sponsor periodic civic forums and to organizations (such as the Parent-Teachers Association and the University Women's Club) which have regularly scheduled meetings. The following advice should be helpful in choosing problems for group deliberation.

1. The problem should be well adjusted to the total situation. As in selecting the subject for a speech or for an oral reading program, you should choose a discussion subject which is appropriate for the speakers, the occasion, and the audience—if it is a public presentation.

The subject will fit the *discussants* if it is a matter of significant concern to them, if it has already stimulated them to reflective thinking, and if it is within the scope of their knowledge and experiences. When he feels no direct or vital association with a problem, the participant may have difficulty in forcing himself to do the necessary research and may feel flat and spiritless during the actual discussion. Unless the individual has conducted some experimental probing of the subject, he probably will lack sufficient information and maturity of thought. Of course, if he understands the techniques of research and is willing to expend the effort, he may be able to compensate for limited background on the subject.

The subject will fit the *occasion* if it is well adjusted to the basic nature of the meeting, the time and place, the remainder of the program, and the amount of time available for the discussion. The analysis of a speaking occasion is familiar to you from your study of Chapter 9. Therefore, it is necessary to emphasize here only the extreme importance of restricting the subject to a compass which can be handled adequately within the time limitations. Broad, sweeping subjects automatically produce superficial treatment. Instead of talking about "the problems of youth," limit your treatment to a single aspect of this broad area, as "What can be done to reduce juvenile delinquency in our community?"

The subject will fit the *listeners* (remember that only public discussions involve non-participating listeners) if it appeals to their interests and if it is suited to their intellectual abilities and background. In selecting a problem for public discussion, keep in mind that the primary purpose of the deliberation is to inform the listeners and to stimulate them to become more concerned with the issue. If possible, poll the potential listeners by questionnaires or phone calls. Otherwise, apply the techniques you learned earlier for analyzing an audience. An average adult audience will be more concerned with "How can the schools be run more economically?" than with "What influence did the Etruscans exert upon Roman culture?" Of course, your subject should be neither above nor below the listeners' level of comprehension and appreciation. Instead of discussing "What is the role of calcium in cell division?" before a lay audience, select a topic like "How is chemistry revolutionizing household appliances?" Also consider that controversial topics spark more interest than do staid, insipid ones. More persons will listen animatedly to "How can we excel the Russians in missile research?" than to "What are the values of thrift?"

2. The problem should be one of inquiry or policy. Problems of inquiry seek answers to questions of "fact" or "value," while problems of policy involve the determination of policies (solutions or courses of action) which will alleviate existing needs.

Problems of inquiry. When applied to discussion questions, the terms "fact" and "value" have specialized meanings. (1) *Questions of fact.* Used in this connection, "fact" does not refer to known truths or to matters which are subject to absolute verification by scientific tests or measurement. If the "fact" in question can be determined with certainty by checking a standard reference work or by employing the yardsticks of science, it is not a rewarding subject for group deliberation. Thus it would be fruitless to attempt to settle these questions by means of discussion: "Which player made the most tackles in the National Professional Football League last year?" (Look up the item in an encyclopedia of sports.) "Did this gun fire the fatal bullet?" (Turn the question over to a ballistics expert for conclusive proof.) "How large is the Sawtooth Primitive Area?" (Consult a map.) The discussion method can be used efficiently only when seeking answers to questions of rhetorical "fact," that is, "facts" which have not yet been proved and which are subject primarily to reasoning rather than to the laws of scientific demonstration. Such questions of rhetorical "fact" concern the probable existence of things or events, their relationships, and the prediction of future happenings. Examples: "Was this worker's accident due to his carelessness?" "Can the market stand an increase in the cost of our product?" "Why did our party lose the last election?" "Who will win the title fight?" (2) *Questions of value.* Problems of value are closely related to those of "fact." They concern an evaluation of the usefulness, importance, merit, or desirability of ideas, persons, or things. Thus value judgments are called for by these questions: "How much reliance can we place on the Gallup poll findings?" "How important to the businessman is training in mathematics?" "How well qualified is the candidate for the position?"

Problems of policy. In applying this type of question, discussants investigate an undesirable situation and attempt to evolve a satisfactory solution or remedial course of action. Unlike those of "fact" or "value," questions of policy call for changes in the *status quo*. Examples: "What is the best method of financing the streets-improvement program?" "How can our department improve its efficiency rating?" "What steps should be taken to alleviate the local teacher shortage?"

3. *The problem should be phrased suitably.* State the discussion problem in the form of a clear, impartial question—preferably, one which cannot be answered by a "yes" or "no."

Use the question form. Avoid fragmentary sentences. They fail to express the purpose of the discussion with sufficient clarity. Although for advertising purposes the topic of a public discussion may be couched as a catchy slogan, it should be phrased as a complete sentence for use by the discussants. Thus, while a poster might read "Tunnels or Bridges?" the actual discussion question would be: "What is the best way of solving the existing traffic problems in crossing the Mirahan River?" Also, avoid declarative sentences or resolutions. They invite argumentation rather than deliberation. The resolution "Medical schools should focus greater attention on the problems of old age" provokes proof and disproof; whereas, the question "To what extent, if any, should medical schools direct greater attention to the problems of old age?" emphasizes that the speakers are *seekers* who will apply reflective thinking in their efforts to find feasible answers.

Employ clear, precise language. The question for discussion and the Specific Speech Purpose for a public speech are very similar; each represents a precisely phrased statement of the exact, restricted goal—the bull's-eye—of the act of communication. The discussion question should state accurately and exactly the problem you are attempting to solve. If vague, abstract, or ambiguous language is used, the problem may lack dimensions. For instance, the topic "High school service clubs" is so inexplicit that it lacks the limitations to give it shape and substance. Rephrased, the question might become one which a group could reasonably expect to answer: "What can be done to encourage high school service clubs to become more active in extracurricular activities?" or "How democratic are the methods by which high school service clubs select pledges?"

State the question impartially. Since objectivity is the essence of the discussion method, the question must be worded impartially. Thus, "How can we improve the out-moded university grading system?" should be restated: "What changes, if any, should be made in the University grading system?" Similarly, "What can be done to change the present unfair methods of enforcing the city's traffic laws?" should become: "What changes, if any, should be made in the present methods of enforcing the city's traffic laws?"

Usually word the question so that it cannot be answered with a "yes" or "no." Ideal discussion is multi-sided rather than two-sided. Questions which evoke "yes" or "no" responses invite division into affirmative and negative sides. Obviously, when this occurs argumentation tends to supplant deliberation. Furthermore, "yes" or "no" questions imply that the scope of discussion has been narrowed to the consideration of only one possible course of action. If a group wishes to examine the relevant methods for acquiring increased revenue for public schools, it should select as its question: "What should be done to secure adequate financial support for the public school system?" or "What is the best method of securing adequate financial support for the public school system?" Such questions logically require the discussants to examine all significant possible solutions. However, the "yes" or "no" question "Should a program of federal aid to education be adopted?" directs primary, if not exclusive, attention on only one of the several possible courses of action. The question "Should restrictions be placed upon the driving of student cars on the campus?" has been answered when the group agrees concerning the *principle* of restriction. As stated, it does not logically provide for the careful analysis of the various possible methods and degrees of restriction. If the group wishes to go beyond mere agreement on the principle involved, the topic should be altered to represent the group's real intent: "What changes, if any, should be made in the policy of the University concerning the driving of student cars on the campus?"

B. Good Discussion Emphasizes Reflective Thinking. The discussant is a thinker at work. In addition to possessing an adequate store of information on the subject, he should also have the ability and willingness to think rationally and to minimize emotionality.

1. Reflective thinking requires adequate knowledge of the problem. The thinking of an individual or a group is no more reliable than the facts upon which it is based. In gathering materials for group discussion, follow the advice contained in

Chapter 11: first, explore your mind to discover what information you already possess concerning the subject; second, determine what additional knowledge you should acquire; and third, to secure the needed ideas and evidence, initiate a program of reading, observing, and communicating with others.

2. *Reflective thinking emphasizes the rational use of evidence and reasoning.* By following the suggestions given in Chapters 8 and 13, you should be able to think rationally and to evaluate critically the thinking of others. As you will recall, specific methods may be applied to test each form of support and each type of reasoning, as well as to protect oneself against the tricks of the propagandist.

3. *Reflective thinking requires a tight rein on the emotions.* By this stage in your reading you are well aware that all persons are subject to strong stresses and tensions. Be alert to the possible influence of emotion in your own discussional participation. Try to forestall emotionalism in others by maintaining a genial attitude of cooperation. If someone becomes irrational, insulting, or passionate, seek to understand the cause for his resort to emotions. Do not respond in kind to negative emotions. You may be unable to prevent a hot flash of anger from arising within you, but you can prevent its being obvious to others. Defend yourself and your ideas, of course. But do so tactfully and pleasantly. Be conciliatory and generous. Never abandon your standards of polite behavior or your spirit of co-operative problem-solving.

C. Good Discussion Is Systematically Organized. The importance of systematic thought development in discussion is demonstrated by experimental studies as well as practical experience. For instance, Harold Guetzkow and John Gyr investigated the discussional behavior of some seven hundred business and government officials during decision-making conferences. In their report, the researchers stressed the importance of straight thinking: "Those meetings in which discussion was orderly in its treatment of topics, and without backward references to previously discussed issues, tended to end in more consensus, despite

large amounts of substantive or affective conflict. When participants discussed but one issue at a time, instead of simultaneously
dabbling in two or three, it was more possible for the group to
reach consensus." [2]

Since group discussion is basically problem-solving, all forms
of discussion and all types of questions can use the following
organizational structure. It should be stressed, however, that this
format is offered as an aid to thought development and not as a
prescriptive pattern to be followed slavishly. In a given case,
circumstances may suggest considerable alteration in arrangement and coverage. (For suggestions concerning the specific
needs of the different *types* of discussion, see the appropriate
sections of Chapter 19.)

Basic Agenda for Discussion

I. What explanations should be made?
   A. What terms in the question require definition?
   B. Are there other terms or concepts inherent in the question which
      need clarification?
II. What is the nature of the problem?
   A. What facts or happenings prompted a consideration of the problem
      by the group?
   B. What is the importance of the problem? Its extent? Its severity?
   C. What are the chief causes of the problem?
   D. What may be the results if the problem remains unsolved?
III. What are the possible solutions (answers) to the problem?
   A. Possible solution (answer) no. I:
      1. Advantages (evidence and reasons supporting its acceptance)
      2. Disadvantages (evidence and reasons supporting its rejection)
   B. Possible solution (answer) no. II:
      1. Advantages (evidence and reasons supporting its acceptance)
      2. Disadvantages (evidence and reasons supporting its rejection)
   C. Possible solution (answer) no. III:
      1. Advantages (evidence and reasons supporting its acceptance)
      2. Disadvantages (evidence and reasons supporting its rejection)
IV. Which is the most desirable solution (answer)?
   A. Why is it superior to the others?
   B. How satisfactory is it?
V. How can this solution be put into effect?

[2] Harold Guetzkow and John Gyr, "An Analysis of Conflict in Decision-Making
Groups," *Human Relations*, August, 1954, pp. 367–382.

1. Application of the basic agenda to problems of inquiry.
A question of inquiry has been answered when the group agrees
upon the verifiability of a "fact" or the relative value of the
topic under examination. Therefore, such discussions omit heading V of the basic format. Here is a brief outline illustrating
how questions of "fact" or "value" might be organized. (This
outline represents a group agenda for a panel discussion before
a civic audience. As you will see presently, a panel group should
meet in one or more "pre-performance" planning conferences
to agree upon the content and arrangement of the group
outline.)

Discussion Question: To what extent would construction of a parking
garage, as proposed by Commissioner Thomas Mahaffey, alleviate congestion in the downtown district?
  I. What explanations should be made?
     A. Clarification concerning the proposed garage?
     B. Clarification of the meaning of "congestion"?
     C. Clarification of the meaning of "the downtown district"?
 II. What is the nature of the problem?
     A. What facts or happenings prompted a consideration of the problem
        by this group?
     B. What is the importance of the problem?
        1. How badly congested is the downtown district?
        2. What are the harmful effects of congestion in the downtown
           district?
           a. Is congestion injurious to downtown business?
           b. Is congestion injurious to the average citizen?
           c. Is congestion injurious to the city itself?
     C. What are the chief causes of the problem?
        1. How important as a causative factor is the recent increase in
           local traffic?
        2. How important as a causative factor is the recent increase in
           through-traffic on highways U.S. 1 and State 19 which intersect
           in the center of the business district?
        3. How important as a causative factor is the fact that much of the
           the downtown district was laid out more than one hundred
           years ago?
        4. How important as a causative factor is inadequate planning by
           the recent generations of city officials?
        5. Other?

    D. What may be the results if the problem remains unsolved?
       1. Will the population growth of the city suffer?
       2. Will the prosperity of the city suffer?
       3. Will new tax sources have to be tapped?
       4. Other?
III. What are the possible answers to the question?
    A. Would the garage have a negative influence on congestion?
    B. If not a negative influence, how beneficial would the garage be?
       1. Will the garage have little positive effect?
       2. Will the garage have a significant positive effect?
IV. Can we arrive at a consensus concerning the probable effectiveness of the garage in alleviating the congestion in the downtown district?

2. Application of the basic agenda to problems of policy. To assert that questions of policy call for the determination of appropriate solutions or courses of action is to be guilty of over-simplification. Actually, considerable variation exists in discussional goals and, therefore, in the application of the basic agenda. Examples: (1) Upon occasion, the members of a public discussion group may realize that it would be impossible for them to agree upon the adoption of a particular policy. As a result, such groups might legitimately omit headings IV and V. (2) Often private discussion groups, such as committees or staff conferences, are charged with suggesting policy changes; the responsibility for officially accepting the recommended policy and for planning its execution may still remain with the parent organization or with higher levels of administration. Such groups would omit heading V. (3) Sometimes, several remedial procedures are required to solve a problem. In such instances, a group would not attempt to determine which *one* of several *essential* steps is the "most desirable."

    The following outline illustrates how a policy formulating group might apply the basic format of thought development. In this hypothetical case, a committee has been directed by the interfraternity council of a university to work out and submit to the council recommendations for improving the academic standing of a fraternity chapter. (This outline might serve effectively as a personal guide for the chairman in directing the committee's deliberations; however, it is probably a little too long to serve as a workable group agenda).

Discussion Question: What can be done to improve the academic standing of the Delta Pi fraternity?

I. What explanations should be made?
    A. Are we concerned exclusively with the academic standing of the members, or with that of both members and pledges?
    B. Is our objective limited to raising to a "C" for this semester the chapter's accumulative average grade level?
    C. What is meant by academic probation as applied to fraternities?
    D. Other?
II. What is the nature of the problem?
    A. What facts or happenings prompted a consideration of the problem by this group?
    B. What is the importance of the problem? Its extent? Its severity?
    C. What may be the results if the problem remains unsolved?
        1. Effects upon the University?
        2. Effects upon the Interfraternity Council?
        3. Effects upon other fraternal organizations on campus?
        4. Effects upon the Delta Pi fraternity?
    D. What are the causes of the problem? [3]
        1. Overemphasis on social aspects of college life?
        2. Overemphasis on campus politics?
        3. Lack of scholastic aptitude?
        4. Underestimation of the importance of study?
        5. Poor study procedures?
III. What are the possible solutions to the problem?
    A. Possible solution no. I: An honor plan?
        1. What is the nature of this plan?
        2. What are the advantages of this method?
        3. What are the disadvantages of this method?
    B. Possible solution no. II: A tutorial system?
        1. What is the nature of this plan?
        2. What are the advantages of this plan?
        3. What are the disadvantages of this plan?
    C. Possible solution no. III: A closely supervised and restrictive study program?
        1. What is the nature of this plan?
        2. What are the advantages of this plan?
        3. What are the disadvantages of this plan?

[3] Notice that in this case the reversal of the headings "C" and "D" of the basic agenda provide a more natural sequence of thought development.

D. Possible solution no. IV: A coercive program?
    1. What is the nature of this plan?
    2. What are the advantages of this plan?
    3. What are the disadvantages of this plan?
E. Other possible solutions?
IV. Which is the most desirable solution(s)?
    A. Can we agree on only one of the proposed solutions, or should we adopt a combination of plans?
    B. Why is the plan(s) agreed upon superior to others?
    C. How satisfactory does this plan(s) seem to be?
V. How can this solution be put into effect?
    A. How can we present our recommendations most effectively to the Council?
    B. What can be done to further the acceptance of our recommendations by the Delta Pi's?

D. Good Discussion Requires Effective Use of Language. In discussion, as in all other forms of oral communication, language should be clear, direct, appropriate, vivid, and impressive. Since all of these attributes are discussed at length in Chapter 4, it is sufficient here to emphasize only the importance of language in promoting a permissive climate. As the chart on pages 450–451 illustrates, appropriate language will help to minimize conflict, promote co-operation, and improve interpersonal relations.

E. Good Discussion Needs Qualified Leadership. If discussants possessed the impersonality and infallibility of electronic calculators, they would move crisply and efficiently through the analysis of each problem to a unanimous acceptance of the best possible solution. No group leader would be necessary. However, as you are well aware, discussants are subject to the customary human imperfections of mind and spirit. The dynamics of group deliberation bring into close and often jarring contact varied personalities, attitudes, subconscious motivations, and so on. To facilitate productive group effort the most skillful kind of leadership is required. The importance of the leadership function is demonstrated by the fact that when the appointed moderator fails to exert adequate direction one or more of the discussants usually attempts to fill the leadership vacuum.

1. Group leaders should possess important qualifications.
Another text has suggested that the leader must serve as
"climate-maker, guardian of the agenda, clarifier, harmonizer,
issue-sharpener, and summarizer." [4] To accomplish such tasks,
the chairman must be well-informed on the topic, possess vital
personal qualities, understand the principles of group dynamics,
and be skilled in oral communication.

a. GROUP LEADERS SHOULD BE WELL-INFORMED ON THE PROB-
LEM FOR DISCUSSION. Although the moderator does not need
to be an expert, he must have an efficient working knowledge of
the subject. By means of careful study or personal experience
he should have arrived at mature interpretations concerning the
dimensions and importance of the problem, the basic issues
involved, and the possible courses of action. Accurate and adequate knowledge is necessary for a leader to guide the discussants
through a rational sequence of thought development. Obviously,
if insufficiently informed, the leader may permit his group to
overlook significant avenues of inquiry, become entangled in a
labyrinth of inessential details, or to substitute non-critical acceptance for discerning evaluation. Also, he may experience
difficulty in fulfilling specific leadership duties, such as stimulating others to reflective thinking, clarifying abstruse statements, correlating divergent contributions, helping to emphasize and evaluate key points, making transitions, and restating
and summarizing.

b. GROUP LEADERS SHOULD POSSESS NECESSARY PERSONAL
QUALITIES. If a discussion leader possessed in superior degree
all the attributes sometimes suggested as necessary, the reflection
from his shiny halo would dazzle the discussants and the audience. The qualities of the ideal leader include being modest—
but not obsequious; being willing to remain in the background—
but not so far back that he is unable to stimulate and integrate
group action; having respect for the ideas of others—but not to
the extent that he fails to submit all claims to close scrutiny;

---

[4] William S. Howell and Donald K. Smith, *Discussion* (New York: The Macmillan Company, 1956), p. 258.

PRINCIPLE	LANGUAGE OF CONFLICT	LANGUAGE OF CONCILIATION
When feasible, accept the blame for failures in communication.	"You weren't listening. You completely missed my point."	"I'm afraid that I didn't state my position as clearly as I should. . . ."
When possible, agree in principle. You may still differ on particulars.	"You are way off base on this matter."	"Under ordinary circumstances your program would probably work nicely. However, this particular case has some peculiar features. . . ."
Express your wish to agree if you could.	"Only an impractical egg head could make such a statement."	"I thoroughly sympathize with Jim's idealism. I wish that human nature was sufficiently altruistic for such a plan to work . . . ."
Recogize that many persons hold similar, if mistaken, beliefs.	"That's a prejudiced statement if I ever heard one."	"Many persons would probably agree with you on that score, Bill. But let's look at the matter a little closer."
Never attack the motives, intelligence, or industry of another discussant.	"If you were intelligently informed on the subject, you would know what Randall had said."	"Everyone is so busy at this time of the year I can understand how you might not have come across this statement. Last week, Charles Randall asserted. . . ."
Always search for common ground.	"Frankly, your plan is a dud."	"I'm willing to go a little way with you on this, Tom. We can agree on . . . But in regard to . . . I have trouble seeing how. . . ."

Give courteous attention to all sincere proposals.

"There's no merit in that proposal. I say let's skip it."

"Let's take a little time to examine Mary's proposal. We can't afford to overlook anything that might bring us closer to a workable solution. . . ."

If criticism is necessary be as "painless" as possible.

"That's one heck of a thing to say, Johnson. Do you have a screw loose?"

"Like most of us, Mike is stirred up about the board's decision. But it's getting late and if we're to come to some effective answer, we need to get on with the job . . . ."

being tactful, courteous, fair-minded, and impartial—but not mistaking superficiality for conciliation; possessing a sense of humor—but not being a "funny man"; possessing enthusiasm—but not being overly forceful; possessing a retentive memory, an agile mind, and a facile tongue—but not obviously out-thinking, out-performing, or out-talking the discussants. Effective leaders are highly attuned to the needs and attitudes of their group members and the listeners. They demonstrate alertness and discernment in making the numerous instant decisions involved in carrying out their leadership duties. Furthermore, their well-integrated personalities enable them to guide others in an unobtrusive, affable manner and, when feasible, to share willingly the leadership functions with the discussants. Unfortunately, until you acquire some personal experience in discussional situations, this analysis of the personal qualities of the leader may seem intangible. Perhaps the most helpful advice is that you remember this essential point: above all, a discussion moderator should be a sensitive, intelligent, and well-adjusted person.

At this point, you may wonder, "If leadership requires sensitivity, emotional adjustment, etc., are leaders born and not made?" Be assured that, although "natural" leaders may develop leadership skills more rapidly, the average person can, with training and experience, become a successful discussion moderator.

c. Group Leaders Should Understand the Principles of Group Dynamics. Naturally, leaders should understand as much as possible about human nature and about the techniques for fostering smooth interpersonal relations. They should grasp the principles governing the logical and psychological use of reasoning and evidence. They should understand the nature, purpose, and procedures involved in the deliberative method. In addition, leaders should recognize the differences between democratic and autocratic leadership and should comprehend the influence exerted upon the leadership function by the size of the group, the purpose of the discussion, the attitudes of the participants, and the necessity for protecting minority rights.

Democratic vs. autocratic leadership. In a given circumstance the style of discussional leadership may represent a position somewhere on the wide axis between democratic and autocratic leadership and may employ elements of both; nevertheless, the dichotomy serves as a useful instructional tool. The group-centered leader is concerned primarily with facilitating group thought. He seeks the maximal realization of the capabilities of each discussant. He shares with the group the setting of goals and concentrates on helping the group evolve what in its judgment is the best consensus. In contrast, the leader-centered leader is *not* primarily concerned with the *process* of deliberation; he is basically interested in the *product* or the results of deliberation. Richard R. Wischmeier summarizes well the opposable characteristics of the two styles of leadership: [5]

GROUP-CENTERED LEADERSHIP	LEADER-CENTERED LEADERSHIP
1. Leader asks a group member to summarize whenever possible.	1. Leader assumes full responsibility for summarizing. He summarizes periodically, emphasizing those ideas which *he* considers most important.
2. Leader clarifies and reflects member ideas without attempting to influence.	2. Leader interprets, rephrases and modifies a member's contributions to conform with what he considers most important.
3. Leader makes few evaluative statements.	3. Leader freely evaluates the statements of the members and expresses approval or disapproval.
4. Leader is concerned with utilizing all of the human resources of the group and thus encourages all members to participate.	4. Leader makes little apparent effort to bring all members into the discussion so long as he feels that the group is progressing satisfactorily.
5. Leader places responsibility for decisions about discussion procedure on the group as a whole.	5. Leader makes most of the decisions concerning discussion procedures.

[5] Richard R. Wischmeier, "Group-Centered and Leader-Centered Leadership: An Experimental Study," *Speech Monographs*, March, 1955, pp. 43–48.

GROUP-CENTERED LEADERSHIP *(Cont'd)*	LEADER-CENTERED LEADERSHIP *(Cont'd)*
6. Leader seldom gives his own opinion: he introduces new information only when he feels it is necessary, i.e., the group is stalled, or the members do not possess the necessary information.	6. Leader does not hesitate to give his own opinions or information.
7. Leader is not concerned with maintaining his position as leader, but attempts to distribute the leadership functions throughout the group.	7. Leader assumes responsibility for performing leadership functions and discourages group members from performing them in order to retain his position.
8. Leader is more concerned with the group *process* than he is with the final outcome.	8. Leader is more concerned with group *product.*
9. Leader method is informal and largely non-directive. Group is relatively free to direct its own course of action.	9. Leader method is more formal and directive.

Usually democratic leadership stimulates greater group effort than autocratic leadership. A safe rule of thumb is that leadership should be shared with the group to the fullest extent *consistent* with the number of persons concerned, the amount of time available for the deliberation, the purpose of the meeting, and the attitudes and abilities of the participants.[6] In contrast to groups which are strongly dominated by the leader, those which employ more democratic procedures usually experience a warmer and more cooperative atmosphere. The discussants feel more comfortable, participate more readily, are more receptive to opposing ideas, and offer somewhat less resistance to modifying their opinions. Furthermore, participants are more apt to find democratic discussions stimulating and enjoyable and are more likely to work actively to carry out agreed upon policies.[7]

[6] A sharp warning against going to extremes in the direction of group control may be found in Robert N. McMurry's "The Case for Benevolent Autocracy," *Harvard Business Review,* January-February, 1958, pp. 82–90.

[7] See these representative, if sometimes conflicting, experimental studies: William M. Fox, "Group Reaction to Two Types of Conference Leadership," *Human Relations,* August, 1957, pp. 279–289; Malcolm G. Preston and Roy K. Heintz,

Influence exerted by the moderator's personality upon his style of leadership. Certain personality characteristics of the moderator may influence his attitudes toward the leadership function. (1) *If he is a high pressure, business only, humorless person,* the moderator may emphasize efficiency and results to the extent that the personally satisfying and enjoyable aspects of discussion are deadened. (2) *If he is an extremely logical, mechanistic, or procedurally-minded person,* the moderator may be inclined to view discussants as mechanical brains and the agenda as an inflexible instrument. An undergraduate science major once suggested that group deliberation can be likened to a train, the discussants to the crew of porters, engineers, and firemen, the moderator to the conductor, and the agenda to the tracks. According to his analogy, the deliberative special should depart upon the order of the conductor; click along at a constant speed over the agenda; pass way marks on an exact schedule; and pull into the solution terminal precisely on time. This student forgot the human equation. He wished to reduce democratic action to a mechanized formula—to a Procrustean system in which individuals lose their uniqueness and their identity. Discussants are not sprockets, or cranks, or cams, or gears, and will not function like the delicately balanced units of a machine. They are human beings and will behave like human beings. (3) *If he is an authoritarian type of person,* the moderator typically adopts a strongly leader-centered style of leadership. Conversely, a more democratic style tends to be preferred by the non-authoritarian.[8] (4) *If he is a retiring, irresolute, or phlegmatic*

"Effects of Participatory vs. Supervisory Leadership on Group Judgment," *The Journal of Abnormal and Social Psychology,* July, 1949, pp. 345–355; Edwin A. Fleishman, "Leadership Climate, Human Relations Training, and Supervisory Behavior," *Personnel Psychology,* Summer, 1953, pp. 205–222; Marvin E. Shaw, "A Comparison of Two Types of Leadership in Various Communication Nets," *The Journal of Abnormal and Social Psychology,* January, 1955, pp. 127–134; William E. Utterback, "The Influence of Style of Moderation on the Outcome of Discussion," *The Quarterly Journal of Speech,* April, 1958, pp. 149–153.

[8] William Haythorn, *et al.,* "The Behavior of Authoritarian and Equalitarian Personalities in Groups," *Human Relations,* February, 1956, pp. 57–74; Franklyn S. Haiman, "A Measurement of Authoritarian Attitudes Toward Discussion Leadership," *The Quarterly Journal of Speech,* April, 1955, pp. 140–144.

person, the moderator may be a "leader" in name only. *Mr. Milquetoast* or *Mr. Abdication* sometimes considers his duties completed by opening and closing the discussion. When a chairman renounces his duties, a leadership vacuum occurs. And unless the discussion is to flounder, one or more discussants must assume the duties of leadership. Too much democracy can mean anarchy. The achieving of an appropriate balance between directed and free deliberation requires skilled, albeit unobtrusive, leadership.

Although the style of leadership in a particular discussion may be influenced by the moderator's personality, it should depend primarily upon the nature of the occasion, the needs of the group, and the purpose of the meeting.

Influence exerted upon style of leadership by the size of the group. As a general rule, the smaller the group, the more democratic should be the style of leadership. As the number of participants increases, member-centered leadership tends to become increasingly unwieldy; more leadership and a different type of leadership is demanded. Why is this so? The answer lies in the psychological influence which the size of the group exerts upon its members. As groups get larger they tend to become less cohesive; less opportunity exists for individual members to speak and, hence, each has more difficulty in realizing a satisfactory feeling of participation; the more reserved members tend to sit back in semi-silence while the more talkative ones monopolize the proceedings; the membership tends to divide into sub-groups with resultant conflicts in loyalties and interests; discussants are less inclined to express themselves candidly and may experience a decrease in feelings of companionship and friendly sharing; and while the potential resources of the group become greater, the motivation of the individual members probably diminishes. Because of these and other characteristics, the large group needs greater help from the chairman in directing the course of thought and in protecting the rights of the majority and of the minority. Particularly if the group exceeds twenty members, the leader may find it helpful to apply standard rules of parliamentary procedure; this is especially true when time is short, tempers high, digressions numerous, or some persons disturbingly loquacious.

Influence exerted upon style of leadership by the purpose of the discussion. Certain group goals do not lend themselves effectively to member-centered leadership. When the purpose of the meeting is to *provide* the discussants with new information or to *assist* the chairman in the performance of his duties, the leader usually will exert more influence over the proceedings. Examples: (1) As you know, the objective of the instructional conference is to help the members acquire needed knowledge and understanding. Ordinarily the leader of such a discussion group is an especially well-qualified person who already possesses the relevant insights and information. Throughout the proceedings there may be a considerable sharing of viewpoints and experiences among the group members: they may ask questions, suggest applications, mention limitations, and offer additional items of information. Nevertheless, because of his greater experience or knowledge, the training leader should usually exert strong influence upon the content and direction of such talk. (2) Staff conferences may be called to help the leader arrive at decisions. In such discussions, the function of the group is not to make decisions, but to stimulate and broaden the thinking of the leader. Therefore, the deliberation will probably be dominated by the chairman. Although other examples might be cited, perhaps these will suffice to demonstrate that the style of leadership is partly dependent upon the purpose of the discussion.

Influence exerted upon style of leadership by the necessity to protect minority rights. We saw earlier that humans have a strong inclination to coerce others into conforming to majority views and that this tendency often displays itself in group deliberation. Unless each person feels free to express himself candidly, without risking obvious disapproval or retaliation, minority members usually will remain silent or appear to accept dominant opinions. When this happens, the personal rights of the individual have been transgressed and discussion represents tyrannical, not democratic, action. Furthermore, since the group loses the benefit of each person's thinking, the intellectual caliber of the deliberation may descend toward mediocrity. As a chairman, you should assume sufficient control over the group to insure the expression of all views, even the unpopular ones.

d. GROUP LEADERS SHOULD BE SKILLED COMMUNICATORS. The leader's tasks require high skill in the use of mind, body, and voice. Previous sections of this book have analyzed in detail the various aspects of effective oral communication. Therefore, it is necessary to suggest here only that the leader should demonstrate by his manner of speaking and listening that he is an objective, genial co-ordinator who is animatedly and impartially interested in all contributions.

2. Group leaders should exercise skillfully the duties of leadership. Because the individual types of discussion require specialized leadership functions, the following passage contains only generally applicable suggestions.

a. PRE-DISCUSSION DUTIES OF THE LEADER. As a chairman you will have several important tasks to accomplish before the actual discussion. (1) Contact each participant. In the case of most public discussions, arrange a face-to-face meeting of the participants so that an understanding can be reached concerning the agenda and the procedures to be employed. In the case of most private discussions, reach each participant by written message or telephone, giving the necessary information about the meeting, stating the major items to be discussed, and requesting suggestions concerning the agenda. (2) To clarify your thinking, construct an outline like the sample ones appearing earlier in this chapter. (3) Prepare yourself psychologically and intellectually by studying and thinking intensely on the subject, by examining the backgrounds, personalities, and speaking abilities of the participants, and by analyzing the probable characteristics of the audience—if one is to be present. (4) Check on local arrangements. Even though a program chairman or some other designated person may be "officially" responsible, make certain that an appropriate room is available, that lighting, heating, and ventilation will be suitable, that a sufficient number of chairs and tables are present and grouped appropriately, and that any necessary equipment (such as blackboard, chalk, charts, easels, ash trays, and name cards) is present.

b. DISCUSSIONAL DUTIES OF THE LEADER. Such duties involve introducing, directing, and closing the deliberations. In the case of public discussions, you will also head the forum period.

(1.) *Introducing the discussion.* The function of the leader in beginning the discussion is very similar to that of the public speaker in opening his address. Both speakers wish to stimulate favorable interest and provide necessary orienting materials. Because the discussion leader's introduction is extremely important in establishing a pleasant, positive, permissive climate and because it should be brief—usually not more than two or three minutes—it must be carefully planned. *DO'S:* Begin the meeting on time. Explain the reasons for the meeting and what you hope the group will accomplish. State the problem to be attacked and stress its importance. Give necessary background information. Explain the procedures to be followed. Introduce the speakers (to each other if they have not met or, if the meeting is public, to the audience). Start the discussion, usually by asking the group a question concerning the first item on the agenda. *DON'T'S:* Don't give a long-winded lecture—let the group cover all except absolutely necessary introductory information. Don't be pessimistic—if you indicate that the problem is too difficult or too involved for meaningful discussion, you will deaden interest; the attitude of the participants (and the audience) will be "If the group can't make any progress in solving the problem, why discuss it?" Don't express personal opinions—as chairman you are supposed to be an objective analyzer, not a convinced believer. Don't read your introduction—achieving instant, close rapport with the participants (and audience) will be more difficult if you read a prepared statement.

(2.) *Directing the discussion.* The main duties of the leader in directing the course of deliberation are to stimulate reflective thinking, steer the sequence of thought, and regulate inter-personal relations.

Stimulating reflective thought during the discussion. To elicit reflective thinking, the leader should *foster a friendly, permissive atmosphere.* By radiating genial interest in the discussants and in the deliberative process, you stir up similar attitudes in others. By refraining from advancing your own opinions on the question, being scrupulously fair to all persons, listening attentively to each speaker, and by expressing few, if any, value judgments concerning the merits of the contributions, you encourage greater spontaneity and freedom from inhibitions. To elicit reflective thinking, the leader should *facilitate the lively, animated exchange and evaluation of ideas and evidence.* By discouraging drawn-out speeches, insisting that participants offer only one idea at a time, and by directing evaluative attention to each significant point immediately after it is made, you will keep the discussion marching toward the deliberative goal. To elicit reflective thinking, the leader should *call for the clarification of all vague, vacuous, enigmatic, or ambiguous statements.* By actuating the examination of cloudy expressions, you will motivate the discussants to think more accurately and express themselves more precisely. To elicit reflective thinking, the leader should *encourage the active participation of each discussant.* By drawing the silent member into the spirited sharing of ideas, you probably will stir him to more vigorous thinking and enable the group to profit from his thinking.

One of the most important techniques in stimulating reflective thinking (and accomplishing other leadership functions) is the skillful use of overhead and direct questions. As its name implies, the direct question is addressed to a particular discussant; perhaps no better method exists to excite cerebral action than to ask a person a question demanding a direct response. Of course, a direct question may prove embarrassing if the recipient is excessively shy or lacks the necessary information. The overhead question is undirected; it is tossed "over the heads" of the participants so that anyone may answer it. Theoretically, each participant should be stimulated to "reach" for the overhead inquiry; however, such a question sometimes may evoke no answer. When this happens, the leader should narrow the focus of the query. Example: "What do you men believe is a major reason for student dissatisfaction with the cafeteria?" *Silence.* "Let me be more specific. Do you believe that students consider the selection of food to be inadequate?" Maximum reflective thinking probably can be excited by combining the overhead and the direct questions: first, throw out an overhead query to capture the interest of everyone; then, ask a particular person to answer it. As: "How rigidly are our traffic laws being enforced? Mike, as a five-year veteran on the police force, what would be your answer?"

Here are other examples of the use of questions to stimulate reflective thinking.

To discourage speechmaking or multiple idea contributions: "Before you continue, Alice, we should direct close attention to the several ideas which you have already given us. Let's go back and pick up the first point Alice made—that the United Fund spends too much money on advertising. Can anyone tell us what the Fund's advertising budget is?"

To evaluate ideas and evidence: "Let's look more closely at the possible effects of this program. For instance, what will happen to the land underneath the roadbed of the proposed bridges and on either side of the approaches? Will this land turn into slums?"

To clarify the obscure: "The word 'Communist' has been used several times in the last few minutes. We all know that such terms have rich personal meanings which vary from person to person. So, for the purpose of our discussion, let's try to agree upon a precise and stable meaning. Who is and who isn't a Communist? Are there some valid criteria or measurements which can be applied to a person to determine whether he is a Communist?"

To stimulate a quiet member to more active participation: "Henry, did I see your eyes light up when Ben mentioned football? The stadium hasn't changed much since you and Jake Miller were churning out the yardage for Gridley some ten years ago, has it? As a former football player and present-day taxpayer, what's your opinion on the mayor's proposal to increase the capacity of the stadium by 5,000 seats?"

Steering the sequence of thought during the discussion. As chairman, you are responsible for *pacing the discussion* so that it moves with sufficient speed to accomplish the discussional purpose within the time limitations but not so rapidly that significant points are overlooked or are treated superficially. To effect this, you should make rough estimates before the program as to the length of time required to cover each major point on the agenda. And, during the deliberation, keep one eye on the clock. When necessary, gently prod the discussants to get to the basic issues more quickly, or unobtrusively check those who wish to gloss over formidable, puzzling, or "uninteresting" items. As chairman, you are responsible for helping the discussants *follow a rational sequence of thought.* You are the principal "guardian of the agenda" and as such should exert discreet and reasonable control over the development of group thought. Try to establish an appropriate balance between the requiring of rigid adherence to the agenda—which usually will stifle spontaneity and freedom of thought—and the abdicating of all authority over the relevance of participation—which typically will mean much wasted time and effort. Only a discriminating judgment can tell the leader when the participants are being handcuffed to the agenda or when a digression is becoming an extended tangent. As chairman, you are responsible for *keeping the participants (and the audience) posted* on what has been accomplished and where the group is in relation to the attaining of the discussional goals. This leadership function is accomplished basically by means of transitions and summaries. Usually at the end of each major item on the agenda, you should make a brief recapitulation of what has just transpired, stressing the areas of agreement and disagreement, and then should employ one or two transitional sentences to link the point just completed to the next one on the outline. Because the leader is somewhat detached from the vigorous give-and-take of deliberation, he usually is the person best equipped to summarize. However, to encourage an increased sense of democratic sharing, some chairmen distribute among the discussants the task of recapitulating. Occasionally a discussion group will appoint a recorder or observer. This person is not a deliberator; his function is to record the course of the discussion. Some chairmen depend upon him to give most or all of the summaries. In some cases, following the actual discussion, the observer is expected to give a critical evaluation of the effectiveness of the group in achieving its goals.

Here are some examples of ways by which the leader can unobtrusively steer the sequence of thought.

To accelerate the tempo: "Although much more undoubtedly could be said about the nature of this problem, time is slipping away. Unless you have objections, let's turn our attention to finding a suitable solution. What remedial action might be taken?"

To decelerate the tempo: "Are there other important causes of the problem which we haven't considered? For instance, do you think that the condition of our streets might be a contributor to the high accident rate?"

To forestall the premature discussion of an item: "Before we attempt to implement the proposal for a new bond issue, let's give Harry a chance to offer a plan which we haven't considered yet."

To link points by transitional statements: "If no one wants to add anything concerning the proposal to introduce an enrichment program, let's move on to another possible solution."

To summarize: "We have covered so much ground in our discussion, it might be wise to take a moment for a brief review."

"Would you agree that a fair summary of the advantages and disadvantages of Charlie's plan would be. . . ?"

Regulating interpersonal relations during the discussion. Admittedly this leadership function overlaps those of stimulating reflective thinking and of steering the sequence of thought. Good interpersonal relations usually will prevail if the moderator is successful in fostering a warm, permissive climate and in keeping the deliberation marching efficiently toward the discussional goal. However, as a leader you should recognize your specific obligation to protect the rights of both the majority and minority and to reduce unnecessary conflict. (1) Careful analysis of the participants prior to the meeting and close observation of them during the discussion should enable you to anticipate unseeming behavior and to apply sufficient direction to prevent its occurrence. If, however, an individual does violate the rights of another person or of the group, you should take appropriate action to prevent its repetition and to minimize its negative influence upon the atmosphere of co-operative, reflective thinking. (2) Unless you as chairman are a stalwart defender of the right of each person to speak candidly, minority opinions may receive insufficient attention or may be unexpressed. (3) One of your important functions as a leader is to distinguish between conflicts which are intellectually necessary to the solving of the problem and those which are not. When a sharp argument arises, the moderator should mentally evaluate it in terms of these questions: Is it germane to the point under consideration and to the basic discussional goal? Is it being conducted in a gentlemanly, albeit vigorous, manner? Is it primarily intellectual in character rather than emotional? Does it seem motivated by a sincere attempt to work out a solution? If the answer to each of these questions appears to be "yes," you probably should permit the argument to continue until it resolves itself or until the passage of time requires the group to move on to the next point. If the answer to one or more of these questions is "no," you should exert suitable restricting influence and, if necessary, terminate the controversy. Personality clashes, emotionalized exchanges, vituperative attacks, and so on, are usually easy to recognize. However, the spotting of rational but extraneous conflict may require somewhat keener perception. As an example, if a group is discussing the desirability of amending the rules for intercollegiate football, one discussant might mention the difficulty of enforcing the existing rule against coaching from the sidelines. Another participant might cite Coach Abercrombie as a frequent and flagrant violator of this regulation. A third might retort that Coach Zonar does as much illegal sidelines coaching as Coach Abercrombie and that Zonar secretly encourages downtown boosters to give presents to the players. A fourth might repeat a rumor that halfback Green of State University has mysteriously come into the possession of a new Oldsmobile convertible. Unless the leader adroitly steers the discussion back on course, the extraneous conflict may spread into an argument over the ethics of various coaches and university athletic programs.

Here are some examples of methods by which the leader can regulate interpersonal relations.

To protect other discussants from the loquacious member(s): "Ruth, before you resume let's see how the rest of our group feel on this point. Jim, what's your opinion?"

To protect other discussants from the arbitrary member(s): "Helen has explained that Dr. Heyser is chairman of the State Advisory Board on Urban Planning and is a nationally recognized authority in his field. Ralph, would you explain the specific reasons why you have labeled this man 'an intellectual fraud' and why you object to our receiving his testimony?"

To protect other discussants from the malicious member(s): "We are confronted with a serious problem that challenges our best corporate efforts. Naturally we are going to have different ideas on what should be done. But we can and must work together in a rational, courteous manner."

To protect minority member(s) from group pressures: "Instead of dismissing Mr. Clarke's suggestion as 'unrealistic,' let's take enough time to become acquainted with it. Mr. Clarke, can you defend your plan against the charge of impracticality?"

To prevent extraneous conflict: "That's an interesting point. Undoubtedly we could spend an enjoyable hour arguing about it. However, since it is not directly related to our question and since our time is limited, we need to put it aside. Until we got sidetracked by the intriguing question of Senator Thompson's morality, we were attempting to determine. . . ."

(3.) *Closing the discussion.* When a consensus has been reached or the allotted time has expired, as chairman you should bring the meeting to a close. Although you might call upon a participant to summarize the course of the discussion or invite each discussant to give a brief statement of his views, the usual procedure is for the leader himself to conclude the discussion with a recapitulation. Naturally the length and character of this final summary will vary according to the purpose and type of the discussion and the nature of the material covered. In general, however, it should review the progress and the achievements of the group, noting both the agreements and the disagreements. To insure the accuracy and fairness of your summation, you usually should invite corrections and additions. In the case of the public deliberation, a period of audience participation typically follows the discussion. Therefore, your summary should also be designed to motivate the listeners to engage actively in the open forum.

(4.) *Conducting the forum.* Since the next chapter analyzes the leader's duties in conducting the forum, it is sufficient to observe here that the audience participation period is an extremely important part of the public program. No matter how successfully the public discussion group fulfills its basic purpose of stimulating reflective thinking on the part of the listeners, maximum resort to cerebration occurs only when the spectators cease to be silent observers and become active participants. The forum provides them the opportunity to share in the pooling of ideas and information.

c. Post-Discussional Duties of the Leader. When the lights have been turned off and the last straggler has disappeared, at least two tasks remain for you as leader. First, you should review your moderating of the discussion by asking yourself such questions as, Did I exert more direction than the group needed? Did I supply leadership effectively and unobtrusively when it was needed? Did the group accomplish its goal smoothly, efficiently, and with a minimum of extraneous conflict? If not, why not? Second, you usually should prepare some sort of written communication concerning the discussion: in the case of a committee meeting, you may draft a report for submission to the parent organization; in the case of the staff conference, you may prepare a summary of the meeting and send a copy to each discussant and to your immediate superior; in the case of a public discussion, you may send to each participant a letter thanking him for taking part in the deliberation.

F. Good Discussion Needs Effective Participation. In addition to qualified leadership, successful deliberation requires the intelligent, co-operative efforts of each discussant. Too many students are inclined to view the leader and the individual discussant through different ends of the same telescope. The discussant is not of minute consequence, a mere adjunct to the towering leader. Strictly speaking, the moderator is not a participant. He may stimulate, integrate, and regulate, but the actual work of problem-solving must be done by the discussants. Ideally the participant should possess the same qualifications and abilities as the leader. Therefore, since much of what has been said previously about the moderator is also applicable to each member, the discussant can be treated in brief compass.

1. The discussant should understand the discussional method and should possess appropriate attitudes. To be an effective discussant, you should understand and appreciate the purposes, values, and limitations of deliberation—as well as the principles of group dynamics. In addition, you should possess proper attitudes toward the deliberative process, the other discussants, the leader, yourself as a participant, and the subject. You should regard discussion not as a gladiator's pit from which one contestant or one side will eventually emerge victorious but as a democratic method by which interested persons can work out appropriate answers to common problems. As a participant, you should expect to receive from other discussants (and, of course, accord to them) respect, congenial and courteous treatment, and a generous encouragement to express your views freely and candidly. Do not apologize to yourself if you take definite opinions to a discussion—faith in one's judgment is essential to effective decision making. However, attempt to avoid the mental rigidity of the unchangeable mind. If logic demands it, be willing to alter your position or abandon non-essential points of difference. No reason exists for you to kowtow to the moderator as to an Oriental potentate; however, you should grant him respect as a colleague who is attempting to fulfill difficult leadership functions. Furthermore, be willing to assist him, when feasible, in the performance of his duties.

2. The discussant should be intellectually prepared for the deliberation. This text has stressed repeatedly that to be an effective participant you must equip yourself for the rigorous mental effort involved in problem-solving. The first step toward intellectual preparedness is to acquire a storehouse of relevant facts and ideas. The second step is to test the merits and limitations of each piece of evidence and reasoning. Only by analyzing and appraising your material can you apply it accurately and fairly. Also, be prepared to document all of your evidence bearing upon controversial matters. The third step is to think deeply and widely concerning the problem and its possible solutions. Try to comprehend clearly and vividly the importance, extent, and ramifications of the problem. Probe until you are confident that you have uncovered the real issues and the basic causative factors. Explore each possible solution until you can formulate tentative judgments about its assets and liabilities, its relative desirability in comparison to other plans, and its potential influence upon the problem. The fourth step is to organize your ideas and information by means of a personal outline. This outline uses the group agenda as its structural framework but is usually more detailed and should indicate the documentation for each significant piece of evidence. The purpose of the outline is to help you to prepare intellectually for discussion by clarifying and directing your thinking and by insuring that you have a sufficiency of relevant, documented material. Its purpose differs from that of the public speaker's outline in that it cannot provide an exact order of thoughts for your oral presentation. The give and take of conversation probably will not provide the opportunity to say everything that you place in the outline nor to follow the exact sequence.

3. *The discussant should think analytically during the deliberation.* Unlike the debater who marshals the most compelling evidence in the most strategic order, you should present your ideas candidly without attempting to camouflage weaknesses, stretch the application of your material, or to exaggerate its worth. Instead of being hypercritical of the evidence and thinking of others and hypocritical toward your own, you should be analytical of all contributions—including your own. Realizing that opinions are no better than the facts upon which they are based, you should constantly seek answers to the questions:

"What are the relevant facts?" "What is their application to the point under discussion?"

4. The discussant should participate cooperatively during the deliberation. One of your most important functions as a cooperative discussant is to help foster an enjoyable, permissive climate. You should take to the meeting a receptive mind as well as a full one. To promote congeniality, you should maintain a friendly, good-spirited manner and occasionally might introduce a touch of relevant humor, mention a personal experience, compliment a member for a particularly lucid contribution, and so on. To facilitate smooth interpersonal relations, subordinate your personal interests to those of the group. When you find it necessary to disagree, do so without being disagreeable. Accept honest criticism of your ideas for what it is and do not mistake it for an attack on your wisdom or character. If you find yourself in the minority, do not pretend agreement, resort to acrimony, or withdraw into morose silence. Instead, continue your good-natured striving to bridge the differences and to help the group reach its discussional goals. Another function of the cooperative discussant is to reinforce the leader when his authority is unfairly challenged or when some untractable member impedes group progress. The third function of the cooperative discussant is to share, when feasible, in discussional leadership. Now let us examine five specific ways in which you can supplement the direction of the leader. (Naturally, any such assistance must be unobtrusive and diplomatic. Otherwise, your efforts may be resented by the group.) (1) In addition to keeping within the confines of the agenda yourself, help others to do likewise. Although the leader is the chief guardian of the agenda, complete responsibility should not be thrust upon him. You and all other participants should mentally test the pertinency of each comment. If the chairman fails to deflect an obviously irrelevant twist, perhaps you should exert gentle pressure to return the deliberation to its true course. (2) Help the group detect and resolve rational but irrelevant arguments, misunderstandings arising from ambiguous or opaque language, or emotionality engendered by defective interpersonal relations or by the spirited exchange of opinions. (3) Help to bring out all pertinent viewpoints. If for some reason a significant point is not introduced, suggest its consideration as a possibly rewarding facet of the subject. (4) Supplement the leader's efforts to delineate the areas of real and potential agreement; to determine the location, nature and relative intensity of disagreements; and to enlarge the areas of assent and minimize those of dissent. (5) Help keep the group advised as to what it has accomplished, where it is at the moment, and what yet remains to be done in order to accomplish the discussional goals. If the chairman neglects to synthesize the individual points, to make occasional summaries, and to offer helpful transitions from one major topic to the next, you could suggest the need for greater coherence or possibly supply it yourself.

5. *The discussant should speak and listen effectively during the deliberation.* The successful application of everything that we have considered so far is dependent upon your possessing adequate skills in oral communication. Do not permit the intimacy of group discussion to mislead you into ineffectual speaking, As in any other communicative situation, employ a lively, conversational mode. Speak enthusiastically, audibly, and directly to the individual listeners. Try to say exactly what you mean in a conciliatory manner. Make a determined effort to be an analytical, co-operative, retentive listener. Demonstrate by your facial expressions and bodily tonus that you are listening alertly to all that is said. In addition to these general suggestions, apply the following specific guides to effective discussional speaking.

Feel free to speak as often as you believe that you have something worth while to say. Some students are unduly afraid that frequent contributions may make them unpopular with other discussants. Such is not the case—as long as you are offering meaningful ideas and are not infringing upon the rights of others.

Unless competition to speak is intense, do not hold up a hand as a request for permission to speak; such a procedure dampens the spontaneity necessary for animated conversation. Although you should not interrupt a speaker, be prepared to begin your remarks the instant he concludes. If you delay starting to speak, you may be crowded out in the vigorous give and take. These observations should not be interpreted to mean that occasional silences are undesirable, particularly in private discussion.

Of great importance: limit each contribution to a single point. A discussion group can give evaluative attention to only one idea or piece of evidence at a time. If you present a series of items, nearly all will be overlooked or given only cursory inspection.

By limiting each contribution to one point, you will find it easier to be brief. Although the length of an uninterrupted comment may vary from a fraction of a second—as for a one-word answer—to perhaps several minutes, the average duration usually should be a minute or less. If you find that you are giving speeches, you are probably making multiple idea contributions.

When a group discussion is characterized by a series of unrelated comments, the participants are usually thinking about what they are going to say next instead of listening to each other. *Every contribution should bear directly upon the immediately preceding one, or should represent a summary or a transition to a new point.* For instance, when you are asked a direct question, answer it precisely and directly. Do not side-step it, answer a different question, or ignore it.

Use discretion when employing notes. Remember that you are a speaker, not an oral reader. Ordinarily notes should be restricted to the presentation of statistics or important quotations.

Do not hesitate to use visual aids if their employment will make ideas clearer, more interesting, or more persuasive. Follow the same rules for presenting visual material that you learned in your study of public speaking. Those rules are applicable to all forms of speaking.

SUMMARY

Because discussion is so widely used and so important as a problem-solving methodology, you should become skilled in its use. Deliberation may be defined as the systematic, objective sharing and evaluating of ideas and information by two or more persons for the purpose of investigating and solving a problem. Although not a panacea, the discussion method possesses certain important values: it can inspire better morale among the participants and a greater willingness to accept a decision; it fosters greater understanding and retention than does passive listening; it often provides better decisions than would be evolved by the discussants working independently; along with debate and parliamentary speaking, it constitutes the essential means by which individuals can share in the democratic process. When discussions fail, the fault lies in one or more of the following factors: insufficient time, inadequate information, faulty evaluation of ideas and evidence, unsystematic development, subjectivity, group pressure, poor human relations, sabotage. Deliberations occurring without an audience include informal group discussions and conferences; those occurring in the presence of an audience include the panel, symposium, lecture forum, and broadcast discussion.

Good discussion possesses the following characteristics: (1) It concerns a subject which is well adjusted to the total situation, which is a question of inquiry or policy, and which is phrased suitably. (2) It emphasizes reflective thinking which requires adequate knowledge, rational use of evidence and reasoning, and close control of negative emotions. (3) It utilizes systematic organization and (4) the effective use of language. (5) It evidences adroit leadership by a moderator who possesses important qualifications and who exercises skillfully the duties of leadership. (6) It manifests effective participation by discussants who understand the discussion method, have appropriate attitudes, possess adequate information, think analytically, participate cooperatively, and speak and listen effectively.

19 ❧❧ *Common Forms*
of Group Discussion

Since the general principles of group discussion were presented in detail in Chapter 18, this chapter is limited to an adaptation of these principles to the specific forms of deliberation.

ENGAGING IN DISCUSSION WITHOUT AN AUDIENCE

Most deliberations occur in private meetings. Customarily, in such discussions each person present is expected to take an active part in the proceedings. The absence of an audience frees the participants from the tensions accompanying a public performance and enables them to concentrate undivided attention on the topic. Therefore, discussants in private meetings are more inclined to be "themselves" and to speak more candidly and freely. Unfortunately, however, when no audience is present to serve as a stimulant and regulator, discussants are less inclined to prepare and plan adequately; they may feel less responsibility to maintain pleasant and cooperative interpersonal relations, and may be either irritatingly outspoken or unconcerned and uncommunicative. Also, we should recognize that policy determination is a unique function of private discussion. Rarely, if ever, is an audience or organization bound by a decison agreed upon by a public discussion group. Virtually always, the authority to determine policies and the execution of policies is vested in private discussion groups or in parliamentary bodies.

    A. Informal Group Discussion.   In this form of deliberation, a group of usually not more than twenty persons meets to talk over a matter of common concern. As a rule no set speeches are presented and no rigid rules of procedure are followed. Informal discussions may occur spontaneously and casually, as when several students enrolled in a particular history course meet accidentally at the coke bar and talk over an approaching examination. We are concerned here, however, with those discussions which are planned and which utilize a fairly systematic development of thought.

The typical purpose of informal discussion groups is to investigate a problem in order to acquire new interpretations and better understanding. Such learning or study groups are exceedingly numerous and vary widely in nature. As examples, a junior high school civics class attempts to assay the probable effects of a recent Supreme Court decision; a score of distinguished scientists and scholars assemble at Pugwash, Nova Scotia, under the sponsorship of Cyrus S. Eaton for the purpose of estimating the moral status of modern man.

1. Planning for informal group discussion. As a leader you have at least eight specific tasks in preparing for informal deliberation. (1) Select and/or analyze the participants. (2) Determine the discussional goals. (3) Prepare an agenda. (4) Prepare yourself mentally and emotionally to conduct the meeting. (5) Notify the participants. Although posters or notices in the local paper are helpful, make direct contact by telephone or written message with as many of the potential group members as possible. Such communications should indicate the name of the sponsoring organization, the purpose of the meeting, the time and place, and the major points to be discussed. (6) Secure appropriate physical arrangements. As illustrated in the accompanying diagram, the ideal seating arrangement for small to moderate-sized groups is the face-to-face situation, preferably about a table. For groups of more than twenty members several tables may be placed in a "U" shape. If no table is available, arrange the chairs in a circle. (7) If you are expected to make some sort of written or oral report to the sponsoring organization at a future meeting, plan either to take adequate notes during the program or appoint a recorder. (8) If you believe that the number of participants may exceed twenty, you may wish to divide the group into smaller "buzz" units. In that event, ap-

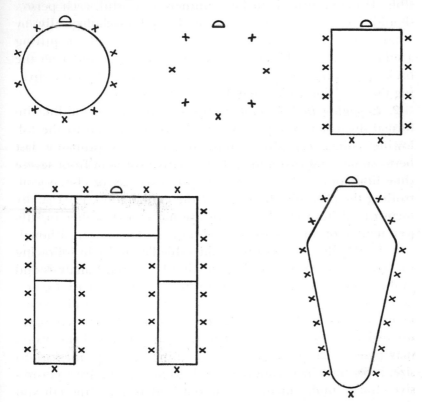

Fig. 13. Seating Arrangements for Private Discussion Groups.

point a competent chairman and a recorder for each potential sub-group (see page 507).

Unfortunately participants often make little, if any, preparation for engaging in informal group discussion. To paraphrase an adage, they seem to believe that there is "knowledge in numbers"—that because perhaps ten or twenty other persons will be present someone undoubtedly will possess sufficient information on any particular point to carry on the discussion. When significant numbers of the discussants hold this attitude, the burden of conducting the deliberation falls chiefly upon a few well-informed persons, making balanced participation impossible. If the meeting is to be genuinely successful, each person should prepare himself intellectually and psychologically by studying the topic as it relates to the proposed agenda, acquiring a sufficient store of knowledge and viewpoints, considering the backgrounds and interests of the other discussants, and anticipating the reception which may be accorded his ideas.

2. *Engaging in informal group discussion.* In guiding informal discussion groups, give special consideration to the following points. (1) Most informal discussions probably last between one and two hours. This relative freedom from severe time limitations relieves you from the necessity of closely controlling the pace and direction of the deliberation. (2) Usually members of informal discussions are not experts either in subject matter or in discussion techniques. Therefore, although you should allow the group considerable flexibility in following the agenda, be especially alert to stimulate careful analysis and evaluations, to promote clear definitions and explanations, and to make generous use of summaries, transitions, and restatements. (3) Informal discussion groups are often larger than other discussional groups. Since that is the case, the size of the group may pose special problems of leadership. As groups increase in size, it becomes increasingly difficult to maintain a free, permissive climate under member-centered leadership. Although you should permit a group to assume as much of the leadership function as it can successfully handle, you probably will need to exert considerable direction in larger groups, especially when they exceed twenty participants. Be alert to the tendency of large groups to divide into sub-groups and cliques. Be sensitive to the increased difficulty in maintaining a representative balance in participation. If necessary, resort to standard rules of parliamentary procedure and, possibly, assign maximum limits for the length and frequency of the individual participations. (4) Do not permit the discussion to run past the announced closing time. When time has expired or the group has achieved its goals, summarize briefly the accomplishments of the group. Try to close the meeting on a positive and enthusiastic note.

When engaging in informal deliberation as a discussant, attempt to adjust your participation to the conditions imposed by the size of the group, the discussional goals, and the prevailing climate. Particularly in a large group, be alert to help with the leadership functions, as in bringing out all relevant aspects of the problem, keeping fairly close to the agenda, stimulating silent discussants to express their views, promoting a genial, cooperative atmosphere, and so forth. Of course, do not appear to compete with the leader or with the other members.

B. Conferences. Unfortunately, writers in the field of discussion have not yet agreed as to the meaning of various commonly used labels. So, a word like "conference" contains enough semantic elastic to permit its being stretched to fit the outlines of almost any discussion method. Its use is restricted here to cover three types of private discussion: committee conferences, staff conferences, and instructional conferences.

1. Committees. Before applying the principles of effective discussion to the committee method, we should analyze the importance, types, membership, functions, and restrictions of committees.

What is the importance of committees? Most of the work of large organizations such as fraternal, professional, or business groups is accomplished by committees. Also, committees perform invaluable service for institutions like universities, foundations, and corporations. Committees investigate problems, determine policies, and may even execute plans or programs. The significance of skilled committee deliberation should become more apparent when we consider that the parent organization customarily endorses the recommendations of its committees and sometimes empowers committees to act in its name.

The utility of the committee lies in its efficiency. Because it is so much smaller than the appointing body, a committee permits greater informality and more freedom in deliberation, longer concentration of uninterrupted thought, and greater ease in scheduling meetings. Because it offers much greater privacy, a committee may resolve sensitive, vexatious, or disagreeable problems with a minimum of publicity and disturbance to the organization.

What are the types of committees? When a committee is appointed solely to accomplish a specific task, it is called a *special* committee. Such a group ceases to exist upon submitting its report to the parent organization. A university homecoming is an example of a special committee. A *standing* committee is one which is asked to perform a particular service for a definite period of time, such as a semester or a year. For instance, the Speech Association of America annually appoints various standing committees, like the "Committee on Public Relations," the "Committee on Publications," and the "Committee on Recruitment and Supply." When a committee is directed to discover facts concerning a specific situation or to recommend policies, it is called a *deliberative* or *investigative* committee. Thus, a faculty senate might appoint a committee to ascertain the academic standards of the university or might direct a committee to recommend a program for reducing cheating. Committees which are appointed to carry out a program or policy already adopted are called *executive* or *action* committees. As an example, a mayor might appoint a committee of civic leaders to direct the city's annual charity drive.

How are committee members and officers selected? The personnel of a committee is either elected by the organization's membership or is appointed by the presiding officer. If one of these methods is not prescribed in the bylaws, the motion which establishes the committee must do so. When the presiding officer appoints the committee, he customarily names the chairman as well. When the organization elects the committee, it may designate the chairman. When no chairman is specified, in some organizations the first-named member is considered the chairman; in other organizations the initial committeeman is expected to call the group together and serve as temporary chairman until the committee can choose its permanent chairman. In small special committees the chairman usually acts as secretary, but in large ones and in all standing committees it is customary to elect a secretary. If a committee is expected to tackle an especially important or formidable task, its leader may be appointed first; this procedure gives him a voice in selecting the personnel of his group. Although parliamentary law does not require it, courtesy suggests that the person who proposed the creation of the committee be named to its membership. In order to coordinate executive and committee efforts, the bylaws of some organizations specify that certain officers shall automatically hold ex officio membership on particular committees; such ex officio members usually have the same functions and obligations as the other members.

What are the qualifications of effective committee chairmen and members? Both the leader and the members should be efficient, willing individuals who are specially well versed on the committee's assignment. They should be well-integrated persons who can work smoothly with the other members. And they should be skilled discussants. In addition, the personnel of deliberative and investigative committees must be carefully selected to represent all of the important viewpoints and interests within the parent organization. Otherwise the deliberations of the committee will not represent fairly the sentiments of the appointing body. In the case of executive committees, all members should be strong supporters of the program they are to implement.

What should be the size of a committee? The number of persons assigned to a committee is usually specified by the constitution, the bylaws, or by the motion which creates it. The appropriate size of a committee depends upon its function. Because committees for action are commissioned to carry out previously determined programs, they should work with streamlined efficiency; this requires that they be small units—usually numbering no more than five members. Because committees for deliberation or investigation must represent all factions and interests in the organization, they may be considerably larger than executive committees—sometimes including fifteen or more members. Unless clearly necessary, however, the number of discussants should not exceed nine. For all types of committees, the arriving at decisions will be expedited if the group has an odd number of members—three, five, seven, etc.

What are the functions and restrictions of committees? The committee is a creature of its parent organization and, therefore, has no separate entity. It possesses only the rights, duties, and authority granted to it in the constitution, bylaws, or the legislation by which it is established. The secretary or president of the organization should give to the committee chairman explicit directions describing the committee's task, defining its powers, stating any established procedures or policies of the organization which might affect the group's activities, and indicating the date when the committee's report should be submitted.

Now that we are better acquainted with the general nature and purpose of committees, *we can turn to the proper procedures involved in planning and conducting committee discussions.*

To help prepare himself and the members for efficient committee deliberation, the chairman should: (1) Study carefully all materials which the parent organization has given or entrusted to him, such as instructions, statements of pertinent organizational policies, and information in the form of papers, reports, or documents. The chairman must understand precisely the nature of the assigned task, the scope of his committee's authority, and the framework of regulating procedures within which the committee must operate. (2) Think intensively on the subject and analyze the backgrounds, personalities, and reputations of the discussants. (3) Prepare an agenda of the items to be taken up at the first meeting. Naturally, the nature of the agenda will depend upon the purpose of the committee, that is, whether its function is to investigate, to make recommendations, or to carry out a program. (4) If possible, contact all of the members to determine a satisfactory time and place for the first meeting. (5) Send to the members a written notice of the first meeting and copies of helpful materials provided by the organization or acquired by the chairman himself in the course of his investigations. The announcement should include the following: the name of the committee; the time, place, and purpose of the meeting; the agenda; an invitation to offer suggestions concerning the agenda; a request that the recipient notify the chairman if unable to attend; and a list of the membership. (6) As a means of organizing and clarifying his thinking, the chairman should prepare a detailed personal outline. He should plan to use this outline, or an abbreviated form, as a guide in conducting the discussion.

Effective committee deliberation also depends upon adequate pre-meeting preparation by the *individual members*. Although the chairman is responsible for summoning the committee together, if he neglects or refuses to do so, any two members can call a meeting. In addition to his duty to insure the meeting of the committee (if he feels that a clear need for such a meeting exists), each member should (1) Study carefully all directives and materials provided by the organization or by the chairman. (2) Explore the committee's task particularly in relation to the proposed agenda of the first meeting and to the policies of the organization. (3) Give to the chairman any suggestions concerning the agenda or any important materials which should be placed in the hands of the members prior to the meeting. (4) Prepare a personal outline to supplement the agenda. (5) Anticipate the interpersonal relationships which possibly will exist during the meeting by analyzing the position, reputation, personality, and viewpoints of each member.

When engaging in committee deliberation, follow the principles of effective leadership and participation discussed earlier. Also, consider these points: (1) Since the committee is in reality a small deliberative assembly, it cannot function legally unless a quorum—a majority of the members—is present. Therefore, make every effort to attend meetings. (2) In small committees, business is conducted very informally and the chairman participates actively in the formulation of the group consensus. In larger committees, the procedure should remain as informal as is consistent with the size and temper of the group. Unless the committee is extremely large, the members should speak from their seats without requesting formal permission from the chairman to speak; the leader may express personal opinions without "leaving the chair"; and motions do not require seconds. When a large committee considers exceedingly important or explosive matters, the chairman probably should limit himself to the role of an objective presiding officer and should enforce strict parliamentary decorum. However, even in such circumstances no restrictions should be placed on the frequency of participation or the length of debate. (3) Committee deliberations are nearly always private. However, if requested to do so, the committee should provide an opportunity for members of the organization to appear before the committee to express their views. Also, the committee may wish to invite outside experts to speak to its members. (4) Adequate minutes should be kept of each meeting. As you know, except in small special committees where the chairman serves as recorder, a secretary should be chosen. Committee minutes are designed for the exclusive use of the membership and should contain all information which may prove helpful in preparing the report to the parent society. The chairman may wish to have the memorandum of each hearing typed and distributed to the members prior to the next meeting. (5) Before a committee concludes one in a series of meetings, it may set the time for the next hearing or may adjourn subject to call by the chair. (6) Both standing and special committees must submit reports to the appointing society at a specified date. If the special committee has not accomplished its discussional goals by that time, it submits a "partial report." A report should be written in the third person and should be as concise as possible. It should state the name of the committee and the purpose for which it was appointed. Also, it may describe tersely the activities of the committee, summarize the results of its investigations, and/or offer recommendations. Formal resolutions to implement the recommendations may accompany the report. A report can contain only those provisions which have been approved in a committee meeting by a majority of those present. Important reports should be signed by the chairman and all concurring members. Dissenters from the majority views may prepare and submit to the society a statement of their position. After voting upon the report, the committee should designate the chairman or some member to present it to the organization. At the appropriate time during the parent society's meeting, the sponsor of the report should introduce it with what he considers to be necessary background explanation. Then, either he or the secretary of the society should read the report orally. If the report contains recommendations, the sponsor should move their adoption. An organization may dispose of a report in various ways: it may adopt a report *in toto;* adopt it partially or with reservations; reject it; reject it in favor of a minority report; simply file it for the information of the members; return it to the committee for further study; or postpone its consideration. The reading of the report, however, constitutes its being "received" by the society. Once its report has been received the special committee ceases to exist. Since standing committees serve a specific period of time, unless the report is its final one it should continue to render its designated service.

2. Staff conferences. When a member of the managerial or supervisory force of an institution, agency, or concern summons his subordinates into consultation, the resulting meeting is called a staff conference. Probably most such conferences are called to answer special, pressing needs. However, in large numbers of business, educational, and governmental organizations, staff conferences are scheduled at regular intervals by the various departments or divisional units. Also, many institutions maintain an integrated discussional program linking the top of the managerial hierarchy through the different levels to the bottom. For instance, a company president may hold planned and regularly scheduled meetings with his officers or executive assistants; each executive assistant also meets periodically with his staff of divisional superintendents; each divisional superintendent meets with his force of department heads; each department head meets with his supervisors; and so on. Such a program of vertically integrated conferences provides an unexcelled means of passing communication up and down the line of command. Directions, information, and policies flow downward through the organizational structure, and the opinions and suggestions of the employees at each level are passed upward by the written and/or oral reports which each conference leader makes to his immediate superior.

In contrast to the usual committee meeting, the staff conference (particularly if it is one of a regularly scheduled series of meetings) may take up several different types of problems. For instance, a particular conference may consider these items: (1) The chairman may explain one of his new directives or one passed along to him by the higher administration. After answering questions, he may encourage his subordinates to share observations concerning the meaning and application of the new policy. (2) The group may investigate a problem in order to acquire a better understanding of its importance, nature, and causes. Example: "Why does our department have a high proportion of articles returned for exchange?" (3) It may study a problem to determine a course of action. Example: "What book should our department adopt as the text in History 132?" (4) It may analyze a problem in order to recommend a policy. Example: "What recommendations should we make to the division manager for improving the present methods of taking inventory?" (5) It may talk over a problem with the leader in order to help him formulate his decision. Example: "What should be the nature and amount of the goods ordered by the chairman for the spring sale?"

In addition to the leader and his subordinates, the membership of the staff conference should include all other persons directly concerned with the discussion subject, as well as those who may be able to contribute significant information or viewpoints. Thus, the director of a university press may wish to invite to a meeting of his staff the following: the university's executive vice-president (to enable the top administration to keep in intimate contact with the activities and problems of the press); the chairman of the art department (to utilize his professional judgment concerning problems of format); and the manager of a local printing shop (to secure his expert advice about production costs). Although staff conferences vary in size according to the circumstances, they should not exceed twenty persons and, if adequate opportunity is to be provided for individual participation, should number fewer than ten persons.

The basic principles of preparation, participation, and leadership apply to staff conferences, with certain special cautions. Although the following advice relates particularly to the chairman, it also concerns the members since they should help when feasible in the leadership function.

To achieve maximal values from staff conferences, *the chairman should make a special effort to foster a democratic, permissive climate.* He should demonstrate by his manner and actions that he welcomes the contributions of his subordinates and considers their conference participation an important asset to the efficient functioning of his department. If he is regarded as an adamant authoritarian, his staff members will not express ideas freely and candidly. As a means of fostering a democratic atmosphere, the chairman should encourage the group to share in the setting of conference goals. Well before the meeting, he should consult his subordinates—all of them if the staff is small, or several ranking members if the staff is large—to secure their advice concerning the time and place of the meeting and the contents of the agenda. He should then send to each staffer a conference notice supplying all necessary details concerning the meeting. The announcement should state these particulars: the job title or organizational identity of the staff (as: "District Sales Managers, Verner's Manufacturing Company," or "Department Chairmen, College of Arts and Sciences"); the time, place, and purpose of the meeting; the names of the participants and guests; the topics on the agenda; a request for suggestions concerning the agenda and for notification if the recipient is unable to attend; the leader's name, job title (as: "Edgar B. Stewart, Regional Sales Supervisor, Verner's Manufacturing Company," or "James L. Maxwell, Dean of the College of Arts and Sciences"), and his signature. If a member of higher management or of some other department has been invited to the conference, the chairman should explain in the announcement, or in the beginning of the meeting, the reason for the presence of the guest. In this way, the leader may prevent unnecessary apprehension on the part of his staff. During the meeting, the chairman should encourage the members to assume as much of the leadership function as is consistent with the discussional purpose and the size of the group. This means that the style of leadership may vary considerably during a particular conference. For instance, if a topic on the agenda calls for the chairman to present an administrative directive or to explain a new work procedure, he inevitably will dominate the discussion; however, if the next topic represents a problem which the staff is expected to solve, the mode of leadership probably should become less chairman-centered and more member-centered. If time permits after the completion of the scheduled agenda, the chairman should invite the members to bring before the group new matters of common interest.

The chairman should explain frankly the discussional goals and the role of the staff members in achieving the goals. If managerial policy precludes their formulating a policy-making decision on a particular matter, he should explain that he wishes to secure their thinking so that he (or the appropriate administrative officer) may be better equipped to make a wise decision. He should not imply nor permit his subordinates to assume that their judgment will determine the course of action.

The chairman should not include too many items on the agenda. When this happens, deliberation becomes hurried and superficial, stretches overtime, or fails to cover all topics. In preparing the agenda, the chairman should estimate the amount of discussion that probably will be provoked by each point and should place at the top of the agenda the topics which must be disposed of before the meeting concludes.

The chairman and discussants should anticipate the need for reference materials such as reports, papers, letters, charts, documents, and books. Too frequently staff conferences are interrupted in order that some necessary information may be located and secured.

Both the chairman and participants should be alert to use the conference period efficiently and to close the meeting at the announced time. Since staff conferences are customarily held during work hours, loyalty to the company demands that the discussion period be used effectively; and in order to plan his work program each participant has the right to anticipate that the conference will end on schedule. If time runs out, the chairman should usually suggest that the pending matter be carried over to the next meeting.

The chairman's report is an especially important factor in achieving full value from staff conferences. Appropriate notes should be taken during the meeting by the chairman or someone he designates, often his personal secretary. Following the conference, the chairman should prepare a concise report which includes the following: the title or job designation of the group; the time, place, and purpose of the meeting; the names of all persons present, including those of any guests; each item discussed and the action taken concerning it; and the name, job title, and signature of the leader. A copy of this report should be sent to each staff member and to the chairman's immediate superior. As we explained earlier, the conference report is a significant means of establishing closer contact between different organizational levels.

3. Training conferences. The main function of training conferences is to instruct employees concerning company policies or to train them to perform their jobs more efficiently. Of course, the method may also be used to inform or train other groups of persons, such as volunteer solicitors for the Red Cross fund-raising campaign, or newly recruited members of the

Ground Observers Corps. This form of conference may be treated very briefly because it is a specialized adaptation of the discussion method and because in many concerns it is part of an integrated in-service training program under the leadership of experienced personnel or supervisory officers. Perhaps it is necessary to point out only that, although the leadership of such conferences is necessarily leader-centered, the exclusive resort to the lecture method should be avoided. When the trainees have some experiences and judgments upon which to draw, the leader should attempt to tap these resources by means of skilled questions. As for any other form of discussion, the more actively the participants can be drawn into the process of problem-solving, the greater becomes their cerebral functioning and the stronger becomes the possibility that they will take away from the meeting new appreciation, insights, and beliefs.

ENGAGING IN DISCUSSION BEFORE AN AUDIENCE

In contrast to private ones, public deliberations are basically performances or programs. The primary function of such "show" discussions is to interest, inform, and stimulate the listeners rather than to determine policies or to enrich the thinking of the participants. Because of their nature and function, public discussions tend to be more formal and, in general, require more planning, greater skill in speaking, better pacing, and a more systematic development of thought.

Since you are familiar with the basic principles, the following passages will be confined to ascertaining for each type of public discussion—panel, symposium, lecture-forum, and radio-television discussion—its unique characteristics, advantages, and limitations, and its peculiar needs of planning, leadership, and participation.

A. The Panel. In popular usage, the term "panel" is applied to almost any kind of public utterance involving more than one person. However, as used in the field of speech a panel discussion is one in which a small group (usually between three and six) utilizes purposeful conversation, under the leadership of a chairman, to explore a question of inquiry or policy before an audience. The typical panel program consists of (1) an introduction of the topic and the speakers by the chairman, (2) the discussion among the panelists, (3) a summary by the chairman, and (4) a forum period during which the audience participates under the coordination of the chairman. Usually the entire meeting lasts between one and two hours, with the panel discussion portion occupying not more than one-half of the total time.

Both the advantages and the disadvantages of the panel method grow out of its use of conversation as the medium of communication. Because conversation is a familiar skill, the average person who is well informed and co-operative may engage efficiently as a panel participant; such a person may, however, lack the public speaking skills necessary for effective performance in the symposium or lecture-forum types of discussion. The panel is the only type of public discussion that affords a continuous interaction among its members; therefore, it is unique in permitting an immediate clarification and evaluation of viewpoints as they are presented. Experimental studies seem to suggest that in comparison to the typical symposium or lecture-forum, the average panel possibly maintains a higher degree of interest among the listeners and may stimulate them to greater amount of reflective thinking.

On the other hand, because the panel utilizes the medium of conversation, it can be used effectively only before relatively small audiences. The intimate and informal atmosphere which is the essence of panel speaking cannot be maintained if the audience is too large. When the listeners number many more than one hundred, the increased problem of audibility and the greater formality of the occasion tend to force the participants to assume the characteristics of public speakers rather than those of conversationalists. The use of a public address system is only partially successful in enabling the panel method to work satisfactorily with large audiences. Admittedly, electronic amplification reduces the necessity for powerful vocal projection; however, it adds to the formality of the situation and its inevitable reverberation and distortion of sound impose restrictions on normal conversational utterance. Therefore, if a large audience is anticipated, the program chairman or sponsor should consider the advisability of using the symposium or the lecture-forum instead of the panel. Another disadvantage is that, in comparison to other forms of public discussion, the panel method requires much more preliminary consulting and planning among the speakers, a higher degree of leadership skill on the part of the chairman, and a greater degree of emotional stability and cooperation on the part of the discussants. A third disadvantage is that, unlike symposium speakers, panel performers must be adequately informed on the entire subject, not on merely a limited segment. A final disadvantage is that the panel method does not permit a participant to develop his contentions in a systematic, uninterrupted manner.

1. Planning for panel discussion. Ordinarily the topic and the speakers should be selected a minimum of two weeks in advance of the program. When the discussion question is to be selected before the naming of the chairman or participants, the program committee or sponsor should analyze the nature, interests, and needs of the sponsoring organization. To ascertain what subjects will be most meaningful, arrangements might be made to submit a questionnaire to the membership of the organization well in advance of the discussion program. Such a questionnaire should request the respondent to indicate his preference concerning the several topics listed and should solicit suggestions for speakers and for additional subjects. If such a procedure seems infeasible, the committee might poll a representative sampling of the membership by telephone or by the questionnaire method. Before definitely settling upon a question, the committee should consider the availability of speakers who are well informed on the subject. When the chairman and the discussants are selected before the topic is determined, the chairman—in conjunction with the program committee and the panelists—should select a subject which is within the scope of the panelists' knowledge, experience, and interest and which is also suitable for the audience, the occasion, the amount of time available, and so on.

In selecting a panel chairman, the program committee should observe the criteria suggested in Chapter 18. Furthermore, because his opening remarks are directed to the audience rather than the panel and because he must lead the forum period, the chairman should be a skilled public speaker.

In selecting discussants, these particular points should be considered. The successful application of the panel method does not demand that discussants be established experts, but they should be competently informed on the problem and its possible solutions or should be willing to undertake the necessary investigation. As in the case of the chairman, the participants should understand and appreciate the discussion method and should be poised, intelligent, emotionally stable and cooperative. To foster the balanced expression of relevant viewpoints, the participants should represent diversified backgrounds and experiences and should possess comparable prestige, knowledge, and speaking ability.

Several days prior to the performance, the chairman and the discussants should meet in order to agree on the procedure to be followed. At this planning conference the chairman may submit copies of a tentative agenda. Such an agenda should be typed, less than two pages long, and should follow basically the format discussed on pages 444–448. It is important that the leader solicit and accept the consensus of the group concerning the nature of the panel outline. If only slight alterations are suggested, the participants can pencil in the changes. Otherwise, as quickly as possible following the meeting, the chairman should have copies of the amended version typed and distributed. At the planning conference the chairman should insure that each participant understands effective panel and forum procedures. He should attempt to foster a warm feeling of friendliness among the discussants and a sense of individual identification with the group. He should be alert to detect competitive attitudes and, if possible, to substitute an endorsement of group effort. The planning conference affords an opportunity for the participants to talk over the topic informally. In this way, they can become acquainted with the viewpoints and attitudes represented in the group. However, most authorities advise against actually rehearsing the panel program. Such practice tends to dull the sparkle and spontaneity which is so important to successful panel performance. A further purpose of the planning conference is to determine whether visual aids are to be used and, if so, how they are to be displayed. Any member or the chairman may present visual aids, providing such materials do not occupy too much time and are suitably prepared for the audience situation.

In addition to attending the planning conference, the performers should prepare themselves for the program by studying the psychological and logical demands imposed by the nature of the audience, the occasion, the other speakers, and the panel method. As you know, each participant should study the question thoroughly, particularly as it relates to the group agenda; and, unless the agenda is unusually detailed, he should prepare a personal outline, indicating documentation for significant points. The chairman's outline guide for conducting the panel probably should indicate time warnings to aid in the pacing of the program and any special techniques which he (or the group) plans to employ, such as the use of charts, notations on a blackboard, and particular questions or transitions.

The arrangement of suitable physical facilities is perhaps more important for the panel than for private discussions. You will recall that the panel leader should usually consult with the chairman of the program committee (or whoever has been placed in charge of the meeting by the sponsoring organization) to arrange for the proper-sized room with adequate lighting, ventilation, and heat; for the appropriate grouping of a table(s) and chairs; for name cards for the participants; and for necessary equipment such as a projector, screen, chart easel, or blackboard.

(The leader should not rely completely upon the program chairman, however, but should check on the physical arrangements prior to the meeting.) If a large audience of perhaps one hundred persons is anticipated, better observation of the speakers can be afforded by seating the panel on a low platform. A high stage should not be used, particularly if it is separated from the audience by an orchestra pit or seatless void; such an arrange-

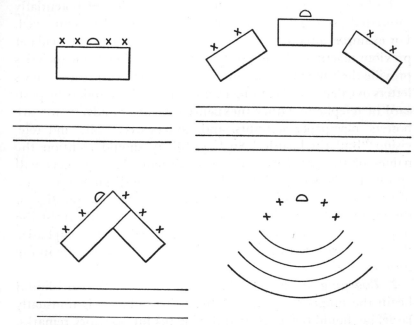

Fig. 14. Seating Arrangements for Panel Discussion Groups.

ment would prevent the attaining of an informal atmosphere. Several ways of arranging the panel and audience are illustrated in the accompanying diagrams. As the drawings indicate, each panelist should have direct visual contact with the other panel speakers and each should be easily seen by the audience.

The distribution of a mimeographed or printed program to the listeners is an excellent means of orienting them to the nature of the meeting and preparing them to engage actively and successfully in the forum period. Such a program might include these particulars: the name of the sponsoring organization; time for beginning and closing the program; place of the meeting; names of the speakers and some identification such as job titles or professional affiliations which indicate their special competency on the subject; blank space for recording notes or for phrasing forum contributions; important definitions, statistics, and graphs; guides for forum participation (see pages 503–507).

To bring the panel program to the attention of potentially interested persons, some sort of publicity should be employed. For example, announcements of the program might be made at previous meetings of the sponsoring organization. Some societies provide their members and interested persons with regular news letters or calendars of coming events and send reminders by postcard or telephone. Other inexpensive means of advertising are posters, newspaper accounts, and notices over radio and television "bulletin boards." Such publicity should mention the names of the panelists and the chairman. The speakers will appreciate the recognition and, if they are well known, the use of their names may attract interest and enhance the prestige of the meeting. In addition, the announcements should stress the importance and application of the topic and should emphasize that each member of the audience is invited to participate in the forum period.

2. Engaging in panel discussion. The chairman should begin the program on time. Unless the audience is unusually large, he should remain seated during his introductory remarks. As for any other type of public discussion, such orienting comments should be concise, ordinarily lasting no more than three minutes. The purpose and contents of the chairman's introduction are very similar to the Introduction of the public speech. Typically the leader should refer to the occasion, the purpose of the meeting, and the significance and timeliness of the topic. If he can do so discreetly, he should stress the direct application of the problem to the listeners, showing how it impinges upon one or more of their basic needs. He may provide definitions or background materials which are necessary to enable the listeners to follow the discussion easily and which he can handle more expeditiously than can the panel. Once he has introduced the subject, he should introduce each discussant, touching upon the person's training or experiences which make him especially well qualified on the subject. (In some panel discussions, each participant is asked to stand while being introduced or is required to rise and introduce himself. To this writer such practices seem stilted and are painfully reminiscent of childhood recitations or prize-ring introductions.) The leader might conclude his opening remarks by throwing out an overhead question concerning the first item on the agenda. Or, he might direct a question at a particular discussant, if he has made previous arrangements to do so. Because it is exceedingly important that the panel get off to a smooth start, the lead-off question should be carefully planned. Sometimes it might even be desirable to rehearse the first question and its answer.

The essential consideration of the panel discussion is that it is a *public* performance, existing for the benefit of the spectators. The leader and discussants must continuously keep in mind that although they are conversing informally among themselves, an audience is "tuned in." What they say must be understandable, interesting, and logical to the listeners as well as to themselves. Of course, the primary task of the discussants is to analyze a problem. If they are too conscious of feedback from the audience, their effectiveness may be reduced.

Here are several specific guides: (1) The chairman should remain impartial and, except under unusual circumstances, should not engage as an active participant. (2) Each discussant should have the opportunity to speak within the first three or four minutes. This will get the panel off to a well-paced beginning and will tend to establish the mode of wide participation and concise, conversational exchanges. (3) The leader and discussants should remain seated, except possibly when presenting a visual aid. (4) Although an audience is listening to their conversation, the speakers should look at each other and speak directly to each other except for the directing of an occasional glance or remark at the audience. Of course, the speakers should speak loudly enough and clearly enough for everyone in the room to hear. (5) To help the listeners to identify the panelists, the speakers should call each other by name, particularly early in the program. First names can be used as a means of stimulating an atmosphere of informality, thus: "That's a good point, Jim, but I think Mary had an even better idea when she suggested. . . ." Naturally, under certain formal conditions and with certain participants the use of first names would be inappropriate. (6) Although the panel should work toward a consensus, do not consider it essential that the group arrive at an agreement on a particular course of action. In fact, on sharply controversial issues, panelists who represent different viewpoints rarely resolve all significant differences in a thirty- to sixty-minute program. If they have presented an intelligent, stimulating analysis of the relevant issues involved in the investigating and solving of the assigned problem, and if the audience has been informed, interested, and stirred to reflective thinking, the panelists have accomplished the function of a public discussion.

When the panel has reached a consensus or when time has expired, the chairman usually summarizes the course of the discussion in one to three minutes. In his recapitulation, he should estimate the accomplishments of the group and point out the major areas of agreement and disagreement. Because of the presence of an audience, the accuracy of the concluding summation is especially important. Therefore, following his comments, the leader should invite the panelists to make any necessary modifications or additions. Instead of summarizing themselves, some chairmen prefer to have each discussant express his position in a brief statement of a minute or less. Such a distillation consumes more time than for the leader to summarize and probably supplies a less satisfactory review. However, because it provides in rapid succession a variety of opinions and speakers, it may be more interesting to the listeners.

Following the summation of the panel discussion, the leader should introduce and moderate the forum. Because all forms of public discussion typically provide for an audience-participation period, and because this portion of the meeting is perhaps even more important than the preceding planned performance, the forum is treated separately on pages 503–507.

Within a day or so following the panel deliberation, the chairman of the program committee, or some other appropriate officer of the sponsoring organization, should write personal letters of appreciation to the panel moderator and discussants.

B. The Symposium. The typical symposium program consists of the following procedure: (1) The chairman should stand and open the meeting with a brief (usually not more than three minutes) introduction of the topic and the speakers. He should follow the guides given earlier for the opening of the panel, except that the introduction of the speakers may be confined to a mere listing of their names and job titles or professions. Thus: "Here this evening to discuss the basic issues of our topic are four distinguished civic leaders: Mayor Charles Hopkins; County Commissioner Thomas Bell; Dr. John Greenfield, Executive Director of Charity Hospital; and the Reverend Mr. James Robertson, pastor of the First Methodist Church." (2) Then, using no more than a minute, the chairman should introduce the first speaker and his segment of the general subject. The purpose of this orientation is to direct favorable attention toward the speaker (by telling briefly of his background that qualifies him to speak on the subject) and toward his subject (by mentioning tersely its significance and appropriateness). The name of the speaker may be withheld until the final sentence and then presented in some such manner as: "Now, let me introduce to you perhaps the most popular mayor in our city's history, the honorable Charles L. Hopkins." (3) The first speaker presents his address. Unless the audience is very small and the mood of the occasion exceedingly informal, he should walk to the speaker's stand or center of the platform to give his talk. (4) The moderator rises to offer a few transitional remarks correlating the contents of the first speech with the topic of the second one. He should not, however, indicate approval or disapproval of what has been said. Then, he introduces the second speaker. (5) The second discussant gives his talk; this is followed by the chairman's transitional comments and his introduction of the third speaker, and so on. (6) Immediately after the final speech, the leader summarizes in one to three minutes the entire scope of the discussion. (7) The chairman then opens, presides over, and, at the appropriate time, closes the forum period (see pages 503–507).

Just as the advantages and disadvantages of the panel method grow out of its use of informal conversation, so the strengths and limitations of the symposium result from its mode of communication—public speaking. Here are some of the advantages of the symposium method: (1) Since symposium performers speak uninterruptedly for an appreciable period of time, each is enabled to present a closely reasoned, well-documented, and systematically integrated development of thought. Thus, if a problem is so complex that it requires considerable factual explanation or if it seems to divide itself into specialized aspects or phases, it perhaps can be presented more effectively by a series of speeches than by the less orderly method of informal conversation. (2) Its speechmaking nature and its adaptability to the use of a public address system enable the symposium to function efficiently before any-sized audience, from the very small to the very large. (3) Symposium programs are easier to arrange than panel programs. If necessary, all of the initial planning can be done by the chairman: he can select the question, divide it into sub-topics, secure suitable speakers, and by means of the telephone and/or mail can notify each participant concerning the nature of the program. (4) Because each performer realizes that he has an uninterrupted period of time at his disposal, he is more inclined to prepare himself adequately. (5) Since each speaker is responsible for only a limited area of the symposium question, he does not have to be intimately acquainted with the entire subject. Therefore use the symposium method when you wish to draw upon the specialized knowledge of individuals who may not be well informed on other phases of the topic. (6) Moderating a symposium is a much simpler process than leading a panel. To stimulate, coordinate, and regulate the contributions of panel members demands broader knowledge of the subject and greater leadership skills than does the chairing of a symposium.

The basic limitation of the symposium is that it provides for almost no interaction among the speakers. To reduce this weakness, at the close of each speech the symposium participants might discuss informally the ideas and evidence just presented, or immediately following the program of prepared speeches the speakers might exchange views in a short panel-like discussion.

Another limitation is that symposiums seem to present more difficulty than panels in maintaining the involuntary attention of the listeners. For this reason symposium participants should be carefully screened for their knowledge of speech preparation and skill in presentation.

In advising you how to prepare for symposium performances, it is perhaps necessary only to suggest guides for the partitioning of the subject and the preparing of the speeches. As the following paired columns indicate, the organization of a symposium program is similar to that of a speech.

SYMPOSIUM	*PUBLIC SPEECH*
Discussion question	Specific Speech Purpose
Chairman's introduction of the discussion topic and the speakers....................	Introduction
Set of symposium speeches	Body:
First speech—on sub-topic no. 1............	I. First major point
Second speech—on sub-topic no. 2..........	II. Second major point
Third speech—on sub-topic no. 3...........	III. Third major point
Chairman's summary of symposium speeches...	Conclusion

As you will remember from your study of speech organization, the speaker should ask himself several questions concerning the partitioning of the Specific Speech Purpose. With only slight adaptations, these questions should be applied to the division of the discussion question: (1) Does the partitioning provide for an adequate coverage of the discussion question? (2) Is each speech topic a direct division of the discussion question? (3) Does each possess relatively the same importance as the others? (4) Is each a separate and independent thought unit? (5) Do strong ties of logical association link together the speech topics? That is, do these subjects follow a natural sequence of thought that will carry the listeners progressively speech by speech toward a fuller understanding and appreciation of the discussion question? The speech subjects may follow a problem-solution sequence: the first speaker may describe the nature of the problem, the second may explain the possible causes, and the remaining speakers may inspect tentative solutions. The following example applies the problem-solution pattern.

Discussion Question: How can the amount of cheating at the University be reduced?

Symposium Speeches:

    Speaker   I: "What is the problem?"

    Speaker II: "Would the establishment of an honor system alleviate the problem?"

    Speaker III: "Would increasing the severity of punishment diminish cheating?"

    Speaker IV: "Would an improvement in student counseling reduce cheating?"

    Speaker V: "Would changes in the present testing procedures decrease cheating?"

Sometimes a topical arrangement of the speakers' topics is feasible. Here is a representative example.

Discussion Question: What can be done to improve the teaching of science?

Symposium Speeches:

    Speaker   I: "At the elementary school level"

    Speaker II: "At the high school level"

    Speaker III: "At the undergraduate level"

    Speaker IV: "At the graduate level"

In preparing for symposium speaking, follow the same procedures for speech development and rehearsal that you learned earlier in this text. In addition, consider these suggestions: (1) Your speech should reflect the spirit of inquiry rather than that of advocacy. (2) Your Introduction should include appropriate references to the remarks of the preceding speakers. Consequently, until the meeting you can make only tentative plans for the opening of your talk. If you are the first speaker, your initial observations should relate to the introductory comments of the Chairman and/or to the audience, occasion, or purpose of the meeting. If your speaking position comes later in the program, perhaps the first 20 per cent of your talk might be devoted to supplementing, corroborating, or disagreeing with what has been said. If you wish to voice dissent, do so tactfully. Be generous and conciliatory rather than magisterial and hypercritical. Since discussion is supposed to represent a co-operative search for the truth and since the preceding speaker has no immediate opportunity to defend himself, your listeners will rightfully resent any grating criticism or disparagement. (3) Unless you are exceptionally skillful in reading from manuscript, you should plan to speak extempore. (4) Plan your speech to conform to the specified time limitations. Unless the chairman has already arranged some sort of warning system, ask him to notify you once near the end of your period and again when time has expired.

C. The Lecture-Forum. Customarily, the lecture-forum program follows this procedure: (1) In a brief introduction the chairman attempts to foster a favorable audience reception for the speaker and his subject. Also, he emphasizes that during the forum period each listener will have an opportunity to participate. (2) The speaker presents an uninterrupted lecture of perhaps thirty to sixty minutes. At the conclusion of his address he usually returns to his seat and remains there during the moderator's opening of the forum period. (3) To provide a bridge between the lecture and the forum, the chairman expresses a few remarks which may include a complimentary reference to the speech, an explanation of the procedures governing the forum, and an attempt to stimulate the listeners to engage actively in the discussion. (4) In the forum following formal lecture programs, audience participation is frequently confined to questioning the speaker. Even when this procedure is not followed, however, the forum usually seems to be somewhat less spontaneous and to die out more quickly than the forums following panels and symposiums. Therefore, the proportion of the meeting which is devoted to the forum might be reduced somewhat from that customarily used for panel and symposium programs. However, the proportion should not become less than one third of the total time available.

The advantages and disadvantages of the lecture-forum method arise from its use of the uninterrupted lecture. An obvious advantage of the method is that it is suitable for any-sized audience. Also, it is clearly the easiest type of public discussion meeting to arrange. Furthermore, when used appropriately the lecture method provides perhaps the most nearly complete and systematic treatment of a complex subject, particularly one which is new to the audience.

Among the significant limitations of the lecture-forum method is that, instead of having the drawing power of several names, it must rely upon only one. Therefore, assuming that other conditions are the same, a lecture-forum might experience more difficulty in attracting an audience than would a panel or symposium. When the speaker is enough of an expert to attract a considerable audience, he usually has directed intense energy to the subject over an extended period of time. As a result of this study and experience, he may formulate such strong opinions that he becomes dogmatic or evangelistic. Unfortunately in the typical lecture-forum, the participation by the audience does not adequately supplement or refute the utterances of the speaker. Another limitation is that the entire responsibility for stimulating the audience rests upon the single speaker. Unlike the panel and symposium, the lecture-forum does not offer the variation provided by different voices, appearances, and individualities nor the interest produced by the interaction of different ideas and personalities. To maintain close attention of his listeners for thirty to sixty minutes, the lecturer must possess superior skill as a public speaker, enjoy exceptional prestige, or have an unusually interesting subject. Although not conclusive, various experimental studies seem to indicate that the average lecture is less successful than the panel or symposium in stimulating the listeners to reflective thinking or in motivating them to share actively in the forum activities.

D. The Forum. First let us review quickly the basic nature of the forum: with the exception of the broadcast type, discussion programs customarily include an audience participation period immediately following the planned discussion; because it offers the listeners an opportunity to share actively in the investigation and solution of the problem, the forum is an exceedingly significant part of the public discussion program; usually the forum constitutes about one-half of the total duration of the panel or symposium meeting and perhaps a somewhat smaller share of the lecture-forum meeting.

1. The function of the chairman. As the leader of the prepared discussion, you also serve as the chairman of the forum. Your function is to stimulate the maximum quantity and diffusion of participation, steer the course of the forum discussion, and regulate interpersonal relations.

In introducing the forum period, you should explain the procedures to be followed. If the planned discussion has been a panel, the mood of the occasion informal, and the size of the audience small, you may remain seated while introducing the forum. Otherwise, you should go to the speaker's stand or the center of the platform. Even though guides for the audience-discussion period may have been printed and distributed to the listeners, your introduction should cover the following: (1) *The nature of the individual participations.* You should explain whether participation is to be limited to questioning the speaker or whether contributions of opinion or information will also be permitted. Although the forum period is often limited to the asking of questions, particularly following a lecture, the session will be more meaningful to the audience members if they are also allowed to state their views, add information, and to differ with the program speakers. (2) *Length of participations.* You should urge the forum members to keep their contributions short. Questions should be precisely phrased in perhaps fewer than twenty-five words and comments restricted to a maximum of two minutes. (3) *Frequency of participations.* You should explain that, in order to afford as many persons as possible an opportunity to participate, no one should ask to speak twice while others are seeking the floor. (4) *Manner of making contributions.* When the occasion is informal and the audience small, you should probably advise the listeners to direct their questions and comments to the discussion group or to an individual member. If the situation is formal or the audience large, you should request that contributions should be directed to you. You will then relay the question to the discussion group or to the appropriate individual.

After your brief introductory remarks, you should open the forum. If no one wishes to speak, you should help the audience break through the psychological barrier which exists between silent listening and active participation. One method is for you to elicit questions which you have previously "planted" in the audience. Another method is for you to pose several intriguing questions to the audience or to direct a question to the discussion group. Once the forum gets under way it may need little, if any, more stimulation. This does not mean that you have no further duties. You should prevent the monopolizing of the discussion by a few persons, clarify questions and comments where necessary, insure the relevance of all questions, and maintain decorum. You should be vigilant in your insistence that each speaker maintain adequate volume. You should seek to spread participation as widely as possible among the members of the planned discussion group as well as among the members of the audience. You should attempt to guide participation in such a way that all major aspects of the problem are covered instead of only one or two. Except in informal situations, you should require that participants be recognized by you before speaking. When the audience is large, you should repeat all questions before directing them to the appropriate person(s) on the panel of speakers. You may remain seated throughout the forum following a panel performance before a small informal audience. For all other situations, you should stand while addressing the audience or receiving questions—usually at the center of the platform or at the speaker's desk; you should retire to an inconspicuous position while a member of the formal discussion group is addressing the audience.

When the time for adjournment arrives or when interest begins to wane, you should close the forum with a brief statement. Although the particular situation will determine the substance of your remarks, you probably should make a capsule summary of the meeting, thank the program discussants for their participation, and express the hope that the audience has had a profitable and stimulating experience.

2. The function of the program discussants. During the forum period your basic function as a program discussant is to answer questions which may be directed to you by the audience, the chairman, or by other members of the planned discussion group. Here are some specific guides: (1) At all times during the forum you should evidence by your positive manner that you are listening attentively to what is going on. (2) When you are a member of a panel which has performed before a small audience under informal conditions, you might receive questions and make replies from your seat. Under other circumstances you should rise and, usually, move to the speaker's stand or to the center of the platform. After making your statement of reply, you should return to your seat. (3) If the chairman does not re-state a question which has been put to you, you should do so. (4) Although you may direct your replies primarily to the questioners, speak loudly enough for all to hear. (5) Try to keep all comments under two minutes in length. Your answers should be crisp and to the point. Do not give speeches. In replying to requests for information, present only relevant and necessary instruction; do not elaborate endlessly. In replying to requests for opinion, state your position tactfully, give one or more reasons why your point is valid, reinforce your reason(s) with some evidence and logic, and then restate your point. (6) Maintain a gracious and generous attitude toward the members of the audience. Do not become overtly offended by opposition to your ideas. When you must disagree, do so as pleasantly and diplomatically as possible. (7) If you observe that a disproportionate number of questions are being directed to you, try to include other members of the panel (or symposium) group in the discussion by soliciting their views.

3. The function of the audience members. Before attending a discussion meeting, you should do some preliminary thinking and reading on the subject. Such intellectual preparation is necessary if you are to receive maximal benefits from the program discussion and the forum. During the planned discussion, listen analytically and objectively. Take notes concerning the points on which you may want to seek clarification or express opinions during the forum. Write down the questions you wish to ask, remembering that they should be brief and trenchant; do not preface a question with a long explanation or observation. If you intend to make a brief talk, prepare a general outline of what you wish to say; such comments should last no more than two minutes and should be tactful and relevant. During the forum period, follow all of the rules mentioned by the chairman in his introduction. Except in small groups, you should not speak until you have been recognized by the chairman. To seek recognition, raise your arm or, in very large groups, rise to your feet. Upon being recognized, customarily you should stand to speak. Channel your questions through the chairman, if he has so prescribed; otherwise, you may address queries directly to the program discussion group or to one of its members. Do not engage in cross exchanges with other members of the audience; if the chairman is bypassed, the meeting easily gets out of hand. Forum speakers often fail to use sufficient volume for easy listening. Employ adequate projection and enunciate clearly and distinctly. If you are close to the front, do not forget that those in the rear also want to hear what you are saying.

4. Buzz sessions. When the audience is unusually large, adequate diffusion of participation during the forum is difficult, and sometimes impossible, to achieve. Also, considerable difficulty may be experienced in stirring the large audience to active participation. To combat these obstacles, some authorities recommend that *buzz sessions* be employed. Under this procedure the chairman of the forum divides the entire audience into small groups of six to twelve persons; each group selects (or is given) its leader and, under his guidance, talks over the topic of the preceding discussion program. At the conclusion of a specified period of time the buzz units dissolve into the original audience and each of the various leaders presents to the entire audience the question or the statement of views agreed upon in his group. A discussion by the entire audience may follow each of these points or may be delayed until all buzz groups have reported. The obvious advantage of the buzz method is that it provides each member of the audience an opportunity to engage actively in the forum. However, much time may be consumed in dividing the audience, selecting chairmen, and in settling down to talk seriously. Furthermore, unless the members have had previous experience with the discussion subject, they may not be sufficiently well informed to speak intelligently. The position of this book is that the buzz session approach should not be used indiscriminately but should be restricted to occasions when the audience is too large to permit a sufficient spread of participation or when the listeners appear to be too phlegmatic to permit the normal forum period to work successfully.

E. The Broadcast Discussion. The broadcast discussion [1] represents an adaptation rather than a distinct type. All of the forms of public discussion are readily adaptable to the medium of broadcasting, with the informality and spontaneity of the panel making it the most widely used.

---

[1] As used here, the term "broadcast" refers to either television or radio transmission, or both.

To understand the adaptations required in presenting broadcast discussions, we should examine briefly the distinctive characteristics of the air audience.[2]

The broadcast audience is nearly always more heterogeneous than a face-to-face discussion audience. Because of the time, inconvenience, and possible expense incurred in attending a discussion meeting, the listeners usually share a sense of "duty" or a greater-than-average interest in the subject. Homogeneity is also fostered by the fact that discussion programs are typically sponsored by a particular organization, held at its meeting place, and, often, restricted to its membership and guests. Admittedly the day of the week, time of day, and the programming policy of the station (for example, some stations are known as "good music" stations and others as educational outlets) may limit the potential universality of the broadcast audience. Nevertheless, the wide diversity of persons within range of the transmitter and the ease of "attending" the broadcast discussion create almost invariably a more heterogeneous type of audience.

The broadcast discussion is beamed to small groups or individuals. Instead of sitting relatively quietly in rows at some meeting hall, the members of the air audience might be standing at a counter of a drug store, reclining on a sofa in a fraternity house, or bending over a work bench in a garage. Like the face-to-face listeners, they may be concerned solely with the discussion program; however, they are more apt to be engaged in some other activity, such as driving, eating, working, dressing, or even bathing. The smallness of the typical audience units and the informality of the listening occasion conditions the auditors to expect an informal, friendly presentation. Since the radio or television discussant is a guest invited into the privacy and warmth of the home, club, and the like, it would be inappro-

---

[2] For a somewhat more extensive treatment of the broadcasting medium, consult Eugene E. White and Clair R. Henderlider, *Practical Public Speaking* (New York: The Macmillan Company, 1954), Chapter 16, or James H. McBurney and Ernest J. Wrage, *The Art of Good Speech* (New York: Prentice-Hall, Inc., 1953), Chapter 27. Full-length treatment may be found in standard references, such as Waldo Abbot and Richard L. Reder, *Handbook of Broadcasting* (New York: McGraw-Hill Book Co., 1956), 4th ed.

priate for him to use the powerful projection, the somewhat slowed rate, and the formal approach that he may employ in speaking to a large "live" audience.

By analyzing the face-to-face speaking situation the speaker customarily can arrive at fairly reliable estimations of the nature of his listeners. However, because it is impossible to anticipate who will listen to a particular station at a specific time, the yardsticks of audience analysis cannot be applied accurately to the air audience.

Since no feedback is possible from the air audience, the broadcaster is unable to observe how his communication is being received. Although this factor may not disturb panel participants, it poses a severe problem of adjustment for many symposium speakers and lecturers.

The air audience is far more difficult to hold. As previously noted, the face-to-face audience has been motivated to attend the meeting because of interest or sense of "duty." After he is seated and the program has begun, the typical auditor is hesitant to embarrass himself and the speaker by walking out. On the other hand, one can with no embarrassment and with slight effort switch from a discussion program to an adult western, a variety show, or a soap opera. Furthermore, the air audience frequently has to contend with extraneous distractions: the driver is forced to make constant adjustments to the road and traffic; the housewife must change the baby, answer the phone, and wash the dishes; the man at the drug store counter must hear the broadcast over the conversation around him. Often such persons will eventually conclude that listening to a thought-provoking "talky" program is too much trouble.

Now, let us turn to the problem of adjusting the discussion method to the peculiar demands of the broadcasting medium.

Obviously, broadcast discussion must possess unusually high interest values. The extent to which potential listeners will be encouraged to tune in can be estimated by applying criteria such as these: Has the program received adequate publicity in the newspapers and in broadcast notices? Are the speakers well known? Do they possess high prestige in relation to the topic? Or, have they had unusual experiences in connection with the subject? Does the topic possess current interest values? Is it highly controversial? Does it affect the immediate wants and needs of the community in an unusually significant manner? The extent to which listeners will be encouraged to remain tuned in can be estimated by applying questions like these: Is the pace brisk? the development of thought clear and logical? the mode lively, buoyant, and communicative? Is language vividly concrete, clear, and impressive? Is maximum utilization being made of the Factors of Interest? Dullness and sluggishness cannot be permitted either in the speaking style of the discussants or in the manner in which ideas are developed. For instance, the use of numerous statistics or involved explanations— even if relevant and meaningful—should be avoided unless critically necessary.

Because time limitations are rigidly enforced, the participants must plan the discussion so that it covers the subject adequately and runs exactly the desired length of time. Although in the case of symposiums and lecture-forums this provision causes little difficulty, the planning of panel discussions may require considerable group preparation. Some panels prefer to work out a detailed group agenda with the responsibility for the introduction of each new phase being assigned to a particular individual. For all panels, the estimation of the time necessary to complete each major section of the outline should be indicated in the margin at the appropriate place.

Although differences of opinion exist on this point, the position of this text is that, unless the discussants are experienced, a broadcast panel should be rehearsed in advance of presentation. Of course, the exact phrasing should not be memorized. If possible, the rehearsal should be recorded and played back. Symposium speakers and lecturers should rehearse in much the same manner as the public speaker.

In radio discussions vocal delivery carries the entire burden of communication. Since the listeners cannot see the speaker, their only contact with him is by means of his voice. Therefore, an effective speaking voice is especially important to the radio speaker. The obvious importance of the voice in radio speaking leads some speakers to believe erroneously that physical delivery is unimportant. However, unless you maintain the controlled, animated bodily expression which is characteristic of your speaking in face-to-face situations, your presentation will probably assume a wooden, unnatural effect.

Because it projects the speaker's physical presence as well as his voice, television is even more intimate than radio. Furthermore, TV listeners have a much closer view of the discussants than they would have as members of a face-to-face audience. (a) For this reason, the speaker's personality, dress, gestures, facial expression, and movement are even more noticeable than in "live" situations. Although your physical delivery should be animated and vigorous, keep in mind the demands of the camera and the air audience. Because the camera may be unable to follow you effectively, especially in close-up shots, avoid using movements and gestures which are too sweeping, rapid, or sudden. Be alert to detect any repetitive nervous mannerisms which, although perhaps relatively inoffensive in the typical face-to-face audience situation, might be highly distracting to the television audience. Although some visual variety is provided by different camera shots and distances, try to provide suitable modifications in your posture, hand movements, facial expressions, and so on. (b) Television speaking should be as conversational and direct as possible. To foster the feeling of intimacy, lecturers and symposium speakers should look directly into the camera at all times except when the lens is aimed at some visual aid or when the speaker makes a necessary reference to his notes. Panelists should look at each other most of the time, but occasionally should look directly at the camera. Because the obtrusive use of memory-aids impairs rapport with the air audience even more quickly than with the "live" one, reduce to the barest minimum the use of notes, off-camera cards, or the teleprompter.

SUMMARY

The various types of discussion may be conveniently divided into two groups: those occurring without an audience and those occurring in the presence of an audience. In private discussions each person present is expected to share in the proceedings. The purpose of such deliberations is to investigate problems and evolve solutions. Private discussions include informal group discussions, committee conferences, staff conferences, and instructional conferences. Public discussions—panels, symposiums, lecture-forums, and broadcast discussions—are primarily programs or shows. Their primary purpose is not to determine policy or to enrich the thinking of the performers; instead, it is to interest, inform, and stimulate the listeners. Because of its peculiar advantages and limitations, each type of public discussion poses specialized needs of planning, leadership, and participation. Except for the broadcast type, public discussion meetings customarily include a forum or audience-participation period. The forum occurs immediately after the planned discussion program and usually constitutes about one half of the total duration of the meeting.

EXERCISES AND ASSIGNMENTS

1. Make a special study concerning the importance of discussion in one of the following areas: student body government; university administration; the profession of law, medicine, dentistry, or education; business; labor unions; local, state, or national government. Report your findings to the class in the form of an essay or a short speech.

2. As part of your investigations for exercise 1, or as a separate project, interview a prominent lawyer, doctor, judge, dentist, teacher, social worker, businessman, or scientist to determine how significant he believes discussion is in his vocation. Prepare an oral or written report of your interview.

3. Make a list of all discussional situations in which you have been involved during the preceding two or three days. Mentally estimate the relative effectiveness of each discussion. What were the desirable and undesirable features of each? If no formal leader was appointed, did one or

more participants assume some of the leadership functions? How? In what manner? Were the attempts to exert direction over the group activities welcomed or resisted by the group? Did the flow of talk move in a relatively systematic manner? Was overt or covert conflict present? What personality or attitudinal characteristics present in the group encouraged the accomplishment of the discussional purpose? Which impeded group progress?

4. After considering the discussions you have heard recently in class and elsewhere, compose a list of the behavior characteristics of leaders and participants which especially irritate you. Then analyze yourself to determine why these characteristics are so repugnant to you. Do you manifest any of these qualities in your own discussional speaking or in other avenues of oral communication?

5. Attend both a college debate and a group discussion meeting. Observe the similarities and differences in the philosophy and methodology of these two types of group speaking.

6. Listen to a radio or television discussion and answer these questions concerning the broadcast:
Was the discussion a modification of one of the basic types of discussion? If so, what adaptations were made? Did these adjustments seem to increase or decrease the effectiveness of the program? Give reasons for your answer. If you believe that the discussion represented a unique type, explain why.

7. Attend a discussion or debate meeting which includes an audience-participation period. Prepare a written critique in which you estimate the relative success of the forum and offer specific criticisms of the leadership and participation.

8. Your instructor will divide the class into groups of four to six persons. Each group will follow this procedure:
(a) Meet in a planning session to choose a chairman and select a subject for a panel or symposium discussion. (For sample topics see exercise 9.)
(b) In the case of the panel, use the planning session to agree upon the group agenda. In the case of the symposium, use the session to determine the division of the topic into the individual speech subjects and to prevent an overlapping in the content of the speeches.
(c) Engage in the discussion before the class. If possible, record and play back the presentation.

9. Study carefully the following sample discussion subjects. Then turn in to your instructor three additional correctly phrased topics for each of

the major categories: campus problems; local and state problems; national and international problems.

Campus problems:

How can we improve the library service at the University?

How can the teaching at the University be improved?

What can be done to improve the student counseling service?

How can school spirit be improved?

What can be done to improve the student health service?

How can testing procedures be improved?

What changes, if any, should be made in the final examination system?

What changes, if any, should be made in the intramural system?

What changes, if any, should be made in the residence hall regulations?

What can be done to make the annual charity drive more successful?

Local and state problems:

What can be done to reduce juvenile delinquency in the community?

How can the amount of vice in the community be reduced?

What can be done to attract more light industry to the state?

What can be done to encourage fair employment practices in the state?

What can the individual citizen do to improve the local government?

What can be done to improve the care and treatment of the mentally ill in the state?

What can be done to remove politics from the county public school system?

What changes, if any, should be made in the state laws governing the licensing of drivers?

How efficient is the local police department?

National and international problems:

What can be done to improve the efficiency of the executive branch of the federal government?

In what way, if any, should the tariff laws be changed?

What can be done to make the UN a more effective agency for peace?

What changes, if any, should be made in the operating procedures of congressional investigating committees?

What can be done to promote better relations in the Western Hemisphere?

To what exent, if any, should the social security program be expanded?

What, if anything, can be done to curb inflation?

What can be done to encourage more persons to vote?

To what extent should the United States assist in the economic development of backward nations?

What changes, if any, should be made in the present methods of training the nation's teachers?

❦❦ Index

515